BEGINNING
ASP.NET WEB PAGES WITH WEBMATRIX

BEGINNING

ASP.NET Web Pages with WebMatrix®

BEGINNING

ASP.NET Web Pages with WebMatrix®

Mike Brind

Imar Spaanjaars

John Wiley & Sons, Inc.

Beginning ASP.NET Web Pages with WebMatrix®

Published by
John Wiley & Sons, Inc.
10475 Crosspoint Boulevard
Indianapolis, IN 46256
www.wiley.com

Published simultaneously in Canada

ISBN: 978-1-118-05048-4
ISBN: 978-1-118-20348-4 (ebk)
ISBN: 978-1-118-20350-7 (ebk)
ISBN: 978-1-118-20349-1 (ebk)

Manufactured in the United States of America

10 9 8 7 6 5 4 3 2 1

For general information on our other products and services please contact our Customer Care Department within the United States at (877) 762-2974, outside the United States at (317) 572-3993 or fax (317) 572-4002.

Wiley also publishes its books in a variety of electronic formats and by print-on-demand. Not all content that is available in standard print versions of this book may appear or be packaged in all book formats. If you have purchased a version of this book that did not include media that is referenced by or accompanies a standard print version, you may request this media by visiting http://booksupport.wiley.com. For more information about Wiley products, visit us at www.wiley.com.

Library of Congress Control Number: 2011936929

ABOUT THE AUTHORS

MIKE BRIND spent the first 20 years of his working life in a series of successful sales and marketing roles, towards the end of which he was introduced to HTML and databases. A dormant inner geek took over and Mike became very much more interested in developing websites than selling advertising space on them.

As well as on books such as those in the Wrox Beginner series, Mike became reliant on the enormous amount of free help provided by online communities while he learned his new craft. Mike is now one of the all-time leading contributors to the official ASP.NET forums at `http://forums.asp.net` and is also a moderator there.

As a result of his contributions to the ASP.NET community via the forums, and through his technical article site at `www.mikesdotnetting.com`, Mike received the Microsoft Most Valuable Professional (MVP) Award for ASP.NET in 2008, 2009, 2010, and 2011. *Beginning ASP.NET Web Pages with WebMatrix* is Mike's first book.

Mike is currently the Operations Director for ITEC Systems, a company that produces specialist software for recruitment agencies all around the world.

Mike lives in Rochester in the UK with his wife of over 25 years, Anna. Together they have two daughters and a grandson.

IMAR SPAANJAARS graduated in Leisure Management at the Leisure Management School in the Netherlands, but he quickly changed his career path into the Internet world.

After working in the Internet business at various web agencies for thirteen years, he started up his own company called *De Vier Koeden* (`http://devierkoeden.com`), a small Internet agency specializing in consultancy and development of Internet and intranet applications with Microsoft technologies such as ASP.NET 4. He's also the technical director of Dynamicweb Netherlands and Dynamicweb North America, two branches of the popular Danish CMS and eCommerce system Dynamicweb.

Imar has written books on ASP.NET and Macromedia Dreamweaver, all published under the Wrox brand. He is also one of the top contributors to the Wrox Community Forum at `p2p.wrox.com`, where he shares his knowledge with fellow programmers.

Since 2008, Imar has been rewarded with Microsoft's Most Valuable Professional (MVP) award for his contributions to the ASP.NET community.

Imar lives in Utrecht, the Netherlands, with his girlfriend, Fleur. You can contact him through his personal web site at `http://imar.spaanjaars.com` or by email at imar@spaanjaars.com.

ABOUT THE TECHNICAL EDITOR

MICHAEL APOSTOL graduated from the University of Oregon with a B.S. in Economics. He started his career working for Microsoft Corporation in Market Development. Michael has worked in both software development and information technology as an I.T. manager, programmer, and consultant for numerous companies in the Western United States in addition to a few trips to Europe as a software instructor. Presently, he is employed as a contractor writing SQL Server TSQL code for a company in Hawaii. He has thoroughly enjoyed his work as a technical editor with his last project being: *Beginning Microsoft ASP.NET 4.0* by Imar Spaanjaars (2010, Wiley Publishing, Inc.). In his free time, Michael tries to get as much time possible with his adopted seven year old Ethiopian son, Geremu, and spouse, Melissa, outside in the sunshine.

CREDITS

ACKNOWLEDGMENTS

I WOULD LIKE TO START by thanking Imar Spaanjaars, my co-author and fellow MVP, for recommending me to Wrox for this project. I am also grateful for the advice and support he has provided as the book became reality. I would also like to thank Paul Reese for listening to Imar and taking a chance on me.

I would also like to thank Michael J. Apostol for his contribution as Technical Editor and for Kezia Endsley for tirelessly translating my English into English. I am particularly appreciative of the efforts of Rosanne Koneval for her patience and diplomacy in guiding this particular author newbie through the process of getting a book done.

Finally, I would like to thank my wife of over 25 years, Anna, for her support and understanding throughout the project. I lost count of how many times she asked "have you finished the book yet?" But at last, I can answer "Yes!"

CONTENTS

FOREWORD

Back in 1997, when I began my career as a professional web developer, I started working with Classic ASP. After a brief training period in a few different programming languages such as C++ and Java, I was thrown in at the deep end and assigned to a project to build an Intranet application for a large consultancy firm in the Netherlands using Classic ASP. Despite the complexity of the project and my lack of experience at the time, I was still able to make valuable contributions to the code base. This was partly due to the great support I received from my more experienced colleagues, but also because of how approachable Classic ASP was. Although it's considered outdated now, Classic ASP had a few great features that made it the technology of choice for many developers for a long period of time. One of the things I really liked about it was how approachable it was. You didn't need complex and overwhelming tools, but instead you could use a simple text editor that had features such as color coding and multiple tabs. Deployment was also very easy: You just uploaded the file to the server and the changes would be applied immediately. For features not supported out-of-the-box (such as image scaling and uploading of files), one of my colleagues would write a DLL in Visual Basic 6 to get the job done. I had great respect for those that possessed these skills as it seemed pretty complicated at that time.

Then in early 2000, ASP.NET was released. It marked a radical change in web development as it approached things from a completely different angle. Rather than having you work with the underlying technologies that make up the Web (such as HTTP , HTML, CSS and more) directly, ASP.NET shields the developer from many of these concepts, and lets you work with a web application in a similar way to how you write desktop applications. As a result, ASP.NET made the hard things easy and the easy things hard. Things that used to take hours or days to develop in Classic ASP — such as building data-driven web pages — could now be done in minutes, simply by dragging and dropping a few controls. But things that were dead-easy before — such as adding an in-line CSS class to a table cell displaying records from a database — all of a sudden turned out to be very difficult.

I clearly recall how the first books on ASP.NET I read stated how unbelievably cool it all was, how it was so much better than Classic ASP, and how it solved so many problems. Although these claims have proven to be true over the past ten years, back then I already started wondering what people would write the day a successor or competitor for ASP.NET would be released, and how all the benefits of ASP.NET would be turned upside down as disadvantages to better promote the new technology.

Fast forward to 2011, and I am ready to find out the answer to that question. But it turns out to be a bit different from what I anticipated. First of all, it's me who's writing the answer to my own question. And secondly, ASP.NET is nowhere near being obsolete nor replaced with a new technology. In the past few years, *ASP.NET Web Forms* (which was the only implementation of ASP.NET when it was first released) is now accompanied by *ASP.NET MVC*, a web development framework based on the popular *Model View Controller* pattern. Under the hood, Web Forms and MVC share all the goodness that the ASP.NET framework brings. ASP.NET MVC has gained a lot of popularity since it was first released, but it's not the perfect framework for each scenario or application you'll ever build. Due to the way MVC works, it has a higher initial learning curve than other web development frameworks.

Realizing that both Web Forms and MVC may not be appealing to every web developer, Microsoft created WebMatrix, a free web development tool designed to help website developers of all skill levels easily create, customize, and publish websites to the Internet. In my opinion, WebMatrix is a great tool for a number of reasons. First of all, it has the openness and approachability that Classic ASP used to have and for which ASP.NET MVC is now getting a lot of credits: You work directly with the core concepts of the web — HTTP and HTML — without some façade on top of these concepts shielding you from the dirty — but important — details. This gives you full control over the program flow and final output. Secondly, it has great tools support. Features you find in Visual Studio such as IntelliSense, site management, and database management made it into the WebMatrix development tool. Thirdly, it's quick to get started with WebMatrix: Within minutes you can download the tool, install it, and view your first WebMatrix page in your browser. Finally, WebMatrix gives you access to all the goodness that ASP.NET and the .NET framework bring, which includes data access, networking capabilities, file management, and a whole slew of other features you need in day to day web development. To summarize, WebMatrix is simple and approachable where possible, and powerful and extensible where needed.

This book gives you an in-depth look at WebMatrix and its accompanying technologies such as IIS Express (the development web server that ships with WebMatrix) and SQL Server. You'll see how to build a website using WebMatrix from the very start of installing the tools in the first chapter, all the way down to deploying that site to a production server in the last chapter. You'll see how to use the tool to build effective websites, and you'll learn the tricks of the trade to make them look and behave great.

If you're still indecisive about whether or not you want to take the plunge into WebMatrix, it's important to realize that you're not locked in once you make the decision. Although not 100% automated, it's relatively easy to upgrade a WebMatrix website to ASP.NET MVC in case you want or need to. On top of that, a lot of what you learn from this book and the experience you gain from building websites with WebMatrix will be usable in ASP.NET Web Forms and ASP.NET MVC as well.

Let me close off this foreword with a slightly modified quote from one of my all-time favorite movies: *The Matrix*:

Welcome to the Web Matrix!

—Imar Spaanjaars

INTRODUCTION

MICROSOFT LAUNCHED ASP.NET, a framework for building dynamic websites more than 10 years ago. Since then, improved versions have been released — in 2003 (version 1.1), 2005 (version 2.0), 2008 (version 3.5), and most recently, version 4.0 in 2010. Not long after the release of version 4.0, a series of blog posts appeared from Scott Guthrie, Microsoft's Corporate Vice President responsible for the Developer Division (which includes ASP.NET). Each of them caused a lot of interest within the ASP.NET development community. The first post announced the launch of IIS Express — a lightweight web server specifically designed to aid in the web application development process. The second blog post concerned the imminent release of a new version of the SQL Server Compact Edition database which could be deployed within a web hosting environment easily. The third post in the series heralded the introduction of a new "View Engine" for ASP.NET, together with a new programming syntax — Razor. The ASP.NET community was giddy with the pace of these announcements. Then along came the final announcement, bringing all these new initiatives together into a totally new web development "stack" — WebMatrix, as well as a new development paradigm leveraging the Razor syntax — Web Pages.

Learning ASP.NET had suddenly got very much easier than it was before.

Until the launch of Web Pages, ASP.NET came in two flavors: Web Forms and MVC. Web Forms has proven pretty popular, and offers a development experience, which is quite close to that enjoyed by Windows application developers. However, web development is very different to desktop development. The two core technologies behind web development — HTTP and HTML are to a large extent hidden from the developer by Web Forms. Web Forms is based on "server-side controls" and has an eventing model, neither of which can be seen in any other web development framework. Web Forms does its best to hide the fact that HTTP is "stateless," by introducing notions such as ViewState to manage the state of these "controls" from one page request to another. HTML is generated as a result of controls, which have been dragged and dropped onto a design surface, rendering themselves when a page is executed on the web server. In trying to appeal to Windows developers, Web Forms introduced a large number of concepts to web development that are totally unique to the framework and not seen anywhere else. While Web Forms is undeniably a hugely powerful framework, it is not the easiest starting point for anyone new to web development. Its learning curve is high.

ASP.NET MVC was introduced in 2008 partly to provide a more "natural" web development experience, and as a result, it very quickly gained traction among intermediate or experienced ASP.NET web developers, as well as a lot of interest from developers who are more accustomed to using competing technologies such as Ruby On Rails. However, ASP.NET MVC is also designed to solve a lot of other problems that advanced developers have with Web Forms — a lack of testability, a need for clearer "separation of concerns," the ability to extend the framework, and so on. These notions are obscure to new web development students, so the one problem that MVC did not solve was to make learning ASP.NET any easier. If anything, MVC's "concept count" is higher than that of Web Forms.

Competing technologies, such as PHP are considered much more accessible in comparison. Even Microsoft's predecessor to ASP.NET — classic ASP — was seen as much easier to learn. Web Pages is designed to provide a much smoother on-ramp to developing dynamic websites with Microsoft technologies, by deliberately keeping this "concept count" low, but by also providing powerful tools that make development easy, and still making the full power of the .NET framework available to newcomers as they need it. That's not to say that Web Pages "dumbs down" web development. The skills you need to learn in order to make use of ASP.NET Web Pages are exactly the same as you need to be effective with PHP or any other server-side technology. And what you learn from working with Web Pages provides a great foundation should you decide to advance to ASP.NET MVC at any stage.

Learning ASP.NET web development should not be difficult. This book and WebMatrix will make it much easier for you than your predecessors found. Over the next 14 chapters, you will build your first site and progressively acquire the skills necessary to embellish it with controlling code and database interactivity. You will be shown how to manage errors in your code, make your site secure from potential hackers, protect areas from unauthorized users and finally deploy it to a web server so that the world can come and visit it. And when you have finished the final chapter, you will find further resources listed for you so that you can continue your progression as a web developer.

WHO THIS BOOK IS FOR

This book is designed for anyone wanting to learn, or wanting to teach how to build dynamic websites using the latest Microsoft technologies. Whether you want to get a simple personal site up and running quickly, or you intend to embark on a career as a professional web developer, this book will provide you with a firm foundation to achieve your goals. No prior experience of web development is assumed. A very basic introduction to the core technologies behind web development is provided to get you up and running if you have no previous web development experience at all.

If you come from another technology, such as ASP classic, or PHP, or if you have previously attempted to tackle ASP.NET development from the Web forms or MVC angle, this book is designed just for you too.

WHAT THIS BOOK COVERS

This book teaches you how to build websites using the latest technology from Microsoft: WebMatrix. The book starts with a description of what WebMatrix is, why Microsoft created it, and how to get hold of it. From that point, each subsequent chapter covers a significant topic relevant to developing web applications with the ASP.NET Web Page framework, and over time, you build on the knowledge acquired in previous chapters to create a working, database driven website. The book is presented in 14 chapters:

➤ Chapter 1, "Getting Started with WebMatrix." This chapter introduces you to WebMatrix and explains what it is, how to obtain it, install it, and how to create a simple one page site. Then you are taken on a tour of the WebMatrix IDE, and shown the key features of the tool that you will use in forthcoming chapters.

➤ Chapter 2, "Designing Web Pages." The basis of the web is HTML or HyperText Markup Language. In this chapter you are provided with an introduction to HTML — what it is and how it works. You are also introduced to CSS or Cascading Style Sheets — a technology used to control the styling of your web pages.

➤ Chapter 3, "Designing Websites." Having learned how to design individual web pages, you need to know how to apply that design consistently across an entire site. This chapter explores the mechanisms available within the Web Pages framework that simplify the application of designs across multiple pages, and make maintaining those pages easier.

➤ Chapter 4, "Programming Your Site." The engine that drives any dynamic site is programming logic. This chapter introduces you to the most popular .NET language, C#, and the basics of programming with that language. You are also introduced to Razor, a templating syntax that enables you to embed C# within your HTML.

➤ Chapter 5, "Adding User Interactivity." The best sites allow users to contribute content or feedback, or to personalize the site according to their preferences. These activities demand that the site developers provide a mechanism by which users can interact with the site. This is done through forms. This chapter examines the fundamentals behind working with forms, including processing and validating user input. You will also see how to send data submitted from a form by e-mail.

➤ Chapter 6, "AJAX and jQuery." AJAX is an important technology for creating rich user experiences. jQuery is a popular third party JavaScript library that provides AJAX management as well as animation and effects. In this chapter, you will learn the basics of jQuery and how to use it to apply effects and AJAX functionality to your site.

➤ Chapter 7, "Packages." Packages are third party code libraries that incorporate specific pieces of functionality. In essence, they save you having to reinvent the wheel for a lot of common tasks. WebMatrix includes a Package Administration tool, and this chapter shows how to use that as well as explaining the benefits of packages. In particular, the chapter focuses on the use of the FileUpload helper which comes within the Web Helpers Package.

➤ Chapter 8, "Working with Files and Images." Once you have uploaded files using the FileUpload helper, you will want to work with them or save them somewhere. This chapter explores how to create files and folders and how to manipulate files. In particular, you examine the WebImage Helper which is designed to make manipulating images easy.

➤ Chapter 9, "Debugging and Error Handling." You will make mistakes when programming your site, and there are tools available to you that help to locate and identify errors. This chapter explores those tools and other techniques that help you create error free applications.

➤ Chapter 10, "Introduction to Data and Databases." You need to understand databases if you want to build truly dynamic sites. This chapter explains what they are and how to create a SQL Server Compact database for use with your website. You will also learn the basics of SQL, the language that databases understand, so that you can programmatically store and retrieve data. The Database Helper is a core component within the Web Pages framework, and you will learn how to use it to communicate with your database.

➤ Chapter 11, "A Deeper Dive into Data Access." You will learn how to communicate securely with your database, and how to create forms for every conceivable data operation: Create, Read, Update, and Delete. You will explore the WebGrid Helper, a component used for displaying tabular data.

➤ Chapter 12, "Security." You may want to secure parts of your website against unauthorized access. This chapter explores the basics behind ASP.NET security, and examines the WebSecurity Helper. You will learn how to create a registration form to enable people to create accounts on your site, and how to manage their level of access based on the roles they are assigned.

➤ Chapter 13, "Optimizing Your Site." Once you have built your website, you want to ensure that it performs well on search engines and on the web server. This chapter explores the tools offered by WebMatrix to help you with Search Engine Optimization (SEO). You also examine caching — a technique for improving performance on the server.

➤ Chapter 14, "Deploying Your Site." Finally, you need to deploy your site to a web host. This chapter provides an overview of the tools offered by WebMatrix to help you locate a suitable hosting company, test their compatibility and to deploy your site to a live server.

HOW THIS BOOK IS STRUCTURED

This book follows the tried and tested formula that has made the Wrox "Beginning" series such a success. It takes a task-oriented approach to learning. As you progress through the book, you will take what you have learned and apply it to a sample website, building on functionality and features as you go.

Concepts are introduced in sections, and then worked through in a step-by-step approach familiar to Wrox readers in Try It Out exercises. Each of these exercises is followed by a How It Works section, which explains how the concepts under examination are applied in practice.

At the end of each chapter, you will find a series of exercise questions which will help you test the knowledge you gained from the chapter. Answers to these questions are provided in the Appendix. Key terms introduced within the chapter are summarized at the end of each chapter.

The focus of this book is on learning how to develop websites using the ASP.NET Web Pages framework and WebMatrix. There are other technologies that you need to know to become a successful developer, and they are touched on in chapters that cover HTML, CSS, and SQL. However, these chapters only provide an introduction to these technologies, and you are encouraged to extend your learning on the topics if you really want to master your art. References to books and other resources that might help you are provided in the relevant chapters.

WHAT YOU NEED TO USE THIS BOOK

All you need is a system which meets the minimum requirements for the installation of WebMatrix and the Microsoft .NET Framework version 4.0:

➤ Windows 7

➤ Windows Server 2008

➤ Windows Server 2008 R2

➤ Windows Vista SP1 or later

➤ Windows XP SP3

➤ Windows Server 2003 SP2

You will be shown how to obtain and install WebMatrix in Chapter 1. To do that, you need an Internet connection.

CONVENTIONS

To help you get the most from the text and keep track of what's happening, we've used a number of conventions throughout the book.

TRY IT OUT

The *Try It Out* is an exercise you should work through, following the text in the book.

1. It usually consists of a set of steps.

2. Each step has a number.

3. Follow the steps through with your copy of the database.

How It Works

After each *Try It Out*, the code you've typed will be explained in detail.

 WARNING *Boxes with a warning icon like this one hold important, not-to-be-forgotten information that is directly relevant to the surrounding text.*

NOTE *The pencil icon indicates notes, tips, hints, tricks, and/or asides to the current discussion.*

As for styles in the text:

➤ We *highlight* new terms and important words when we introduce them.

➤ We show keyboard strokes like this: Ctrl+A.

➤ We show file names, URLs, and code within the text like so: `persistence.properties`.

➤ We present code in two different ways:

```
We use a monofont type with no highlighting for most code examples.
```

```
We use bold to emphasize code that is particularly important in the present
context or to show changes from a previous code snippet.
```

Also, the WebMatrix code editor provides a rich color scheme to indicate various parts of code syntax. That's a great tool to help you learn language features in the editor and to help prevent mistakes as you code. To reinforce WebMatrix colors, the code listings in this book are colorized using colors similar to what you would see on screen in the code editor when working with the book's code. In order to optimize print clarity, some colors have a slightly different hue in print than what you see on screen. But all of the colors for the code in this book should be close enough to the default WebMatrix colors to give you an accurate representation of the colors.

SOURCE CODE

As you work through the examples in this book, you may choose either to type in all the code manually, or to use the source code files that accompany the book. All the source code used in this book is available for download at `www.wrox.com`. When at the site, simply locate the book's title (use the Search box or one of the title lists) and click the Download Code link on the book's detail page to obtain all the source code for the book. Code that is included on the website is highlighted by the following icon:

Available for download on Wrox.com

Listings include the filename in the title. If it is just a code snippet, you'll find the filename in a code note such as this:

Code snippet filename

NOTE *Because many books have similar titles, you may find it easiest to search by ISBN; this book's ISBN is 978-1-118-05048-4.*

Once you download the code, just decompress it with your favorite compression tool. Alternately, you can go to the main Wrox code download page at `www.wrox.com/dynamic/books/download .aspx` to see the code available for this book and all other Wrox books.

ERRATA

We make every effort to ensure that there are no errors in the text or in the code. However, no one is perfect, and mistakes do occur. If you find an error in one of our books, like a spelling mistake or faulty piece of code, we would be very grateful for your feedback. By sending in errata, you may save another reader hours of frustration, and at the same time, you will be helping us provide even higher quality information.

To find the errata page for this book, go to `www.wrox.com` and locate the title using the Search box or one of the title lists. Then, on the book details page, click the Book Errata link. On this page, you can view all errata that has been submitted for this book and posted by Wrox editors.

 NOTE *A complete book list, including links to each book's errata, is also available at* `www.wrox.com/misc-pages/booklist.shtml`.

If you don't spot "your" error on the Book Errata page, go to `www.wrox.com/contact/techsupport .shtml` and complete the form there to send us the error you have found. We'll check the information and, if appropriate, post a message to the book's errata page and fix the problem in subsequent editions of the book.

P2P.WROX.COM

For author and peer discussion, join the P2P forums at `p2p.wrox.com`. The forums are a Web-based system for you to post messages relating to Wrox books and related technologies and interact with other readers and technology users. The forums offer a subscription feature to e-mail you topics of interest of your choosing when new posts are made to the forums. Wrox authors, editors, other industry experts, and your fellow readers are present on these forums.

At `p2p.wrox.com`, you will find a number of different forums that will help you, not only as you read this book, but also as you develop your own applications. To join the forums, just follow these steps:

1. Go to `p2p.wrox.com` and click the Register link.

2. Read the terms of use and click Agree.

3. Complete the required information to join, as well as any optional information you wish to provide, and click Submit.

4. You will receive an e-mail with information describing how to verify your account and complete the joining process.

 NOTE *You can read messages in the forums without joining P2P, but in order to post your own messages, you must join.*

Once you join, you can post new messages and respond to messages other users post. You can read messages at any time on the Web. If you would like to have new messages from a particular forum e-mailed to you, click the Subscribe to this Forum icon by the forum name in the forum listing.

For more information about how to use the Wrox P2P, be sure to read the P2P FAQs for answers to questions about how the forum software works, as well as many common questions specific to P2P and Wrox books. To read the FAQs, click the FAQ link on any P2P page.

1

Getting Started with WebMatrix

WHAT YOU WILL LEARN IN THIS CHAPTER:

➤   What WebMatrix is all about

➤   How to acquire and install WebMatrix

➤   How to create a simple site with WebMatrix

➤   Where to go within WebMatrix to get things done

➤   What file types you are likely to be working with

➤   How to structure a website

In the early days of web development on the Windows platform — in the 90s of the last decade — Microsoft offered a relatively simple and approachable technology, now referred to as Classic ASP, which enabled inexperienced web developers and even non-programmers to build simple websites. Getting started with Classic ASP was easy; all you needed was a text editor and a hosting account to run your site. With the release of ASP.NET and Visual Studio .NET in early 2002, the web development landscape changed considerably. Although extremely powerful, ASP.NET is not easily approachable, and certainly not so for non-programmers. It has a pretty steep learning curve and requires experience in programming. The tool used to build ASP.NET websites — Visual Studio — is also a lot more complex to use than a simple text editor. In addition, it takes a fair bit of time to download and install Visual Studio.

Although the advent of ASP.NET and Visual Studio addressed the needs of experienced and professional programmers and was generally seen as a major leap forward, Microsoft no longer had a good option for people starting out with web development. To accommodate this group of users and make it easier for them to start developing websites on the Windows platform, Microsoft developed *WebMatrix* that was first released in January 2011. In this book, you'll get an in-depth look at WebMatrix and how to use it, starting with instructions on acquiring and installing WebMatrix in this chapter, all the way down to deploying a fully functional website to a production environment in Chapter 14.

In the next section you'll learn what WebMatrix is and how to install it. The section that follows introduces you to ASP.NET Web Pages — the development framework you'll be using in WebMatrix. The second half of this chapter then gives you an extensive tour of the WebMatrix user interface.

INTRODUCING WEBMATRIX

In this introductory section you'll learn what WebMatrix is and why you should use it. In addition, you'll learn how to acquire and install it, setting you up for the many exercises you'll find throughout this book.

What Is WebMatrix?

Many people tend to refer to WebMatrix as the lightweight tool to create web pages using the new Web Pages Framework and Razor syntax. However, WebMatrix is more than just the tool. WebMatrix is a stack of software components required to build web applications delivered seamlessly in one package. There are four core components to the stack: a web server (IIS Express); a development framework (.NET 4.0); a database platform (SQL Server Compact Edition 4.0); and a lightweight web authoring and management tool.

IIS Express is a lightweight web server used to serve up pages and other requests made by the browser. It offers all of the core features of the full version of IIS 7, the web server that is typically used in production hosting scenarios on server editions of Windows. It doesn't require administrator privileges to run, nor does it require complex configuration. It can run on any operating system from Windows XP upwards (including Home Edition).

The .NET Framework is a huge collection of code libraries, which offer pre-built solutions to many, many common programming problems. The framework also includes a common language infrastructure, which enables developers to pick from many languages to write their applications in. The most popular languages are C# and VB. ASP.NET is a web development framework that sits on top of the .NET Framework.

SQL Server Compact Edition (SQL CE) is a file-based database system, which you use to store your data in. Since it is file-based, SQL CE does not require you to run a setup program or install and configure a database server in order to use it. Databases are stored as files on disk with an SDF extension (similar to an Access database), and are easily copied to a web server or other machine via FTP, X-Copy, or similar. The database engine runs in memory within the application and shuts down automatically when it is no longer needed. It has a relatively slim set of features compared to the full version of SQL Server, which makes it very easy to work with.

The WebMatrix UI provides a host of tools for creating websites from templates or from scratch, downloading pre-built Open Source applications and customizing them, managing files, databases, publishing your web application to a web server, testing and configuring your site, optimizing your site for search engines, and more.

Why Should You Use WebMatrix?

There is a wide choice of programming languages and frameworks available to those who are just beginning web development, including PHP, Ruby on Rails, Java, ColdFusion, and even classic ASP — so why choose WebMatrix?

WebMatrix provides a relatively simple approach to web development, which can help you become productive very quickly. But don't let the simplicity of the development tool fool you. Behind the scenes you have access to the full power of the .NET Framework. The .NET Framework is composed literally of thousands of libraries of pre-written code covering nearly every programming requirement you will ever need. Microsoft is constantly expanding the framework, and of course fully supports it. Furthermore, a huge and active community of volunteers actively supports ASP.NET at places such as Wrox's own forums (`http://p2p.wrox.com/`) and the official Microsoft ASP.NET forums (`http://forums.asp.net`), where the authors of this book actively participate and try to answer your questions.

When planning WebMatrix, the development team at Microsoft decided that simplicity is key, and everything they do is driven by a desire to keep the "concept count" low for beginners to web development. There is stuff that every developer of dynamic websites needs to know, regardless of the framework they choose: HTML, CSS, some JavaScript, SQL, and server-side code. To varying degrees, all frameworks obscure some of the unnecessary details relating to these fundamentals. In doing so, some frameworks introduce a new range of concepts to learn and become familiar with. The upside of this is that once the new concepts are learned, you can enjoy a consistent development experience that encourages RAD, or Rapid Application Development. The downside is that learning the new concepts can take a long time and might overwhelm the beginner.

WebMatrix goes back to the roots of web development. It encourages you to immerse yourself in HTML, CSS, JavaScript, and more, which are accessible technologies common to all web development platforms. It also includes a range of "helpers," which are wrappers around some of the common tasks you will perform when developing a website, such as data access, managing security, and sending e-mail. These helpers provide shortcuts more than anything, and they are very easy to learn and use. You typically access these helpers from your web pages using either Visual Basic or C# code. The examples in this book all use C# as the language of choice, but you could follow along with Visual Basic if you prefer.

Another great feature of WebMatrix is its price: It's completely free. This means you can follow along with all the examples from this book, and build great production-ready websites without spending a dime.

How Do You Acquire WebMatrix?

In theory, it's possible to create ASP.NET Web Pages applications using any text-editing package, such as Notepad. In theory, it's also possible for you to commute to work or college on your hands and knees. I wouldn't recommend either as a sensible option. Get a bus or train, drive a car, or cycle to work or college, and use WebMatrix for Web Pages development.

Usually, before you attempt to download and install all the bits that form a web development framework, you would be advised to check that your system meets the minimum requirements. Then you might find yourself hopping around the Internet locating and downloading the various parts that make up the whole. But those days are gone. Microsoft released a product called the Web Platform Installer (WPI), which simplifies the whole process. WPI analyzes your system and identifies if parts of what you need are already installed. It knows which items are dependent on which other items, so all you need to do is select WebMatrix from the list of options, and let WPI do all the work. Your development machine's operating system must be compatible with version 4.0 of the .NET Framework which means you can use any of the following operating systems:

➤ Windows 7

➤ Windows Server 2008

➤ Windows Server 2008 R2

➤ Windows Vista SP1 or later

➤ Windows XP SP3

➤ Windows Server 2003 SP2

> **NOTE** *When you install WebMatrix, you also get a copy of IIS Express, the light-weight web server. This web server requires your Documents folder to be on a local hard drive. You'll run into problems if this folder is stored on the network. If this is the case, locate your Documents folder in Windows, right-click it and choose Properties and switch to the Location tab. You can click the Move icon to move your Documents folder to a local drive, such as your C drive. You can choose to move your existing files to this new location, but this is not required.*

WebMatrix is a small download — about 15MB if you already have .NET 4.0 installed, rising to about 50MB if WPI needs to fetch .NET 4.0 for you as well.

TRY IT OUT Installing WebMatrix

This exercise guides you through the simple process of acquiring, downloading, and installing WebMatrix using the Web Platform Installer.

1. You can download WebMatrix via the Web Platform Installer (WPI) from this Microsoft site: www.microsoft.com/web/webmatrix/. If this link ever changes, you can also find the WPI at www.microsoft.com/web. If none of these links works, search the main Microsoft.com website for "WebMatrix" or "Web Platform Installer."

2. At the WebMatrix or WPI website, look for a button such as Install WebMatrix or Install Now and click it. This starts the WPI, which guides you through installing WebMatrix. If you started your download at the WebMatrix site, you'll see a screen similar to the one shown in Figure 1-1.

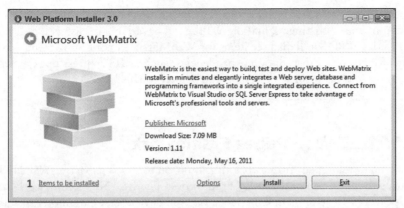

FIGURE 1-1

3. Click Install and follow the on-screen instructions to complete the install. If you started a WPI download instead, you'll see a screen similar to Figure 1-2.

FIGURE 1-2

4. Locate Microsoft WebMatrix in the list (you can use the Search box at the top to find it), add it to the list of downloads by clicking Add, and then click the Install button.

No matter how you started the installation of WebMatrix, your files are now downloaded and installed for you. Within minutes (depending on your Internet connection speed), WebMatrix should be completely installed, and you're ready to roll with the remainder of this book.

How It Works

Rather than going to many different websites finding the latest bits and pieces you need to install separately, Microsoft has released the Web Platform Installer, your one-stop download and installation tool for many of Microsoft's developer applications, such as WebMatrix and Visual Web Developer Express

Edition, as well as many Open Source tools and frameworks. The first time you install Web Platform Installer, it also installs an icon in your Start menu, making WPI readily available in case you need to install additional software. Besides WPI, you'll also see items for WebMatrix in your Start menu. You won't see any additional icons for the other installation dependencies, such as IIS Express or SQL Server CE. You'll learn how to access these tools from within WebMatrix later in this book.

Introducing the ASP.NET Web Pages Framework

ASP.NET Web Pages is a web development framework. It is built on top of the existing ASP.NET Framework, which in turn is built on top of the .NET Framework. The ASP.NET Framework provides an extraordinarily powerful development experience for web developers. Common tasks are wrapped into easy-to-use classes. Authentication, membership and roles management, file management, data access… all of these have their own APIs (Application Programming Interfaces), which make working with them very easy compared to other approaches. The ASP.NET Framework was conceived with the enterprise developer in mind, and reflects the demands that maintaining large, ever-changing sites impose.

Traditional ASP.NET development encourages a separation of code from the presentation layer, using a model called "code behind." Code is placed in separate files in the same way developers of desktop applications had been doing for years. User Interface (UI) elements result from the rendering of so-called server controls, which emit HTML to the browser, shielding the developer from building up that HTML manually.

Other web development frameworks follow a different pattern, in that the HTML is not hidden away. You work directly with it. The Web Pages Framework follows this pattern, which means that the development experience is not unlike the one that PHP or classic ASP developers are used to. Server code is intermixed with HTML using the Razor syntax, which again is a similar experience to other frameworks. And it is easier to learn, mainly because there is not so much to absorb. Razor syntax is a very succinct way to define markup (such as HTML) mixed with server side programming logic. Chapter 4 gives you an in-depth look at Razor and how to use it in your WebMatrix websites.

Despite the fact that Web Pages is easier to learn, it still sits on top of the .NET Framework (and the ASP.NET Framework), which means that sites you develop using Web Pages can be as complex and functional as any built by enterprise developers. The key point, however, is that Web Pages makes building simple sites a simple task. It removes a lot of the configuration steps involved in building sites using either the Web Forms model or the newer MVC model. You simply open WebMatrix, create a new site, and start coding — as you'll see how to do in the next exercise.

TRY IT OUT   Creating Your First Web Pages Application

Now that you have downloaded and installed WebMatrix, it's a good time to build a simple web application to test that everything works correctly on your system. This section shows you how to do that, and then explores a bit of the details behind it in the "How It Works" section.

1.   Start WebMatrix from the Windows Start menu. You should be presented with the Quick Start screen, as shown in Figure 1-3.

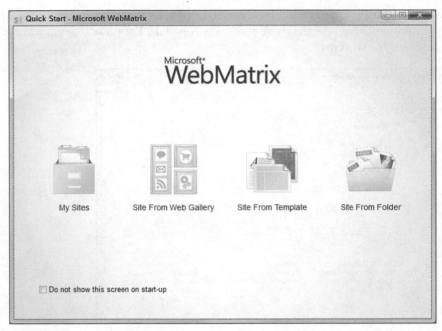

FIGURE 1-3

Notice the option in the bottom-left corner where you can choose not to see this screen in the future. If you accidentally turned it off now, you can turn it on later by clicking the main WebMatrix button and then choosing Options. You find the option to turn on the Quick Start screen in the General Options for Working with WebMatrix section.

2. Ignoring the other three options for the moment, click Site From Template.

3. Click the Empty Site template to select it from the options available. You can name this site anything you like in the Site Name box at the bottom. For this exercise, call the site **My First Site**, and click OK. You should see a message that your site is being created from the chosen template, which is then replaced with a confirmation that your site has been started successfully. The confirmation message appears temporarily at the bottom of the screen.

4. By default, WebMatrix always opens your site with the Site option selected in the left pane and the Site workspace visible, as shown in Figure 1-4.

    You will explore the various workspaces later in the chapter, but for now, click the Files button in the lower-left corner. You will be shown a screen that invites you to add a new file to your site. You can also see that the Empty Site template is an appropriate name — there are no files there to begin with except a file called robots.txt, which is explained later in this book.

5. There are three ways to add a new file to your site. The first is simply to click the link in the middle of the workspace. The second option is available from what is called the *Ribbon Bar* — the main toolbar at the top of the WebMatrix window. This hosts a collection of icons and text used to represent many of the tasks and actions you can perform with WebMatrix. In the second group of items — Files — you can see the word New under a document icon. If you click that, you are offered

the option to add a new file or folder. Finally, you can right-click on the site name at the top of the left pane. The first option provided by the context menu is New File. For now, though, just click the link in the middle of the workspace.

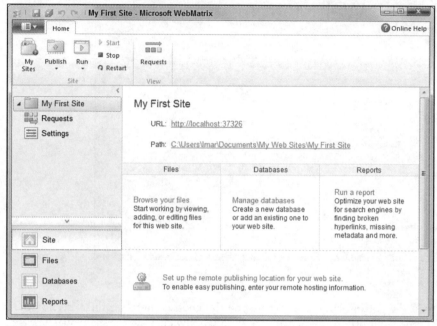

FIGURE 1-4

6. The next step is to choose a file type. The options available to you will depend on which category — Common, Suggested, or All — is selected at the top left of the screen. You will explore the various file types later in this chapter. In the meantime, choose CSHTML, which is a *C# Razor* file; leave the filename to its default of Page.cshtml; and click OK.

7. Add the following bold text and code between the opening and closing body tags:

```
<body>
  <h1>Welcome to the WebMatrix!</h1>
  <p>I began to become a web developer on @DateTime.Now.ToString()</p>
</body>
```

Whenever you see bold text and code in this book, you only need to type that. Any non-bolded text should already be present in the file you are working on, if you have followed along correctly.

Don't let the @ sign bother you too much at this point. This is an intrinsic part of the Razor syntax, and over the next few chapters, you are going to become great friends with it.

8. Press Ctrl+S to save the changes to the page, and press F12 to run it in your default browser. If all goes as planned, you should see something similar to Figure 1-5.

If you get an error message instead, there are two possible causes. If the error summary message is HTTP Error 403.14 - Forbidden or HTTP Error 404.20 - Not Found, you have probably not requested your new page directly, but its parent folder. In that case, go back to WebMatrix, double-click your page in the Files list, and try again.

FIGURE 1-5

If the error message relates to a compilation error, chances are that you have a spelling mistake in your code. C# is case-sensitive, so make sure that you have used exactly the right combination of upper- and lowercase letters in DateTime.Now.ToString().

NOTE *If you get a message from Internet Explorer about Intranet settings, click the button that lets you turn on these Intranet settings. You may want to follow the Help option first to learn more about this feature.*

9. Assuming that you managed to run the page successfully, make a note of the time that you began your web development career, and then refresh the page in the browser by pressing F5. You should see that the time has just been updated.

Congratulations, you just completed your first web application!

How It Works

When you added the CSHTML file to the site, it started life with some *HTML* or *Hypertext Markup Language* already added by WebMatrix by default. The two lines of code that you added consist of a mixture of more HTML (the items enclosed in angle brackets), static content ("Welcome to the WebMatrix" and "I began to become a web developer on") and some server-side code — the part preceded by the @ symbol. When you requested the page in your browser, the web server — IIS Express — was called into action. Its job is to serve web pages as HTML so that the browser can understand the result and display it. HTML is a language that is used mainly by web browsers like Internet Explorer and Firefox so that they can recognize the structure and content of a document. IIS Express comes preconfigured to recognize the file types that are being requested and served. Some file types, such as images and static HTML files (ending with HTM or HTML), are served without any fuss at all. Others, like C# Razor files (with a CSHTML extension), are mapped within IIS Express to separate processing engines to transform the file from its raw server-side format (with the code blocks in it) to something that the browser understands. In the case of CSHTML files, they are mapped to ASP.NET. On your development box, the client (your browser) and the server (IIS Express) are located on the same physical machine. After you've put your site in production, the client and server parts of your site will be on different machines. Your site's files are hosted and served up on a server running IIS (the web server on Windows machines) while clients (potentially from all over the world) make requests for your pages using their browser. Chapter 14 digs deeper into deployment and shows you how to copy your site to one of the on-line services offering WebMatrix hosting facilities.

ASP.NET's role is to examine the content of the file and identify whether any server-side code embedded within it needs to be executed. You will most often use server-side code to generate content dynamically, depending on certain conditions. In the previous "Try It Out," the dynamic content was the current date and time. When you refreshed the page, the content was updated according to the system clock on the server at the point the code was executed.

If you have closed the browser, press F12 again or click the Run button on the Ribbon Bar in WebMatrix.

Now right-click anywhere on the page in the browser and select the relevant browser menu option to view the page source. The HTML source code that reached the browser should open in your default text editor. If you examine it, you can see that nearly all of it is identical to the code in the CSHTML file you created, except that `@DateTime.Now.ToString()` has been replaced with the current date and time in plaintext.

In the following section you'll get a more detailed look at what happens when you request a page in your browser.

How the Web Works

One of the most important aspects to becoming a successful web developer is to understand the relationship between the user's web browser and the web server. Judging by the type of questions that regularly appear in the ASP.NET forums — even from people who seem to have been programming websites for some time — this relationship is very often misunderstood or not considered at all. Although you saw some aspects of this relationship in the preceding section, it's now time to examine this issue in more detail.

Imagine that you are sitting in a restaurant. The waiter comes over and asks you for your food order. He takes out his pad and notes which table you are sitting at, and details of the menu items you would like. Then he disappears. A while later the waiter reappears with your order. You don't know where your meal came from or how it was prepared. You probably don't care as long as the meal is edible.

While he or she was gone, the waiter passed your food order to the chef in the kitchen. The chef sprang into action and prepared the order. A part of the order may have been fulfilled without any real work, such as a plain bread roll. Or the order may have needed special processing, such as frying or grilling. These tasks would have been passed to specialists within the kitchen to manage. Once complete, the order is passed to the waiter for delivery. The chef doesn't know what happened to the food that was prepared or where it went. He doesn't care (as long as he receives no complaints). His job is purely to process incoming requests and serve appropriate responses.

Web applications are like this. The browser or client plays the diner's role. The chef is the web server, the waiter is the transport mechanism for the *request* (the meal order) and the *response* (the prepared meal), and the waiter's order pad is the equivalent of the *HyperText Transfer Protocol* (HTTP). The client makes a request, which is conveyed to the correct web server, given the URL of the request. The server examines the request and decides if it can be fulfilled without further ado, or whether some processing is required. The part of the request that is examined primarily is the file extension. This may have been registered with the server and mapped to special processors, such as ASP.NET or PHP; or, in the case of an image or HTML file, there is no need for processing. The raw content of the file is served as a response.

Web Pages files (CSHTML and VBHTML) are mapped to the *ASP.NET run time*. This is part of the Microsoft .NET Framework, which is designed specifically to process web requests. When the ASP.NET run time is asked to process a Web Page file, it looks for two things:

➤ **Static Content:** This includes HTML and textual content. It may also include embedded styling information contained in CSS and JavaScript code. These elements are sent to the browser directly — exactly as they appear in the original file.

➤ **Dynamic Content:** In the previous "Try It Out," you saw that you can embed programming logic inline within HTML in a Web Pages file. Although you used C# in the example, you could do the same with VB. As you progress through this book, you will discover that you can also place code in special blocks or in separate files altogether. ASP.NET is responsible for executing and processing this code, which will most likely produce different results depending on the conditions within the code. For example, you might use code to perform calculations, detect who the current user is, and see if she is permitted to view the current page, hide or reveal data, or process user input supplied via forms. You will see this in a lot more detail beginning in Chapter 4, "Programming Your Site." Before that, Chapter 3, "Designing Websites," shows you how this type of code can help you manage the appearance of your site consistently across pages.

Once the file has been processed and the finalized response is ready, this is sent to the browser for consumption. The web server has no further contact with the browser. It just sits there, waiting for the next request.

To get the most out of WebMatrix, you also need to be familiar with its user interface and the many buttons, panels, and workspaces it contains. In the next section, you'll take a look at the WebMatrix UI, which will prepare you to build your first real site in the following chapter.

A TOUR OF WEBMATRIX

WebMatrix is a very lightweight, but powerful, integrated development environment (IDE). It has been developed specifically for building ASP.NET Web Pages applications, but it can also be used for ASP.NET Web Forms, ASP.NET MVC, PHP, and classic ASP applications. It is known as an *integrated* development environment because it brings together all the tools you need to develop web applications in one place. Each of the tools has its own workspace, and each of the workspaces is accessible through the Workspace Selector at the bottom of the left pane. Before examining each work-space in detail, close WebMatrix if you haven't done so already, and then start it up via the Start menu in Windows. If you ticked the box to prevent the Quick Start screen from appearing in future, WebMatrix should open the last site you worked on. At the moment, this should be "My First Site." If you made no changes to the Quick Start screen, you should be presented with the same four options as illustrated in Figure 1-3, previously. This time choose My Sites, and then select My First Site and click OK. You will be taken to the first workspace — the Site workspace.

The Site Workspace

The primary purpose of the Site workspace is to provide you with a simplified one-page dashboard for accessing the key tasks and information related to managing your sites. To help you familiarize yourself with this workspace, take a look at Figure 1-6, which highlights the main features.

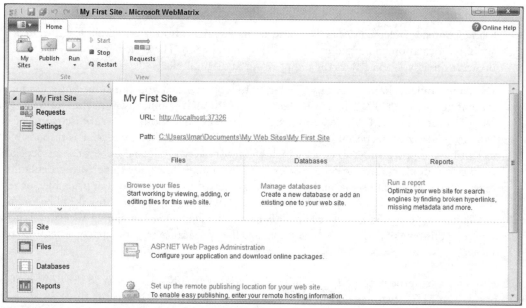

FIGURE 1-6

The Ribbon Bar

At the top of the screen, just below the Windows title bar, you'll see the familiar Ribbon Bar found in many other everyday Microsoft applications. The Ribbon Bar can be divided in tabs, and each tab can contain a number of groups. The only tab available in Figure 1-6 is the Home tab. The first group — Site — stays visible regardless of which workspace you are in, but the other options change depending on the task you perform. You will take a more detailed look at the functions available from the Site group later in the book, along with the purpose and features of the Requests option to the right of the Site group.

Left Pane

The left pane is collapsible. If you click the little arrowhead in the top-right corner, you can expand the right pane by collapsing the left one. Clicking the arrow again reverses this operation. The thin vertical line between the left and right panes is a splitter, and enables you to increase or decrease the width of the panes without collapsing the left one completely by dragging it to the left or right. In the Site workspace, the left pane contains two options — Requests and Settings. The Requests option is duplicated from the Ribbon Bar. Both items will be examined later in the book.

Workspace Selector

The Workspace Selector appears in the same position in all workspaces, below the left pane, and provides easy navigation between the four workspaces. This area is also collapsible.

Right Pane

This is the main work area within WebMatrix. When in the Site workspace, the right pane provides you with details of the currently selected site. These include its URL, which is typically `http://localhost` followed by a random port number. IIS chooses the port number. It is usually a large number, and one that outside sources find difficult to detect, for security reasons. If you click this link, your current site will fire up in a web browser.

You can also see the file path to the current site. By default, when you create a new site, it is added to a folder called My Web Sites within your Documents folder. Clicking this link will open the location of your current site within Windows Explorer. The three options that follow are alternative ways to navigate to the other three workspaces.

The final options in the bottom part of the workspace relate to configuring your site, obtaining a web hosting account if you don't already have one, and publishing your site to a live web server. You will make use of these options in Chapter 14, "Deploying your Site."

At the bottom of the Site workspace is the notifications area, which shows various messages such as whether your current site has been started by IIS or has been stopped. This area is not always visible, as the notifications come and go as appropriate.

If you press and hold down the Alt key, something rather interesting happens, as shown in Figure 1-7.

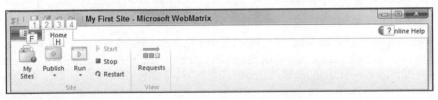

FIGURE 1-7

Just like in Microsoft Office and some other Microsoft applications, letters and numbers appear in specific positions on the Ribbon Bar. These are shortcut keys to the actions on the Ribbon Bar. For example, if you now press H, more letters appear on each item in the various Ribbon Bar groups, providing keyboard shortcuts to the options available. Note that this behavior is not limited to the Site workspace; you can use it anywhere in WebMatrix.

The Files Workspace

The Files workspace (shown in Figure 1-8) is where you are likely to spend most of your time within WebMatrix.

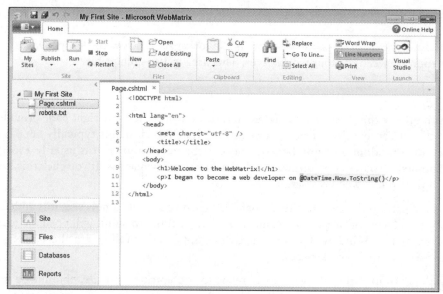

FIGURE 1-8

You can use the Files workspace to add new folders to your site, and work with files from the many types available, including Razor files, HTML files, CSS and JavaScript files, a site configuration file, VB or C# code files — even text and XML files. The options on the Ribbon Bar provide many common text-processing functions associated with working with files. The final option allows you to open the current site in Visual Web Developer 2010 Express Edition or Visual Studio 2010 if you have either of those tools installed. You will see how this could be useful in Chapter 9, "Debugging and Error Handling."

The left pane displays the entire folder structure of your website in a tree view. Files are opened in separate tabs within the right pane, providing you with the ability to have multiple documents opened at any one time. Each opened document displays its filename in the tab itself. You can navigate from one tab to another in a number of ways: You can simply click the tab you want; you can double-click the file in the tree menu in the left pane; you can click the down arrow at the top-right corner of the right pane and select a file from the menu that appears; or you can cycle through all the currently opened documents by pressing Ctrl+Tab.

The Databases Workspace

You will explore the databases workspace in a lot more detail in Chapter 10, "Introduction to Data and Databases." For the time being, all you really need to know is that this workspace makes working with databases very easy. You can create new databases from here and modify them by adding tables and columns. Once you have added database tables, you can open them and view, add, and edit data within them. You will be able to test your queries to ensure that they return the correct data prior to coding them into your website, and there is even a tool for migrating your SQL CE database to the full version of SQL Server.

The Reports Workspace

Once you have built your site, you will probably want people to visit it, but how are they going to know your site exists? The best way to publicize your site is to submit it to search engines. However, will the search engines like your site? Will they understand it? Will they be able to categorize your site in the correct search results? Search Engine Optimization is the practice of making websites highly accessible to search engines so that they index your site for the most appropriate search phrases. Chapter 13, "Optimizing Your Site," explores this topic in a lot more detail. It covers, among other things, how to use the Reports workspace to analyze and report on your existing site, or on other external sites, in order to show what needs fixing or improving to make the sites search-engine friendly.

The Reports workspace is unique to WebMatrix. Even the professional ASP.NET development environments — Visual Web Developer and Visual Studio — don't include this fantastic tool!

Common WebMatrix Templates

To make creating new sites and pages as quick and easy as possible, WebMatrix ships with a number of predefined templates for new files and websites. The next section explains the most commonly used file types, followed by an overview of the available site templates.

File Types

During the "Try It Out" earlier in this chapter, you added a new file to your website. At that time, you were presented with the Choose a File Type dialog box (shown in Figure 1-9), which showed a selection of file types.

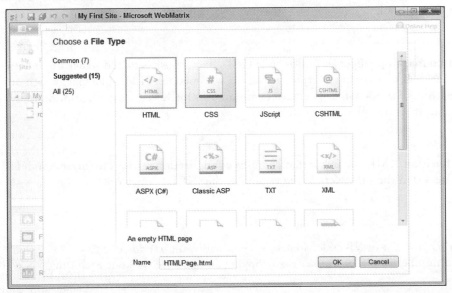

FIGURE 1-9

This section explores the more common file types available to you and explains what they are used for.

HTML

The HTML file type is used for static HTML documents. The content is text based, and served directly by the web server. You will use this file type as part of exercises that are designed to show HTML and CSS. Otherwise, you are unlikely to need this file type for Web Pages development.

CSS

CSS (Cascading Style Sheet) files are used to control the presentation and formatting of web pages. You will learn much more about how to use this kind of file in Chapters 2 and 3.

JScript

JScript is Microsoft's implementation of ECMAScript, which is also the basis of JavaScript. JScript is a client-side (browser-based) scripting language, which is most often used to provide a richer user experience than HTML can offer. For all intents and purposes, JScript and JavaScript are the same thing. For convenience, the term JavaScript will be used throughout this book when referring to JScript files.

CSHTML/VBHTML

Razor syntax can be implemented using either C# or Visual Basic. CSHTML files are ASP.NET Web Pages files that are designed to work with Razor using C#, whereas the VBHTML extension is used for files that contain Razor code using Visual Basic. Note that Razor code can be (and often is) mixed with plain HTML in a CSHTL or VBHTML file.

ASPX (C#/VB), Classic ASP, and PHP

WebMatrix is not just a tool for developing Web Pages sites. You can also develop ASP.NET Web Forms sites with it, as well as sites with Classic ASP or PHP. Web Forms, Classic ASP, and PHP are beyond the scope of this book.

XML

XML is a text-based mark-up language similar to HTML. Its purpose is to add structure to data so that humans and machines can easily interpret it. Data is wrapped in HTML-like tags, which are defined by the creator of the XML file. The most common uses for XML are configuration files, and for transporting data from one platform to another.

Web.Config (4.0)

The Web.Config file is an XML document that contains configuration settings for your ASP.NET Web Pages site. The 4.0 in the title refers to the version of the .NET Framework that the file is set up to use.

Class (C#/VB)

A Class file contains pure C# or VB code. Sometimes you will want to add code to your site that might be used in a number of places. Rather than copying and pasting the code each time you want to use it, you create a routine using pure C# code, and call that routine wherever you need it. You'll see how to make use of class files later in this book.

Besides templates for files, WebMatrix also has templates for complete websites, helping you jump-start your site development.

WebMatrix Site Templates

WebMatrix includes a range of site templates. You have already seen the Empty Site template, which lives up to its name. Now you will explore the other templates and see how they can be used to give you a head start in your website development.

The Starter Site

The Starter Site is just like the Empty Site in that it is blank. It has no theme. Its purpose is to give you a starting point for building a site that makes use of the Web Pages security and membership features, which you will explore in detail in Chapter 12, "Security."

The Bakery Site

The Bakery Site is an example of an e-commerce site. The site content is driven from a database, and the workflow includes a simple online ordering system. You will learn how to use databases to power your site in Chapters 10 and 11.

The Calendar

The Calendar is one of the most advanced sites among the templates and serves as a starter site for an online Calendar application, similar to Outlook Web Access or Google Calendar. It offers features such as adding and viewing events, sharing your calendar with others, downloading event details, and user selectable themes.

The Photo Gallery

The Photo Gallery also includes security and membership and its content is database-driven. The real point behind the Photo Gallery is to showcase some of the built-in WebMatrix features for managing images.

ANATOMY OF A WEB PAGES APPLICATION

You have already been introduced to the types of files you will use most often in your Web Pages development. Using the Calendar as a guide, you will see where the various types of files go, and also learn about some of the special folders offered by WebMatrix. You can either create a new site based on this template in WebMatrix to follow along with this section, or refer to Figure 1-10, which shows the Files workspace for a new Calendar website.

Default Folders in a Web Pages Application

An ASP.NET Web Pages website can contain a number of special folders, each one briefly described in the following sections.

FIGURE 1-10

App_Code

Within ASP.NET, App_Code is a special folder. It is the place where you will add C# or VB Class files containing only C# or VB code.

By default, the web server is configured not to allow users to browse this folder and download its contents. In the Calendar template site, App_Code, contains a number of custom helpers written purely in C#. You will learn more about creating your own helpers in Chapter 4.

App_Data

Like App_Code, the App_Data folder is a special ASP.NET folder. It is also protected from being browsed by users and is primarily used for placing database files. You can put any kind of data in here, including SDF files (for SQL Server Compact), CSV files, XML files, and so on.

Bin

The Bin folder is the place for binary files and compiled assemblies (DLLs). When you use the Package Manager (explored in more detail in Chapter 7, "Packages"), any DLL files will automatically be downloaded and added to the Bin folder. If you find yourself needing to use third-party components, such as those required for managing PDF creation, you will place their library files in the Bin folder. Again, the web server is preconfigured not to serve the contents of this folder to users.

The previous folders all have special meaning in ASP.NET, and their names are important. The following folders are named the way they are by convention. Each of the template sites follows the same naming policy for consistency, but you are free to rename the folders as you like.

Account

When you use the Membership features, you will place your account-management files in the Account folder. In the Calendar sample site, you can see that the files are all CSHTML files, because they need to access a database or perform other server-side tasks. Renaming this folder will require a small configuration change to your site, which you will learn about in Chapter 11, "A Deeper Dive Into Data Access."

Content

By convention, your images and other media files are placed here, along with style sheets (covered in Chapter 3).

Scripts

JScript files containing JavaScript code are placed in the Scripts folder.

Shared

In most articles and books on WebMatrix, the Shared folder is the location for Layout pages (examined in Chapter 3) and reusable blocks of content.

Although you can rename these folders, I advise against it. There are two reasons for that advice: The first is that following a consistent naming convention makes it much easier to locate items in the future. You may not think so now, but it is very easy to forget how your site is structured when you look at it at some time in the future. You will be thankful that you worked consistently when you are asked to add new features to a site you have long forgotten. The second reason is that the folder structure offered by the WebMatrix templates follows the ASP.NET MVC templates. The upgrade process will be a lot simpler if you don't have to rename your folders to follow the slightly different rules that apply to MVC, where for example, the Shared folder does have special meaning.

The Root Folder

There is one more very important folder in an ASP.NET Web Pages site, and that's the Root folder. You won't see this appear in the file and folder view labeled "Root," but it is the top-level directory in which all other folders and files reside. When you look at the folder structure in the left pane, it is the folder that appears at the top of the listing as a grey icon and is labeled with the name of your site.

SUMMARY

In this chapter you learned what WebMatrix is. You learned that it is composed of four integrated parts — a web server, a database platform, a development framework, and a tool for developing websites using Microsoft technologies.

You also learned how to obtain WebMatrix, and how to download and install it very simply using the Web Platform Installer. You tested that your installation was successful through a simple exercise that announced to the world that you are on your way to becoming a web developer. You were introduced to the various workspaces within WebMatrix, which will help you use the tool most effectively when managing different aspects of web development.

Understanding the relationship between the client and the server is fundamental to becoming a successful web developer. This chapter explored that relationship and explained the important roles played by each party in the relationship. It also covered, in simple terms, how ASP.NET works on the web server, and its role in differentiating between HTML, CSS, and code to generate web pages dynamically.

You explored the types of files you are likely to use most often with WebMatrix, and learned their role in helping you build your site. Finally, you looked at the site templates offered by WebMatrix and explored the Calendar site template to understand how to manage your folders and files within a Web Pages application.

In the next chapter, you will learn more about HTML and CSS, and learn how important these technologies are for building websites.

EXERCISES

1. What's the best way to acquire and install WebMatrix?

2. What's the difference between a CSHTML and a CS file?

3. Name at least two special ASP.NET Web Pages folders and explain what types of files they contain. Besides the types of files these folders contain, can you mention another reason why these folders are special?

4. What's the difference between static and dynamic files?

Answers to the Exercises can be found in the Appendix.

▶ **WHAT YOU LEARNED IN THIS CHAPTER**

TOPIC	KEY CONCEPTS
WebMatrix	A stack of software components to build web applications. There are four core components to the stack: A web server (IIS Express); a development framework (.NET 4.0); a database platform (SQL Server Compact Edition 4.0); and a lightweight web authoring and management tool. Often, the "lightweight web authoring tool" is simply referred to as WebMatrix.
IIS Express	A lightweight web server designed specifically to be used during development.
SQL Server Compact Edition 4.0	A file-based database system used to store data.
Web Platform Installer (WPI)	The unified download tool for many of Microsoft's developer products.
Razor syntax	A simple programming syntax for embedding server-based code in a web page. It enables you to mix plain HTML and server-side logic in a very succinct way.

Designing Web Pages

WHAT YOU WILL LEARN IN THIS CHAPTER:

➤   An overview of HTML

➤   The basic syntax of HTML

➤   An overview of cascading style sheets

➤   The basic syntax of CSS

➤   How to bring the two technologies together

In the previous chapter, after you downloaded and installed WebMatrix, you tested your installation by creating a page in a new website and modified its content before running the page in the browser. When you created the new page, you saw that WebMatrix had already added some HTML mark up to the file before you modified it. HTML is fundamental to web development, so this chapter will provide you with a basic introduction to the topic and show you how to work with HTML to construct web pages.

Construction of web pages is obviously a crucial first step. However, it is only a first step. Managing the presentation and styling of the content is important if you want to create attractive pages. During the course of this chapter, you will also learn how to do that using *cascading style sheets* (CSS).

INTRODUCING HTML

HyperText Markup Language, or HTML, is a means by which structure and format is applied to a text-based document which is primarily intended to be displayed by a web browser. HTML was originally introduced in 1991, and together with the specification for the *HyperText Transfer Protocol* (HTTP), this formed the birth of the World Wide Web. HTML has undergone a number of version changes since then, the most recent of which is HTML 4.01, which was agreed as a Recommendation in 1999. Each Recommendation builds on the previous one, adding functionality and clarifying rules. The next major revision of HTML, version 5, is currently at Working Draft stage. You will hear more about *HTML5* later in this chapter.

At this point, it is worth mentioning Extensible HyperText Markup Language or *XHTML*. XHTML was introduced in 2000, not long after HTML 4.01 became a Recommendation. A Recommendation is the final stage in the process that the World Wide Web Consortium (The W3C) follows when creating standards and protocols that define the "World Wide Web." XHTML is a subset of XML, which has much stricter rules than HTML (which is an application of Standard Generalized Markup Language, or SGML), and it was introduced primarily to allow a much wider variety of devices to work with web documents, without having to add processing overhead just to be able to parse HTML. Since XHTML follows the strict rules that govern XML, simple XML parsers can parse the content. Web browsers are very lenient when it comes to parsing HTML, and they cater for all sorts of broken rules. This comes at a cost because a lot of processing power is needed. Lower powered devices need a lighter-weight processing engine and XML parsers fit the bill.

HTML is made up of a series of *tags* which surround content, and contain structural and formatting information, which is intended to define how the document should be understood and displayed. When a web browser receives HTML or XHTML from a web server as described in the previous chapter, it parses the HTML and applies some styling and formatting to the document for display based on the instructions in the tags. The styling applied to HTML documents by browsers — the *default style sheet* — can differ from browser to browser in small ways, but by and large, they all follow the same conventions when interpreting and implementing the rules laid down in the Recommendations.

HTML Elements and Tags

Most HTML *elements* follow the same tag format:

```
<open-tag>Some text for display</close-tag>
```

HTML *tags* are enclosed in angled brackets. The difference between the opening tag and the closing tag is that the closing tag is preceded by a forward slash (/) before the tag name. A handful of tags do not follow this format. They are known as self-closing tags, and they look like this:

```
<self-closing tag />
```

You will see the most commonly used self-closing tag shortly. Before that, have another look at the code you added to the Razor file in the previous chapter:

```
<h1>Hello WebMatrix!</h1>
<p>I began to become a web developer on @DateTime.Now.ToString()</p>
```

The text "Hello WebMatrix" is enclosed in <h1> tags. Altogether, the opening tag, the content, and the closing tag form an element. This particular element is a top-level heading. Further up the document, you see the opening tag for the body element. Towards the end of the document, you see the closing tag for the body element. The h1 and p elements that you added are *child* elements of the body element. Elements can contain text and/or other elements.

When the browser encounters an `<h1>` tag, it typically displays the content within the heading using a large and bold font. There are five further heading levels, numbered from two to six. Recalling the way that this text was displayed when you ran the page, you will remember that "Hello WebMatrix" appeared large and bold, but it also appeared on a line of its own. Headings are *block-level* elements. Block-level elements begin on a new line by default. The fact that the text you added appears on separate lines within the file has nothing to do with the resulting display. If you placed both lines on one, the rendered result would have been the same. Browsers ignore line breaks and most of the white space in HTML, except in one specific instance — when the `<pre>` tag is used. You will test this out shortly.

Another type of element is known as an *inline* element. These don't start new lines, but offer a way to tell the browser that their content needs particular treatment, or has special meaning. One very common example of inline tags is `<strong>`. Any text contained within a `strong` element is rendered using a bold font by the browser. To force a new line without using a block-level element, you use the `<br />` tag, which is the promised example of the most commonly used self-closing tag.

A full description of all HTML elements is way beyond the scope of this book. Table 2-1 summarizes the more important elements, but you can refer to the W3C site (the organization responsible for maintaining the HTML Standards) for more information here: `www.w3.org/TR/html401/index/elements.html`.

TABLE 2-1: Common HTML Elements

TAG	DESCRIPTION	EXAMPLE

`<html>`	Delimits the beginning and end of an HTML document.	`<html>`
		`… All other content`
		`</html>`

`<head>`	There can only be one `<head>` section, and it contains information about the document such as the title and description.	`<head>`
		`… document related information`
		`</head>`

`<title>`	Appears in the head and is displayed in the browser's title bar.	`<title>Beginning WebMatrix</title>`

`<body>`	Denotes the displayable content within the document.	`<body>`
		`… all displayable content`
		`</body>`

`<div>`	Used to define sections within an HTML document. A block-level element which forces a new line after its content.	`<div>`
		`First section of content goes here`
		`</div>`
		`<div>`
		`Second section goes here and displayed on a new line`
		`</div>`

continues

TABLE 2-1 *(continued)*

TAG	DESCRIPTION	EXAMPLE

`<p>`	A paragraph element. Like div, this is also a block-level element that forces a new line at the end of its content.	`<p>`
		`First paragraph of text goes here.`
		`</p>`
		`<p>`
		`Second paragraph appears on a new line.`
		`</p>`

`<span>`	An inline container used mainly to provide a means to apply styles to parts of a block of text.	`<p>` `This is normal text while <span style="background-color:yellow"> this part has a yellow background </span>`
`<strong>` `<b>`	Enclosed text is rendered with a bold font. Speech-based browsers might attach semantic meaning to `<strong>` but not to `<b>`.	`<strong>This text</strong> will be displayed in a bold font`
`<em>` `<i>`	Enclosed text is rendered in italics. Speech-based browsers will attach emphasis to `<em>` but not to `<i>`.	`Please go to the fire point <em>immediately</em>`

`<ul>`
`<ol>`
`<li>`
	Used to define bulleted lists. `<ol>` is an ordered list in which each item is numbered sequentially. `<ul>` is an unordered list in which each item is prefixed by a bullet point. `<li>` denotes the individual items in the list.	`<ol>`
		`<li>First item numbered 1</li>`
		`<li>Second item numbered 2</li>`
		`</ol>`
		`<ul>`
		`<li>First item with a bullet</li>`
		`<li>Second item with a bullet</li>`
		`</ul>`

`<table>`
`<tr>`
`<td>`
	Used to display tabular data. `<table>` indicates the start of the table, `<tr>` represents each row, and `<td>` represents a single cell within the table.	`<table>`
		`<tr>`
		`<td>Top left cell</td>`
		`<td>Top right cell</td>`
		`</tr>`
		`<tr>`
		`<td>Bottom left cell</td>`
		`<td>Botton right cell</td>`
		`</tr>`
		`</table>`

TAG	DESCRIPTION	EXAMPLE

`<form>`	Denotes the beginning and end of a form.	`<form>`
		`... inputs go here`
		`</form>`

`<fieldset>`	Groups related form elements.	`<fieldset>`
		`Name: <input type="text />`
		`Email: <input type="text" />`
		`</fieldset>`

`<legend>`	Provides a caption for a `<fieldset>` element.	`<fieldset>`
		`<legend>Register Now</legend>`
		`...`
		`Other inputs`
		`...`
		`</fieldset>`

`<input>`	Depending on the value provided for the `type` attribute, this will render some kind of data entry field in a form.	`<input type="textbox" />`
		`<input type="radio" />`
		`<input type="submit" />`

`<select>`
`<option>`
	Renders a drop-down list of choices for the user. An `<option>` represents an individual item in the list.	`<select>`
		`<option>Pick One!</option>`
		`<option>Pick me!</option>`
		`<option>No - pick Me!</option>`
		`</select>`

`<textarea>`	Provides the user with a multi-line data entry field.	`<textarea> Some multi-line content</textarea>`
`<img>`	Specifies that an image should be rendered.	`<img src="myimage.gif" />`
`<a>`	Generates a hyperlink.	`<a href="mypage.htm">Click here</a>`

`<pre>`	Maintains the formatting of the text it contains, including white space and new lines. Displays the content in a monospace font by default. Typically used for code listings.	`<pre>`
		`Some content`
		`here`
		`</pre>`

Tag Attributes

HTML tags can contain one or more *attributes* that provide additional information about the element. You may have noticed this in the description of the `<input>` element in the preceding table, where the `type` attribute is used to specify how the input element should be rendered. Attributes are always specified in the opening tag, and consist of name/value pairings. Some attributes are required. For instance, an `img` element must contain an `src` attribute whose value is the URL of the image file. Some of the more common attributes that you will work with are listed in Table 2-2 together with an explanation of their meaning and use.

TABLE 2-2: Common HTML Attributes

ATTRIBUTE	PURPOSE	EXAMPLE USAGE
src	Points to the URL of an image or script. Used mainly in `<img>` and `<script>` tags. Required.	`<img src="myimage.gif" />` `<script src="myscript.js"></script>`
id	Provides a unique identity for an element. Useful for referencing individual elements with JavaScript or CSS.	`<div id="maincontent">`
name	Used to reference a form field.	`<input type="text" name="firstname" />`
style	Defines an inline style.	`<span style="color:red">Some text</span>`
class	Specifies a CSS class name for the element.	`<div class="error"></div>`
title	Provides extra information about an element or its content. In most browsers, this appears in a pop-up tooltip.	`<span title="Important Information"></span>`

type	Works with the `input` element to specify the nature of the item to be rendered.	`<input type="textbox" />`
		`<input type="radio" />`
		`<input type="submit" />`

href	Defines the destination of a hyperlink or the source of a resource.	`<a href=http://www.wrox.com>Visit the Wrox site</a>`

In the next section you will put some of these tags and attributes together into an HTML document so that you can familiarize yourself with them and see how they behave in the browser.

TRY IT OUT   Inline and Block-Level Elements

1. Open WebMatrix and create a new site from the Empty Site template. Name the site **Trying Out HTML**.

2. You are going to add a file. Click Browse Your Files in the middle of the Sites workspace. Since the site is empty, you can click the Create a New File button in the middle of the Files workspace. (See Figure 2-1.)

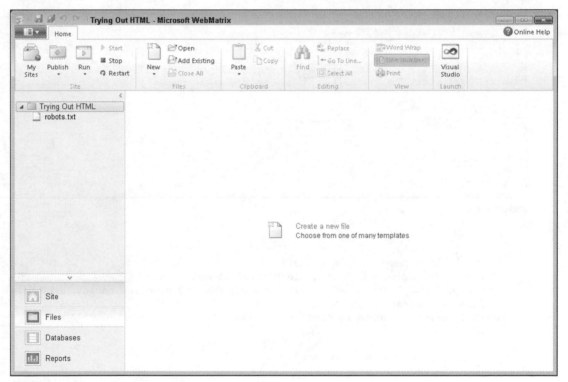

FIGURE 2-1

From the list of available file types, choose HTML File and name the file **Page1.html**.

3. Add the following code within the body element. As you do, notice how the *IntelliSense* feature within WebMatrix comes into play, which is shown in Figure 2-2. You will learn more about IntelliSense shortly.

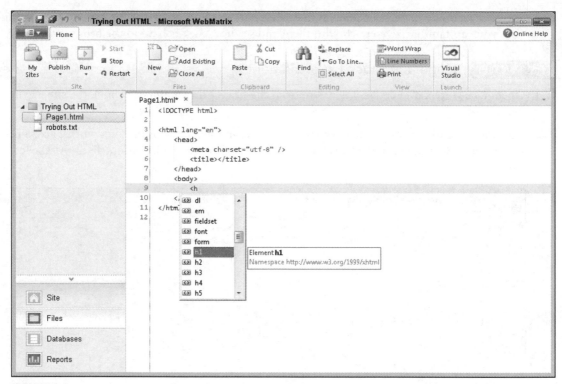

FIGURE 2-2

```
<body>
    <h1>HTML Block Level Elements</h1>
    <div>This is a div, which is a block level element.</div>
    <div style="background-color:yellow">This div has a yellow background.</div>
    <p>This is a paragraph.</p>
    <p>This paragraph contains some <span style="background-color:yellow">
        highlighted</span> text.</p>
    <div title="White space ignored!">HTML ignores
        linebreaks and white space
            in the
        source…
    </div>
    <pre>
                … except when
                the &lt;pre&gt; tag
                is used.
    </pre>
</body>
```

4. Press F12 to run the page in your default browser. It should resemble Figure 2-3.

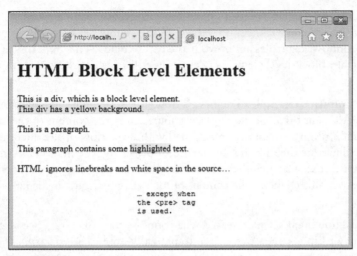

FIGURE 2-3

Have a look at the browser's title bar in particular. It should show `http://localhost:nnnnn/ Page1.html`, where *nnnnn* is a randomly generated number as in Figure 2-4. You can also see *localhost* in the browser's tab.

FIGURE 2-4

5. Go back to the page you named Page1.html and add the following between the opening and closing `<title>` tag

```
<title>HTML Block Level Elements</title>
```

6. Run the page again. This time, you should notice that the browser tab contains the text you added to the `<title>` tag just like in Figure 2-5. If your browser has a title bar, you should also see the title displayed there.

FIGURE 2-5

How It Works

In the first chapter, you added a heading and a paragraph. You saw that line breaks are automatically created between them by the browser. You also saw that h1 headings are rendered with a larger bold font. In this example, you can see that this is always the case. You can also see a difference between div elements and paragraphs. The two div elements below the heading do not have any vertical space between them. However, you can see that browsers apply spacing to the top and bottom of the paragraphs.

Notice something else when you look at the second `div` as it appears in the browser. You applied a style using the `style` attribute, which gave it a yellow background. However, the yellow background is visible across the full width of the browser window, regardless of how far the text extends. This experiment helps to illustrate the fact that by default, block-level elements occupy the full width of their containing element.

There are three other items to note from this example. The first is how inline elements behave. You applied a background color to a `span` element through the `style` attribute. Only the content of the `span` element received the styled background. Inline elements are positioned within the flow of the document. The next point of the exercise was to illustrate the fact that by default, browsers ignore line breaks in content. Although the last `div` contained text that included line breaks, the entire content was rendered on one line. If you hover your mouse over this element, the content of the `title` attribute is displayed in a tooltip.

Finally, notice how the white space and line breaks are preserved when you use the `<pre>` tag. See also how the browser displays the content within a `<pre>` tag — it automatically applies a *monospace* or fixed-width font by default. The angle brackets surrounding the `pre` tag are rendered using special *HTML entities*. This is the way in which you render reserved characters, which might otherwise be seen as part of HTML by the browser. A list of common HTML entities is provided in Table 2-3.

The `title` element is very important. It gives your page an identity. The `title` is used by search engines in search results, and it is used by the browser to identify your page in History or Bookmark listings. You saw that applying an identity to your page is achieved by providing meaningful text within the `<title>` tags.

HTML Entities

Table 2-3 shows the most commonly used HTML entities. Entities can be expressed through an *entity name* or an *entity number*. Most browsers recognize most names for entities, but numbers are supported more widely. Some of the less commonly used entities do not have a name, only a number.

TABLE 2-3: Common HTML Entities

ENTITY NAME	ENTITY NUMBER	CHARACTER	DESCRIPTION
&lt;	&#60;	<	Less than
&gt;	&#62;	>	Greater than
&copy;	&#169;	©	Copyright symbol
&apos;	&#39;	'	Apostrophe
&quot;	&#34;	"	Double quote
&euro;	&#8364;	€	Euro symbol
&reg;	&#174;	®	Registered trademark
&deg;	&#176;	°	Degree

ENTITY NAME	ENTITY NUMBER	CHARACTER	DESCRIPTION
&amp;	&#38;	&	Ampersand
&frac14;	&#188;	¼	One quarter
&frac12;	&#189;	½	One half
&frac34;	&#190;	¾	Three quarters

IntelliSense

IntelliSense is provided to make you more productive. As soon as you type the opening tag for an HTML element (<), a list pops up offering suggestions. As you type, the list scrolls to entries starting with the first letter, or letters, that you typed. Once an entry has turned blue, you can use the Enter or Tab key to commit it to your page. If the item you want is semi-selected (it has a dotted border, but the background has not turned blue), you can use the Tab key to select it. IntelliSense also helps you by closing your tags for you.

If you are within the angle brackets of an HTML element but IntelliSense has not appeared, press the spacebar to get it to appear. Pressing the Esc key will clear it away again. You can get IntelliSense to appear anywhere within your document by pressing Ctrl+spacebar. If you do this in a web page, you are presented with all HTML tags, and when you choose one, the opening bracket is provided. If you invoke IntelliSense like this, and want to start typing to save scrolling, make sure you type the opening bracket.

IntelliSense is clever enough to know what type of document you are in and where you are within it. If your cursor is positioned within the <body> element of a web page file, the options presented in the list are appropriate for that element. A much more restricted set of options appears when your cursor is placed in the <head> element. When you are working with CSS (which you will see later), you are presented with a completely different set of options.

It's time to employ IntelliSense again, this time with some other common HTML Elements — hyperlinks and lists.

TRY IT OUT   Hyperlinks and Lists

In this exercise you will create some hyperlinks and lists. Hyperlinks are probably the most important element in HTML because they provide a way for users to navigate your site. Without hyperlinks, the Web simply would not work.

1. Click the New button on the Ribbon Bar (it's on the left side of the Files section) and add another HTML file to your site. Name it **Page2.html**.

2. Add the following line of HTML to the existing content within the <body> tags:

```
<body>
    <h1>Links and Lists</h1>
</body>
```

3. Using the same technique, add another HTML file called **Page3.html**. Add the following code to it between the `<body>` tags:

```
<body>
    <h1>Links and Lists</h1>
    <a href="/Page2.html" title="Click to go to Page 2">Go to Page 2</a>
</body>
```

4. Run the page in the browser by pressing the F12 button, and notice the hyperlink. It appears in a blue font and is underlined in contrast to the black font of the rest of the text. Hover your mouse over the link for a couple of seconds. You should see the content of the title attribute ("Click to go to Page 2") displayed in a tooltip. Now click the link. Page2.html should load in the browser.

5. Returning to WebMatrix, add the following code to Page2.html:

```
<body>
    <h1>Links and Lists</h1>
    <ul>
        <li>First bullet point</li>
        <li>Second bullet point</li>
    </ul>
    <ol>
        <li>First numbered item</li>
        <li>Second numbered item</li>
        <ul>
            <li>First bullet point</li>
            <li>Second bullet point</li>
        </ul>
        <li>Third numbered item</li>
    </ol>
    <a href="/Page3.html" title="Click to go to Page 3">Go to Page 3</a>
</body>
```

6. Run the page in the browser. The result should look like Figure 2-6.

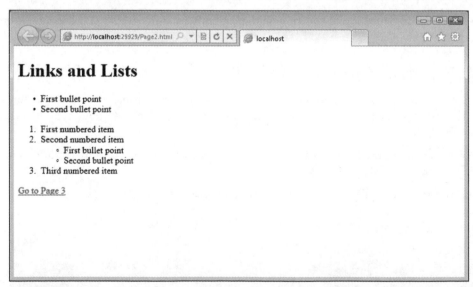

FIGURE 2-6

How It Works

Hyperlinks are not difficult to work with. The browser sees an anchor element — <a> — and knows that it should navigate to the resource located at the href address. Hyperlinks are inline elements. You also saw that there are two kinds of lists available through HTML — the *ordered* list and the *unordered* list. Ordered lists are defined by the <ol> tag. By default, all the major browsers use numbers to define each item within an ordered list, although you can change this behavior yourself using CSS (which you will see in the next section). Individual items in unordered lists (created using the <ul> tag) are denoted by default with a black bullet point by major browsers. Again, this is something you can change via CSS. Individual items are added to both the ordered list and the unordered list in exactly the same way — using the <li> tag. By observing their behavior, you can tell that lists and list items are block-level elements.

HTML5

HTML5 introduces some exciting new elements and capabilities to the HTML toolset. At the time of writing, support for the newer HTML5 elements varies from browser to browser, with Internet Explorer (IE) 8 providing the least support. IE9 includes a significant level of support for HTML5. Development work is already underway on version 10 of Internet Explorer, which will see the browser extend its support for HTML5. It is intended to be released during 2012 as part of the new Windows 8 operating system. So what is this goodness that HTML5 offers? To begin with, there are a number of new elements. Some of these are semantic, which means they describe the structural nature of the content. Within HTML 4, the only way you can meaningfully describe the structure of content is through the use of <h1>-<h6> tags, or the <p> tag. The new semantic tags are described in Table 2-4.

TABLE 2-4: New HTML5 Semantic Tags

TAG	MEANING
<article>	Defines a standalone item of content such as a news story, blog post, or comment.
<aside>	Defines an item of content that's separate from the main content but related, such as a sidebar.
<footer>	Defines the footer area for a page or a <section> element.
<header>	Defines the header for a page or a <section> element.
<hgroup>	Denotes the heading of a section. It can group <h1>-<h6> elements, if more than one is used.
<mark>	Denotes an item of text that's marked for highlighting or reference purposes. Could be used for highlighting keywords found in a search result, or to relate an item to a footnote, for example.
<nav>	Identifies the area on the page that contains the major navigation.
<section>	Defines a logical block of content, typically with a heading such as a chapter.
<time>	Denotes a time or date.

These new tags will help screen readers, and other semantically aware user agents, to describe the structure of the document to the reader. Cool. But I promised "exciting." Okay, here goes.

How about drawing on a web page? I don't mean placing images within a page, but actually drawing? At the moment, you can only do this using a plug-in such as Silverlight or Flash, but HTML5 offers a new <canvas> element that will support drawing via client side script. HTML5 also provides support for video and audio. You will meet the standard form elements in Chapter 5, but HTML5 introduces a lot of new ways to do things here too. The new elements are really exciting in that they allow you to do away with all kinds of client side scripting for validation, focusing on a particular field, offering the user a calendar for picking a date and providing default text as placeholders. Elements can be set so that users can edit their content, complete with spell checking. And drag-and-drop features will be possible with minimal client side scripting. You have met the common HTML 4 attributes already, but HTML5 will allow you to define your own custom attributes, by prefixing them with data-.

Unless you can control the browser that your audience uses, it would be unwise indeed to rely solely on the new possibilities offered by HTML5 at this stage. Browser support is patchy, but expanding. Nevertheless, there is a growing number of third party, mostly open source (free), libraries available to help you build sites that take advantage of these new features. It is definitely worthwhile familiarizing yourself with the official documentation, which can be found at http://dev.w3.org/html5/html-author/.

 WARNING *IntelliSense was a last-minute addition to WebMatrix. It wasn't included in any of the Beta releases, which prompted a lot of calls for its appearance from the community who are accustomed to using IntelliSense in WebMatrix's more advanced cousins — Visual Web Developer and Visual Studio. The WebMatrix team appears to have finally relented, but the version of IntelliSense that was included in the final release of WebMatrix was "borrowed" from Visual Studio. The default* doctype *within Visual Studio is XHTML, and the existing version of IntelliSense conforms to that. Consequently, none of the newer HTML5 tags is available in WebMatrix 1.0.*

Back to the current day, in the next section you will learn how to control the style and position of your HTML elements through cascading style sheets.

CASCADING STYLE SHEETS

In the preceding section you created two examples to test some aspects of HTML. These examples show that HTML provides structure to your document and in some cases will provide something in the way of formatting (think about the h1 tag). However, you have to admit that the results look fairly plain when viewed in a browser. They are hardly likely to create a memorable impression (in any kind of good way, at least) in the minds of your visitors. Browsers have a default set of styles that they work with. Text is black on a white background, with Times New Roman as the usual default font. Links are blue and underlined, until they are visited, when they turn purple. Your visitors can change these styles by configuring their browser options. However, the properties they can influence are limited, and most users are unlikely to know how to make the necessary changes. On the other hand, as a web developer, you have a great deal of control over the design aspect of your site. The technology you will use to manage the presentation of your pages is cascading style sheets (CSS).

CSS is a relatively new technology. It wasn't until 2000 before any web browser offered near full support for the first specification (CSS 1.0), which was finalized in 1998. Since then, two further versions have been introduced: CSS 2.0 and CSS 2.1. CSS 3.0 has been under development since 2005. All the major web browsers offer support for 2.1, although how they implement that support differs a little from browser to browser.

Prior to the introduction of CSS, the only way to control the typeface in a web page was to use the (now deprecated) `<font>` tag:

```
<font face="Arial" size="-1" color="#666666">Hello World!</font>
```

For simple pages this worked. However, as pages grow, and the variety of font styles required on the page increases, maintenance becomes very difficult. Consider the scenario in which the customer decides that the new corporate brand demands that Tahoma, in a slightly bigger font and darker color, is the "new black." It would take the developer forever to affect a change such as this across potentially hundreds, or thousands, of pages. CSS solved this problem by offering an easy way to separate the structure and content (the HTML) from the presentation.

Using CSS, you can control the position of elements, their size, color, and even their behavior. You can style groups of elements depending on their type — `<p>`, `<div>`, `<span>` and so on — or their *class* attribute. You can even target individual elements based on their unique `id` attribute.

Styles can be defined in a number of ways:

➤ They can be embedded inline within an HTML element as part of the `style` attribute. You have seen an example of this in the preceding Try It Out when you applied background colors to a `div` and a `span`.

➤ They can be *declared* in one `style` element, usually within the `head` section of an HTML document.

➤ They can be defined in a separate style sheet (a text-based file with a *.css* extension), which is accessed via a `link` element, again, in the `head` section of an HTML document.

➤ Styles can be applied by the browser, also known as the browser's *default style sheet*.

➤ Users can create their own custom style sheets.

With styles coming from all directions, which ones take precedence? The order of priority is defined by the *cascade*, which is where the term "cascading style sheets" comes from. At the weakest end of the cascade is the browser's default style sheet. This is followed by the user's custom style sheet. At the strongest end is the author's style sheet (the rules you apply). Then, proximity to the element being styled takes effect. External styles are overridden by embedded styles, which in turn are overridden by styles declared within the `style` attribute of the element itself.

CSS Structure and Style Rules

When you start to style a document, you generally want to affect the presentation or behavior of individual elements or groups of elements. Cascading style sheets provide a means to target specific elements through *selectors*, and to define the presentational styling information through *rules* or *rulesets*. The structure of a style rule or ruleset is as follows:

```
selector
{
    property: value;
    property: value;
}
```

The selector identifies what the rule should be applied to. The three most commonly used selectors are as follows:

➤ An HTML element, such as `div` or `p` (the *type* selector)

➤ A CSS class (the *class* selector)

➤ The `id` attribute of the target element (the *ID* selector)

A Type Selector Example

The following rule will set the font color in all paragraph elements to red.

```
p
{
    color: red;
}
```

A Class Selector Example

In this example, any element having a class value of `.special` will be displayed in red text.

```
.special
{
    color: red; }
```

An ID Selector Example

Where an element has an id of "special", its font will appear red if this rule is applied.

```
#special
{
    color: red; }
```

The property is the part of the HTML element that the style should affect. Examples of valid CSS properties include *color, font-family, border, margin,* and *background*. Each property has a range of permissible values, depending on the nature of the property being set. IntelliSense is a great help here, in that it will list only the valid range of property values for a given property. Comments are applied to CSS using the following notation: `/* … */`. The forward slash followed by the asterisk denote the beginning of the comment, and is terminated by the reverse syntax — asterisk followed by a forward slash. The browser ignores everything in between these marks.

TRY IT OUT Applying CSS

In this exercise you will create a simple HTML file and add some valid HTML elements to it. Then you will apply some styling via CSS. You have seen an example of the first way to define styles — by applying them to the `style` attribute of an HTML element. It's time now to look at the second method. Your CSS rules controlling the elements you add to the file will be placed in a `<style>` block within the head of the document. Finally, you will test the result by running the page in the browser.

1. Open the site you created in the last exercise. This should be called **Trying Out HTML**.

2. Add a new HTML file to the site and name it **CssDemo.html**.

3. Add the following code between the `<body>` tags:

```
<body>
    <h1>CSS Demo</h1>
    <div>Divs have been styled with a blue border,
        yellow background and Arial font.</div>
    <p>Paragraphs have been styled with an italic default font at 20px.</p>
    <div>Blue border, yellow background, and Arial</div>
    <div> </div>
    <p>Italic default 20px</p>
</body>
```

4. Run the page as it is. You should see something similar to Figure 2-7.

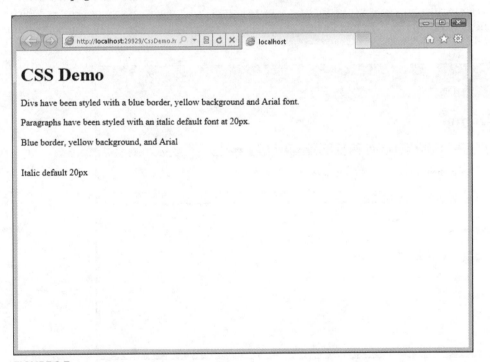

FIGURE 2-7

5. Add the following just before the closing `</head>` tag:

```
<style type="text/css">
    h1 {
        color: red;
    }
    div {
        border: 1px solid blue;
        font-family:  Arial;
        background-color: yellow;
    }
    p {
        font-size: 20px;
        font-style: italic;
    }
</style>
```

6. Run the page in the browser. This time, you will see that the heading has turned red, and that each of the `<div>` elements has a blue border and yellow background, and that the font is no longer the default font. There is even an empty `<div>` glued to the bottom of the second `<div>`. The paragraph content, on the other hand, still uses the browser default font, but this has been italicized and is larger than the contents of the `div`. If any of these changes that appear in Figure 2-8 did not take place, carefully read through the CSS rules you typed and make sure they are exactly the same as in this example. If you make a spelling mistake in a property name or value, the browser will ignore your rule. Some selectors are case sensitive. It is not always easy to remember which ones, so the general advice is to match case at all times. Typographical errors, of course, will not be tolerated.

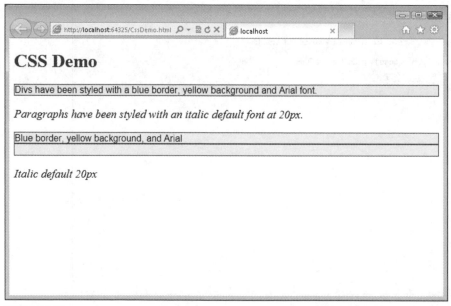

FIGURE 2-8

How It Works

In this exercise, you applied a set of CSS rules within a `<style>` element. The `<style>` element has a required attribute called `type`, which is set to the value `"text/css"`. Even though the rules were applied within the same page as the elements they controlled, the content of the `<style>` block is still known as a style sheet. This particular style sheet consists of three rulesets: one for all `<h1>` tags; one for all `<div>` tags; and one for all `<p>` tags.

This exercise demonstrated the use of *type* selectors. Type selectors ensure that all elements of the specified HTML element type will be styled according to the rules. You saw this in action when all three `<div>` elements received the same style — a blue border, yellow background, and Arial as the font. When you specify a property and value for that property you effectively override the default styles applied by the browser for that property. All other properties are styled according to the browser's default style sheet. The `<div>` font size and style were the browser defaults, for example, as were all other unspecified properties belonging to the `<div>`.

You saw also that styles are applied to elements even when there is no visible content in them. This was the case with the third `<div>`, although ` ` is considered content. It's the HTML entity for a non-breaking space. If you remove ` ` from the content of the `<div>` and ran the page in the browser again, you will notice that the yellow background disappears, but the border remains.

Rulesets consist of a selector, an opening brace, one or more *declarations,* and a closing brace. A declaration takes the form of a property, followed by a colon (:) and a value. Individual declarations are separated by a semicolon (;) at the end of the value. White space in a style sheet is meaningless, so

```
p{font-size: 20px; font-style: italic;}
```

is identical to

```
p
{
    font-size: 20px;
    font-style: italic;
}
```

The semicolon following the last declaration is not required.

NOTE *Although the semi-colon that follows the last declaration is not required, I tend to add them out of habit. When you are in the process of developing a site and tweaking its appearance, you will find yourself adding extra declarations to rulesets a bit at a time. It is very easy to forget to terminate existing declarations with the semicolon when adding new declarations, and then wonder why your new declaration isn't taking effect.*

Do you remember the problem definition that CSS is intended to solve? CSS is designed to separate content from presentation. You have now seen the first two options for applying style rules: by adding them to style attributes within an HTML element; and by adding a <style>element to the <head> section, and creating rulesets within it. The first option obviously doesn't solve the problem statement. Styling information is embedded at element level, and needs to be repeated for each element that it affects. The second option certainly moves styles away from their elements, and helps to solve the problem to a certain extent, but if you declare your styles at page level, they will affect only that page. If you want to apply the same styles to other pages, you have to use copy and paste. Any changes you make will need to be made on every page, although you will only have to make the change in one place within each page.

The final method for applying CSS styles — defining them in a separate file — solves all these problems. All of your styles can be made available to all pages by linking from the pages to the file itself. Any change you make to a style declaration in the file will take effect immediately across all pages that reference the style sheet file.

In the next exercise you will add a new page that will be styled through a separate style sheet file.

TRY IT OUT   **Using an External Style Sheet**

In this exercise, you will add two files. The first file will be a new HTML page within which you will add some elements. Then you will add a style sheet file to the website and link to it from the newly created HTML file. Finally, you will add a combination of selectors to the style sheet to control the presentation of the elements in the web page.

1. In the Ribbon Bar, click New ➪ New File and add a new HTML file to the site called LinkedStyle.html.

2. Within the <body> section of the new page, add the following HTML code. The | is known as the pipe character. On my keyboard, it can be obtained by holding Shift down and typing a backslash (left of the Z key):

```
<body>
    <div id="header">This is the head content</div>
    <div id="maincontent">
      <div id="nav">
        <a href="home.cshtml" class="current">Home</a> |
        <a href="about.cshtml">About</a> |
        <a href="contact.cshtml">Contact</a>
      </div>
      <div id="content">This is where the rest of the page content goes</div>
    </div>
    <div id="footer">This is the footer area</div>
</body>
```

3. Add a new file to the site. From the Choose a File Type dialog box, select CSS. Leave the file name as the default StyleSheet.css. Notice that there is a selector already in the file, which is for the HTML <body> element. Add the following declarations within the curly braces:

```
body {
    margin: 0;
    padding:0;
```

```
    font-family: Arial;
    font-size: 80%;
}
```

4. Ensuring that `LinkedStyle.html` is selected in WebMatrix (either by clicking once on its tab in the Files workspace or clicking it in the File Explorer to the left side of the IDE), click the Run button to launch the page in your default browser. Notice how the appearance is dictated by the browser's default style sheet. The font is most likely Times New Roman, and there is a space between the content and the top and left edges of the browser window. To apply your new styles and change the font to Arial, you need to link the style sheet to the page. You do this using a `<link>` tag, which goes into the `<head>` section. Change the `<head>` section to include a `<link>` in `LinkedStyle.html` as shown here:

```
<head>
    <meta charset="utf-8" />
    <title></title>
    <link href="/StyleSheet.css" rel="stylesheet" type="text/css" />
</head>
```

5. If you run the page again, you should notice that the font has been changed to Arial, but the change has been applied across the whole document.

6. Add the following to the `StyleSheet.css` file:

```
#maincontent, #header, .footer {
    width: 60%;
}
#header {
    height: 80px;
    border-bottom: 2px solid blue;
    font-size: 200%;
    font-weight: bold;
}
#nav a {
    color: red;
    text-decoration: none;
}

#nav a.current {
    color: blue;
}
#content {
    background-color: #c0c0c0;
}
.footer {
    font-size: 90%;
    font-style: italic;
    color: #555555;
}
```

7. Run the page in the browser again and study the changes, which should replicate those in Figure 2-9. Note that when you run the page in the browser, the hyperlinks to other pages will not work, as you have not created the target pages.

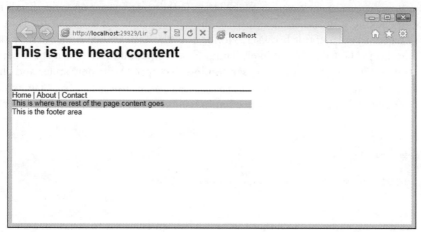

FIGURE 2-9

How It Works

You have applied styles using a mixture of selectors. The <body> is styled using a type selector, which you were introduced to in the previous Try It Out. All padding and margins were removed, which results in the content moving to the top-left corner of the browser window. Some of the div elements have been styled using the ID selector. These are recognizable by the fact that the id value from the div has been added to the style sheet, but the value has been prefixed with the hash or pound sign (#). The last div was styled using a class selector. The div element was given a class attribute with the value of footer. This value was used in the style sheet, but prefixed with a dot (.).

You set the width of the content by *grouping* selectors. Each one is separated by a comma as shown here:

```
#maincontent, #header, .footer{ … }
```

This is an expedient way of applying the same rule to multiple selectors. You could just as easily have applied the width declaration to each selector individually, but maintenance is less easy as you would have to make multiple changes if you decided to change the width to say, 70% in the future.

Did you see that one of the links was blue while the others are red? You achieved this effect by targeting a specific element through *combining* selectors. You created a rule for all links:

```
a{ color:red;}
```

Then you created a new rule that specifically targeted any link in the element identified as *nav*, which has a class attribute with a value of *current*:

```
#nav a.current {
    color: blue;
}
```

You will see this type of approach being used quite often on sites to change the appearance of the link pointing to the current page.

CSS Positioning and the Box Model

Before there was widespread browser support for CSS, developers used HTML tables to manage the layout of their pages. Tables offer some benefits: They are relatively simple to understand and they create a rigid structure. On the other hand, the W3C specifications recommend that the use of tables should be considered for presenting tabular data only, so using them for structuring layout is inconsistent with the idea of semantic HTML, or using HTML appropriately based on the tag's implied meaning.

There are also practical disadvantages to using tables for layout. It creates code "bloat." To generate a content holder using tables, you need to create a table row to house the table cell, which results in a minimum of three HTML elements needed for one piece of content. As a consequence, pages based on tables can contain considerably more HTML than those where CSS has been used for layout, and that results in slower downloads and more bandwidth being used. They are also harder to maintain.

Before you can successfully use CSS to control the layout of your pages, you need a fundamental understanding of the *CSS box model*. In the exercises you have completed so far, one thing should have become obvious, and that is that every element on a web page is a rectangle or box. Some of these elements naturally occupy all of the space available to them (block-level elements) and some stretch only as far as needed to constrain their content (inline elements). However, they are all essentially boxes.

The box is composed of four parts: the *content, padding*, *border*, and *margin*. These parts are illustrated in Figure 2-10.

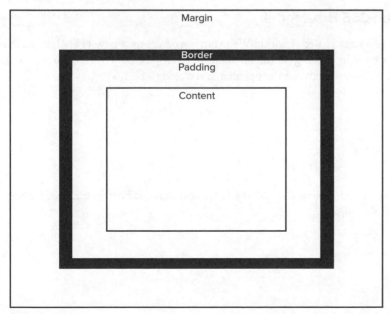

FIGURE 2-10

Padding is the space between the content and border. This can be adjusted in equal measures all around via the element's `padding` property. You can exert finer control over padding by applying values to the `padding-top`, `padding-right`, `padding-bottom`, and `padding-left` properties. Padding is optional — you can remove all padding by setting the property's value to zero (0).

The border is the area between the padding and the margin. Like padding, borders can be styled via the `border` property, or `border-top`, `border-right`, `border-bottom`, and `border-left` properties. Borders are optional. Finally, the margin is the space outside of the border. This can be controlled via the `margin` property, or on each side as with borders and padding. Like padding and borders, margins are optional.

To calculate the width of the space an element occupies, you need to add the left margin width, left border width, left padding width, right padding width, right border width, and right margin width. The height is calculated in a similar fashion from the top margin to the bottom margin. Browsers have differing default values for margins and padding that can make control over an element's size and positioning difficult when attempting to apply an identical layout across different browsers. You can overcome this problem using a technique called a *CSSReset*, which removes default padding and margins from elements. There are a variety of ways to apply this technique, but the most common approach is to use the universal selector (*) and to set padding and margins to zero:

```
*{
    padding:0;
    margin:0;
}
```

This removes padding and margins from every element on the page. In the next exercise, you will explore more about positioning HTML elements via CSS.

TRY IT OUT   **Exploring the CSS Box Model**

1. Open `Trying Out HTML`, if you have closed it within WebMatrix and create a new HTML page called **CssPositioning.html**. Do this by right clicking on the site name at the top of the Files Explorer pane and choosing New File. Add the following between the opening and closing `<body>` tags:

```
<div id="wrapper">
    <div class="box"></div>
    <div class="box"></div>
    <div class="box"></div>
    <div class="box"></div>
</div>
```

2. Create another new file, this time choosing the CSS file type, and name it **Positioning.css**. Replace the existing code with the following:

```
body {
    padding: 0;
    margin: 0;
}

#wrapper{
    width: 400px;
```

```
        min-height: 200px;
        margin: 20px;
        border: 1px solid black;
}

.box{
        float: left;
        width: 100px;
        min-height: 100px;
        border: 1px solid red;
}
```

3. Modify `CssPositioning.html` to link to the style sheet you just created and to provide a title:

```
<title>CSS Positioning Example</title>
<link href="Positioning.css" rel="stylesheet" type="text/css" />
```

4. Run the page in the browser by pressing F12. Notice how the first three boxes line up horizontally, but the fourth box drops below the previous three and its red border appears outside of the bottom of the containing `div` — the one with the black border. See Figure 2-11.

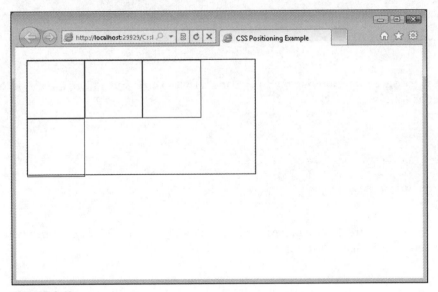

FIGURE 2-11

5. Modify `Positioning.css` with the amendments highlighted here:

```
.box{
        float: left;
        width: 98px;
        min-height: 98px;
        border: 1px solid red;
}
```

6.   Run `CssPositioning.html` in the browser again, and see how all four boxes line up horizontally, as in Figure 2-12.

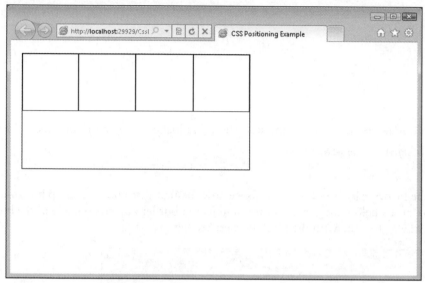

FIGURE 2-12

7.   Amend the style sheet once more, altering the `width` and `min-height`, and adding a `margin` to the `.box` class ruleset as follows:

```
.box{
    float: left;
    width: 88px;
    min-height: 88px;
    margin: 5px;
    border: 1px solid red;
}
```

8.   Finally, run the page once more. Notice that each of the boxes appears on one line horizontally, with some space between them, as shown in Figure 2-13.

How It Works

Your HTML page is simple — it contains a wrapper `div` and four child `div` elements, each with the CSS class of `box` applied to it. To start with, you removed all padding and margin from the `body` in the style sheet, and set some simple properties on the existing `div` elements. You constrained the containing wrapper `div` to 400 pixels wide, and gave it a black border so that it can be seen. All elements that have the `box` class applied to them have widths and heights of 100 pixels, and a 1-pixel wide red border. They also have a `float` property applied to them. The `float` property changes the behavior of block-level elements so that they are positioned in the direction of the value applied — in this case `left` — and other content can wrap around them. It is one of the most important properties for page layout.

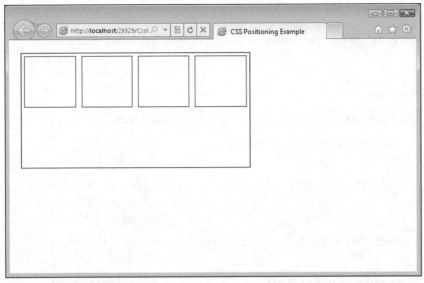

FIGURE 2-13

When you ran the page, you saw that the first three boxes lined up horizontally (due to `float: left` and a `width` being applied to them), but the fourth box fell underneath and began a second line of boxes. There isn't room for the fourth box on the top line, despite all boxes appearing to be 100 pixels wide and the container being 400 pixels wide. This is because all the boxes have a border specified at 1 pixel. If you remember from earlier, the total width of an element extends from its outer margins, and takes into account the width of borders and content. With no margins, each "box" is 102 pixels wide — 1 pixel left border, 1 pixel right border, and 100 pixels for the content. When you removed two pixels from the width property of each box, you adjusted the total width, including borders to 100 pixels exactly, which is why the boxes fit on one line.

Finally, you gave each of the boxes a 5-pixel *margin*. If you recall, the margin is the space between the border of one element and another. Consequently, each box will need an additional five pixels of space all round it. To adjust for this, you removed 10 pixels from the width of each box (five pixels per side), and they all lined up on the same row with some spacing between them.

Using the CSS box model to position elements on your page can seem a little daunting at first. Hopefully this example will have helped illustrate how the box model works, and how to use the `float` property to get elements to line up against each other. This hasn't by any means been an exhaustive study of CSS, and you are recommended to invest as much time up front to learning the basics, especially through experimentation. It will become second nature very quickly, and what you learn will make your job a lot easier in the long run. An excellent source of information on CSS is *Beginning CSS: Cascading Style Sheets for Web Design, 2nd Edition* by Richard York (ISBN 978-0-470-09697-0). For more information on HTML, check out *Beginning Web Programming with HTML, XHTML, and CSS* by Jon Duckett (ISBN 978-0-470-25931-3).

In the meantime, the following section examines some of the other more common CSS properties.

CSS Properties

Table 2-5 examines the more common CSS properties according to their usage, together with examples of usage.

TABLE 2-5: Common CSS Properties

PROPERTY	DESCRIPTION	EXAMPLES
color	Determines the color of the font	color: red; color: #fff000;
font-size	Sets the size of the font.	font-size: 10pt; font-size: 90%; font-size : 15px;
font-style	Specifies the font style.	font-style: normal; font-style: italic;
font-weight	Specifies the weight of the font.	font-weight: bold;
font-family	Determines the font face.	font-family: Verdana;
padding	Determines the space between the content and the border. Note: When used as in the example, the values apply to the top, right, bottom, and left of the element, in that order.	padding: 10px 0 0 10px;
margin	Sets the spacing between one element and others. Note: When used as in the example, the values apply to the top, right, bottom, and left of the element, in that order.	margin: 10px 0 0 10px;
padding-top padding-right padding-bottom padding-left	Sets the padding on one side only.	padding-left: 10px;
margin-top margin-right margin-bottom margin-left	Sets the margin on one side only.	margin-left: 3px;
border	Enables you to set multiple border properties in one declaration.	border: 1px solid black;
border-width	Specifies the border width only.	border-width: 10px;

PROPERTY	DESCRIPTION	EXAMPLES
border-style	Specifies the border style only.	border-style: dotted;
border-top border-right border-bottom border-left	Specifies the properties of one border only.	border-top: 1px solid black;
background	Specifies multiple background properties in one declaration.	background:#ffffff; url('myimage.jpg') no-repeat;
background-image	Specifies an image to appear as the background.	background-image: url('/images/myimage. gif');

Tips for Working with CSS

Always use an external style sheet rather than applying styles inline or within <style> tags at the top of a page. This will help to make your website more maintainable as you have only one place to go to make alterations and amendments, and they will take effect on every page that references your style sheet.

Group your style rulesets logically. As your style sheet grows, it can become difficult to find the specific rule or declaration you need when looking to change it in any way. A common way of structuring a style sheet is to place all of your Type declarations at the top, followed by those that apply structure to your site through ID selectors. You can use comments within the style sheets to label sections.

You may have a specific set of rules that you apply to all forms on your site. You will already have set base styles using type selectors for all input elements or button elements, but you may also have some custom classes that apply to forms only. You can segregate them using comments like this:

```
/*
-----------------------------------
FORM STYLES
-----------------------------------
*/
.submitButton{
    color: #cc00ff;
}
```

The forward slash followed by the asterisk denotes the beginning of the comment, and it is terminated by the reverse syntax — asterisk followed by a forward slash. The browser ignores everything in between.

Familiarize yourself with the wide variety of properties supported by CSS, and the ranges of valid values they accept. You can often find sample sites to download. A good learning exercise is to study the style sheets that come with these, and to make alterations to individual declarations and observe the effect the change had on the page's structure or appearance.

SUMMARY

You are now familiar with the two key technologies you need to know in order to be able to style web pages — HTML and CSS.

HTML is the language of the Web. HTML is primarily used for adding structure and some formatting to your web pages and is constructed from elements that appear in angled brackets as tags. It's important to remember that each opening tag needs a closing tag, although some elements are self-closing. This chapter showed the difference in behavior between block-level elements and inline elements, and you learned the purpose of the most commonly used elements.

HTML elements can seem daunting to newcomers, but there is a limited set of them, and it should not take much time to familiarize yourself with their purposes.

Cascading style sheets are used to apply much more control over the formatting of HTML elements as well as their appearance. Each of the commonly used ways in which you can declare CSS rules was examined in this chapter — through type selectors, ID selectors, and class selectors. You can group and combine selectors to apply a rule across elements referenced by different types of selectors.

CSS declarations are constructed from setting values against properties. Like HTML, there is a finite set of properties that CSS supports, and each of them accepts a finite number of valid values. The most common of those were described in this chapter.

HTML and CSS are fundamental to designing web pages and managing their appearance. This chapter gave you a solid foundation on which you can build effective and attractive sites. However, it only explored design at the page level. The next chapter will take what you have learned so far, and apply these technologies at site level to create a consistent appearance across the site in an easily maintainable manner.

So far, you have been introduced to website design in a theoretical manner. The topics you have learned are very important and general to web development. From here on, you will take what you learn and apply it to building a real website.

Wrox Classifieds is a working site that includes all of the main features provided by ASP.NET Web Pages. Once you have built the site, visitors will be able to:

➤ Browse existing listings.

➤ Create an account on the site.

➤ Add items for sale.

➤ Bid for items offered by other account holders.

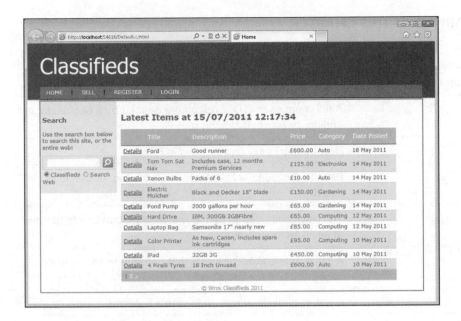

Site administrators will be able to:

➤ Manage listing categories.

➤ Manage user accounts.

Each chapter will provide you with the knowledge required to progressively add this functionality. There is a lot to cover, but it doesn't matter what level you are currently at — it's all very doable. I learned how to build websites by reading a book, just like you are now.

EXERCISES

1. What is the difference between a block-level HTML element and an inline element?

2. What are the three principal ways of applying CSS styles to specific HTML elements?

3. Taking what you have learned from this chapter, create a page with a content area of 900 pixels wide, containing a header and footer occupying the full width. Add three vertical columns of content — each equal in width, with 10 pixels of space between them, and five pixels of space between the columns and the containing element. Set the text of the first column to red, the second to blue, and the final column to green. You must use an external style sheet for this exercise.

Answers to the Exercises can be found in the Appendix.

► **WHAT YOU LEARNED IN THIS CHAPTER**

TERM	DEFINITION
HyperText Markup Language	HTML — The language that browsers use to render a web page.
Element	A fragment of an HTML document defined by a beginning and ending, or by a self-closing tag.
Tag	How elements are represented in HTML
Attributes	Provide additional information about the tag, or define its behavior.
CSS	The language used to define the presentation and formatting of an HTML document.
Declaration	A value applied to a property that determines the behavior/appearance of the property.
Ruleset	A group of declarations applied to a Selector.
Selector	A means of grouping elements by type, ID, or CSS class.
CSS Class	An HTML attribute that can be referenced in CSS to specify rules for all elements sharing the same class value.
Inline Styles	CSS rules applied within the HTML tag via the `style` attribute. They only affect the element in which they are declared.
Embedded Styles	CSS rules specified in the `<style>` element of an HTML document. They only take effect on the contents of the document.
External Style Sheet	A separate file containing rulesets, which affect all documents that reference the file via a `<link>` element.

3

Designing Websites

WHAT YOU WILL LEARN IN THIS CHAPTER:

➤   How Razor layout pages work

➤   How to create small blocks of reusable content

➤   How to pass data between content and layout pages

In the previous chapter, you learned that HTML and CSS are the basic building blocks in website development. Their purpose is to provide structure and style to your web pages. You were advised to use external style sheets to assist with the maintainability of your site's design. The skills you have learned so far are applicable to all kinds of websites, not just those built on the ASP.NET Web Pages framework.

Maintainability is an important concept within web design. One of the core principles behind maintainability is the *DRY principle*, which stands for Don't Repeat Yourself. In essence, the idea behind this philosophy is that you should minimize the number of places in which you need to make changes should alterations be required. The advice in the previous chapter to use external style sheets as opposed to page level style sheets follows this principle.

Most sites feature the same content on every page, or within a large number of pages. Headers, footers, and navigation systems are just some examples. Adding the same header to every page in your site breaks the DRY principle. If you need to change the appearance of the header, you need to edit every page. The sample site you will begin building in this book has a header, footer, login panel, search bar, and other areas that will feature on most if not all pages. It also has a consistent layout across the site. In this chapter, you learn how to create headers and other repeated items as reusable blocks of content which can be plugged in wherever you like, providing an efficient way for you to manage and maintain your site content and appearance.

You will use some Razor syntax while working through the examples in this chapter. The concepts are quite simple, so you should not worry if they are not explained in detail. A full explanation of the Razor syntax is provided in the next chapter.

SITE TEMPLATES FROM LAYOUT PAGES

Whenever I begin working on a site, I usually have a set of simple illustrations or images to work from. Sometimes I produce these myself, or a designer provides them. They provide information on the structure of each page within the site. They show where the header, footer, and navigation should be, and where the content differs from page to page. Figure 3-1 shows a layout of an example site.

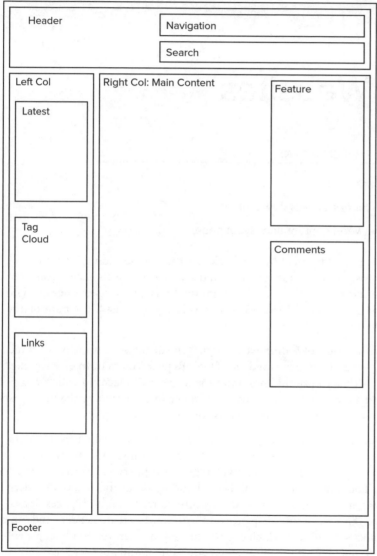

FIGURE 3-1

So far as the Wrox Classified site is concerned, you have the benefit of the screen shots at the end of the previous chapter to work from. Using these screen shots as a guide, you will begin working up a representation of the structure of the site using HTML and CSS, which you learned about in the previous chapter. This acts as the beginning of a site template, which you will use to manage the rest of the pages.

In the next exercise, you create a simple page containing HTML elements to provide a framework for the content.

TRY IT OUT Creating a Page Structure

1. Create a new site within WebMatrix using the Empty Site template. Call the site **Classifieds**.

2. Add a new CSHTML page using either the New button (and choose File) or by right-clicking on the site name in the File Explorer pane on the left side and choosing New File. Name the file **Template.cshtml** and add the following code to the `<body>` element.

```
<body>
    <div id="header">
        <div id="head">This is where head content goes</div>
    </div>
    <div id="navstrip">
        <div id="nav">This is where the navigation goes</div>
    </div>
    <div id="wrapper">
        <div id="left">
            <div id="search">This is where left content goes</div>
        </div>
        <div id="content">
            <p>This is where main content goes</p>
        </div>
        <div id="footer">
            <p>This is where the footer goes</p>
        </div>
    </div>
</body>
```

3. Using the same method as before, add another new file to the site, but choose the CSS file type this time and leave the filename as `StyleSheet.css`.

4. Replace the existing code in the style sheet you just created with the following:

```
/*
--------------------------------------------------
HTML ELEMENTS
--------------------------------------------------
*/
body {
    font-family : Verdana, Helvetica, sans-serif;
    font-size: 80%;
    color: #5f5f5f;
    padding: 0;
    margin: 0;v
    background-color: white;
}
```

```
/*
----------------------------------------------------
SITE STRUCTURE
----------------------------------------------------
*/

#header, #navstrip{
    width: 100%;
    background-color: #4b4b4b;
}

#header{
    min-height: 70px;
    color: white;
}
#navstrip{
    border-bottom: 2px solid #c3c4c8;
}
#head, #nav, #wrapper{
    width: 900px;
    margin: auto;
}
#head{
    font: normal 4em Tahoma;
    line-height: 2em;
}
#wrapper{
    background-color: white;
    border: 2px solid #717171;
}
#nav{
    background-color: #717171;
    line-height: 25px;
    color: white;
}

#nav a, #nav a:hover, #nav a:visited{
    color: white;
    font-size: 1.0em;
    text-decoration: none;
    text-transform: uppercase;
    padding: 5px 15px;
}
#left, #content{
    float: left;
    min-height: 400px;
}

#left{
    width: 180px;
    background-color: #e8e8e8;
}
```

```
#content{
    width: 700px;
    background-color: white;
    padding: 10px
}

#footer{
    clear: both;
    font-size: 90%;
    color: #999;
    text-align: center;
}

#nav, #login {
    border-bottom: 1px solid black;
    padding-bottom: 4px;
}
```

5. Add the following `<link>` element to the `<head>` section of `Template.cshtml`:

```
<head>
    <meta charset="utf-8" />
    <title></title>
    <link href="StyleSheet.css" rel="stylesheet" type="text/css" />
</head>
```

6. Make sure that `Template.cshtml` is selected in the File Explorer, and click the Run button. The result should look like Figure 3-2.

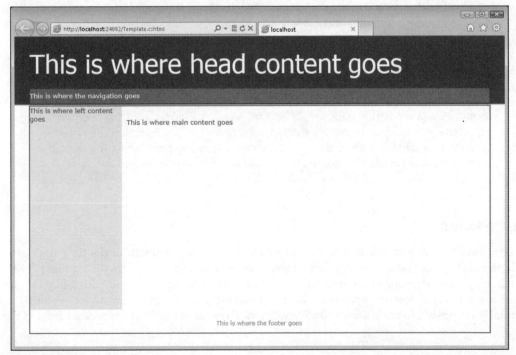

FIGURE 3-2

How It Works

Notice how the element that promises to show where all of the site's action will happen appears to the right of the block that will contain page related instruction, rather than underneath it? How did that happen? They are both `<div>` elements, which, as you learned in the previous chapter, are block-level elements. One of the characteristics of the block-level element is that it forces a new line, but that hasn't happened here.

The cause of this behavior is the CSS `float` property. The `<div>` element with the ID of `left` has a width applied to it, and is told to go as far left as possible, which allows any other content to sit to the right of it. Since the next `<div>` has a width that fits the remainder of the space provided by the wrapper, it duly sits to the right. The `float` property is the basis of CSS multi-column layouts.

Another interesting thing to note about the page is where the content starts. As you have seen so far, elements align horizontally to the left, but there is a space between the visible content below the navigation bar and the browser's left edge. This space increases and decreases depending on how wide you have your browser. The content of the section has a fixed width — 900px — which has been applied to a surrounding `<div>` element with the ID of `wrapper`, and its margins have been set to `auto`. The same has been done to the `nav` and `head` div elements. This effectively centers the content of the element within the containing element, and again, is a common way for developers to set their layouts.

 WARNING *A lot of developers only test their work using one browser. The problem with this approach is that browsers render HTML slightly differently in certain cases. While you are learning HTML and CSS, you are likely to search for solutions to certain requirements online, and hopefully, you will find just the right snippet of HTML or CSS to deliver what you need. However, some of these samples may have been written for a specific browser, and will not work as expected in other browsers. Or they may have been created to circumvent a bug in an older browser that no longer exists. For these reasons, you should test your pages in as many browsers as possible. The options under the Run button include one that invites you to open your site "in all browsers." You should do this periodically. There is nothing worse than having to unpick your HTML and CSS when you have nearly finished your site — or worse, when you have launched your site and a user complains that parts of it are not working in their browser.*

Layout Pages

You now have the basis of a structure for every page in the completed site. In the early days of web development, the only options available to developers were to copy and paste the outline HTML into each separate page and try to maintain each one separately, or to use something like Frames. Frames are generally frowned upon these days as introducing different maintenance problems, and potentially seriously affecting a site's usability. Frames have actually been deprecated from HTML5 (although browsers will still render them). Now, suppose you adopted this approach and decided some time down the line that you wanted to modify some aspect of the site design. Your only option would be to go into every page file separately and make that modification. Currently, a modification to the site structure will not likely be too much trouble to accommodate, but consider how it will be made more complex when you have a large number of pages with actual content added to the structure.

Most web development frameworks offer solutions to this problem. WebMatrix is no different. Its solution is called a *layout page*. The layout page acts as a template for all pages that reference it. The pages that reference the layout page are called content pages. Content pages are not full web pages like you have been creating in the exercises so far. They contain only the content that varies from one page to the next. In the Classifieds samples site, the content that appears in the `<div>` element with the ID of `content` is the main content that varies. You could probably have guessed that!

In the next exercise you will create a layout page for the Classifieds sample. Then you will create your first content page. You will also start managing your files and folders according to the recommended structure covered at the end of Chapter 1.

TRY IT OUT   Creating a Page Layout

1. If you haven't already done so, start the *Classifieds* site in WebMatrix.

2. Click New ⇨ New Folder and add a folder called **Shared** to the site.

3. Add another folder to the site called **Content**. Make sure that the site name is selected in the left pane when you do this, otherwise you may inadvertently add the Content folder to the Shared folder. You don't want to do that.

4. Move the StyleSheet.css file you created earlier from the root folder to the Content folder. The easiest way to do this is to select the file by clicking once on it. Then click Cut in the ribbon bar (the button with the scissors icon), select the Content folder, and then click Paste (just to the left of Cut).

5. Using the same Cut and Paste technique, move the Template.cshtml file from the root of the site to the Shared folder.

6. Rename `Template.cshtml` to **_Layout.cshtml**, making sure that you add the leading underscore to the filename. You can rename files by right-clicking on them and choosing Rename from the options provided to you. At this stage, your site structure should look like Figure 3-3.

FIGURE 3-3

7. You need to make some changes to the layout page. The first step is to change the reference to the style sheet you just moved. Amend the `<link>` element so that it looks like this:

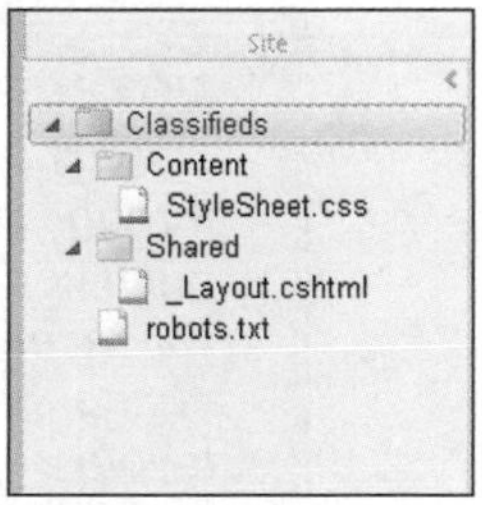

```
<link href="@Href("~/Content/StyleSheet.css")" rel="stylesheet" type="text/css" />
```

Don't worry about the strange `href` value for the moment.

8. Replace the text in the `<div>` called `"content"` with the following:

```
<div id="content">
    @RenderBody()
</div>
```

9. Add a new CSHTML file to the root folder and call it **Default.cshtml**.

10. Replace all of the existing text with just the following:

```
@{
    Layout = "~/Shared/_Layout.cshtml";
}
<p>All of the site action will appear here via content pages</p>
```

11. Making sure that the Default.cshtml file is selected in the left pane, click the Run button. When you do, you should see no visible changes from the previous example.

How It Works

Default.cshtml is a *content page*. What makes it a content page is the single line of server-side code at the top (ignore the curly brace business for the moment). That line of code specifies the physical location of a layout page. When any page is requested via the browser, any server-side code at the top of the page is executed. In this particular case, the code at the top of Default.cshtml effectively says "My layout can be found in the file called `_Layout.cshtml` in the `Shared` folder, which is inside the site's root folder." The tilde (~) is a special ASP.NET symbol that translates to "root."

When this line of code is encountered, the layout file is located, and a call to the `RenderBody` method is located within it. That method call is what defines a layout page as a layout page. If you remove the call to `RenderBody` from `_Layout.cshtml` and try to run `Default.cshtml` again, you will get an error message complaining that the layout page doesn't contain a call to the `RenderBody` method.

When the call to `RenderBody` is successfully located, ASP.NET merges the layout page content with that of the content page, emitting the output from the content page at the point where `RenderBody` appears within the layout markup, as illustrated in the Figure 3-4. The merged result is sent to the browser.

> **NOTE** All of the layout pages, and other files that aren't meant to be served directly by your web server, have names that are prefixed with underscores (_) throughout this book. You don't have to prefix the filename with an underscore, but if you do, and then you select it in WebMatrix and click the Run button, you will receive an error message telling you that files with leading underscores cannot be served. If you remove the leading underscore and try to run the layout page directly, another error message tells you that the file cannot be called directly because it contains a call to the `RenderBody` method. So either way — leading underscore or not — you cannot directly request a layout page. However, prefixing your layout filenames with an underscore gives the clearest indication that they are not intended to be requested by the server.

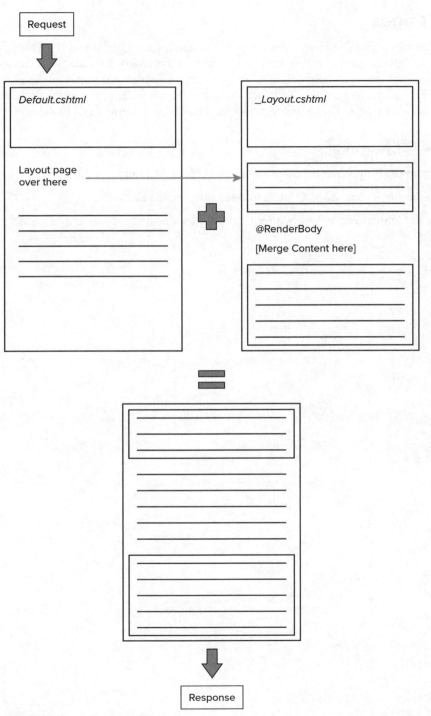

FIGURE 3-4

Nesting Layout Pages

It is possible to nest layout pages. You might consider using nested layout pages if you were building a corporate site for a global company, for instance, that's composed of many divisions, each having its own look and feel. There may be a common look and feel for the header and footer of the site, but the navigation and content changes in both structure and appearance depending on which division of the company is being featured. The next exercise explores how this effect can be achieved.

TRY IT OUT   **Nested Layout Pages**

1. Create a new site from the Empty Site template and name it **Nested Layouts**.

2. Add two folders to the site — one called **Content** and the other called **Shared**.

3. Add a new CSS file to **Content** and leave it with the default filename of `StyleSheet.css`. Add the following code to it:

```css
body {
    font-family: Arial, Helvetica, sans-serif;
    font-size: 80%;
    padding: 0;
    margin: 0;
}

h1{
    color: #0093c0;
}

#wrapper{
    background-color: #c1dfde;
    padding: 10px;
    width: 800px;
    margin: auto;
    min-height: 600px;
}

#electronics, #automation{
    min-height: 400px;
}

#electronics{
    background-color: #8ec1da;
    width: 650px;
    float: left;
}

#automation{
    background-color: #ffe8d3;
}

#electronicsnav{
    background-color: #fff;
```

```
    min-height: 400px;
    width: 150px;
    float: left;
}

#automationnav{
    background-color: #dedede;
}

#automation h3{
    color: #997d63;
}
```

4. Add a CSHTML file to the Shared folder and name it **_MainLayout.cshtml**. Change the existing code so that it looks like this:

```
<!DOCTYPE html>
<html lang="en">
  <head>
    <meta charset="utf-8" />
    <title>@Page.Title</title>
    <link href="@Href("~/Content/StyleSheet.css")" rel="stylesheet" type="text/css" />
  </head>
  <body>
     <div id="wrapper">
       <div id="header"><h1>Global Enterprises</h1></div>
       <div id="nav">
         <a href="Home">Home</a> |
         <a href="About">About</a> |
         <a href="Engineering">Engineering</a> |
         <a href="Electronics">Electronics</a> |
         <a href="Automation">Automation</a> |
         <a href="Contact">Corporate</a> |
         <a href="Contact">Contact Us</a>
       </div>
     @RenderBody()
     </div>
  </body>
</html>
```

5. Add another CSHTML file to the Shared folder and name this one **_AutomationLayout.cshtml**. Replace the existing code with this:

```
@{
    Layout = "~/Shared/_MainLayout.cshtml";
}
<div id="automationnav">
    <a href="Products">Products</a> |
    <a href="Services">Services</a> |
    <a href="Support">Support</a> |
    <a href="Team">The Team</a> |
</div>
<div id="automation">
```

```
    @RenderBody()
</div>
<div id="footer">The Automation Division Footer</div>
```

6. Now add a third CSHTML file to the Shared folder. Name it **_ElectronicsLayout.cshtml**, delete the existing code, and add the following:

```
@{
    Layout = "~/Shared/_MainLayout.cshtml";
}
<div id="electronicsnav">
    <a href="Products">Products</a> <br />
    <a href="Services">Services</a> <br />
    <a href="Support">Support</a> <br />
    <a href="Team">The Team</a> <br />
</div>
<div id="electronics">
    @RenderBody()
</div>
<div id="footer">The Electronics Division Footer</div>
```

7. Nearly there. Add a CSHTML file to the root folder. Name this one **Automation.cshtml** and replace the existing code with this:

```
@{
    Layout = "~/Shared/_AutomationLayout.cshtml";
    Page.Title = "Automation";
}
<h3>Automation Home Page</h3>
```

8. Finally, add another CSHTML file to the root folder and call it **Electronics.cshtml**. Replace the existing code with the following:

```
@{
    Layout = "~/Shared/_ElectronicsLayout.cshtml"
    Page.Title = "Electronics";
}
<h3>Electronics Home Page</h3>
```

9. Making sure that the Electronics.cshtml page is selected in the left pane, click the Run button to launch the page in your browser. Notice that the second navigation has a white background and the main area has a blue background (Figure 3-5).

10. Click the Automation link in the top navigation. See how the colors change? The main content is a brownish-pink color, as is the secondary navigation. The heading in the main content area changes color too. Most obviously, the Electronics navigation is displayed vertically whereas the Automation navigation is horizontal (Figure 3-6).

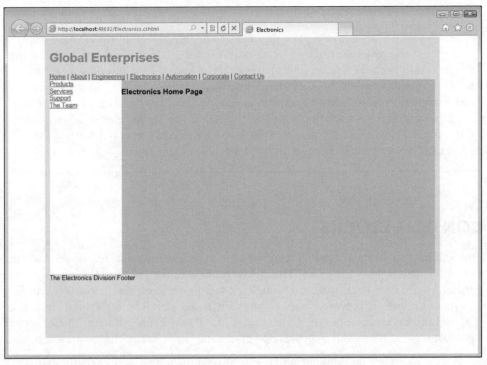

FIGURE 3-5

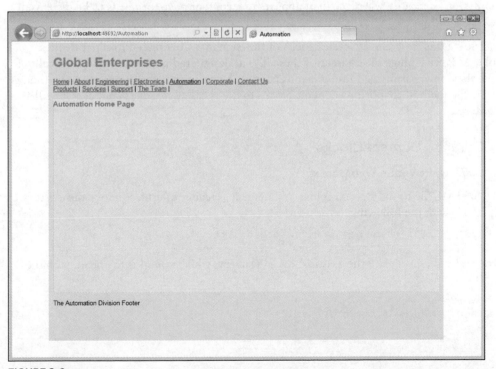

FIGURE 3-6

How It Works

Do you remember what it is that defines a layout page? It's a call to `RenderBody`. In this exercise you created a layout page from _MainLayout.cshtml by placing `@RenderBody()` in the file, and by matching that with `Layout` declarations in both the _AutomationLayout.cshtml and _ElectronicsLayout.cshtml files. You also added calls to `RenderBody` in both of those files, thus turning them into layout pages. Electronics.cshtml and Automation.cshtml each contained `Layout` declarations pointing to their own layout page, completing the content-layout relationship. There is no limit to the number of layout pages you can nest. The design of the pages won't win any awards, but this exercise serves to illustrate that nesting layout pages can offer a very flexible solution to certain problems.

REUSABLE CONTENT BLOCKS

You have just explored how to create a reusable template to manage the look and feel of your whole site, or parts of your site, through layout pages. This helps conform to the DRY principle you learned about earlier. As you browse through the completed sample site, you also encounter another situation where parts of the site are repeated throughout, such as the search box, the login area, the header, the footer, and the navigation options. Other parts, such as the Featured Items block, appear on some pages, but not others. When such features do appear, they are exactly the same each time.

Placing these blocks of content in a layout page will certainly help make your site easier to maintain. There will be just one place to go to make changes, if they are needed. However, that doesn't provide a full answer, especially when the item appears in a content page, or needs to be displayed based on certain conditions.

Content blocks solve this problem. Discrete blocks of functionality are created in separate files, and at run time, ASP.NET plugs the content of these files at designated positions within the calling page, much like the content is merged into a layout page at the point that the `RenderBody` method is called. However, the method that brings content blocks to life is called `RenderPage`, as you will see in the next exercise.

TRY IT OUT Creating Content Blocks

1. Open the *Classifieds* site within WebMatrix.

2. Add a new CSHTML file to the `Shared` folder and name it **_Header.cshtml**. Remove the existing text and replace it with the following:

```
<div id="head">This is where head content goes</div>
```

3. Open _Layout.cshtml and replace the existing `<div>` element, which contains the head, with the following:

```
<div id="header">
    @RenderPage("~/Shared/_Header.cshtml")
</div>
```

4. Making sure that Default.cshtml is selected in the left pane, click the Run button. The result should look like Figure 3-7. There should be no visible difference between this and the previous version.

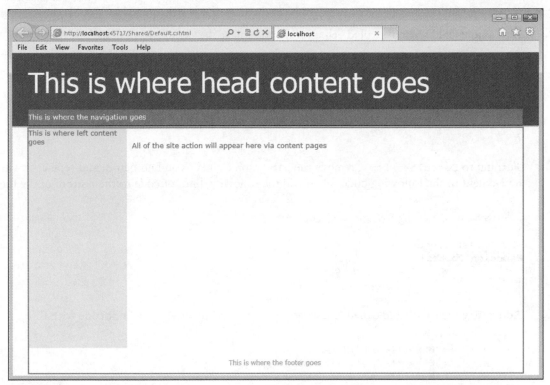

FIGURE 3-7

How It Works

You created a content block in a separate file called _Header.cshtml. The prefixed underscore prevents the file from being served by the web server if it is requested directly, which makes sense. What use would it be to a site visitor on its own? Our old friend the `Shared` folder came into play again as a storage location for the content block. When Default.cshtml was requested by the browser, the code within it was executed. As you learned earlier, the layout page was merged with the body contained in Default .cshtml, but not before the `RenderPage` call was executed in the layout page, inserting the content of _Header.cshtml at the point where `RenderPage` appears. The final output from merging all three files was sent to the browser.

There is no limit to the number of content blocks you can place in any page. Adding them is extremely simple, as you have just seen. But this approach has one limitation: Sometimes, you might not want a block of content to be shown in the calling page. When you use `RenderPage`, you *must* supply content. If none is supplied, you will receive an error. The `RenderSection` method, discussed next, is designed as a way to manage optional content.

TRY IT OUT   Using RenderSection for Managing Optional Content

This exercise builds on the previous exercise to illustrate how the `RenderSection` method differs from `RenderPage`. To follow along, make sure you have the Classifieds site opened in WebMatrix.

1. Add a new CSHTML file called **Sell.cshtml** and replace the default content as follows:

```
@{
    Layout = "~/Shared/_Layout.cshtml";
}
<h2>Post Your Advertisement</h2>
@section footer{
    This is a footer for the Sell page
}
```

2. Turning to `Default.cshtml`, remove the paragraph element you had before and replace it with the h2 element in the following code. Then add the following lines of code to the bottom of the file:

```
@{
    Layout = "~/Shared/_Layout.cshtml";
}
<h2>Latest Items</h2>
@section footer{
    &copy; Wrox Classifieds @DateTime.Now.Year
}
```

3. Add a new file to `Shared` called **_Navigation.cshtml** and replace the default code with this:

```
<div id="nav">
    <a href="@Href("~/")">Home</a> |
    <a href="@Href("~/Sell")">Sell</a> |
    <a href="@Href("~/Account/Register")">Register</a>
</div>
```

4. Finally, make the following modifications to `_Layout.cshtml`:

```
<body>
    <div id="header">
        @RenderPage("~/Shared/_Header.cshtml")
    </div>
    <div id="navstrip">
        @RenderPage("~/Shared/_Navigation.cshtml")
    </div>
    <div id="wrapper">
        <div id="left">
            <div id="search">This is where left content goes</div>
        </div>
        <div id="content">
            @RenderBody()
        </div>
        <div id="footer">
            @RenderSection("footer")
        </div>
    </div>
</body>
```

5. Make sure that `Default.cshtml` is selected in the left pane, and click the Run button. See how the footer with the copyright notice appears at the bottom of the page? Now click the "Sell" link. If everything has been done correctly, you should see that the footer area contains different content than the previous page.

6. Go back into the `Sell.cshtml` file and remove the following lines:

```
@section footer{
    This is a footer for the Sell page
}
```

7. If you re-run the Sell page now, you will see an error message like the one in Figure 3-8.

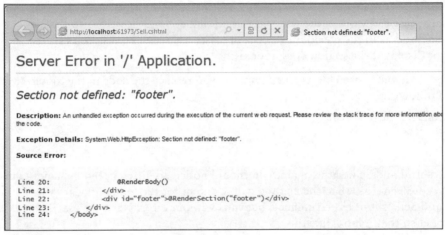

FIGURE 3-8

8. Modify `_Layout.cshtml` so that the call to `RenderSection` looks like this:

```
<div id="footer">
    @RenderSection("footer", required: false)
</div>
```

9. Now run the Sell page again. You should see that no errors occur and no footer appears.

How It Works

The `RenderSection` method looks for named *sections* and inserts their content at the point where the method call appears. Just like the `RenderBody` and `RenderPage` methods, the content is glued together at the point of page execution and the combined output is rendered to the browser. If you just pass the name of the section to the `RenderSection` method, a section declaration is required. Because the layout page is used by the `Default` and `Sell` pages, they both need to provide their own declaration for a footer section. The actual declaration doesn't need to be the same across both pages, as you have seen.

When you removed the section declaration from `Sell.cshtml`, you received an error page. If you read the details of the error message, you can see that the problem arises from the fact that no section called `footer` is defined in `Sell.cshtml`. As the method call stands at the moment, you have to define a section called footer. One change was required in the layout page, and that was to specify that the section is not required. You achieved that by adding `required: false` to the `RenderSection` method call in the layout page.

The `RenderSection` method is a very useful addition to the methods you have already seen that make content reusable. It has two advantages over the `RenderPage` method: You can define different content for the section from page to page and you don't have to provide any content, as long as you specify that it is not required in the method call itself.

IsSectionDefined

An alternative method for managing optional sections is available through the `IsSectionDefined` method. Essentially, this can work in the same way as adding `required: false` to the `RenderSection` method as in the previous exercise, but with an added bonus: You can specify default content for display if the section does not exist.

Taking the current _Layout.cshtml file as an example, if you replace the code in the footer `<div>` element with the following:

```
@if(IsSectionDefined("footer")){
    @RenderSection("footer")
}
```

and run Default.cshtml and Sell.cshtml again, you should notice no difference in behavior compared to adding `required: false` to the method call. Content for the footer appears when you run Default.cshtml, and Sell.cshtml has no content, but runs without error. Nevertheless, if you extend the previous snippet so that it looks like this:

```
@if(IsSectionDefined("footer")){
    @RenderSection("footer")
} else {
    <p>This is the default footer content</p>
}
```

you will find when running both pages that the default content for the footer appears as if no section has been defined.

PASSING DATA BETWEEN CONTENT AND LAYOUT PAGES

At this point, your layout page controls the `<title>` of your page. This is an important part of the page, as it's the description that most browsers use to identify a page that's been bookmarked. It is also the value that search engines use to label your page when they list it in their search results page. Not only that, but keywords found in the title can have an influence on how relevant search engines see your page. Having the page title set in one place throughout the site could be problematic, in that every page in the site will share the same title, reducing its relevance and making it more difficult to identify the correct entry in a series of bookmarks. You really need to be able to set the title value at the page level, maximizing its relevancy to the actual content. This is a job for the `PageData` property of your content pages.

`PageData` is a dictionary, which is a type of collection. You will learn more about collections in Chapter 4, but for the mean time, it should be enough to say that items are stored in `PageData` using a *key/value relationship*. You add values to the `PageData` collection using the following syntax:

```
PageData["MyValue"] = "Some value";
```

The key in this case is *MyValue*, and the associated value for that key is *some value*. When you want to retrieve an item from the `PageData` dictionary, you reference it by its key so that `PageData["MyValue"]` will return "some value" for you.

There is a shorthand version for adding items to a `PageData` dictionary, which makes use of C# 4.0's dynamic properties. This is the option you will use from now on:

```
Page.MyValue = "Some value";
```

In this case, you have created a property dynamically called *MyValue*, which belongs to a `DynamicPageDataDictionary` object. The `DynamicPageDataDictionary` object is, for all intents and purposes, the same as `PageData`, but it uses a cleaner and more concise syntax. ASP.NET Web Pages makes good use of a couple of important features that were added to the C# language in version 4.0, and you will see these covered in a little more detail in the next chapter.

There is no limit to the number or types of values you can store in a `PageData` dictionary, but you should be aware that the contents you store are available only with the current content/layout page combination.

TRY IT OUT   Using the PageData Dictionary

In the next exercise, you will make use of the `PageData` dictionary to manage your page titles from the content page.

1. Open _Layout.cshtml if you have closed it and add the following to the `<title>` element:

```
<title>@Page.Title</title>
```

2. Open Default.cshtml, if necessary, and add the following code to the code block you started earlier:

```
@{
    Layout = "~/Shared/_Layout.cshtml";
    Page.Title = "Home";
}
```

3. Open Sell.cshtml and add the following to the code block at the top:

```
@{
    Layout = "~/Shared/_Layout.cshtml";
    Page.Title = "Post Your Advertisement";
}
```

4. Save all the changes and run Default.cshtml. If you look at the browser title bar, you should see that the page title has now been set to "Home." If you click on the link to the Sell page, you will see that the title has changed to "Post Your Advertisement."

How It Works

The `PageData` dictionary is a collection of arbitrary values defined at the content page level. When the content page is merged with the layout page, this dictionary is made available to the resulting completed page. Consequently, values can be used within the layout page. Figure 3.9 shows how this relationship works.

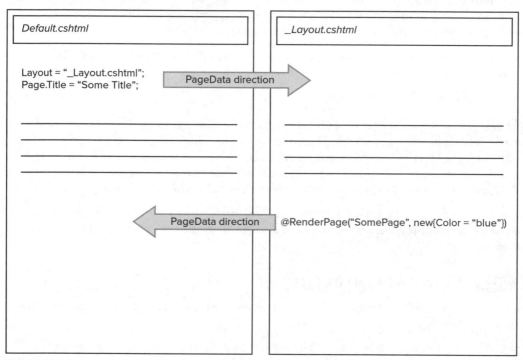

FIGURE 3-9

The page title was passed as a piece of text for display. The other value, `ShowLogin` was passed as a *boolean* value (either `true` or `false`), and used by the Razor code to determine whether to display a particular part of the page. So far, you have passed values from content pages to layout pages, but data can also be passed in the opposite direction — from a layout page to a content page. The `RenderPage` method call takes an additional parameter that can contain values that you want to pass from the layout page to the section it displays. In the next exercise, you amend the layout page to incorporate a separate file for the footer, and then pass data to the footer.

TRY IT OUT Passing Data from the Layout to a Section

1. Open Default.cshtml if you have closed it and remove the lines of code that define a footer section:

```
@section footer{
    &copy; Wrox Classifieds @DateTime.Now.Year
}
```

2. Open _Layout.cshtml and make the following change to the footer area so that the code looks like this:

```
<div id="footer">
    @RenderPage("~/Shared/_Footer.cshtml", new {Year = DateTime.Now.Year})
</div>
```

3. Add a new CSHTML file to the Shared folder and call it **_Footer.cshtml**. Replace any existing markup in the file with the following:

```
&copy; Wrox Classifieds @Page.Year
```

4. Making sure that Default is selected in the left pane, click the Run button to launch the page in a browser. If all went well, you should see the footer displayed at the bottom of the page with the current year as part of the copyright line.

How It Works

This time, you defined the data that was added to the PageData dictionary from within the layout page. You did this by passing in an additional argument to the RenderPage method call. The second argument, which is optional, is known as an *anonymous type*. It begins with the new keyword, and then an opening curly brace ({). After that, you are free to define values in exactly the same way as you did earlier — you specify a key and an associated value. In this case, the key was Year and the value you assigned to that was C# code for the current year. Then you closed with another curly brace (}). If you want to provide more than one value via the RenderPage method, you must simply separate each one with a comma:

```
@RenderPage("~/Shared/_Footer.cshtml", new {Color = "blue", Number = 10})
```

Each value will be added to the PageData dictionary individually. To reference them in the section page, you can use either method introduced earlier:

```
PageData["Color"]
PageData["Number"]
```

or

```
Page.Color
Page.Number
```

Both methods will yield blue and 10, respectively.

This exercise illustrated how values can be passed between content pages, layout pages and sections via the PageData dictionary. There are other ways to pass data between pages, and across all pages in a website. These include:

➤ Cookies

➤ Query strings

➤ Hidden form fields

➤ Session variables

You will see these covered in more detail throughout the book.

PRACTICAL TIPS WHEN DESIGNING LAYOUTS

The following tips will help you to reduce complexity and repeated code when designing layouts for your site:

➤ **Always start with a visual outline of your web pages.** These can be in any format that works best for you. Ideally, this work will be done by someone else and presented to you as a series of graphics. However, simply sketching the outlines on pieces of paper works for me quite often. From these sketches, you can quickly identify the page elements or sections that repeat, and those that do not.

➤ **Start all new sites with a layout page.** It doesn't matter how simple or complex the site is. This way, if you decide to add a new repeating feature to your site at a later date, you can insert it into your layout page. Then, all content pages that make use of the layout page will automatically benefit from the new feature.

➤ **Keep your layout page as "skinny" as possible: Avoid adding too much server-side code to the layout page.** Make use of `required: false` or `IsSectionDefined` to manage optional content as much as possible; move all of your CSS definitions to an external file so that they don't intrude on your layout page. This will keep your layout pages lightweight and easy to read and maintain.

SUMMARY

Understanding the structure of your site from the start is a very important aspect to successful web development. If you attack the project in a piecemeal fashion, you will find managing the development of the site, especially in the area of making changes, more and more complex. This chapter, together with the advice provided in the previous chapter, has shown you how to separate your site's style and layout into separate files for easy maintenance. You were also shown the key features offered by WebMatrix to manage the structure of your site and to maximize reuse of page content blocks. You have also seen how to share data between content and layout pages in both directions.

WebMatrix makes it super easy to manage a consistent look and feel for your site through these features. Through the exercises, you have learned that you can maintain a powerful level of control over your site's structure with the minimum of server-side code.

You should have a good grounding in the fundamentals of web *design* by now. Web *development* requires a keen grasp of server-side code, and the next chapter provides you with the basic fundamentals of programming within WebMatrix, together with an examination of the Razor syntax.

EXERCISES

1. How should you name a layout file, and why?

2. What does the `RenderBody` method do, and how does it differ from `RenderPage`?

3. Name two ways to include optional content within a page, and explain the difference between them.

4. How do you pass data from a layout page to a content page?

Answers to the Exercises can be found in the Appendix.

▶ **WHAT YOU LEARNED IN THIS CHAPTER**

TOPIC	KEY CONCEPTS
Layout page	A file that defines the structure of pages that reference it.
Section	A snippet of code that can be displayed in a layout page.
RenderBody	A method that defines where the default content will appear in a layout page.
RenderPage	A method that causes the content of other named files to be included within a layout page, but allows the layout page to pass data to the included file.
RenderSection	A method that causes the content of a section to be rendered within a layout page.
PageData	A container of key/value pairs that are accessible by layout and content pages.
IsSectionDefined	A method that determines whether a section has been defined before attempting to render it.

4

Programming Your Site

WHAT YOU WILL LEARN IN THIS CHAPTER:

➤ Where Razor, C#, and VB fit within ASP.NET Web Pages

➤ Programming fundamentals

➤ The basics of the Razor syntax

➤ Separating code and functionality

➤ Creating your own reusable functions

➤ The key objects you will work with in Web Pages

The primary purpose of programming is to exercise control over the behavior of your application. When you first conceive your website, you know what purpose it is intended to serve. It may provide your visitors with news stories on demand. It may provide a means for visitors to locate and order an item they wish to purchase. It might simply provide them with a means to view your personal photo album, but in an order and manner they choose. How your application behaves will depend on the set of programming instructions you embed within it. You will decide what your visitors can and cannot do or see. You will decide what options you want to provide them with, and under what *conditions* these will be made available. You determine the *logical behavior* of your application and embed that logic through the programming language available to you.

Your application will need to make decisions based on conditions that you define. For example, if the current user is authenticated, your application might provide them with a means to administer content. If the user selects a particular option within a form, your application will present certain data to them. If they make a different selection, your application will be programmed to show different data. You will use programming to control the application's flow.

Your application will need to be aware of *data*. This data can take the form of single values, such as the current user's name, or a more complex collection of values, such as those passed to the web server when someone submits a completed registration form. This data will need to be stored, albeit temporarily in most cases, for later retrieval. Sometimes, your application will need to compare one value with another, or perform calculations on a series of values. For instance, of all the news stories available to it, your application may need to compare the date they were created with the current date to ensure it only shows today's news.

Endowing your website with controlled *behavior* through server-side programming is the essence of dynamic web development. This chapter introduces you to the most important programming concepts you need to learn if you are to provide your visitors with the right type of experience.

THE .NET FRAMEWORK, C#, VB, AND RAZOR

The .NET Framework supports a number of programming languages, of which C# (pronounced "see-sharp") and *Visual Basic* (VB) are the most popular. WebMatrix, on the other hand, supports only C# and VB, which simplifies your choice concerning which language you should use. You are free to use either of the options available. All the examples in this book are provided in C#.

Why C#?

At the time of writing, all of the site templates that come as part of the WebMatrix package are written in C#. Consequently, if you want to work with them, you need to understand C#. Articles and other resources available within the blogger community are primarily provided in C#. Again, an understanding of C# is important if you envisage making use of these resources. There is an additional value to learning C#, which is that C# is very similar in syntax to JavaScript. Accordingly, familiarity with C# may help you to learn JavaScript, the foundation of AJAX, more quickly. Finally, the Razor syntax itself is based on C#.

Where Does Razor Fit In?

Whereas C# is a programming language, Razor is a *template syntax*. As you have seen so far, server-side programming code within ASP.NET Web Pages is intermixed with HTML. When your page is requested by a browser, it is processed by a special *Razor Parser*, which locates and identifies the server-side code. Razor includes a number of rules and symbols that help the parser identify where code is placed, and what type of code block it has encountered. As you learned in the first chapter, Razor already knows whether the code is C# or VB from the file extension (CSHTML or VBHTML).

PROGRAMMING FUNDAMENTALS

Before you take a look at a wider range of Razor rules, you will explore the basics of programming. As you have seen, Razor is a means of adding C# code to your pages, but further discussion on how to do this is unlikely to make sense unless you know what the code does and how it works. If you are comfortable with the basics of programming in C#, you can skip the next few sections. If you already know a programming language, but do not know C#, the next sections should provide a useful basic primer. This is not intended to act as a full introduction to the C# language, but will provide most people with enough to get started. As you build the sample application, any further code constructs that require explanation will be covered as you go along. The topics this section looks at include:

➤ Variables and data types

➤ Statements

➤ Objects, properties and methods

Variables and Data Types

Variables are containers for storing values in memory for later use. You will most often create a variable using the `var` keyword:

```
var theYear = DateTime.Now.Year;
```

In the previous example, the value of `DateTime.Year.Now` is stored in a variable called *theYear*. Providing a value to the variable (using the equals sign) is known as *initializing* the variable. When you use the `var` keyword to create or declare a variable, you must initialize it.

C# keywords and variable names are case-sensitive, so when you refer to the variable later in your code, you must use the same case. Look at the following example:

```
var a = 0;
var A = 1;
```

This is legal, as the variables *a* and *A* are considered different due to their case.

 NOTE *I'll say it again: C# is a case-sensitive language.*

Naming Variables

Although the preceding example is legal, you should strive to name variables so that their purpose and meaning is clear. As your code grows and becomes more complex (and it will, trust me!), the last thing you want to do in a year's time is to try to understand the logic within a block of code packed with cryptic variable names. You can name your variables anything you like, but there are some simple rules that you must follow:

➤ You may only use letters, numbers, and the underscore character in your variable's name.

➤ You may not include spaces in your variable names.

➤ The first character must be a letter or an underscore.

➤ You may not use C# keywords as variable names.

➤ As was mentioned earlier, case matters.

 NOTE *Visual Basic variables and keywords are not case sensitive.*

The following are all legal C# variable names:

```
theYear
TheYear
_theYear
year6
year
```

The following are all illegal:

```
year-6
6year
the year
public
```

The first example includes a hyphen (-), which is an illegal character. The second starts with a number. The third includes a space in the variable name and the fourth is a C# keyword.

 NOTE *Public with a capital P is a legal variable name in C#. This is because C# is a case-sensitive language. (I've said that before, haven't I?) I would recommend, however, not capitalizing C# keywords so that you can use them as variable names. Doing so adds potential confusion to your code.*

Data Types

Each variable contains data of a particular *data type*. It might be a character, or series of letters, or a number. It might also be a special type. The .NET Framework defines and understands many different types through a standard known as the *Common Type System* (CTS). The purpose of the CTS is to ensure that objects of a particular data type from one .NET-compliant programming language are interoperable with a matching type from another. The result of this interoperability is that you can, if you like, freely add both VBHTML and CSHTML files to your Web Pages website, although you cannot mix languages within the same file.

The most common data types that you are likely to use within your C# code are listed in Table 4-1.

TABLE 4-1: Common C# Data Types

DATA TYPE	DESCRIPTION	EXAMPLE
string	Stores text as a series of Unicode characters. The default value is null.	`string theString = "Mike";`
int	Stores whole numbers between -2,147,483,648 and 2,147,483,647. The default value is 0.	`int theNumber = 5;`
bool	Used to store a Boolean value, true or false. The default value is false.	`bool theBool = false;`

DATA TYPE	DESCRIPTION	EXAMPLE
DateTime	Stores a date and time.	`DateTime theDate = new DateTime(2010, 11, 1, 0, 0, 0);`
char	Represents a single Unicode character.	`char theChar = 'c';`
float	A single-precision floating point number. Notice that the fractional value requires the letter "f" as a suffix to differentiate it from a double.	`float theFloat = 63.98f;`
double	Stores a double-precision floating-point number.	`double theDouble = 1.59;`
decimal	Stores very large fractional numbers with more accuracy than double. Notice that the fractional value requires a letter "m" as a suffix to differentiate it from a double.	`decimal theDecimal = 1.597613m;`

The var Keyword and Strong Typing

C# is *strongly typed*, which means that the data type should be specified or be able to be inferred at the point a variable is declared. Strong typing provides *type safety*, which reduces the potential for errors in your code. You have seen the var keyword used to *declare* (create) and *instantiate* (specify a value for) variables in all examples so far. However, var can be used only if the variable's data type can be inferred from the value given to it. In all of the examples provided in Table 4-1, variables have been declared explicitly using the specific data type keyword and initialized with a value. Consider this example:

```
string theString = "Mike";
```

In every one of these examples, the var keyword could have been used instead:

```
var theString = "Mike";
```

The compiler can see what value has been provided and can determine the correct data type. This is known as *implicit typing*. Sometimes you may need to declare a variable without instantiating it. Whenever you do this, you must do so explicitly, specifying the type. You cannot use the var keyword without providing a clue to the variable so that the compiler can "see" what data type the variable should be:

```
string myString; // declared with no value
myString = "Mike"; // assigned

var myString // Will not work
var myString = "Mike"; // declaration and assignment together
```

Once you have set the data type for a variable, you cannot change it by simply assigning a completely different type of value to it. The following will not work:

```
var theValue = "Mike";
theValue = 0; // Attempt to change a string to an int
```

Some data types allow implicit conversion. For example, a float can implicitly be converted to a double, although loss of precision may occur. Equally an int can be implicitly converted to a double, float, or decimal. Conversions the other way must be explicit — that is the data type which the value is being converted to must be stated. This can be done by placing the target data type in brackets before the value to be converted.

```
int theIntValue = 10;
float theFloatValue = theIntValue //implicit conversion from int to float
float theFloatValue = 1.5f;
int theIntValue = (int)theFloatValue; // Explicit conversion from float to int
```

However, you can change its value to another of the same type:

```
var theValue = "Mike";
theValue = "Pete";
```

Working with Strings

The *string* data type is probably the one that you will work with most often in your Web Pages applications. When you create a string, you must enclose the value in double quotes ("):

```
var thestring = "Mike";
```

If your string includes a double quote, this can be escaped using a backslash:

```
var theString = "Norman \"Bite Yer Legs\" Hunter";
```

Alternatively, you can create a *verbatim string* by prefixing the value with the @ symbol, and doubling the double quotes:

```
var theString = @"Norman ""Bite Yer Legs"" Hunter";
```

 NOTE *Norman Hunter is a well-known former English footballer who was particularly noted for his "committed" style of play — hence the nickname ("Bite Yer Legs"). It should be noted that no evidence exists to suggest that Mr. Hunter did actually sink his teeth into an opponent's legs at any stage during his playing career.*

You can also use a verbatim string to manage a value that contains a backslash:

```
var thePath = @"C:\Users\My Documents";
```

Or alternatively, you can double the backslashes to escape them:

```
var thePath = "C:\\Users\\My Documents";
```

Converting Strings to Other Data Types

Although you are unable to change the data type of a string variable, you can convert the value to other data types represented by another variable. This is important if you want to be able to perform arithmetical calculations on a value that has been presented to you as a string. You will need to do this quite often, as all values presented to you by a site visitor will initially reach your server-side code as strings. WebMatrix includes a number of simple methods for converting strings to a variety of other types; these are detailed in Table 4-2. You will see how to apply these later in the chapter.

TABLE 4-2: Conversion Methods in Razor

METHOD	PURPOSE	EXAMPLE
AsInt()	Converts the string to an integer. If the conversion is unsuccessful, returns 0.	`var x = "25";` `var y = x.AsInt();`
AsBool()	Converts the string to the Boolean true or false. Returns false if the conversion is unsuccessful.	`var x = "true";` `var y = x.AsBool();`
AsFloat()	Converts the string to a float. If the conversion is unsuccessful, returns 0.	`var x = "63.98";` `var y = x.AsFloat();`
AsDecimal()	Converts the string to a decimal. If the conversion is unsuccessful, returns 0.	`var x = "63.98";` `var y = x.AsDecimal();`
AsDateTime()	Converts the string to a DateTime type. If the conversion is unsuccessful, returns 01/01/0001 00:00:00.	`var x =  "2010.9.3";` `var y = x.AsDateTime()`

Collections

All of the data types you have seen so far represent one single value. Within ASP.NET Web Pages, you will often have to work with multiple values stored together in one variable, in other words, a *collection* of values. You will do this every time you reference the values submitted by a site visitor through a form, for example. A collection is a data structure that enables you to store multiple values. The .NET Framework provides many types of collections, each having its own advantages, disadvantages, and specialized usage. Moreover, you are free to create your own type of collection, but discussion surrounding that is outside of the scope of this book.

Arrays

Arrays are the simplest type of collection. When you create an array, you have to specify its capacity, or the number of items it will hold. You do that in one of two ways. Either you provide the items when you initialize the array, or you explicitly tell the array how big it will be. The following example illustrates both approaches by creating an array of strings that will hold three values:

```
string[] people = new string[]{"John", "Simon", "Anna"};

string[] people = new string[3];
people[0] = "John";
people[1] = "Simon";
people[2] = "Anna";
```

Notice how the array is declared in both cases. The data type (string) is followed by square brackets ([]). In the first example, the array is populated by the three values it will contain in the curly braces ({}). In the second example, each *element* (an individual item in an array) is added to the array by addressing its *index* or position within the array. By default, the array index is zero-based, which means that the first element is at index 0. You reference the elements by using this index, so regardless how you created the array, the following code will create a new string variable called *person* with the value "Simon" by referencing the item at Index 1 in the *people* array:

```
var person = people[1];
```

Arrays are fixed size structures. You cannot alter the number of elements they hold once they are created. The simplest way to get around this is to create a new array and copy over the elements you need from the original array:

```
// Create a new array called temp
var temp = new string[4];
//Copy the contents of the people array to temp
Array.Copy(people, temp, people.Length);
// Re-assign the people array so that it hold the contents of temp
people = temp;
```

Other Types of Collections

Arrays are simple to use, but limited. A much more flexible alternative is the *generic list*. Generics provide a way to create strongly typed data structures. If you remember the discussion around the var keyword, working with strongly typed data is preferred as it provides a measure of protection against errors creeping into your code. Generic lists will allow only the data type you specify, so you cannot add the wrong type of data to it. When you see the generic list referred to in documentation, you will see List<T>. The capital T in angle brackets is the telltale signature of a generic collection. The T stands for any type you like. It's up to you to decide what data type your list should hold. If you want to create a strongly typed list of strings, it will be declared like this:

```
var myList = new List<string>();
```

A strongly typed list of integers is declared as follows:

```
var myList = new List<int>();
```

Lists expose a lot more functionality than arrays. You do not need to declare their size. You can add and remove items at will. Here's how you use a `List<string>` to add your people to:

```
var people = new List<string>();
people.Add("John");
people.Add("Simon");
people.Add("Anna");
```

Notice that the list was created without specifying a size. Items were added after it had been instantiated. You can go on adding items as often as you like.

You can initialize this list in another way, through a *collection initializer*, which looks very similar to the way that your first array was created:

```
var people = new List<string>(){"John" "Simon", "Anna"};
```

Once that is done, you can still add additional elements:

```
people.Add("Kevin");
```

Generic collections are the recommended way to manage collections of data simply because they are strongly typed.

One final collection to look at is the *NameValueCollection*. The `NameValueCollection` is a special type of collection that holds *key/value pairs*. It is used in a number of places within ASP.NET as a container for a series of values associated to a key. One area where you will work with a key/value pairs extensively is when processing user input supplied via a form on a web page. You explore the subject of working with forms in more detail in the next chapter, but when you address elements within a `NameValueCollection`, you do so by referencing the name of their key:

```
var name = Request.Form["FirstName"];
```

This example assumes that an item with the key `"FirstName"` exists in the `Request.Form` collection. Its value is passed into the variable `"name"`. Notice that the key acts in the same way as an array indexer, and needs to be placed in square brackets. You will see more of this in Chapter 5.

Statements

Statements are the set of instructions you provide to your program to tell it how to behave. You have already seen many examples of statements at work. You have seen *expression statements* being used to assign values to variables in the preceding section. Now you will look at *selection statements*, which provide a mechanism for making decisions in code based on conditions, and *iteration statements*, which allow you to perform actions repetitively either a known number of times, or until a certain condition has been met. Before you do that, you will take a tour of the common *operators* provided by the C# language.

Operators

Operators are symbols that specify what action should take place regarding one or more *operands*. Operands are expressions when used as arguments. A variable might be an operand, a literal value, or an integer. The C# language reference categorizes operators according to their usage:

ARITHMETIC OPERATORS	
+	Addition. Also used for string concatenation.
–	Subtraction
*	Multiplication
/	Division
%	Modulus

The first four operators are self-explanatory. The last one, the modulus operator, calculates the reminder after one number has been divided by another. If the modulus of a division by 2 is 0, the number being divided is even. This is useful when you want to apply alternating styles to rows of data. The result of 10%4 is 2.

RELATIONAL OPERATORS	
==	Is equal to
!=	Is not equal to
<	Is less than
>	Is greater than
<=	Is less than or equal to
>=	Is greater than or equal to

 NOTE *Notice the first operator here. In Visual Basic, you compare equality using the equals sign (=). In C-like languages (C#, JavaScript, Java, C, and so on), equality is tested by doubling the equals sign. Forgetting to use two equals signs (==) when testing equality is a common source of errors for people just beginning with C#.*

ASSIGNMENT OPERATORS	
=	Equals
+=	Addition assignment
-=	Subtraction assignment

The addition and subtraction assignment operators act as a kind of shorthand. For example:

```
a += b;
```

is the same as:

```
a + a = b;
```

LOGICAL OPERATORS	
&&	Logical "and"
||	Logical "or"
!	Logical "not"

The logical "and" and "or" operators are known as *binary operators*. Both sides of the equation must be *logical expressions*. That is, they must either evaluate to true or false on their own. Take a look at the following pseudo-code:

```
If the sun is out && the temperature is over 70°f…
```

In this example, the sun must be out *and* the temperature must be over 70°f for the test to pass, whereas in the next example, which uses the logical "or,"

```
If the sun is out || the temperature is over 70°f…
```

either the sun must be out, *or* the temperature must exceed 70°f for the test to pass. In both examples, "the sun is out" will evaluate to `true` or `false` on its own, as will the statement "the temperature is over 70°f."

Selection Statements

You have been introduced to operators, but how do you use them to evaluate expressions or test conditions? The importance of being able to do so cannot be understated. You will often need to test conditions and make decisions based on the result. This is what allows you to transfer control over to a specific flow of execution. For example, you may need to determine whether the current user is authorized to see the page she is requesting, or you may need to determine whether a user has submitted a form for validation. The construct you will use most often is the `if` statement. An `if` statement, optionally combined with an `else` statement, provides a simple way to control the flow of execution based on the result of the test. Its syntax, using pseudocode, follows this format:

```
if(condition to test){
    do something
}
```

When an `else` statement is used, the syntax follows this pattern:

```
if(condition to test){
    do something
} else {
```

```
        do something different
    }
```

The "condition to test" is presented in parentheses (brackets) as an expression, or as a series of expressions separated by && or ||, depending on what combination you are testing. It is followed by a pair of curly braces, within which the operation to be performed is placed. In C# code samples that you find in other books or online, you may see the curly braces omitted if a single line code block follows the if statement:

```
    if(condition to test)
        do something;
```

This is perfectly legal. However, within ASP.NET Web Pages, the Razor syntax does not allow it. You must provide the curly braces every time you use the if statement.

In the following pseudo-code examples, you have a Boolean variable called valid and a numeric variable, x. The examples will test a variety of conditions that include one or both of the variables so that you can see how the logical operators work:

```
    bool valid = false;
    //if valid is equal to true
    if(valid == true){
        do something
    }
```

You do not need to use the equality operator to test if a Boolean is true or false. The following snippet is identical in operation to the previous one:

```
    bool valid = false;
    //if valid is equal to true
    if(valid){
        //do something
    }


    //if x is equal to 3
    if(x == 3){
        //do something
    }

    //if valid is true and x is equal to 3
    if(valid && x == 3){
        //do something
    }

    //if valid is true or x is equal to 3
    if(valid || x == 3){
        //do something
    }
```

If you have a large number of conditions to test, you can continue with a series of else statements as long as you like. However, another construct that is available to you is the switch statement. This is the preferred method for testing multiple conditions. In the following example, you are assumed to have calculated the difference in goals between two teams playing a football match and stored it in *theResult*. Depending on the size of the margin in the score, a different message is created:

```
var theMessage = "";
switch(theResult){
    case 0:
        theMessage = "It's a drawn match";
        break;
    case 1:
        theMessage = "A close win";
        break;
    case 2:
        theMessage = "A comfortable win";
        break;
    case 3:
        theMessage = "A convincing victory";
        break;
    case 4:
        theMessage = "A thrashing!";
        break;
    default:
        theMessage = "Out of sight!";
        break;
}
```

If there is no difference in the number of goals scored by both teams, the result is a draw. As the margin gets progressively larger, the message changes to reflect that. Each test case (case statement) is terminated with the break keyword. This prevents further test cases from being evaluated if one succeeds. If all fail, the default test case is executed. In the example, the default means that any margins of five goals or more result in the message "Out of sight!" The default case will also execute if theResult is negative. In C#, the condition (the part after case) must be a *constant expression*. That means that you cannot use other operators in it. This differs from the equivalent Visual Basic Select Case statement, where multiple expressions or ranges can be used.

Iteration Statements

Every programming language provides a means to execute code repetitively, either until a particular condition is met, or for a fixed number of iterations. These are known as iteration statements. Sometimes you will know in advance how many times you want the code to execute. Sometimes you don't. Other times you will want code to execute until a specific external condition has been met. These are the factors you take into account when choosing the appropriate construct.

The for Loop

The for loop is used when you know in advance how many times you want the code to execute. For example, you might want to render the numbers 1–10 to the page. In this case, you know that the code to render a number needs to execute 10 times:

```
for (var i = 1; i <= 10; i++){
    //do something
}
```

The `for` loop syntax follows this structure:

```
for (initial state; condition under which loop continues; iterator){
    code to execute on each iteration
}
```

The initial state in this example is that the variable `i` is declared and instantiated with a value of 1. All the time that `i` is less than or equal to 10 (the condition under which the loop continues), the code within the curly braces will execute. On each iteration, `i` is incremented by 1. As soon as `i` equals 11, the condition test fails, and the loop stops executing.

If you want to iterate over an entire collection, you could use the collection's `Count` property, or an array's `Length` property as part of the "condition under which loop continues" segment:

```
string[] people = new string[]{"John", "Simon", "Anna"};
for(var i = 0; i < people.Length; i++){
    //do something
}
```

In the previous example, your array has three elements. The `Length` property will give you a value of 3. Since you are referencing elements by index, using the iterator, you do not want the iterator's state to exceed the index of the last element. That's why the loop must terminate when the iterator reaches a value equal to the total number of elements. If you try to reference an element with an index of 3, you will get an `"Index was outside the bounds of the array"` error message because arrays have a zero-based index, and the highest index in a 3 element array is 2.

foreach

There's a simpler way to iterate the items in a collection using a `foreach` loop, and it avoids the confusion some people have with balancing the index values against the absolute number of elements in an array. The syntax for a `foreach` statement is as follows:

```
foreach (var person in people){
    //do something
}
```

while

The `while` statement causes code to execute until a condition or expression is false. The conditional test takes place before the first iteration, which means that any code in the *statement body* — the part that appears within the opening and closing curly brackets — may never execute:

```
var x = 5;
while(x < 10){
    x++;
}
```

In this example, x starts at 5. The loop will continue to execute all the time that x is less than 10, and on each iteration, x will increment by 1. If x was initiated to 15 to begin with, the loop would never execute. 15 is clearly more than 10.

do... while

The do loop will execute at least once, in contrast to the while loop. This is because the condition appears outside of the statement body. The following code will always result in x being incremented to 16 despite the fact that the while expression appears to restrict the operation to only those conditions where x is less than 10:

```
var x = 15;
do{
    x++;
}
while(x < 10);
```

Objects, Properties, and Methods

The next section looks at some of the fundamental concepts you need to know to be able to understand how to use the built-in objects within Web Pages as well as to begin constructing your own objects should you need to. It is far from a primer on Object Oriented Programming, but will provide a foundation from which you can build your knowledge. Object Oriented Programming is a vast topic, and way beyond the scope of this book. The concepts provided here are the minimum you need to know to become productive with ASP.NET Web Pages.

Objects

An *object* is the basic building block of programming within the .NET Framework. They are things that you control through programming. All of the variables and collections you have met so far are different types of object. WebMatrix includes a large number of built-in objects that you will work with, such as a Database object to help you work with data stored in a database, or a WebGrid object, which allows you to display data in tabular fashion. Moreover, the .NET Framework has thousands of objects that you will also make use of during your site development. Objects often model real-world things like files and images.

Objects are created from *classes*. Books on C# programming have different ways to describe exactly what a class is. Some compare them to cookie cutters or blue prints. I see them as the formal definition of an object. They contain the details and rules concerning what an object created from them can do, and what it looks like. In that respect, they are very much like templates in a word processing application. As well as the pre-built classes that come with .NET, you are free to create your own classes, from which you can instantiate your own *custom objects*. WebMatrix provides an option to add a file of type "Class (C#)". If you select this option, you are presented with the following templated code:

```
using System;
using System.Collections.Generic;
using System.Web;

/// <summary>
/// Summary description for ClassName
/// </summary>
public class ClassName
{
```

```
    public ClassName()
    {
        //
        // TODO: Add constructor logic here
        //
    }
}
```

This code needs a bit of explaining. The first three lines are called *using directives*. Classes within the .NET Framework are organized into logical groupings called *namespaces*. The System namespace contains all the basic classes that the rest of the .NET Framework relies on. The most important one of these is the Object class, from which all other objects ultimately derive. Other important classes are String and Array. System.Collections.Generic contains classes that define generic collections, like the List<T> you saw earlier. System.Web is another namespace, which incorporates classes related to ASP.NET functionality. Using directives makes the classes in these namespaces available to the code in the class file. The three namespaces that have been made available in the template code may, or may not be needed, but it seems that the template authors feel that they are the ones you will most likely use.

Lines of text that begin with three forward slashes (///) are XML comments. Other IDEs such as Visual Studio and Visual Web Developer, which have a fuller version of IntelliSense built-in, make use of these comments and display them as you code. They serve no real purpose within WebMatrix at the moment.

Next is the class declaration. In this case, a class called ClassName is defined. ClassName is now a type. So not only can you use the built-in data types such as String, DateTime, and Boolean which you saw earlier — you can create your own types. To instantiate an object of type ClassName, you use the new keyword:

```
ClassName c = new ClassName();
```

You could just as easily use var here:

```
var c = new ClassName();
```

Your variable c is now an instance of the ClassName type, but it doesn't do anything. It has no *members*. Members give a class a reason for existence. You will look at the two most common types of class members next.

Properties

Like real-world objects, .NET objects have characteristics or features. These are known as *properties*. In the real world, eyes have a color property. A sound has a volume property. In some cases, you can set and retrieve the value of the property. In others, you can only retrieve the value. Earlier, you used the Length property of an array object to manage a condition. When you did so, you referenced the value of the property using *dot notation*:

```
int x = myArray.Length;
```

The Length property belongs to the array object known as *myArray*, so it is joined to the object using the dot. All properties have a data type. In the case of the Length property of an array, the data type is an `int`. Taking the template Class file as an example, here's how properties might be assigned to a class. Before adding properties, I have modified the code so that the class has a meaningful name, and removed the *default constructor* code that was added there, as well as the unnecessary `using` directives:

```
using System;

/// <summary>
/// Summary description for Car
/// </summary>
public class Car
{
  public string Make { get; set; }
  public int NumberOfDoors { get; set; }
  public DateTime Registered { get; set; }
}
```

Using the `new` keyword again, you can instantiate an object of type `Car` like this:

```
var car = new Car();
```

You can set its properties:

```
car.Make = "Ford";
car.NumberOfDoors = 4;
car.Registered = DateTime.Now;
```

You can also read its properties:

```
if(car.Make == "Ford"){
    //it's a Ford
}
```

You can also use an *object initializer* to instantiate the `car` object, which is a more concise option:

```
var car = new Car { Make = "Ford", NumberOfDoors = 4, Registered = DateTime.Now };
```

CONSTRUCTORS

Every class must have a constructor. The constructor is a special method that gets called when you use the `new` keyword. The constructor's job is to initialize the object you create from the class. Often, for simple classes, the constructor doesn't have to do anything at all. Sometimes, however, you need to execute extra code to create a valid instance of the class, and the constructor is where you put that code. As the `Car` class code stands at the moment, the value for the `NumberOfDoors` property will be 0, which is the default value for an integer. You might decide that no one can use your `Car` class without having the value for `NumberOfDoors` set at 4 to start with. If this was the case, you would set `NumberOfDoors` to 4 in the constructor. If you do not want to add code to the constructor that is provided by the template file, you can remove it. The C# compiler will create a default empty constructor for you when the code is compiled.

The Car class is still not very interesting. It provides a convenient way for you to store values associated with a particular type of object, but that's it. Sometimes that is all that is needed. Such custom objects are quite commonplace within .NET development as simple data containers. However, things get more interesting when you begin to bestow behavior on your objects in the form of *methods*.

Methods

Objects can have behavior, or things they can do (or that you as a programmer can make them do). These are known as *methods*. Earlier on, you saw that a List can have things added to it. The method that you use to do this is the List's Add() method. You also saw that strings can be converted to different data types using a variety of methods such as AsInt() or AsBool(). Methods on objects are *called* using the same dot notation you use for referencing an object's properties, but methods are always followed by brackets (which is mainly how they differ in appearance from properties).

A car is pretty useless unless it starts, so the Car class could do with a method that gives it this behavior:

```
using System;

/// <summary>
/// Summary description for Car
/// </summary>
public class Car
{
  public string Make { get; set; }
  public int NumberOfDoors { get; set; }
  public DateTime Registered { get; set; }
  public int Speed { get; set; }

  public void Start()
  {
    //starts the car
  }
}
```

Now the Car class has a Start method. The method body is empty, so it doesn't do anything but you can start the car by calling the method:

```
Car.Start();
```

Any code that you add to the method will be executed.

Sometimes you provide additional information within the brackets when you call a method. You might add one piece of information, or a number of items separated by commas. These items of information are known as *arguments*. The type and number of arguments you pass are defined in the *parameter list* provided as part of the method's *signature*. The signature for the Start method is

```
public void Start()
```

The word `public` specifies that the method can be called from outside of the `Car` class itself. It is known as an *access modifier*. If you do not set an access modifier on your method, it will default to `private`, which means that only code within the `Car` class can call the method. The next part of the signature specifies the data type of the return value. Often, methods will return a value to the calling code. It might be a `string`, `DateTime`, `bool`, or any other type. In this case, the `Start` method does not return a value of any type, so the keyword `void` is used to indicate that. If the method requires arguments, they will appear in the brackets after the method name. I will add an `Accelerate` method to the Car class to illustrate this:

```
using System;

/// <summary>
/// Summary description for Car
/// </summary>
public class Car
{
  public string Make { get; set; }
  public int NumberOfDoors { get; set; }
  public DateTime Registered { get; set; }
  public int Speed { get; set; }

  public void Start()
  {
    //starts the car
  }
  public void Accelerate(int speed)
  {
    Speed += speed;
  }
}
```

I have also added a new property: `Speed`, which is of type `int`. The `Accelerate` method requires an argument of type `int`. The body of the method simply increments the `Speed` property's value by whatever value is passed in to the `Speed` parameter:

```
var car = new Car();
car.Accelerate(20); // car.Speed now equals 20.
```

In the large majority of cases, all parameters require a value to be passed in to them when you call a method. The latest version of the C# language, C# 4.0, saw the addition of *optional and named parameters*. Since WebMatrix was built on version 4.0, a number of its objects' methods make use of optional parameters. Simply put, parameters are made optional simply by having a default value applied to them by the class. If you pass no value in when calling the method, the default value is used. Since you might not pass values to all parameters, you need to provide the names of the ones for which values are being supplied. Here is a modified version of the `Car` class, which has a constructor defined:

```
using System;

/// <summary>
/// Summary description for Car
/// </summary>
```

```
public class Car
{
  public Car(DateTime registered, string make="Ford", int doors = 4)
  {
    Registered = registered;
    Make = make;
    NumberOfDoors = doors;
  }
  public string Make { get; set; }
  public int NumberOfDoors { get; set; }
  public DateTime Registered { get; set; }
  public int Speed { get; set; }

  public void Start()
  {
    //starts the car
  }
  public void Accelerate(int speed)
  {
    Speed += speed;
  }
}
```

When you instantiate a Car object, you have to provide at least one argument. This is for the registered value. It is a required parameter, as it has no default value set. The other two parameters have default values set, so they are optional parameters. If you do not provide a value, the default values are used. If you choose to instantiate a Car object with three doors, you need to pass a value to the doors parameter:

```
var car = new Car(DateTime.Now, doors: 3);
```

Your Car object will now have three doors, its make will be a Ford (the default), and its time of registration will be the point at which the instance was created. You can also use an object initializer, even with optional parameters:

```
var car = new Car(DateTime.Now){ NumberOfDoors = 3, Make = "Audi" };
```

Notice that this time, the property name NumberOfDoors has a value applied to it, rather than the optional parameter doors in the constructor method's parameter list.

This has been by no means a comprehensive introduction to programming with C#, but should have provided you with enough of the basics for the code that follows in this book to make sense to you. If you want to further your C# knowledge, a great starting point is *Beginning Visual C# 2010* by Watson, Nagel, et al. (ISBN 978-0-470-50226-6). Where other programming topics are introduced later on in this book, they will be explained as necessary. In the next section, you will look at how to apply your C# code to Web Pages using the Razor syntax.

INTRODUCTION TO THE RAZOR SYNTAX

As you have learned before, *Razor* is a simplified syntax that allows you to mix server-side code with static content within the same file. The static content might be HTML, text, or JavaScript. One of the chief design goals behind Razor was that it should be simple to learn. By that, the designers of Razor wanted to allow developers to leverage their existing language skills in C# or VB, and get up to speed with using Razor as quickly as possible. It is not a new or different language. It simply provides a means to mark up C# or VB so that it can be parsed easily and executed. Razor has a small number of quite simple rules that must be followed to avoid errors.

Rule number one: Razor code always starts with the @ character. The Razor parser assumes that if the @ sign is the first character on a line and there is no space after it, or if there is a space before it (and no space after it), you are writing code:

```
@DateTime.Now
```

There are occasional issues with this rule. Take comments on a blog site, for example. Some blog sites employ a technique that threads comments, so that if someone is responding to a previous poster, there is a strong visual cue that shows that one comment is posted in reply to another. Other sites show a "flat view" of comments. A conventional way to show that you are addressing your comment to a previous poster in flat view is to prefix their name with the @ sign. Here's how it might look:

Posted by Dave on 17/9/2011 12:36pm
How do I learn more about WebMatrix?

Posted by Mike on 17/9/2011 12:48pm
@Dave: Buy my book :o)

If you were to add this to a CSHTML or VBHTML file as it is at the moment and then ran the page, you will get a *compiler error* as your reward. Chapter 9 discusses compiler errors in a lot more detail. The compiler will complain that `"The name 'Dave' does not exist in the current context"`. Razor assumes that Dave is a code variable, because it is preceded with an @ sign, which is the first character on the line. To prevent Razor from making that assumption, you *escape* the @ sign by doubling it:

```
@@Dave: Buy my book :o)
```

WebMatrix includes *syntax colorization* to help you recognize these kinds of issues. As soon as you add the @ sign to a page, the syntax highlighter provides a gold background as it assumes you are starting to write code. As you continue to type code, WebMatrix makes further decisions. If the @ sign is preceded by text, and immediately followed by text, as in an e-mail address, WebMatrix knows that you are not typing code, and the gold background disappears. If WebMatrix still believes you are writing code, it applies a shaded background. When you break out of the code block, the background returns to white. If you add another @ sign immediately after the first, the gold background disappears, telling you that Razor recognizes you intend to render a literal @.

Razor code can appear as statements in an inline statement or expression, or code block. You have already seen examples of both.

Inline statements or expressions:

```
@RenderBody()
@DateTime.Year.Now
```

Code block:

```
@{
    Layout = "~/Shared/_Layout.cshtml";
}
```

Inline expressions might be method calls as in the first line above, or used to render the value of variables. The second line renders the current year to the browser. Code blocks begin and end with curly braces { }. There must be no space between the @ sign and the opening brace. You should try to keep your code block at the top of the page so that your files are as organized as possible. Code blocks can contain multiple statements:

```
@{
    Layout = "~/Shared/_Layout.cshtml";
    var theYear = DateTime.Now.Year;
}
```

Each statement in a code block must be terminated with a semicolon. This follows standard C# rules. Inline expressions and statements are not terminated with semicolons. For readability purposes, you should put each statement in a code block on a separate line, but you don't have to. The following works just as well as the previous example:

```
@{
    Layout = "~/Shared/_Layout.cshtml"; var theYear = DateTime.Now.Year;
}
```

So long as the first brace immediately follows the @ sign, you can place single-line statements on one line within a code block:

```
@{ Layout = "~/Shared/_Layout.cshtml"; }
```

Mixing Razor and HTML

You have read an awful lot about programming and code, so it's about time you fired up WebMatrix again. Mixing Razor and HTML is a lot easier to describe if you can see how it works, so the next exercise will have you do just that.

TRY IT OUT   **Mixing Razor with HTML**

1. Open WebMatrix and create a new site using the Empty Site template. Name the site **Chapter4**.

2. Add a new CSHTML file and name it **Razor.cshtml**. Add the following highlighted code to what is already in the file:

```
@{
    var people = new List<string>(){"John", "Simon", "Anna"};
    var myInt = 3;
}
```

```html
<!DOCTYPE html>
<html lang="en">
    <head>
        <meta charset="utf-8" />
        <title></title>
    </head>
    <body>
        <p>There are @myInt people</p>
        <ul>
        @foreach(var person in people){
            <li>@person</li>
        }
        </ul>
    </body>
</html>
```

As you type, notice how WebMatrix adds a gold background to the first @ sign and assumes that you are entering code. When you type the opening brace ({), WebMatrix automatically adds the closing brace for you. All of the content between the braces has been shaded. WebMatrix sees this as a code block. The code block goes at the top of the page. This is the recommended placement position for code blocks. It helps to keep your Razor files tidy.

Look at how the syntax highlighter treats different types of text: C# keywords are turned blue. Strings appear brown. If you start typing a string and it appears in black text, you probably forgot the opening double quote. Numbers are highlighted in a pink color.

When you added the foreach statement, you prefixed the foreach keyword with the @ sign. Immediately, your code acquired a shaded background. This continued until you opened the curly braces and they were closed automatically. All of the content between the curly braces was shaded until you added the <li> tags. As soon as you closed the <li> tag, shading disappeared from behind them. WebMatrix sees the <li> tags as HTML.

3. If you click Run to launch the page in a browser, the result should show the three people's names with bullet points, as in Figure 4-1.

FIGURE 4-1

How It Works

This exercise demonstrated how to mix HTML with Razor syntax. You created a collection of people in a Razor code block at the top of the page. The code block began with an @ sign and an opening brace.

It was terminated with a closing brace, separating the code from the static HTML of the page. You saw how WebMatrix provided a colored background to the code block, helping you to minimize mistakes. If the colored background stops too early, or continues beyond the point you expect it to, your opening and closing braces are likely to be mismatched.

Once you started to work with Razor within the static HTML of the page, you saw how variables to be rendered to the page are prefixed with the @ sign, and that useful background color comes into play again. This is true of statements that are interwoven into the HTML, as you saw with the `foreach` statement.

Inline variables are placed at the point in the HTML that you want the resulting values to appear. You see this where `@myInt` is placed as if it is part of the text. Iteration and selection statements can be prefixed with the @ sign without the need for braces when they are used inline. If you want to render text and HTML output within a code block, you need to help Razor recognize the difference between code and text. There are three ways to accomplish this:

➤ Wrap the line in matching HTML tags. The previous example shows the item to be rendered wrapped in matching `<li>` tags. You can see that they are not shaded. Razor knows that they are not server-side code. Razor also recognizes self-closing tags like `<br />` like this:

```
<body>
    <p>There are @myInt people</p>
    <ul>
    @foreach(var person in people){
        <li>@person</li>
    }
    </ul>
</body>
```

➤ If the line doesn't include HTML, but mixes verbatim strings with inline expressions, prefix the first instance of the static text with the @ sign, followed by a colon (:)

```
@foreach (var person in people) {
    @:* @person - Manager
}
```

Only one @: is needed per line which is why it appears before the asterisk (the first instance of static text) and not "- Manager" (the second instance of static text). Do you remember HTML entities from Chapter 2? Here's how to output the alphabet in uppercase using HTML entities:

```
@for(var i = 65; i <= 90; i++){
    @:&#@i; 
}
```

➤ In cases where the text to be rendered is multi-line, wrap the entire block in `<text>` tags. These are not HTML tags. They do not affect the output and will not be rendered.

```
<body>
    @foreach (var person in people) {
        <text>
        The next person is @person<br />
        who is a manager
        </text>
```

```
    }
</body>
```

The `<text>` tags can be used to tidy up the output of the HTML entities in the previous alphabet example as well:

```
@for(var i = 65; i <= 90; i++){
    <text>&#@i; </text>
}
```

Inline expressions are placed in brackets. The following code loops through numbers from 1 to 10, and renders the remainder from dividing each number by 2. The modulo operation is an inline expression:

```
@for (var i = 1; i <= 10; i++) {
    @(i % 2)<br />
}
```

Finally, server-side comments that are not intended to be rendered within the HTML source code are wrapped in @*... *@ symbols:

```
@for (var i = 1; i <= 10; i++) {
    @* 1 for odd numbers, 0 for even *@
    @(i % 2)<br />
}
```

Reusable Code

A lot of the code you produce will serve a page-specific purpose. However, there will be times when you want to perform the same actions across a number of pages, or across the entire site. There may also be times when you want a variable to be available to the whole site or some parts of it. As you have learned earlier, you should aim not to repeat yourself (remember DRY?). Any code that you add to a page is generally available only within the context of the page it appears in. But the Web Pages framework includes a number of ways in which you can create reusable code or values so that they can be used in more than one place.

Global Values and _AppStart.cshtml

One type of variable that you have not met yet is the *constant*. This can be any data type, but its value is fixed and cannot be changed through code. There are a number of situations where constant values are suitable, such as your user name and password for mail server authentication. Every time you want to send e-mail from your site, you need to supply these values. You wouldn't really want to set the values on each page that sends e-mail, just in case you change your mail service provider, and need to go through the entire site updating the values. The _AppStart.cshtml file provides a place to set these types of value once so that they are accessible throughout the site.

If an _AppStart.cshtml file exists, it is executed when your application starts for the first time (or restarts), before any requested page is executed. See Figure 4-2. Any variable initialized in this file is held in memory across the application until the application stops (because the server was powered down or reset, or you made a change to _AppStart.cshtml, for example). Many of the helpers require some initialization before they can be used. _AppStart.cshtml is the perfect place to set the initialization values.

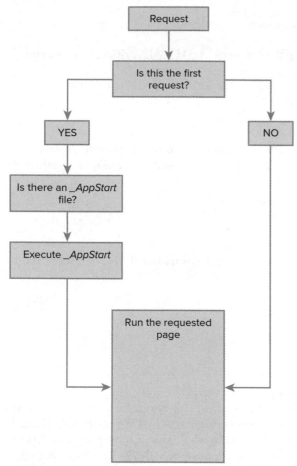

FIGURE 4-2

To set a value, you use the AppState property, which behaves in a similar way to the NameValueCollections you met earlier, except that your global variables do not have to be strings:

```
AppState["Discount"] = 10;
```

Just as with PageData, which you met in the previous chapter, you can also use a shorthand version, which is what you will see throughout the rest of this book:

```
App.Discount = 10;
```

TRY IT OUT Setting Global Variables

In this simple exercise, you will set the standard purchase discount amount for a site. This is a constant value and does not change dynamically. You will therefore apply the value in the _AppStart.cshtml file so that it is available to all pages within the site.

1. If you have closed it previously, open the Chapter4 site that you started in the previous exercise.

2. Add a new file to the site called **_AppStart.cshtml,** using the CSHTML file type. Make sure that the name of this file is correct, including the underscore and the capital A and S. The file must be added to the root folder of the site.

3. Replace the existing code with the following:

```
@{
    App.Discount = 20;
}
```

4. Add a new CSHTML file called **Page.cshtml** and add the following code to the top of the file:

```
@{
    var purchasePrice = 120;
}
```

5. Within the <body> section, add the following code:

```
<body>
    Your discount is @(purchasePrice * App.Discount/100)
</body>
```

When you run the page, the value supplied to App.Discount in the _AppStart.cshtml file has been used to calculate the discount amount available as a percentage of the purchase price, and should result in 24. Notice the syntax in use here — the calculation of the discount is an *expression*, which is why it has been placed in parentheses after the @ sign. If you want to amend the site's standard discount amount in future, you only need to go to one file.

How It Works

The _AppStart.cshtml file is executed once in the lifetime of a Web Pages application — when that application begins. As such, it is the perfect place to initialize variables that persist for the lifetime of the application. In this exercise, you use the _AppStart.cshtml file to set the discount rate for your application using the shorthand App.*property* syntax. Whenever you reference App.Discount, the value will always be the same — unless you reset the value somewhere else in code.

 WARNING *Application level, or global variables should be used sparingly and carefully. They should only be used for values that apply for all users of the application, and for the life of the application. To prevent them from being accidentally reset anywhere through code, you should consider prefixing the data type with the* const *keyword when the variable is declared and the value is assigned.*

As you progress through building the sample site, you will use a number of helpers that require initialization before they can be used. The _AppStart.cshtml file is the perfect place to do this. You will return to this file a few times before you reach the end of this book.

Sharing Values Across Pages with _PageStart

In the previous chapter, you saw how layout and content pages combine to generate the final output in response to a request. In each example, the layout page was set in a code block at the top of the content page. If you have a lot of pages, it will require a lot of copying and pasting to set the layout page for each content page. _PageStart.cshtml is a special file that you can use to set the layout page for all pages within a particular folder and any subfolders of that folder. It can also do a lot more than this. You can set variables within _PageStart.cshtml that are accessible to any page in the same folder, or its subfolders. In fact, you can run any logic that affects the pages that reference the _PageStart.cshtml file both before and after the contents of the page are executed, as illustrated in Figure 4-3.

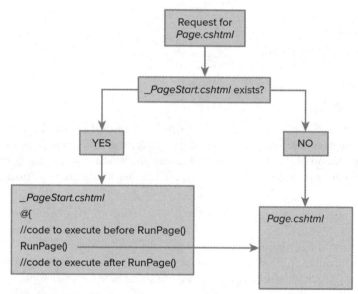

FIGURE 4-3

The RunPage method that you see in the middle of the _PageStart.cshtml file in Figure 4.3 causes the requested page to be executed, but it is not necessarily required. If you omit an explicit call to RunPage, it will be called automatically after all code in the _PageStart.cshtml file has been executed. You would include the RunPage method call if you wanted to execute code after the requested page has executed. You might want to do this to set the values of global variables based on the outcome of the requested page, for example. Then you would add the call to RunPage at a point just before you add code to set the global variables.

In the next exercise, you will explore how _PageStart.cshtml files work within the folder hierarchy of a site. This will show how each gets executed in turn.

Testing _PageStart.cshtml

In this exercise, you add a hierarchy of folders to the Chapter4 site you built earlier. You also add some
_PageStart.cshtml files to the hierarchy, and set some variables as well as layout pages for some content
pages that you will also create.

1. Open your Chapter4 site if you have closed it. Add a new folder named **Shared** to the site, and
within that, create a new CSHTML file called **_Layout1.cshtml**. Change the existing code so that
it reads as follows:

```
<!DOCTYPE html>

<html lang="en">
    <head>
        <meta charset="utf-8" />
        <title>@Page.Title</title>
        <style type="text/css">
            body{
                background-color: NavajoWhite;
            }
        </style>
    </head>
    <body>
        <h3>This is Layout 1</h3>
        @RenderBody()
    </body>
</html>
```

2. Add a new file to the root of the site and name it **_PageStart.cshtml**. Replace the existing code with
the following:

```
@{
    Layout = "~/Shared/_Layout1.cshtml";
    PageData["Colors"] = new []{"LightCyan", "Gainsboro","Chocolate"};
}
```

3. Add a new file to the root folder of the site called **Default.cshtml** and replace the existing code with
the following:

```
@{
    Page.Title = "Start page";
}
<h1>Testing _PageStart</h1>
@foreach(var color in PageData["Colors"]){
    <p style="background-color:@color">
        This paragraph is @color
    </p>
}
<p><a href="/Level1/">Click</a> to visit Level 1</p>
```

4. If you run the page now, you should see it has a pink background and that each paragraph is displayed in a different color, like in Figure 4-4.

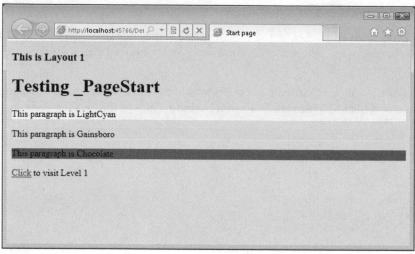

FIGURE 4-4

5. Add a new folder called **Level1** to the site. Create a new file in this folder called **Default.cshtml**. Replace the existing code with the following:

```
@{
    Page.Title = "Level 1 Start page";
}
<h1>Testing _PageStart From Level 1</h1>
    @foreach(var color in PageData["Colors"]){
        <p style="background-color:@color;">
            This paragraph is @color
        </p>
    }
```

6. If you run this page, you should see almost an identical result to Figure 4-4. Notice that the page's title has changed.

7. Add another file to the Shared folder and name it **_Layout2.cshtml**. The code for this page is almost the same as _Layout1.cshtml:

```
<!DOCTYPE html>

<html lang="en">
    <head>
        <meta charset="utf-8" />
        <title>@Page.Title</title>
        <style type="text/css">
            body{
                background-color: PaleGreen;
            }
        </style>
    </head>
    <body>
        <h3>This is Layout 2</h3>
        @RenderBody()
```

```
      </body>
</html>
```

8. Turning back to the newly added Default.cshtml file (the one you added to the Level1 folder), add the following line of code:

```
@{
    Page.Title = "Level 1 Start page";
    Layout = "~/Shared/_Layout2.cshtml";
}
```

9. Run the page again, and see how the background color has changed, but the paragraphs are still displayed in the same colors as seen in the Default.cshtml page you added to the root folder.

10. Add a file to the Level1 folder called **_PageStart.cshtml**. Replace the existing default code with the following:

```
@{
    Layout = "~/Shared/_Layout1.cshtml";
    PageData["Colors"] = new []{"LightCyan", "Gainsboro","Chocolate"};
}
```

11. Alter the code within the Default.cshtml file that sits in the Level1 folder to look the same as the following:

```
@{
    Page.Title = "Level 1 Start page";
    Layout = "~/Shared/_Layout2.cshtml";
}
<h1>Testing _PageStart From Level 1</h1>
@{
    var i = 0;
    foreach(var color in Page.Colors){
        <p style="background-color:@color; font-family:@Page.Fonts[i];">
            This paragraph is @color
        </p>
        i++;
        }
}
<p><a href="/Level1/Page">Click</a> to visit Level 1</p>
```

12. Add one more file to the Level1 folder. Choose the CSHTML file type and leave the name as Page .cshtml. Make the following highlighted changes to the template code:

```
@{
    Layout = null;
}
<!DOCTYPE html>

<html lang="en">
    <head>
        <meta charset="utf-8" />
        <title></title>
        <style type="text/css">
```

```
            body{
                background-color: LightSteelBlue;
            }
        </style>
    </head>
    <body>
        <h1>Testing _PageStart From Level 1</h1>
        <p>This page overrides the layout set in PageStart</p>
    </body>
</html>
```

13. Now if you run Default.cshtml in the Level1 folder, you should see that each paragraph retains its background color, but that each one is displayed in a different font. If you click the link on the page, you are taken to Level1/Page.cshtml, but the background color has changed again, and there is no header proclaiming that the current page is making use of a layout page.

How It Works

This exercise was designed to illustrate how a _PageStart.cshtml file in one particular folder can influence all files within the same folder, as well as all files within subfolders. When you added the layout declaration to the root _PageStart.cshtml file, you saw that it affected the layout page for the Default.cshtml file in the root folder, as well as the one in the Level1 folder. If you don't want subfolders to use the same layout pages as top-level files, you can either set a new layout page in a separate _PageStart.cshtml file, or you can simply set the layout page on a per file basis. In this exercise, you set the layout to null in the Page.cshtml file in Level1.

The exercise also demonstrated how values can be shared across pages. In the top-level _PageStart.cshtml file, you created a PageData value consisting of an array of colors. These were available to the top-level *Default.cshtml* file, and you used them to provide a background color to a number of paragraphs. When you added a _PageStart.cshtml file to the Level1 folder, you created a PageData value consisting of an array of fonts. However, you could still reference the PageData colors array set in the top-level _PageStart.cshtml file. This part of the exercise also illustrates the fact that each _PageStart.cshtml file is executed in turn, as depicted earlier in Figure 4.3.

You have now learned two ways to share *values* across pages. However, you will also want to share *behavior*. In the next section, you will learn how to create functions once, and have them available throughout your site.

Reusable Functions

As you build up your .NET experience, you will find yourself creating a variety of utility functions to perform the same task again and again. For example, you might want to check that a string purporting to be an e-mail address that has been provided to you is in a valid format. What you define as "valid" is largely up to you and the demands of the application you are working on at any one time. Some people might be happy that the string that's been presented to them has an @ sign somewhere in it, with a dot at a position at least three characters further on in the string, followed by some more characters. Others might want to go the whole hog, and not only test that each character within the string is in its right place, and conforms to the range of acceptable characters according to an international standard for e-mail addresses, but they might also want to perform some kind of remote mail server lookup to verify that the domain exists.

Taking the example of e-mail address validation, you don't really want to have to copy and paste it wherever you are validating an e-mail address within your application. If your requirements change, you have to go through all of your code and make the same code change everywhere to accommodate the new requirement. In the next exercise, you will create one e-mail validation function, which can be called from anywhere within your site.

TRY IT OUT Creating a Reusable Function

1. Open your Chapter4 site, if you have closed it and create a new folder called **App_Code**. Make sure that you type the name exactly as it is shown here.

2. Add a new CSHTML file to the new App_Code folder and name it **Functions.cshtml**.

3. Replace the existing code with the following:

```
@using System.Text.RegularExpressions;

@functions {
    public static bool IsValidEmail(string s)
    {
        string pattern = @"^[\w-\.]+@([\w-]+\.)+[\w-]{2,4}$";
        return Regex.IsMatch(s, pattern);
    }
}
```

4. Add a new CSHTML file and name it **ValidEmail.cshtml**. Add the following code to the <body> element:

```
<body>

    mike@wrox.com is a valid email address:
    @Functions.IsValidEmail("mike@wrox.com")<br />
    www.wrox.com is a valid email address:
    @Functions.IsValidEmail("www.wrox.com")<br />
</body>
```

How It Works

If you run the page, you should see that mike@wrox.com passes the IsValidEmail test and returns true. The web address fails the test, returning false.

The first line that you added to the Functions.cshtml file references a particular namespace within the .NET Framework, which exposes classes for working with *regular expressions*. Regex, as they are commonly known, provide an advanced way to search and match strings or substrings when simple string methods are inadequate. A full discussion of Regex is beyond the scope of this book. However, the Regex engine works by matching strings against "patterns" that are defined using a set of *metacharacters*.

Then you added @functions, which is the syntax for wrapping methods in Razor. Within that you can add as many C# methods as you like, although in this example, there is just the one: IsValidEmail. Notice that the method is declared with the static keyword. This is the recommended way of declaring utility methods. It means you do not have to instantiate an instance of the class the method belongs to in order to execute the method. Notice also that the method returns a Boolean true or false, and that it accepts a string and a parameter.

The body of the method establishes a Regex pattern. Without going into too much detail about the construction of the pattern itself, as that's not the focus here, it looks for certain types of characters in a particular order. If the incoming string matches the rules defined in the pattern, the Regex.IsMatch method returns true; otherwise it returns false.

When you run the application, items in the App_Code folder are compiled to C# classes, which take the name of the file. So you have a class called Functions, with a static method called IsValidEmail. This is what you call in your test web page when you add @Functions.IsValidEmail(). Keep this function. You will need it later in the book.

If you are interested in learning more about the magic and power of *Regular Expressions, Beginning Regular Expressions* by Andrew Watt (ISBN: 978-0-764-57489-4) provides comprehensive coverage in a range of programming languages and on a range of platforms, including .NET.

Reusable Custom Helpers

The function you just created is purely a logical thing. It isn't intended to render anything to the browser. Helpers, on the other hand, are all about emitting HTML to the browser. You can combine server-side code and HTML to create your own reusable helpers. In the next exercise, you will create two helper methods that you can reuse again and again. One of them will render <script> tags, which will reference JavaScript files. The other will render a <link> element for referencing style sheets. The script file and the JavaScript file featured in the code below don't actually exist, but do not let that obscure the point of the exercise.

TRY IT OUT   Creating Custom Helpers

1. Open your Chapter4 site, and add a new CSHTML file to the App_Code folder and name it **Helpers.cshtml**.

2. Replace the existing code with the following:

```
@helper RegisterJs(string folder, string[] scriptLibs)
{
 foreach (var script in scriptLibs)
   {
     <script src="@folder/@script" type="text/javascript"></script>
   }
}

@helper RegisterStyles(string folder, string[] styleSheets)
{
```

```
    foreach (var sheet in styleSheets)  {
      <link href="@folder/@sheet" rel="stylesheet" type="text/css" />
    }
  }
```

3. Open ValidEmail.cshtml, which you created in the last exercise, and add the following to the <head> element:

```
    <head>
        <meta charset="utf-8" />
        <title></title>
        @Helpers.RegisterJs("/Script", new[] {"myScript.js"})
        @Helpers.RegisterStyles("/Content", new[] {"Main.css"})
    </head>
```

4. Run the page in a browser and then use the browser's menu option to view the source code. You should see something similar to the following:

```
<head>
  <meta charset="utf-8" />
   <title></title>
   <script src="/Script/jquery.min.js" type="text/javascript"></script>
   <link href="/Content/Main.css" rel="stylesheet" type="text/css" />
</head>
```

How It Works

Helpers work in just the same way as Razor functions, except that they allow you to mix HTML with Razor code. Since they are placed in the App_Code folder, the file contents are compiled to a C# class with the same name as the file. Both of the helpers you created are essentially the same, except for the HTML they render. One renders a <link> element for style sheets, whereas the other renders <script> tags for JavaScript files. They both take a string as a parameter, indicating the folder that contains the relevant files, and an array of strings, representing the filenames. Although you only provided one filename for each helper when you used them in your Razor page, they cope with multiple files via the foreach loop. A new <script> tag or <link> element will be rendered for each file.

SUMMARY

This chapter has provided a bit of a whirlwind introduction to programming with C#, including how you apply that knowledge using the Razor syntax to your Web Pages site. As you saw, getting started with programming is not very difficult, but this chapter only provided you with a starting point.

A core part of programming is data, which is held in variables. Variables can be one of a large number of data types, and you were introduced to the most common ones during this chapter. You also learned about explicit typing and implicit typing using the var keyword. You explored how to work with the String data type in a little more detail, being one of the types you will use most often. You also saw a number of varieties of numeric data types, and learned how they differ from one another. You also met some more complex types, such as arrays and other collections, which provide containers for groups of objects into one variable.

Statements are instructions that tell your application how to behave. You learned about operators, and then you looked in more detail at different types of statements. Selection statements allow you to make logical decisions and branch code based on conditions; iteration statements are used to manage code execution loops. Then you were introduced to the topic of properties and methods, which are responsible for managing data and behavior, respectively.

The core of ASP.NET Web Pages is the Razor syntax, which allows you to combine HTML and server-side code in the same file. You saw that there are some quite simple rules to follow when applying Razor code to a CSHTML file. All code begins with the @ sign. Code blocks are enclosed in braces, and items to be rendered to the page should be enclosed in matching HTML tags or Razor <text> tags.

In the final part of the chapter, you were reminded that you should strive to write code only once and reuse it wherever you could. You were shown a number of ways in which Web Pages offers you help to organize your code. You learned that the _AppStart.cshtml file is the place to initialize global values so that they are accessible across the site, whereas _PageStart.cshtml files allow you to define code to run before and after a page in a particular folder is executed. You saw how to create your own reusable functions using the @functions syntax. You also learned how to call the function in a page using the @helpers syntax, which allows you to mix code and markup in a reusable way.

The next chapter builds on what you have learned here, and applies your newfound programming knowledge to processing user input on the server. You will also learn how to validate that input, before sending it in an e-mail from your site.

EXERCISES

1. Describe three ways in which you can mix Razor syntax and HTML markup within a Razor file.

2. The HTML entity for a capital letter A is A. The capital letter Z is generated from Z. Using logical deduction, and one of the looping constructs you learned in this chapter, use Razor to generate the letters A–Z on one line, with spaces between them.

3. Create a custom helper to generate an array as an unordered list, like the one that you tried in the first exercise in this chapter. Then provide code to make use of the helper to render a list of film titles to a page.

Answers to the Exercises can be found in the Appendix.

▶ **WHAT YOU LEARNED IN THIS CHAPTER**

TOPIC	KEY CONCEPTS
Razor	A template syntax language for use with ASP.NET Web Pages.
Variable	A unit of storage for values.
Data type	The way different types of values are categorized.
Collection	A data structure for storing multiple units of values.
Statement	A programming instruction. Categorized by type, including selection and iteration.
Operator	A symbol that dictates the operations to be performed on one or more operands.
_AppStart.cshtml	A file that runs at the point the application first starts up, which can be used to set global values.
_PageStart.cshtml	A file that is executed before any page in the same folder or subfolder. Can be used to set values or execute code that affects the page that's requested.
@function	Razor syntax for creating a reusable block of code.
@helper	Razor syntax for creating a reusable block of code intended to return HTML.

5

Adding User Interactivity

WHAT YOU WILL LEARN IN THIS CHAPTER:

➤ What forms are and how to create them

➤ How data entered into forms is received by the web server

➤ How and why you should validate data

➤ How to send user input elsewhere by e-mail

If you visit my little blog site, you can interact with it. You can add content by providing comments to articles, or you can use the rating system to indicate your displeasure with my efforts and thereby alter the total number of ratings and the average score for each entry on my site. You can define your own filtered view of the content to an extent by using the Search facility. Opportunities to interact with my site are somewhat limited, but they exist nevertheless.

Huge sites like Amazon and eBay simply wouldn't work if they did not provide a means for you to interact with them. You can specify your preferences, choose items to purchase, make payments, post reviews, provide feedback, register your details with them, and have them remember all of this for future visits. In fact, they are so packed with interactive features that most people will tell you that they *use* Amazon or eBay, whereas the few people who happen to land on my site will more likely describe their activity as *visiting* the site. If you want *users* rather than *visitors*, you need to provide a way for people to interact with your site. You need to be able to accept and process their input. You need to allow them to personalize their experience, record their preferences, and make use of the services you offer.

CREATING FORMS

There are a number of ways in which you can invite users to submit their input, but the primary method is via a form. Some forms can be as simple as a text box and a button. Others might span multiple pages, such as ones that gather your details for insurance quotes. The ratings system on my blog site doesn't look like a form at all — it's a series of colored stars — but behind the scenes, there is a form.

GET versus POST

In the first chapter, you were introduced to the subject of HTTP requests. If you recall, an HTTP request is a call to a web server to perform some action on a resource at a particular location. HTTP includes a set of methods, called *verbs,* which are used to signify the nature of the desired action. In the vast majority of cases, the desired action is retrieval of data, and the HTTP method to signify this is GET. Sometimes, the desired action is the modification of data, or the addition of new data located at the resource address. The method used to signify this type of action is POST. This is the method most often used when submitting data via a form.

It is possible to submit form data using a GET request. The data is appended to the URL as a collection of name/value pairs, each separated by an ampersand (&). The collection is separated from the URL by a question mark (?), and the result is referred to as a *query string*:

```
http://www.domain.com/somepage.htm?name=value&name2=value2
```

You see this when you look at the URL in your browser's address bar for the results page of search engines. However, URLs, including the query string, are limited in size. What the actual limit is varies from browser to browser, but this fact alone makes query strings an unsuitable means for submitting large amounts of data. When the POST method is used, the data is sent within the Request body instead, where no such restrictions apply.

CREATING A FORM TO OBTAIN USER INPUT

Forms are created using the `<form>` tag. Between the opening and closing `<form>` tag, you place all the HTML elements which the site visitor will use to enter or select data to be sent to the server. If you place any of these elements outside of the `<form>` tags, their contents will not be included as part of a submission:

```
<form action="" method="post">
...
</form>
```

The `form` element takes two attributes at a minimum. The first is called `action`, and it provides the location to which the form should be submitted. In the previous example, the form will be submitted to itself because the value is empty. In the next example, the form will be submitted to a page called `Thanks.cshtml`:

```
<form action="/Thanks.cshtml" method="post">
...
</form>
```

The second attribute — `method` — indicates the HTTP verb that is used for the request. In nearly every case, this will be POST for the reasons discussed in the previous section.

You also need a way for users to submit the form. The `input` element does this job, but the `input` element comes in a number of varieties, indicated by the value of the `type` attribute. When you specify that `type="submit"`, a form submission button is rendered as shown in Figure 5-1:

```
<form action="/Thanks.cshtml" method="post">
    <input type="submit" />
</form>
```

FIGURE 5-1

Looking at Figure 5-1, you can see that the default text on the button is Submit Query in Internet Explorer 8. It is plain Submit in most other browsers, but you have full control over ensuring the same value is applied across all browsers. You can change this text (see Figure 5-2) by adding a `value` attribute, and setting its value to whatever you like:

```
<form action="/" method="post">
    <input type="submit" value="Click Me" />
</form>
```

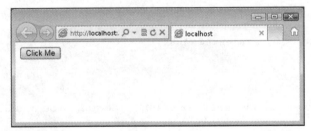

FIGURE 5-2

So far so good, but the form is pretty useless as it is. There is no way for users to provide data to submit. You need some form fields. If you recall from Chapter 2, there are a range of form field elements available to you, but the one you are likely to use most often is the text box so users can provide single lines of text. This is another `input` element, but the type in this case is `text`, which is also the default for `input` elements. Figure 5-3 illustrates that text boxes are rendered if you don't specify a value for the `type` attribute, as well as when you specify the `type` as `text`:

```
<form action="/" method="post">
    <div>Please enter your name</div>
    First name: <input name="firstname" /><br />
    Last name: <input type="text" name="lastname" /><br />
    <input type="submit" value="Click Me" />
</form>
```

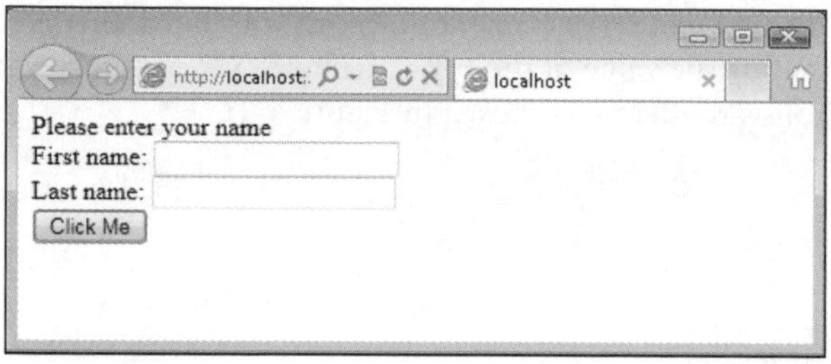

FIGURE 5-3

At the moment, if you enter your name into this form and click the button, the page refreshes, the text boxes are cleared in most browsers, and nothing else appears to happen. The data you entered was sent to the server as a POST request, but there is no server-side code to do anything with it.

The Web Pages framework includes an object called `Request`. This object contains information about the current HTTP request. It knows the type of browser you are using and its capabilities. It knows what method was used for the request — GET, POST, PUT, or DELETE — which page, or resource was requested and a lot of other things. The `Request` object also has a number of collections including one for form data: the `Request.Form` collection. This is a `NameValueCollection`, which if you recall from the previous chapter, allows you to reference values using the name of the element. Referring back to the HTML code for the text boxes in the previous example, you see that they have been given a name attribute with a value of `"firstname"` and `"lastname"`. When the form is submitted, whatever has been entered into the text boxes will be available by referencing it in the collection as follows:

```
Request.Form["firstname"]
Request.Form["lastname"]
```

Alternatively, you can use the shorthand way of referencing the value:

```
Request["firstname"]
Request["lastname"]
```

If you had also provided a name attribute to the submit button, for example `"action"`, you would be able to reference that in the `Request` collection too. It would have returned `"Click Me"`, since that is what has been provided to the value attribute.

REFERENCING REQUEST COLLECTIONS

You will see examples using the shorthand `Request` method very frequently, but there is one danger to using it. There are other collections within the `Request` object, and you will meet some of them later. ASP.NET will search each of the collections in turn for an item with the key `"firstname"`. If one of these collections also includes an item with the same key, you may get that value returned instead of the one you expect. Mostly, when working with the Form collection this won't be an issue because the Form collection is the second collection to be searched after the QueryString collection, but it is an issue to bear in mind if you do not see the values you expect to see.

TRY IT OUT Creating a Form

In the following exercise, you are going to create a simple page that displays a message. You will also provide a form and ask the users to enter their name. When they submit the form, you will use server-side code to process the value and change the message to incorporate the value they provided.

1. Create a new empty site within WebMatrix and call it **Chapter5**.

2. Switch to the Files workspace and press Ctrl+N. Add a new CSHTML file called **Default.cshtml**.

3. Add the following code to the <body> element:

```
<form action="" method="post">
    @if(IsPost){
        <div>You entered: @Request["yourname"]</div>
    }else{
        <div>Please enter your name</div>
    }
    <input type="text" name="yourname" /><br />
    <input type="submit" value="Click Me" />
</form>
```

4. Run the page and enter a value in the textbox. Then click the Submit button. You should see the default message replaced with the name you entered.

How It Works

You added an opening <form> element to the page and set its method attribute to POST. You also specified, via the action attribute, that the form should post to the same page in which it appears. You added a conditional check to see if the page was requested using POST. This is what the if(IsPost) expression does. You will use this method for checking that a form was submitted, or *posted*, a lot as you move forward. You also added a textbox for the user to enter a value into and gave it a value for its name attribute — "yourname". You also added a Submit button. This was customized using the value attribute to say Click Me rather than the default Submit Query.

When the page was first run, it was requested using GET, which is the default method for HTTP. Since the page was requested using GET, IsPost returned false and the else part of the condition was executed, resulting in the message "Please enter your name" appearing.

When you clicked the button, the request method was dictated by the form's method attribute, and POST was used. This time, the conditional check if(IsPost) returned true, so the first message was displayed. This took the value associated with "yourname" from the Request.Form collection and displayed it.

 NOTE *Always include the name attribute and provide it with a value when adding a form element, otherwise ASP.NET cannot reference the value associated with the element.*

Other Form Elements

Textboxes are not the only way to capture data from the user, and they have some limitations. Let's suppose, for example, that you wanted the users to provide the name of the country they live in. If they come from where I live, they might enter United Kingdom. Or, they might enter Great Britain, or UK, or England. If you wanted to send an e-mail to everyone in my country, you would have a bit of a problem managing all the variations that have been submitted, and that's ignoring the ones that were mistyped. What you really need to provide is a way to force the users to select one option from a predefined list, but with around 200 possible countries, you don't want that list to appear in full on the page. That would be a scrolling nightmare. Similarly, you might want the users to be able to pick more than one option, or you might want them to have to choose one of a small number of options. There are a number of other form elements that serve specific purposes like the ones described here, and in the next exercise, you will be introduced to some of them.

TRY IT OUT   Testing Form Elements

This exercise features a fictitious admin page from a blog site or news site. It is designed to permit users to add a new story, and to set some options that ensure the story is displayed in the right area of the site. The users will be able to add a headline, an introduction, the main part of the story, and then specify which section of the site the story should appear in, whether the option to allow comments should be provided, and finally to indicate whom the author or authors of the story were. In this fictitious case, more than one person can contribute to the creation of the story.

1. Open your Chapter5 site within WebMatrix if you have closed it.

2. Add a new CSHTML file called **AddStory.cshtml**.

3. Add the following code to the <body>:

```
<body>
    <h3>Add your story</h3>
    <form action="" method="post">
        <div>Headline</div>
        <input type="text" name="headline" />
        <div>Introduction</div>
        <textarea name="introduction"></textarea>
        <div>Story body</div>
        <textarea name="body"></textarea>
        <div>Choose Section</div>
        <select name="section">
            <option>General News</option>
            <option>Business</option>
            <option>Technology</option>
            <option>International</option>
            <option>Politics</option>
            <option>Sport</option>
            <option>Education</option>
            <option>Health</option>
            <option>Travel</option>
        </select>
        <div>Allow Comments?</div>
        <input type="radio" name="comments" value="yes" /> Yes
        <input type="radio" name="comments" value="no" /> No
        <div>Authors</div>
```

```
        <input type="checkbox" name="author" value="James" />James<br />
        <input type="checkbox" name="author" value="Karen" />Karen<br />
        <input type="checkbox" name="author" value="Stephanie" />Stephanie<br />
        <input type="checkbox" name="author" value="Alfie" />Alfie<br />
        <input type="checkbox" name="author" value="Molly" />Molly<br />
        <input type="submit" value="Add Story" />
    </form>
</body>
```

4. At the top of the <body> area, add the following code:

```
<body>
    @if(IsPost){
        <div>You submitted:</div>
        <div>Headline: @Request["headline"]</div>
        <div>Introduction: @Request["introduction"]</div>
        <div>Story Body: @Request["body"]</div>
        <div>Section: @Request["section"]</div>
        <div>Allow Comments: @Request["comments"]</div>
        <div>Author(s): @Request["author"]</div>
    }
```

5. Click the Run icon to bring the page up in a browser and enter some text into the Headline and Introduction boxes. Add some text to the Story Body box. Ignore the Section and Comments fields, and then select at least two authors. Now submit the form. The resulting page should look something like that depicted in Figure 5-4.

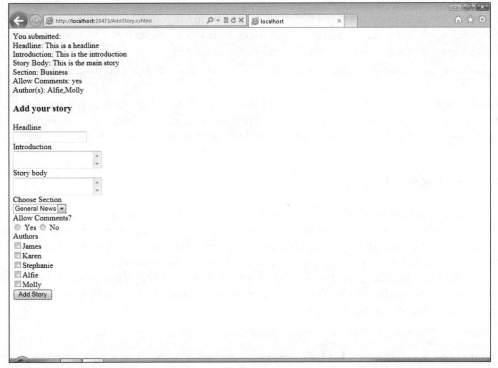

FIGURE 5-4

How It Works

You provided a range of form elements for different purposes. The `<input type="text">` has already been explained, and is used to capture a one-line headline. To capture multi-line text such as the introduction and the story body, you use a `textarea` element. You used a `select` element to present the user with a list of predefined options from which they could choose one Section for the news item. Then you used radio buttons for a mutually exclusive selection. Finally, when you wanted the user to select one or more items from a list to indicate who authored the item, you presented them with `<input type="checkbox">` elements.

When the form was posted back, you should have noticed that there was a value for `Section`, even though you did not choose an item from the list. The reason for this is that General News, the first item in the list was visible. The select list provides the text between `<option>` and `</option>` as a form value unless you explicitly provide a `value` attribute to the `option`. To stop default options being accepted as having been chosen like this, when they weren't, you normally add your own default, and set the option's value to an empty string:

```
<option value="">Pick one</option>
```

Radio buttons do not behave in the same way. In fact, if you do not check a radio button, it isn't even included in the Form collection. Your radio buttons were both given the same name. This has the effect of *grouping* them, so that you cannot select more than one radio button with the same name. That is why they are generally used for mutually exclusive options. If you run the page again and select Yes, choosing No clears the Yes button. If you do not supply your own value to radio buttons, the default value that's passed to the server is on.

Check boxes work in much the same way as radio buttons, in that if you do not select any, they do not appear in the Form collection. However, if you select more than one with the same `name` attribute (which also has the effect of grouping them), the values are passed in a comma-separated string.

You should now have a clearer idea of how forms work in ASP.NET Web Pages, and you have seen a variety of form elements and learned how their behavior differs. In the next section, you will learn how to validate what the user enter into a form, and why validation of user input is important.

VALIDATING USER INPUT

You saw in the previous exercise that the user can safely ignore form fields when submitting a form, but in the real world, you would not want your users to do this as they please. What good is a registration form unless the user is compelled to provide a user name? Equally, there was nothing to stop a user from entering invalid data. A user can enter words instead of numbers. If you try to process the resulting data as a number, you are in for problems. What good is a living person's date of birth value if it is some time in the future? You must validate form data when it has been submitted, and when you validate the data, you usually test for three things:

➤ **Presence:** Has a required piece of information been provided?

➤ **Data type:** Is the submitted value's data type compatible with what you expected?

➤ **Range:** Is the submitted value within the bounds of an acceptable range of values?

Server-Side or Client-Side Validation?

There are two places where you can perform validation: on the client within the browser before the form has been submitted, and on the server, after the form has been submitted. A debate used to rage about which approach to validation was best. One school of thought declared that client-side validation was the way to go, because it prevented the server from having to process a request that might be rejected. This, so the argument went, prevented overloading the server resources unnecessarily. To be fair, this line of reasoning was particularly prominent about 10 years ago, when servers were extraordinarily expensive, and ridiculously under-powered by today's standard. However, I still see remnants of this argument appear in the ASP.NET forums even now.

Those who hold the view that client-side validation trumps server-side validation were wrong then, and still are very wrong. Client-side validation relies on scripting, mainly JavaScript running in the user's browser. Every browser provides the user with the option to disable JavaScript, which means that code that relies on it will not work. In other words, validation on the client will not happen. It's also pretty easy to copy a web page, save it locally, edit it to alter the client-side code to do something different than what the original developer intended, and then use it to submit a form to a website.

Validation *must* be performed on the server. Client-side validation is no more than a courtesy to the user. It provides them with instant feedback, often before they have completed the form. Server-side code is the gatekeeper to your site's security and integrity.

In the next section, you are going to add server-side validation to your form to ensure that the user has provided values for all fields. You will also display a helpful message to them to let them know what they did wrong, if the form fails validation.

TRY IT OUT   Adding Server-Side Validation

1.   Return to the AddStory.cshtml page you created previously, and amend the code just at the top of the `<body>` element to the following:

```
<body>
@if(IsPost){
    var errors = String.Empty;
    if(Request["headline"].IsEmpty()){
        errors += "<li>You must provide a headline</li>";
    }
    if(Request["introduction"].IsEmpty()){
        errors += "<li>You must provide an introduction</li>";
    }
    if(Request["body"].IsEmpty()){
        errors += "<li>You must provide story body</li>";
    }
    if(Request["section"].IsEmpty()){
        errors += "<li>You must choose a section</li>";
    }
    if(Request["comments"].IsEmpty()){
        errors += "<li>You must specify whether comments are allowed</li>";
    }
    if(Request["author"].IsEmpty()){
        errors += "<li>You must select at least one author</li>";
```

```
    }
    if(errors.IsEmpty()){
        <div>You submitted:</div>
        <div>Headline: @Request["headline"]</div>
        <div>Introduction: @Request["introduction"]</div>
        <div>Story Body: @Request["body"].Replace("\n","<br />")</div>
        <div>Section: @Request["section"]</div>
        <div>Allow Comments: @Request["comments"]</div>
        <div>Author(s): @Request["author"]</div>
    }else{
        <h3>The following errors need correcting:</h3>
        <ul>
            @Html.Raw(errors)
        </ul>
    }
}
    <h3>Add your story</h3>
```

2. Make sure that the AddStory.cshtml page is selected in the left pane, and then press your F12 key to launch the page in a browser.

3. Add a value for the headline and click the Add Story button. You should receive a result similar to Figure 5-5.

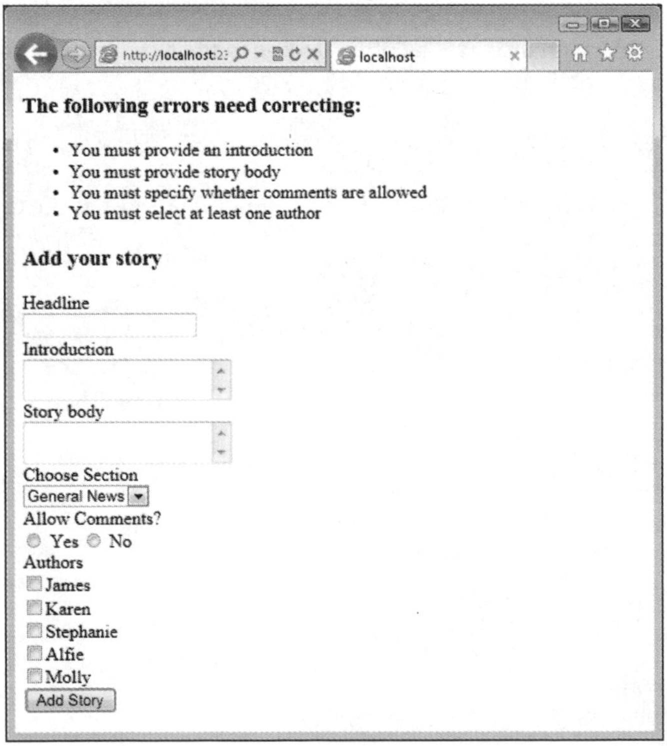

FIGURE 5-5

How It Works

You added a new variable to the code block which already checks to see if the page is posted back to the server. The variable is called *errors* and is initiated to an empty string. Then you use the IsEmpty test on each form field in turn. This test establishes whether a value was supplied by the user. If no value was supplied, the IsEmpty test returns true. As you test each input in turn, if there is no value present, you build a string consisting of <li> elements explaining what went wrong, and apply it to the *errors* variable using the addition assignment operator (+=).

Once you have tested each field in turn, if the form has failed your validation — in other words, if any of the required fields are empty — the *errors* variable will no longer be an empty string. However, if it is empty, you display the summary of what was posted as in the previous exercise. In the event that there are errors, the resulting value of the *errors* variable is written to the browser between opening and closing <ul> tags.

HTML Encoding

Did you notice how the errors were rendered to the browser via the Html.Raw() method? By default, all strings rendered via Razor are HTML encoded. This means that angle brackets < > and ampersands (&) are converted to their HTML equivalents, which are <, >, and & respectively. What this means in practice is that the user would see:

```
<li>You must provide a headline</li>
```

rendered literally, rather than as a bulleted list item. There would be no line breaks, so the result would look strange as far as the user is concerned.

Why is output HTML encoded? Simply put, this is one of Web Pages built-in security measures. It is designed to prevent malicious users or hackers from injecting HTML that would alter the appearance of the page (at best) or execute a cross-site scripting (XSS) attack (at worst). Without going into too much detail, XSS attacks are one of the leading vulnerabilities that websites can be subject to, and could for example lead to any form you include in your page being redirected to post the content, including user names, passwords, and other sensitive data to some other site.

The Html.Raw method tells Web Pages to render the HTML included in any string as raw HTML, and not as an encoded string. You will meet another of Web Pages built-in security features that helps prevent XSS attacks towards the end of the chapter.

Persisting Values Across Postbacks

Back to the exercise: You have provided your users with a helpful series of pointers to missing data they need to provide in order for the form to be accepted. But they provided a perfectly valid headline, and now they have to provide that again. In fact, this wouldn't be so much of a problem if they had missed most fields, but it would be if they had successfully completed most fields in a larger form. You need to provide a mechanism to persist the data they provided so that they don't have to enter it all over again. Fortunately, this is easy to do, especially with a couple of custom helpers.

Persisting Values Across Form Submissions

1. Create a new folder in the Chapter5 site called **App_Code**. Make sure that the name is correct, with the underscore between App and Code.

2. Add a new CSHTML file called **Helpers.cshtml** to the App_Code folder.

3. Replace the existing code within the Helpers.cshtml file with the following:

```
@helper Selected(string option, string value){
    if(HttpContext.Current.Request[option] != null){
        var values = HttpContext.Current.Request[option].Split(',');
        if(values.Contains(value)){
            <text>selected=\"selected\"</text>
        }
    }
}


@helper Checked(string option, string value){
    if(HttpContext.Current.Request[option] != null){
        var values = HttpContext.Current.Request[option].Split(',');
        if(values.Contains(value)){
            <text>checked=\"checked\"</text>
        }
    }
}
```

4. Return to the AddStory.cshtml file, and make the following amendments to the form elements:

```
<form action="" method="post">
<div>Headline</div>
<input type="text" name="headline" value="@Request["headline"]" />
<div>Introduction</div>
<textarea name="introduction">@Request["introduction"]</textarea>
<div>Story body</div>
<textarea name="body">@Request["body"]</textarea>
<div>Choose Section</div>
<select name="section">
    <option value="">Pick one</option>
    <option @Helpers.Selected("section","General News")>General News</option>
    <option @Helpers.Selected("section","Business")>Business</option>
    <option @Helpers.Selected("section","Technology")>Technology</option>
    <option @Helpers.Selected("section","International")>International</option>
    <option @Helpers.Selected("section","Politics")>Politics</option>
    <option @Helpers.Selected("section","Sport")>Sport</option>
    <option @Helpers.Selected("section","Education")>Education</option>
    <option @Helpers.Selected("section","Health")>Health</option>
    <option @Helpers.Selected("section","Travel")>Travel</option>
</select>
<div>Allow Comments?</div>
<input type="radio" name="comments" value="yes"
            @Helpers.Checked("comments","yes") /> Yes
<input type="radio" name="comments" value="no"
            @Helpers.Checked("comments","no") /> No
<div>Authors</div>
<input type="checkbox" name="author" value="James"
            @Helpers.Checked("author","James") />James<br />
```

```
<input type="checkbox" name="author" value="Karen"
         @Helpers.Checked("author","Karen") />Karen<br />
<input type="checkbox" name="author" value="Stephanie"
         @Helpers.Checked("author","Stephanie") />Stephanie<br />
<input type="checkbox" name="author" value="Alfie"
         @Helpers.Checked("author","Alfie") />Alfie<br />
<input type="checkbox" name="author" value="Molly"
         @Helpers.Checked("author","Molly") />Molly<br />
<input type="submit" value="Add Story" />
</form>
```

5. Save your changes, making sure that the AddStory.cshtml file is selected in the left pane. Click the Run button to bring the form up in your default browser.

6. Leave the headline field blank, but provide values for the other text boxes, and select Yes or No in the comments. Also, select a section and choose an author or two.

7. Click the Submit Story button so that the form posts back. Depending on what you entered, the result should look like Figure 5-6.

FIGURE 5-6

How It Works

Persisting form values for text inputs is very easy. You just need to add `@Request["myValue"]` to the value attribute of the input element, where *myValue* corresponds with the name attribute of the form field. You did this for the headline using `@Request["headline"]`. When the form is redisplayed, if a corresponding value in the Request collection is found, it is applied to the variable and displayed. Text area elements are slightly different, in that they require an opening and a closing tag. Any text that they hold should be placed between these tags, which is why you placed the `@Request["myValue"]` syntax in that position. Fundamentally, they work in the same way as text inputs.

Select lists work in a different way. If you choose whatever source view option that your default browser offers, you can see that the item you selected prior to posting the form has some additional text inside its `<option>` element: `selected="selected"`. This is how the browser knows to retain this value as the selected one in the select list. The helper you wrote called *Selected* is the one that manages this for you. It's time to examine that helper more closely:

```
@helper Selected(string option, string value){
    if(HttpContext.Current.Request[option] != null){
        var values = HttpContext.Current.Request[option].Split(',');
        if(values.Contains(value)){
            <text>selected=\"selected\"</text>
        }
    }
}
```

The helper accepts two strings. The first one represents the name of the form field that it is being applied to. In this case, it's the `<select>` element's `name` attribute, which is "`section.`" The second string is the value of the option, which should be present in the Request collection if it has been selected.

Notice the long version used to reference the `Request` object:

```
HttpContext.Current.Request
```

You have to use this longer format if you want to reference the current `Request` context from outside of the page you are working with. This includes situations where you reference it within helpers, functions, or other C# classes.

The first thing that the helper code does is to establish whether the item in the `Request` collection actually exists. This is important, as any attempt to reference an object that doesn't exist will result in an error when you run the page. If it exists, the code checks whether the value can be found within the form collection item. Remember, some form fields are capable of holding multiple values as a comma-delimited string so the `string.Split` method is used to separate each value out into elements of an array. Then the array is checked to see if it contains a value matching that of the current option.

Finally, if the current value being sought is found, `selected="selected"` is rendered as part of the `<option>` tag.

The other helper that you created — *Checked* — is used for the other two form element groups: the radio and the check boxes. As you can see from the code, it is almost identical to the *Selected* helper, except in terms of what it renders.

One important point to note: persisting user input is an important part of making your site usable. There is nothing more frustrating for a user to be told they have missed a password or something similar, only to find that the developer has not persisted the values they posted that passed validation. Persisting values across form posts is, as you have seen, not very difficult, but it does rely on forms being posted to themselves for processing rather than to another page.

Practice makes perfect, it is said. Now that you have learned the different types of form elements available to you, and how to validate and persist user input, it's time to put what you have learned into practice to continue building the sample site.

In the next section, you are going to build a form so that users of your Classifieds site can post new items they are offering for sale. You will also create server-side code to ensure that the data they submit meets your application's requirements. In the event of any breaches of validation, you will display helpful messages telling the user what mistakes they made and how to fix them before resubmitting the form. You will also persist the data they submitted so that they can correct any mistakes without having to complete the form all over again.

Before you start, you need to consider what data you want to capture, and what rules you want to enforce to ensure that the data provided by the user is in a valid state. Table 5-1 summarizes the form fields and the rules that apply to them.

TABLE 5-1: The Form's Business Rules

FIELD	DATA TYPE	RULES
Title	String	Required, not exceeding 200 characters in length
Description	String	Required
Duration for posting	Integer	Required, restricted options
Condition of item	String	Required, restricted options
Price	Decimal	Required, must be greater than 0
E-mail address of seller	String	Required, must be in a valid format

All of the fields are required, or mandatory. At this stage that shouldn't be a surprise: you are collecting the barest minimum amount of data. The Title is restricted to 200 characters, which suggests a single line of text, so an `<input type="text">` element will suffice. The Description is not limited. You want to give your users a fair chance of selling their item, so you will provide a `<textarea>` element. You will provide five predefined values for the length of time in days that the item will remain visible on the site. You could use radio buttons to manage this, but a `<select>` element will be tidier. However, you will use radio buttons for the three options you provide to describe the condition of the item for sale. Finally, `<input type="text">` elements will capture the price and seller's e-mail address.

Now you know what HTML elements you will use, and you know what rules you want to apply, what are you waiting for? Hold up there... before you go any further, it's time to introduce the subject of *HTML Helpers* and *ModelState*.

HTML Helpers

I'm going to take you back to the beginning of ASP.NET. When Microsoft launched the framework back in 2002, one of the things it introduced from the outset was the notion of server controls.

For people who were familiar with desktop application development, these server controls were quite a welcome sight. They act in a similar way to controls found in Windows Forms, in that when you place one on a Web Form, such as a `TextBox` control, you can reliably expect an `<input type="text" />` HTML element to be rendered on the web page when it appears in a browser: all clever stuff, which *abstracts* the fact that the browser renders HTML. For Windows developers, this is very helpful. It means that they don't really have to learn HTML — or at least, they can make some significant progress in developing web applications without touching HTML at all. Web Forms server controls could be thought of as the first ASP.NET "HTML helpers," although that was not a term that was ever officially applied to them.

ABSTRACTIONS

An *abstraction* is a software development term for hiding the underlying technology to make something easier. Software development is full of abstractions. Your word processing application is an abstraction. It provides you with a familiar experience if you want to create a document. You have Save buttons, New File dialog boxes, and so on. These hide from you the underlying details concerned with creating data and saving it to a computer's hard disk. Most often, abstractions are extremely helpful timesavers. I have never had to learn how to program against the underlying Windows Operating System simply to persist some nicely formatted text to be sent as a letter.

Sometimes, abstractions can be harmful. The ASP.NET Web Forms server controls have been criticized by people who consider themselves "true" web developers, simply because they do not encourage Web Forms developers to get to grips with HTML, CSS, HTTP, and other core web development technologies. You have been introduced to these technologies in earlier chapters because they are important, and knowing how the web works is essential if you want to do anything more than the trivial with your websites or applications. The team behind WebMatrix understands this point, which is why WebMatrix exposes you to raw HTML rather than having something that hides what the Web is all about.

ASP.NET MVC introduced the first formal HTML helpers. They are designed to provide a shorthand method for rendering HTML to a *View* (the "V" in MVC, which represents the *User Interface*, or what the browser renders). The vast majority of these helpers render form fields. There are helpers for textboxes, check boxes, text areas, select lists, and so on. The Web Pages framework also includes helpers, which are very similar to their MVC cousins.

To see how they work, take a look at this HTML markup for a text box from the earlier form you built:

```
<input type="text" name="headline" id="headline" value="@Request["headline"]" />
```

The helper equivalent is as follows:

```
@Html.TextBox("headline", Request["headline"])
```

The resulting HTML that gets rendered is identical to the previous snippet. These form helpers assist in keeping your code terse. Beyond that, they contain no special magic. Most of them have multiple *overloaded methods* which allow you to exercise fine-grained control over your rendered HTML. The previous example takes a string representing the name of the form field, and an object, which represents the value. Another option allows you to additionally pass in an object that contains name/value pairs that will ultimately render as HTML attributes. A call to this overload might look like this:

```
@Html.TextBox("headline", Request["headline"],
              new {@class = "special", title = "Enter a headline"})
```

This will render as:

```
<input class="special" id="headline" name="headline"
         title="Enter a headline" type="text" value="" />
```

> ### OVERLOADED METHODS
>
> You were introduced to methods in the previous chapter, which as you learned, define the behavior of an object. You also learned that you can pass parameters into methods. The parameters you supply are defined in the method's signature. Most programming languages support *optional parameters* but prior to version 4.0, C# was not one of those languages. Again, this is something that was touched on in the previous chapter. Up until the release of version 4.0, the way that C# developers could provide alternative ways to invoke a method was to provide different versions of the same method, or to *overload* it. The HTML helpers for forms that come with ASP.NET Web Pages are based on the ones originally introduced in MVC, which was written prior to C# 4.0. Consequently, the overloaded methods from MVC appear in Web Pages. Keeping all the overloaded methods, rather than replacing them with one method that uses optional parameters, means a lot less work if you upgrade your Web Pages site to MVC at some stage in the future.

Notice that the last value passed in is an *anonymous type*. It is not assigned to a named variable explicitly, but is a convenient way to move read-only values around the .NET Framework. Look at the values. The first one creates a property on the object called class, with a value of "special". The second creates a property called title, with a value of "Enter a headline". However, the first — class — has been prefixed with the @ sign while the title property hasn't. The reason for this is because class is a C# keyword. The @ symbol in this case simply tells the C# compiler that in this particular context, the keyword is not being used, and to use "class" as a literal name for the property. This should not be confused with the Razor usage of the @ symbol.

Table 5-2 looks at the helpers you can use to replace the main form elements.

TABLE 5-2: HTML Helpers for Forms

FORM ELEMENT	EXAMPLE
Check box	`@Html.CheckBox("checkbox")` Output: `<input id="checkbox" name="checkbox" type="checkbox" />`
Hidden field	`@Html.Hidden("hidden")` Output: `<input id="hidden" name="hidden" type="hidden" value="" />`
Label	`@Html.Label("label")` Output: `<label for="label">label</label>`
Password	`@Html.Password("password")` Output: `<input id="password" name="password" type="password" />`
Radio button	`@Html.RadioButton("radio", false)` Output: `<input id="radio" name="radio" type="radio" value="False" />`
Text area	`@Html.TextArea("textarea")` Output: `<textarea cols="20" id="textarea" name="textarea" rows="2"></textarea>`
Text box	`@Html.TextBox("textbox")` Output: `<input id="textbox" name="textbox" type="text" value="" />`

Should you use these helpers? Well, that depends. If you are very comfortable working with HTML, you might like the fact that they save a lot of typing and keep your code files cleaner. They also produce valid error-free HTML, which can help you save time. Most of the helpers map to a counterpart in ASP.NET MVC, so if you are considering moving up to MVC in due course, using the helpers now could save you quite a bit of time migrating your UI code to Views. You should be warned, though, that the helpers in MVC do not always behave in exactly the same way as Web Pages helpers. For example, in MVC, the Checkbox helper actually renders a Hidden field in addition to the check box.

If you are new to HTML, I would recommend against using them to start with. These helpers are not transferrable to other technology platforms, such as PHP, and a thorough understanding of HTML is, as I said earlier, an essential skill for anyone wanting to become a serious web developer. For that reason, these particular helpers will not be used in this book. However, there are also a set of helpers for validation. When combined with the *ModelState* dictionary, these become very powerful, so you shall look at them next.

ModelState and Validation Helpers

ModelState was introduced in ASP.NET MVC, where it is a storage container for incoming form values. It also does a lot more than that within its MVC context. The Web Pages framework has a version of ModelState that doesn't do anywhere near as much as the MVC version, but one feature the Web Pages version does share with its MVC counterpart is that you can manually register validation errors in it. And this feature, combined with the Validation helpers, can really tidy up your code.

ModelState is a dictionary. As with previous dictionaries that you have met so far, items are stored in it using key/value pairs. To store an item, you use the `AddError` method, which takes two strings:

```
ModelState.AddError("firstname", "Fill this in!");
```

This registers an item with the key `"firstname"` and the value `"Fill this in!"`. ModelState also has an `IsValid` method which returns `true` if it contains no errors. If you use the `AddError` method to register an item within ModelState, the `IsValid` method returns `false`.

In the previous exercise, you saw how to build a string to display details of any errors back to the users. ModelState provides a much neater way to build a collection of error details. When you rendered the error details in the previous exercise, you used the `Html.Raw` helper to provide a summary at the top of the form. A lot of websites do this, and I find it really irritating. If I miss a required field, or do not provide the right type of data somewhere, I usually find myself scrolling between the form fields halfway down the page and the error message stuck at the top repeatedly trying to satisfy any broken rules. I much prefer to have the error message as close to the form field as possible, and the Validation helpers make this really easy to do from your point of view.

Assume you have registered an error in ModelState using the previous code example. If you want to render the error message, you would use the `ValidationMessage` helper:

```
@Html.ValidationMessage("firstname")
```

Wherever you place this code, the value associated with the `"firstname"` entry in ModelState will be rendered, so failure to meet the validation rules that have been applied to `"firstname"` will result in `"Fill this in!"` appearing. And this means it's really easy to display the error message next to the relevant form field. Alternatively, you could display all validation errors in one place if your design requires it (and you like to annoy me) using the `ValidationSummary` helper:

```
@Html.ValidationSummary
```

There is also an overloaded version of `ValidationSummary` that prevents the individual form errors from displaying, but still produces a summary message: `ValidationSummary(bool excludeFieldErrors)`. You simply pass `true` into this method to prevent individual field errors from appearing in one place:

```
@Html.ValidationSummary(true)
```

Now that you have met some new things to play with in form validation, you will continue from where you left off and use them in the Classifieds form.

TRY IT OUT Validating Form Input

1. Open the Classified site if you have closed it.

2. Add a new CSHTML file to the site and name it **_PageStart.cshtml**. Replace the existing code with the following:

```
@{
    Layout = "~/Shared/_Layout.cshtml";
}
```

3. Add a new folder called **App_Code**. Add a new CSHTML file to App_Code and call it **Helpers .cshtml**.

4. Within that file replace the existing code with the code from the Chapter5 site Helpers.cshtml file. Here it is again for convenience:

```
@helper Selected(string option, string value){
    if(HttpContext.Current.Request[option] != null){
        var values = HttpContext.Current.Request[option].Split(',');
        if(values.Contains(value)){
            <text>selected=\"selected\"</text>
        }
    }
}

@helper Checked(string option, string value){
    if(HttpContext.Current.Request[option] != null){
        var values = HttpContext.Current.Request[option].Split(',');
        if(values.Contains(value)){
            <text>checked=\"checked\"</text>
        }
    }
}
```

5. Open the Sell.cshtml page you created earlier and remove the line in the code block that sets the layout page. Then add the following markup in place of the <h2> heading:

```
<form id="post-advert" action="@Href("~/Sell")" method="post">
    <fieldset>
        <legend>Post Your Advertisement</legend>
        @Html.ValidationSummary(true)
        <div>
            <label for="title">Title*</label>
        </div>
        <div>
            <input type="text" name="title" value="@Request["title"]" />
            @Html.ValidationMessage("title")
        </div>
        <div>
            <label for="description">Description*</label>
        </div>
        <div>
            <textarea name="description">@Request["description"]</textarea>
            @Html.ValidationMessage("description")
        </div>
        <div>
            <label for"duration">Duration*</label>
        </div>
        <div>
            <select name="duration">
                <option value="">--Choose one--</option>
                <option value="1" @Helpers.Selected("Duration","1")>1 Day</option>
                <option value="3" @Helpers.Selected("Duration","3")>3 Days</option>
                <option value="7" @Helpers.Selected("Duration","7")>7 Days</option>
                <option value="14" @Helpers.Selected("Duration","14")>14
                Days</option>
```

```
        </select>
        @Html.ValidationMessage("duration")
    </div>
    <div>
        <label for="price">Price*</label>
    </div>
    <div>
        <input type="text" name="price" value="@Request["price"]" />
        @Html.ValidationMessage("price")
    </div>
    <div>
        <label for="condition">Condition*</label>
    </div>
    <div>
        <input type="radio" name="condition" value="Fair"
                @Helpers.Checked("Condition","Fair") />Fair
        <input type="radio" name="condition" value="Good"
                @Helpers.Checked("Condition","Good") />Good
        <input type="radio" name="condition" value="As New"
                @Helpers.Checked("Condition","As New") />As New
        @Html.ValidationMessage("condition")
    </div>
    <div>
        <label for="email">Your Email Address*</label>
    </div>
    <div>
        <input type="text" name="email" value="@Request["email"]" />
        @Html.ValidationMessage("email")
    </div>
    <div>
        <input type="submit" name="Submit" value="Post" />
    </div>
    </fieldset>
</form>
```

6. Add a new CSHTML file called **Functions.cshtml** to the App_Code folder and replace the existing markup with the following:

```
@using System.Text.RegularExpressions;
@functions{
    public static bool IsValidEmail(string s){
        string pattern = @"^\w+([-+.]\w+)*@\w+([-.]\w+)*\.\w+([-.]\w+)*$";
        return Regex.IsMatch(s, pattern);
    }
}
```

You should recognize this as the e-mail validation helper from the previous chapter.

7. Returning to Sell.cshtml, add the following code to the code block at the top of the page, just under the sole line which sets the page title:

```
if(IsPost){
    if(Request["title"].IsEmpty()){
        ModelState.AddError("title", "Please provide a title");
    }
```

```
    if(Request["title"].Length > 200){
        ModelState.AddError("title", "Your title cannot exceed 200 characters");
    }
    if(Request["description"].IsEmpty()){
        ModelState.AddError("description", "You must provide a description");
    }
    if(Request["duration"].IsEmpty()){
        ModelState.AddError("duration", "Please choose a duration");
    }
    if(Request["price"].IsEmpty()){
        ModelState.AddError("price", "Please provide a price");
    }
    if(!Request["price"].IsDecimal () && !Request["Price"].IsEmpty()){
        ModelState.AddError("price", "Please provide a valid number for the price");
    }
    if(Request["condition"].IsEmpty()){
        ModelState.AddError("condition", "Please state the condition of your item");
    }
    if(Request["email"].IsEmpty()){
        ModelState.AddError("email", "Please provide your email address");
    }
    if(!Request["email"].IsEmpty() && !Functions.IsValidEmail(Request["Email"])){
        ModelState.AddError("email", "Please provide a valid email address");
    }
    if(!ModelState.IsValid){
        ModelState.AddFormError("Please fix the errors below before submitting the
form");
    }
}
```

8. Open StyleSheet.css from the Content folder and add the following to the end of the file:

```
/*
-------------------------------------------------
FORM
-------------------------------------------------
*/
legend{
    color: #84a24a;
    font-size: 1.3em;
    text-transform: uppercase;
    font-weight: bold;
    font-family: "Arial Narrow";
}

.field-validation-error, .validation-summary-errors{
    color: red;
}
```

9. Now test the form by submitting it without entering any values. You should get a result similar to Figure 5-7.

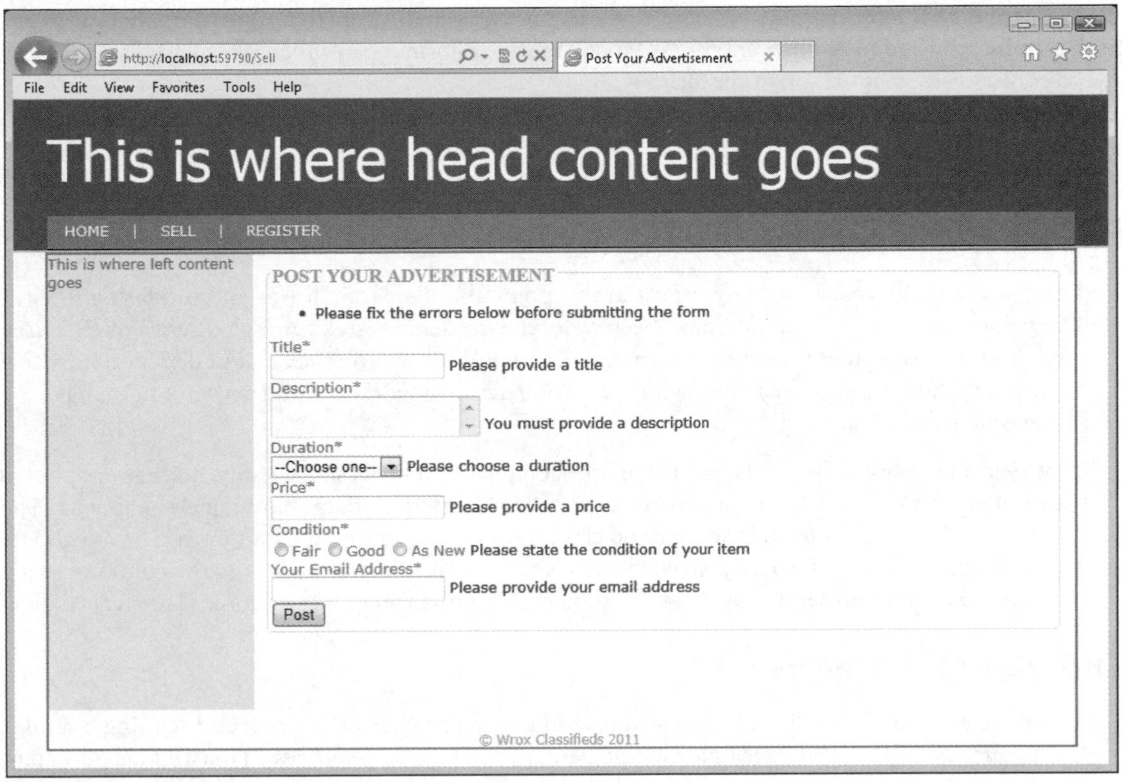

FIGURE 5-7

How It Works

You added some new HTML elements to your form this time: the `fieldset`, `legend`, and `label` elements. By default, the `fieldset` element results in a border being added around its child elements. The `legend` element acts as a caption for a `fieldset` element. The `label` element associates a label with its form element, which can provide some usability enhancements to your forms, especially for people who use screen readers or a mouse. You can click on the label and the associated form element will receive focus in some cases.

You added an `Html.ValidationMessage` to each form element, which is responsible for displaying the details of any error arising from the value entered into the specific field. Notice that the string passed into the `Html.ValidationMessage` method call relates to the form field it appears next to. You also added an `Html.ValidationSummary` method call to the top of the form, but specified that it should only display a summary message by passing `true` to the `excludeFieldErrors` parameter.

In the code block at the top of the page, you tested to see if the form had been posted back, and if it had been, you began to test each form field value against your business rules, as defined in Table 5.1. If any of the tests failed, you added a field entry into the ModelState's `Errors` property using the `ModelState.AddError` method, defining the error message to be displayed. You also passed in a key value representing the form field, which ties a particular message to a particular `ValidationMessage` method call within the form. Then you used the `IsValid` method to test whether there were any entries in the ModelState's

`Errors` property. If it returns `false`, there is at least one entry, indicating that something went wrong. At that point, you added another entry into ModelState — a Form error, which is displayed as part of the `ValidationSummary` at the top of the form.

PROCESSING USER INPUT

There is not really much more to discuss at this point about creating forms and validating input. The principles behind validation have been well rehearsed and tested through a series of exercises now. You have also met most of the form inputs you will likely ever use, and understood how they behave, and how they differ from each other. You have also worked with two ways to manage server-side validation.

However, one thing still stands out. If the user completes all fields successfully, all that happens at the moment is that the form is presented back to them with their data. Nothing else happens. The point behind creating a form is so that you can do something with the data that you have validated. Typically, you will save it to a database, which is covered in Chapter 9. An equally common scenario is to take the data and send it by e-mail to someone. That is what you will look at next.

The WebMail Helper

The WebMail helper has been introduced to simplify the process of creating and sending e-mail from your ASP.NET Web Pages site. Sending e-mail is a two stage process: First you need to configure your mail server options, which include specifying which one to use and logging on to it; and second, you need to construct an e-mail and send it. Your mail server options very much depend on what service is available to you. You may have an ISP who offers e-mail sending as part of your package, in which case they will be able to provide you with the correct details. It is also possible to send e-mail via one of the online providers such as Google, Yahoo, or Windows Live Mail/Hotmail, as long as you have a valid and current account with them. Finally, you may have access to your own SMTP (Simple Mail Transport Protocol) server which you can use.

The WebMail helper provides access to a number of properties that you can use to configure the options you need to make use of whichever mail service you plan to take advantage of. Table 5-3 shows the various settings that need to be considered when configuring the server details.

TABLE 5-3: Configuring the WebMail Helper

PROPERTY	DESCRIPTION
`SmptServer`	The name or address of your SMTP server. This may take the form smtp.domain.com or 127.0.0.1.
`SmtpPort`	The port number you should use. This is usually 25, but some ISPs block traffic on Port 25 as an anti-spam measure, forcing use of 587 instead.

PROPERTY	DESCRIPTION
EnableSsl	Determines whether encryption should be used for transmission. False by default.
Username	Your mail account user name.
Password	Your mail account password.
SmtpUseDefaultCredentials	If true (it's false by default), this allows you to connect to the mail server using the currently logged on user account.
From	The e-mail address that the message is sent from.

Once set, these values are not likely to change across the site. Consequently, they make a great candidate for the AppStart file you met in the previous chapter:

```
@{
    WebMail.SmtpServer = "mail.domain.com";
    WebMail.SmtpPort = 25;
    WebMail.EnableSsl = false;
    WebMail.UserName = "your user name";
    WebMail.Password = "your password";
    WebMail.From = "user@domain.com";
}
```

Versions of Windows up to XP Professional used to include an SMTP server as part of their Internet Information Services installation, but these have been removed from later versions as an anti-spam measure. If you don't have access to an SMTP server from your development machine, but simply want to test the creation and sending of e-mails, you can set the location of a "pickup" directory in a configuration file. The pickup directory is simply a location where applications (such as your website) save e-mails they generate for later processing by an SMTP server. Assuming that you use this option, your configuration initially will be very simple:

```
@{
    WebMail.SmtpServer = "127.0.0.1";
    WebMail.From = "user@domain.com";
}
```

The From address is any random, but validly structured e-mail address, but the SmtpServer value is 127.0.0.1, which is the local loopback address for a Windows machine if the service you are trying to connect to resides on the same machine as the code that attempts the connection. Port 25 is the default port number for mail, which is why it is the default value for the WebMail's SmtpPort parameter. This means you don't need to set this value explicitly. The WebMail helper has a Send method. Some of the parameters this method takes are required, while some are optional. Table 5-4 explores them all in more detail.

TABLE 5-4: The WebMail Helper's Send Parameters

PARAMETER	DESCRIPTION
to	The e-mail address that the mail should be sent to.
subject	The subject of the e-mail.
body	The e-mail body content.
from (optional)	If you have not set the WebMail.From property, you can use this parameter to set the e-mail address that the e-mail will be sent from. You are more likely to use this parameter if you want to set the From address dynamically.
cc (optional)	If you want to send a copy of the e-mail to someone else, provide their e-mail address here.
filesToAttach (optional)	You can attach files to the e-mail using this property.
isBodyHtml (optional)	Determines whether the body content is HTML or plaintext (the default).
additionalHeaders (optional)	Allows you to create additional headers.

TRY IT OUT Creating and Sending an E-mail

In this exercise you will modify the page containing the form that you just worked on so that it generates and sends an e-mail if the input is valid.

1. Add a new CSHTML file to the root of your Classified site called **_AppStart.cshtml**.

2. Replace the existing code with the following, ensuring that the values you provide are valid for the SMTP server you are using:

```
@{
    WebMail.SmtpServer = "127.0.0.1";
    WebMail.SmtpPort = 25;
    WebMail.EnableSsl = false;
    WebMail.UserName = "your user name";
    WebMail.Password = "your password";
    WebMail.From = "user@domain.com";
}
```

If you use the pickup directory option, you can use the previous code snippet I provided. You will need to follow this extra step. Add a new Web.Config (4.0) file to the site. Do not change its name. Add the following to the file just before the closing </configuration> tag:

```
<system.net>
    <mailSettings>
        <smtp deliveryMethod="SpecifiedPickupDirectory">
```

```
        <specifiedPickupDirectory pickupDirectoryLocation="C:\Mail\"/>
      </smtp>
    </mailSettings>
</system.net>
```

You should ensure that you create a folder called "Mail" in the root of your C: drive, or change the name and/or location of the folder to match one that you have access to and can create.

3. Open Sell.cshtml and add the following code at the end of the code block where you added your validation code:

```
if(!ModelState.IsValid){
    ModelState.AddFormError(@"Please fix the errors
                            below before submitting the form");
} else {
    var message = "<p>Details of your item for sale:</p>";
    message += "Title: " + Request["title"] + "<br />";
    message += "Description: " + Request["description"] + "<br />";
    message += "Duration: " + Request["duration"] + " days<br />";
    message += "Price: " + String.Format("{0:c}", Request["price"].AsFloat());
    message += "<br />";
    message += "Condition: " + Request["condition"];
    WebMail.Send(
            to: Request["email"],
            subject: "Advertisement confirmation",
            body: message,
            isBodyHtml: true
            );
    result = "Your advertisement details have been sent to you by email";
    }
}
```

4. Add another line of code to the top of the code block which instantiates the variable result:

```
@{
    Page.Title = "Post Your Advertisement";
    var result = "";
    if(IsPost){
```

5. And finally, add a line of code to the top of the form so that the result variable will be displayed:

```
<div>@result</div>
<form id="post-advert" action="@Href("~/Sell")" method="post">
    <fieldset>
```

6. While you are at it, you can change the header for the site so that it makes more sense. Open the _Header.cshtml file in the Shared folder, and replace "This is where the head content goes" with "Classifieds."

7. Save your changes and run the page in a browser. If you are not using the pickup directory approach, make sure that you enter your own e-mail address in the E-mail Address field. Enter valid values in all the other fields, and submit the form. Check your e-mail client if you have used an SMTP server. If you used the pickup directory method, check the folder you specified. You should find a new .eml file. Double click it, and it should open in your default e-mail client. See Figure 5-8.

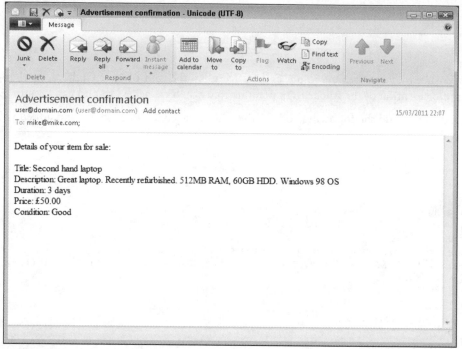

FIGURE 5-8

How It Works

In this particular example, you chose to set the e-mail format to HTML by passing `true` to the `isBodyHtml` parameter. As you constructed your message body as a string, you provided HTML tags to format it nicely. You also used the `String.Format()` method to take the numeric value provided as the `price`, and display it as a currency. There are a wide range of formatters within the .NET Framework that save you the effort of having to convert the value to a string, and then manipulate it yourself. Once you had built the entire e-mail body in the `message` variable, you applied that to the `body` parameter of the `Send` method and applied the value that was posted in the form as the e-mail address to send the message to.

Your SMTP configuration has already been set for the entire application in the _AppStart.cshtml file, so whenever you send mail, you don't need to repeat the set up.

HTML and Request Validation

In the section about HTML encoding, I promised that you will learn another built-in security feature that helps to prevent XSS injection attacks. That feature is called *request validation*. How it works is this: If you attempt to submit anything that looks like HTML tags through the form you have just created, ASP.NET will throw an exception such as the one in Figure 5-9.

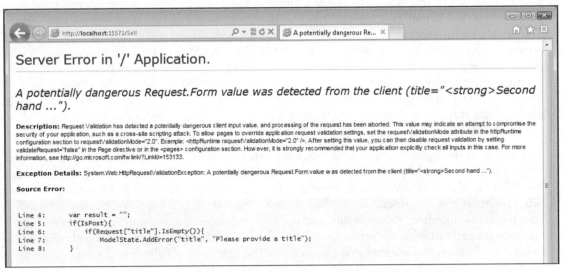

FIGURE 5-9

Sometimes you will want to allow users to submit HTML via your form. You might be building a content management system (CMS) so that they can maintain the content of their pages, or you might decide to allow them to embellish their sales item's description with the addition of some HTML in the Classifieds site. You can do this by disabling Request Validation at a granular level on specific form fields, or indeed any other route by which users can provide input, such as query string, cookies, or server variables. Assuming that you want to allow users to include HTML tags in the Description field in your Sell.cshtml form, you would use the `Request.Unvalidated()` method like this:

```
var description = Request.Unvalidated("Description");
if(description.IsEmpty()){
    errors += "<li>Please provide a description</li>";
}
```

This opens up a potential security hole. If you are developing a site for internal use, such as a CMS, and you know that the users who can take advantage of this hole are benign (no one will deliberately sabotage their own site), this may not be a concern at all for you. However, if your site is open to the general public, it is open to hackers, and hackers just love to probe any site for breaking points. Consequently, you still need to validate the input to screen out any potentially dangerous values — particularly `<script>` tags.

SUMMARY

This chapter has provided you with a good understanding of how forms work within Web Pages. By now, you should understand the difference between various form input types and other fields. You should know which ones to use and how their behavior differs when values are passed to your server-side code. You learned how to control the HTTP verb (POST or GET), which governs how the form values are submitted through configuring the `method` attribute on a form, as well as the location to which the values are submitted via the `action` attribute. The `name` attribute is very important when creating form elements. The value you apply to it acts as a key for referencing whatever the user entered, or selected. You learned how to test whether a form had been submitted using the `IsPost` method.

You looked at the importance of validating values that come from users. You examined a number of built-in methods that help you to test the presence or type of data that has been supplied, and you looked at creating your own helper to perform more complex validation. The importance of server-side validation was explained, as was the role that client-side validation plays. Then you looked at how to persist submitted values in the form if it failed server-side validation. You examined two methods for validating on the server — one that depends on building a string to display validation failures to the user, and another that makes use of the `Validation` helpers and `ModelState` to manage the registration and display of validation error messages.

Finally, you were introduced to the WebMail helper and shown how to configure it to send e-mails containing form data.

In the next chapter, you learn about jQuery, a client-side library that makes adding JavaScript to your pages easy. You will also extend the form to manage client-side validation via a jQuery plug-in.

EXERCISES

1. Which is more important — client-side validation or server-side validation — why? What are the three things to test during validation?

2. GET and POST are two HTTP verbs that can be used to pass form data to the server. Which one is preferred and why?

3. What is the role of the `Html.Raw` method? Why is it needed?

4. How do you tell ModelState that validation failed? How do you test for failure?

5. Name two ways in which you can set the From address in the WebMail helper, and the difference between them.

Answers to the Exercises can be found in the Appendix.

▶ **WHAT YOU LEARNED IN THIS CHAPTER**

TOPIC	KEY CONCEPTS
HTTP POST	A method for passing values from a form to the server in the body of a request.
HTTP GET	A method for passing values to the server as a query string appended to a URL.
Business rules	The rules you decide should apply to values within certain aspects of your application.
Server-side validation	The process of testing values using server-side code to ensure they meet business rules.
Client-side validation	Validation that takes place within the user's browser using client-side code such as JavaScript.
HTML encoding	The process that happens when HTML tags are converted to their HTML entity equivalents so that they are rendered literally to the browser.
ModelState	A dictionary for maintaining validation errors.
WebMail helper	A helper for managing e-mail.
SMTP server	Software for managing the sending of e-mail.

AJAX and jQuery

WHAT YOU WILL LEARN IN THIS CHAPTER:

➤ How jQuery works

➤ How to include jQuery in your pages

➤ jQuery basics

➤ How to manipulate page elements using jQuery

➤ AJAX basics

➤ How to use the JSON helper

➤ Using jQuery plug-ins

The days of the static web disappeared with the introduction of server-side technologies. Developers began producing web applications instead of websites. These applications began to replace desktop software. However, as web-based software grew in abundance, it lacked a key feature often found in its desktop-related counterparts: usability. If parts of the page content changed as a result of user input, the user often had to wait for a full page refresh to see these changes. The interface was still static.

In the late 1990s, attempts to liven up web pages were made using *Dynamic HTML* (DHMTL), which relied on client-side scripting, most often using JavaScript to manipulate the underlying HTML in the browser. Some of these efforts were crass — you can still find sites where your mouse cursor is stalked by a trail of stars. Other attempts sought to solve usability problems by hiding and showing segments of the page as a result of mouse movement or click events, such as sliding menus and news tickers.

There is a fundamental problem with JavaScript: Different browser vendors create their own implementations. As browser vendors rushed new browsers out into the market during the early part of this century, they started developing their own custom features, and web developers started to write hacks to accommodate all browsers. For most web developers, including JavaScript goodies in their site usually involved an exercise of search, copy, and paste, and finally keeping their fingers crossed that the next generation of browsers didn't break the code snippet they had borrowed while barely understanding how it worked.

AJAX (Asynchronous JavaScript and XML) is a group of technologies with JavaScript at its core. AJAX revolves around asynchronous HTTP requests, which allow the client to communicate with the server.

INTRODUCTION TO JQUERY

A number of people released JavaScript libraries designed to make working with JavaScript easier without having to learn advanced JavaScript programming, or having to understand how browsers differed. Adoption rates varied, depending on the library's complexity, but one library stood out above all others — jQuery. The key to jQuery is its simplicity. Its catchy tag line is the "Write Less, Do More" JavaScript library. It has a concise syntax and is very readable. In fact, it proved so popular that Microsoft has adopted it, and ships it as part of the default template for Web Form and MVC sites. Microsoft also provides product support for the library, so that makes jQuery the obvious choice for incorporating JavaScript when building ASP.NET Web Pages sites.

The core raison d'être behind the jQuery library is to simplify common client-side tasks. Probably the most common task is to get a reference to a page element so that it can be manipulated. jQuery uses the same approach to referencing elements as you found in CSS — by tag name, ID, or CSS class. It also offers some other advanced mechanisms for referencing elements. Having obtained a reference, you want to do something with the element, or group of elements, such as change their style, hide them, add something to them, change their text or HTML content, fade them out, or add event handlers to them. jQuery exposes an API of methods that are succinct and easy to use.

There are three elements to jQuery:

> **The Core library:** A small download that contains all the methods you need for accessing and manipulating elements in a page, and for using AJAX functionality.

> **jQuery UI:** A customizable library that includes common UI elements such as date pickers, tabs, dialog boxes, drag and drop, and animation effects.

> **jQuery plug-ins:** Currently numbering in excess of 4,000, these extend the functionality of jQuery to provide menus, data display templates, slide shows, enhanced animations and effects, form extensions, image croppers, advanced color pickers, and just about every other kind of client-side widget you might need.

HOW TO INCLUDE JQUERY IN YOUR PAGES

The jQuery library is a free download available from `http://jquery.com`. The current version at the time of writing is 1.6.2. There are usually a number of files for each release, which differ in size. You can obtain the Development version, but this is the largest file and is intended for use with debugging tools. It contains comments and the code itself includes a lot of whitespace for readability. Whitespace increases the file size dramatically. A minified version — the Production version — is also available, and has been subject to a process that removes white space and comments and changes variable names to shorter versions. This results in a file size that's a fraction of the source and is recommended for production use.

To keep your site files organized, you should consider creating a folder for script files. In the samples, I always use a folder called Scripts for script files. Call me unadventurous if you like. Once you have saved the file there, you use a standard <script> tag to reference it:

```
<script src="@Href("~/Scripts/jquery-1.6.2.min.js")" type="text/javascript"></script>
```

You use the Href helper here to ensure that the relative path generated by the Razor code is compatible with all browsers. You should also notice that the opening <script> tag has a closing </script> tag. Some browsers require this, so avoid using a self-closing <script /> tag.

Ideally, the <script> tags should be placed in the head element of your document. If you are using a Layout page, this is where your reference to jQuery will go. This option also has the added convenience that it will make jQuery available to all pages that make use of the Layout page in question. Once the visitor has downloaded the library, it is cached by the browser and available without being downloaded again.

Content Delivery Networks

An alternative method to including jQuery is to use a *Content Delivery Network* (CDN). There are a number of CDN options available, and their primary role is to make data available at various points within a network (the Internet) so that download times are improved. Once a file from a particular domain has been downloaded, it is usually cached by the user's browser. Further requests for the same file result in the cached version being used rather than another round trip over HTTP. The real beauty of this is that if a visitor to your site has previously visited another site using the same CDN, they already have the file in their browser cache. That means that you save on bandwidth, and the user doesn't have to wait for your script to download. The two most popular CDNs for jQuery are offered by Microsoft and Google. To make use of either of these services, use the following link (amending the actual filename to reflect the version you want to use):

➤ Google:

```
<script src="http://ajax.googleapis.com/ajax/libs/jquery/1.6.2/jquery.min.js"
        type="text/javascript"></script>
```

➤ Microsoft:

```
<script src="http://ajax.aspnetcdn.com/ajax/jQuery/jquery-1.6.2.min.js"
        type="text/javascript"></script>
```

Now that you have a reference to jQuery, how do you use it? In the next exercise you will create your first jQuery page. It will be a simple one and does nothing more than tests to see if you have referenced the file correctly.

TRY IT OUT   Your First jQuery Page

1. Create a new site within WebMatrix based on the Empty Site template. Name it **Chapter6**.

2. Within the root of the site, create a folder called **Scripts** and either download a copy of jQuery, or copy it from the sample download accompanying this chapter. Place the jquery-1.6.2.min.js file in the Scripts folder.

3. Add a new CSHTML file to the root folder of your site and call it **default.cshtml**.

4. Within the `<head>` element, add the following code:

```
<script src="@Href("~/Scripts/jquery-1.6.2.min.js")" type="text/javascript"></script>
```

As an alternative, you can use one of the CDNs instead.

5. Add the following code to the `<head>` element, after the reference to jQuery:

```
<script type="text/javascript">
    var colors = ["red", "blue", "green", "yellow"]
    $(document).ready(function(){
        $('#colorchanger').click(function(){
            $('p').each(function(index, value){
                $(this).css('background-color', colors[index]);
            });
        })
    });
</script>
```

6. In the `<body>` element of the page, add the following code:

```
<body>
    <p>This paragraph will turn red</p>
    <p>This paragraph will turn blue</p>
    <p>This paragraph will turn green</p>
    <p>This paragraph will turn yellow</p>
    <input type="button" id="colorchanger" value="click me" />
</body>
```

7. Save the page, and click the Run button to bring the page up in your default browser. When you click the button, you should see that each of the paragraphs gets a different background color, holding out the promise hinted at in their text content.

How It Works

After the jQuery library was made available to the page, you added another `<script>` block, within which you added some JavaScript code. The first line of that code created an array containing four strings. Each string is a color name. You also added four paragraphs to the page, each one showing some text that suggested that they will change color. The order in which the colors are referenced in the paragraphs matches that of the array. Finally, you added a button to the page. You gave it an ID of `colorchanger`.

Going back to the script block, you added more code. The first line after the array declaration begins with a dollar sign ($) and `(document).ready(function()`. The dollar sign is a shorthand version of `"jQuery"`, which is not just the name of a library, but a global object. You could have written the first line like this:

```
jQuery(document).ready(function(){
    ...
```

The `ready` part of the code is actually an *event handler*. Once the event it refers to has fired, the code within the subsequent function call is executed. But which event does `ready` listen out for? It's actually waiting for the Document Object Model (DOM) elements to be fully loaded into the browser. Once that has happened, the (document).ready event fires.

 NOTE *The Document Object Model is a standard for representing and interacting with elements in an HTML document via JavaScript particularly. Not all browsers implement the DOM in the same way. The jQuery* (document).ready *function hides this fact from you nicely, and saves you having to write a lot of code to cover all browsers. You cannot reference HTML elements within a page via JavaScript until they exist. Once the browser has parsed the HTML and created a "DOM tree," it is safe to attempt to reference any element within that tree.*

There is in fact an even shorter version of (document).ready, which is simply this:

```
$(function(){
... .
```

Once the DOM tree has been created within the browser, the function that you defined in the event handler is executed. The first line of the function references the element with the ID of colorchanger. That's your button. It adds an onclick event handler to the button. Event handlers in jQuery are named almost the same as their JavaScript counterparts, but without the "on" prefix. The event handler is fired in response to the button being clicked, and calls another function, which first gathers up all <p> elements on the page into a collection. Then the jQuery .each() function is called, which iterates over the collection. As it does, it applies a CSS style to the current <p> element, using the current element's index in the collection to reference the corresponding color in the array by its index. The function then applies that value to the background-color property.

Simple, isn't it? Well, actually it's not — at least if you weren't using jQuery, you would have written substantially more than three lines of JavaScript to achieve the same effect. Remember — although you are using the jQuery syntax, this code is still pure JavaScript. jQuery doesn't replace JavaScript — it simply provides an easier way to code with it. Although the example might not make an awful lot of sense right at the moment, it serves to illustrate the power of jQuery and why it has established itself as a firm favorite within the web developer community. If the example still leaves you a little confused, fret no more. The next few sections take a much closer look at the foundations on which jQuery is built.

JQUERY SELECTORS

jQuery is primarily concerned with providing you with an easy way to manipulate DOM elements. As you have already been shown, the key to being able to manipulate elements is to get a reference to them in the first place. That's the role of *selectors*. A selector is a means of targeting one or more elements on the page. If any elements on the page match your selector, they are returned as a *matched set*, or *wrapped set*. As you discovered in the previous exercise, the set of matched elements makes up a collection.

The basic syntax for a selector starts with the dollar sign — $. Thereafter, the elements you want to reference appear in brackets within quotes:

```
$('selector')
```

Once you have a matched set, you can start doing things with it. For example, you could pass it to a variable:

```
var paragraphs = $('p');
// now you can do something with paragraphs
```

You will more likely use *method chaining*. Most jQuery methods return a *jQuery object*, which consists of the matched set. That means you can keep chaining method calls as you like:

```
$('p') //returns a matched set of p elements
.css('someclass') //applies the CSS someclass element to them
.hide('slow') // makes them disappear
.show('slow'); //makes them reappear
```

This works because white space is ignored within JavaScript, but most often, chaining appears on the same line:

```
$('p').css('someclass').hide('slow').show('slow');
```

Method chaining is not exclusive to jQuery. It appears in many languages. Here's an example of chaining string methods in C#:

```
var input = "  some string that needs to be worked in";
var output = input.Replace(" on", " in").Trim().ToUpper();
```

Basic Selectors

jQuery uses the same basic CSS syntax to target elements that you were introduced to in Chapter 2. These are detailed in Table 6-1.

TABLE 6-1: jQuery Selectors

SELECTOR	DESCRIPTION	EXAMPLE
Universal selector	References all elements on the page	`$('*')`
ID selector	References elements with a specific ID	`$('#colorchanger')`
Element selector	References elements by type e.g. p or div	`$('p')`
Class selector	References elements according to their class value	`$('.myclass')`

You saw in Chapter 2 that you can group CSS selectors to apply styles, and jQuery understands this too:

`$('ul, ol')` — references all ul and ol elements

jQuery also understands combining selectors:

$('p.myclass') — references all p elements with a class of myclass

 NOTE *The examples in this book show literal strings being referenced with single quotes ('), but you may also come across examples that use double quotes ("). For example, you might see that last example written like this:*

> $("p.myclass")

Either way will work, but you must be consistent. You cannot open with a single quote and close with a double quote, for example. Is one way preferred over another? Well, even the official jQuery documentation switches between single quotes and double quotes in its examples, but my preference is for single quotes, so that is what you will see throughout this book.

Selectors with Filters

Things would become quite awkward if you could only select elements using the basic selectors. For example, if you wanted to add a particular CS style to alternate rows in an HTML table, you would have to perform a certain amount of JavaScript gymnastics to iterate a matched set of rows to apply the style to every other one. The jQuery team thought of that and came up with a very flexible solution called *filters*.

Filters are kind of like a query expression, in that you can specify that only the first element that matches the selector should be returned; or every even numbered one; or ones that have an index greater, lesser, or equal to the one you specify. Filters are a lot more advanced than that. You can select elements based on the position they occupy in the document, what text they contain, or what they don't contain. You can select elements based on the presence or absence of attributes — even specifying what the attribute's value is. Table 6-2 details some of the more commonly used filters, but full details of all filters are available in the online jQuery documentation at http://docs.jquery.com/.

TABLE 6-2: jQuery Filters

FILTER	DESCRIPTION
:first	The first item in a matched set. $('p:first') returns the first paragraph.
:last	The last item in a matched set. $('p:last') returns the last paragraph.
:odd	Returns all odd-indexed items in a matched set. $('tr:odd') returns table rows indexed at 1, 3, 5, and so on.

continues

TABLE 6-2 *(continued)*

FILTER	DESCRIPTION
`:even`	Returns all even-indexed items in a matched set. `$('tr:even')` returns table rows indexed at 0, 2, 4, and so on.
`:has`	Returns all elements in a matched set that have a child element specified. `$('p:has(span)')` returns all paragraphs containing a span element.
`:eq`	Returns the element with the matching index. `$('p:eq(1)')` returns the second paragraph in a zero-based indexed collection.
`:lt`	Returns elements placed lower than the specified index position. `$('p:lt(2)')` returns the first and second paragraphs in a zero-based indexed collection.
`:gt`	Returns elements placed higher than the specified index position. `$('p:gt(2)')` returns the fourth and subsequent paragraphs in a zero-based indexed collection.
`:contains(x)`	Returns all elements containing the text x. `$('div:contains(foo)')` returns all div elements with the text foo in them, or in descendants of the div.
`[attr^=x]`	Returns elements with the specified attribute having a value starting with x. `$('p[title^=foo]')` returns all paragraphs with a title attribute whose value begins with foo.
`[attr$=x]`	Returns elements with the specified attribute having a value ending with x. `$('p[title$=bar]')` returns all paragraphs with a title attribute whose value ends with bar.
`[attr*=x]`	Returns elements with the specified attribute having a value containing x. `$('p[title*=baz]')` returns all paragraphs with a title attribute whose value contains baz.

MANIPULATING PAGE ELEMENTS WITH JQUERY

Once you have a reference to elements on the page, you obviously want to do something with them. You may want to hide them, fade them out, animate them, change their appearance through CSS, add to them, or remove them entirely. The jQuery API contains simple methods to do all this and more. You are going to explore some of these methods now, and then apply what you have learned in an exercise.

Applying CSS to Elements

I really like the BBC Sports site (`http://news.bbc.co.uk/sport`). During the football season, the BBC provides a text-based commentary on the Premier League matches. One of the really nice features they offer is a live update of the scores across all the matches. As goals are scored, the match in question is highlighted briefly and the text becomes bold. It's a neat way to draw the eye to what's happening. After a couple of seconds the highlighted, bold entry fades back to the same style as the other matches. The BBC use jQuery to create this effect — altering the CSS of the individual row — and there are a number of methods provided by jQuery for doing this kind of thing.

css(name, value)

You used this method in the first exercise when you changed the background color of each paragraph. The first argument — `name` — accepts a valid CSS property (`background-color`, `height`, `border`, and so on), and the second argument is a valid value for that property:

```
$('h1').css('font-family', 'Arial');
$('h1').css('color', 'red');
```

css(map)

The preceding method allows you to affect one CSS property, but the `map` method is a lot more powerful. The parameter is a series of properties and their values passed in to the method in a *JavaScript Object Notation* (JSON) map of key/value pairs. You will learn more about JSON later in this chapter, but for the time being, suffice it to say that the syntax for the map follows this pattern:

```
{key: value, key: value}
```

The `map` opens with a curly brace ({), and each key/value pair is separated by commas. The key and its value are separated using a colon (:). The map is then closed with a closing curly brace (}):

```
$('h1').css({'color':'red', 'font-family': 'Arial'});
```

addClass, removeClass, and toggleClass

When you looked at CSS in Chapter 2, one of the things you were advised to do was to keep styling information in a separate file using CSS selectors. The previous methods all allow you to manipulate the style of particular elements, but they require you to define that styling information within the jQuery code. If you decided that you want to change the color or the font family, you would have to go into your jQuery code to do this, which can become a bit of a maintenance nightmare if you have a lot of jQuery in a large site. The `addClass` and `removeClass` methods allow you to reference styles that have been defined in your external style sheets and apply them or remove them easily. The `toggleClass` method works in a similar way to the simple toggle method, in that it applies a style if it hasn't already been applied to the element, or removes it if it has.

Assuming that you have created a style declaration in your CSS file like this:

```
.customStyle{color:red; font-family: Arial; border: 1px solid red;}
```

you can switch it on and off like this:

```
$('h1').toggleClass('customStyle');
```

In the following exercise you will use what you learned about selectors and filters, and combine them with ways to apply CSS to elements to alter the appearance of various items on a page.

TRY IT OUT   Setting Styles with Selectors and Filters

1.   Open your Chapter6 site and add a new file to it named **filters.cshtml**.

2.   Add a reference to jQuery 1.6.2 to the head element in the same way as you did in the previous exercise and make the title **jQuery Filters Demo**.

3.   Add the following code to the body:

```
<h1>jQuery Filters</h1>
<div>
    <input type="button" id="font" value="Font" />
    <input type="button" id="odd" value="Odd" />
    <input type="button" id="even" value="Even" />
    <input type="button" id="contains" value="Contains" />
</div>
<table width="300">
    <thead>Sample table</thead>
    <tr><td>1st col cell 1</td><td>2nd col cell 1</td></tr>
    <tr><td>1st col cell 2</td><td>2nd col cell 2</td></tr>
    <tr><td>1st col cell 3</td><td>2nd col cell 3</td></tr>
    <tr><td>1st col cell 4</td><td>2nd col cell 4</td></tr>
</table>
<div>
    <input type="button" id="toggle" value="Toggle" />
    <input type="button" id="starts" value="Start" />
    <input type="button" id="ends" value="End" />
    <input type="button" id="anywhere" value="Anywhere" />
</div>
<div>
    <a href="http://www.google.com"
        title="Visit Google">Click to visit Google</a><br />
    <a href="http://www.facebook.com"
        title="Visit Facebook">Click to visit Facebook</a><br />
    <a href="http://www.wrox.com"
        title="Visit Wrox">Click to visit Wrox</a><br />
    <a href="http://www.bbc.co.uk"
        title="Visit The BBC">Click to visit the BBC's site</a><br />
</div>
```

4.   At the top of the page, just after the reference to jQuery, and before the closing `</head>` tag, add the following code:

```
<script type="text/javascript">
    $(function(){
        $('#font').click(function(){
            $('*').css({'font-family': 'Arial','font-size': '13px'});
        });
```

```
        $('#odd').click(function(){
            $('tr:odd').css('background-color', '#ccffbf');
        });
        $('#even').click(function(){
            $('tr:even').css('background-color', '#99ff80');
        });
        $('#contains').click(function(){
            $('td:contains(2nd col)').css('background-color', '#ffbfdc');
        });
        $('#toggle').click(function(){
            $('a').toggleClass('links');
        });
        $('#starts').click(function(){
            $('a[title^=Visit]').css('color', 'red');
        });
        $('#ends').click(function(){
            $('a[href$=uk]').css('color', 'blue');
        });
        $('#anywhere').click(function(){
            $('a[title*=Face]').css('color', 'green');
        });
    });
</script>
<style type="text/css">
    .links{
        color:#b36b00;
        text-decoration:none;
    }
</style>
```

5. Run the page in a browser by pressing F12 or clicking the Run button. The resulting page should resemble Figure 6-1.

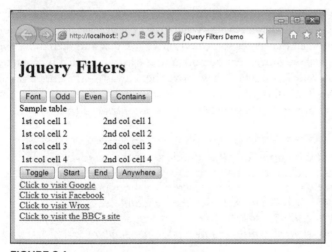

FIGURE 6-1

6. Click each button in turn and examine the changes that take place on the page.

How It Works

You have managed to test quite a few of the filters offered by jQuery here. You added a table and some links to the page. You also added a number of buttons. Each button was bound to a click event handler through its ID selector. In each of those event handlers, different elements were targeted, based on the filters you used. The Font button was given the task of finding all elements on the page through the universal selector and applying an Arial font to them. Notice that a map was passed in to the `.css` method, with two properties having values set at the same time — the `font-family` property and the `font-size` property. The Odd button applied a light green background to every other table row. That might not have worked as you expected — the second and fourth rows were affected, but 2 and 4 are even numbers, so what's going on there? Remember, the collection of elements in a jQuery object has a zero-based index, so as far as jQuery is concerned, the second and fourth rows are at index 1 and 3, respectively. The Even button applied a darker green background to the remaining elements at index 0 and 2. The final table button — *Contains* — located all table cells (`td` elements) that contain the text `"2nd col"` through this syntax: `td:contains(2nd col)`, and applied a pink background color to them.

Moving to the set of hyperlinks, you gave each one a title. The Toggle button applied the style defined in the `.links` declaration in the `<style>` block to all links. If you clicked it again, it would have removed that style. When you clicked the Start button, the filter looked for all links (a elements) with a `title` attribute whose value starts with `"Visit"`. Because they all match this condition, all hyperlinks were turned red. The End button created a matched set of all a elements with a `href` attribute whose value ends with `"uk"`, which is just the link to the BBC's site. The text was set to blue. Finally, the Anywhere button returned a matched set of links with `"Face"` anywhere within the value of the `title` attribute, and the Facebook link turned green.

Event Handling

As your visitor moves about your site's pages, all sorts of client-side *events* occur. As you have already seen, an `onclick` event fires when the user clicks something. When users change the selected item in a list, an `onchange` event fires, as it does when they enter some text into a textbox and then move their mouse away. An event fires even if the visitors move their cursors into the area occupied by a particular element — the `onmouseover` event, and again when they move them away — the `onmouseout` event. jQuery provides a means for handling all these events, and more, unobtrusively. In fact, one of jQuery's main reasons for being is to provide an easy way to utilize *unobtrusive JavaScript*.

 NOTE *Unobtrusive JavaScript is an approach that encourages the removal of JavaScript behavior from the structure of a web page. Remember, HTML is a structural markup language and should only really be used for that purpose — to define the structure and content of a document. In much the same way as you are encouraged to separate the presentation aspects of the document into an external file, you should also look to separate the behavior in a similar way.*

Unobtrusive JavaScript is more than just separation of behavior. It also concerns the management of differing behavior across browsers, and the graceful degradation of pages so that they still function when JavaScript is not available.

Prior to jQuery, you would normally see JavaScript event handlers hard-wired into the element that they relate to:

```
<input type="button"  id="click" onclick="someFunction();" value="Click" />
```

This code ensures that when the button is clicked, a JavaScript function called `someFunction()` is executed. However, this example illustrates behavior being mixed with structure and content. jQuery allows you to bind event handlers in a separate code block very easily. Table 6-3 explores some of the most common event handlers and how they are applied using jQuery.

TABLE 6-3: Common jQuery Event Handlers

HANDLER	DESCRIPTION
`.click()`	Binds an `onClick` event handler to an element (a single click), or triggers the event on an element.
`.hover()`	Binds an `onHover` event handler to an element (the mouse entering and leaving it), or triggers the event on an element.
`.change()`	Binds an `onChange` event handler to an element (the element's `value` being changed and losing focus), or triggers the event on an element.
`.select()`	Binds an `onSelect` event handler to an element (the selection being changed), or triggers the event on an element.
`.submit()`	Binds an `onSubmit` event handler to a form (the form being submitted), or triggers the form to submit.
`.focus()`	Binds an `onFocus` event handler to an element (the element receiving focus), or triggers the event on an element.
`.keypress`	Binds an `onKeyPress` event handler to an element (a key being pressed), or triggers the event on the element.

Effects

There are a number of methods available that affect the visibility of a particular element, or set of elements. Some of them simply toggle the visibility on or off, whereas others apply a transition effect to the element as its visibility is altered. You will look at the most commonly used methods here, including:

➤ show

➤ hide

➤ animate

show()

This method instantly makes an element visible. No animation effects are applied, unless you provide them as a parameter. Valid parameter values are constants like slow, fast, or the number of milliseconds that it should take for the transition to take place.

```
$('h1').show();
$('h1').show('fast');
$('h1').show(900);
```

hide()

This works in the opposite way to show in that it removes the element from the page. It doesn't remove it from the DOM — it effectively has the same effect as applying display: none as a CSS property. Again, you can add some animation by passing an acceptable value as a parameter:

```
$('h1').hide();
$('h1').hide('fast');
$('h1').hide(900);
```

toggle()

The toggle method acts as a combined hide and show method in that it hides or shows the matched elements based on their current state. If they are visible, they will be hidden. If they are hidden, they will become visible. As with hide and show, you can add effects as a parameter:

```
$('h1').toggle();
$('h1').toggle ('fast');
$('h1').toggle (900);
```

fadeIn()

The fadeIn method works in a similar way to show, except that the element reveals itself from being transparent to opaque:

```
$('h1').fadeIn();
$('h1').fadeIn('fast');
$('h1').fadeIn(900);
```

fadeOut()

The fadeOut method works in the opposite way to fadeIn:

```
$('h1').fadeOut();
$('h1').fadeOut('fast');
$('h1').fadeOut(900);
```

fadeToggle()

fadeToggle works in a similar way to toggle, except that the element reveals or hides itself by adjusting its transparency:

```
$('h1').fadeToggle();
$('h1').fadeToggle('fast');
$('h1').fadeToggle(900);
```

Three other effects are worth looking at as well: `slideUp`, `slideDown`, and `slideToggle`. The first of these hides a matched set with a sliding motion, and the second reveals a matched set with the reverse sliding motion. The last of these methods toggles between the two states, depending on the starting point. All three accept the same kind of arguments as the other effects' methods do to control the speed.

In the next exercise, you will respond to a variety of events with jQuery, and apply some effects to elements to explore how these concepts combine.

TRY IT OUT Event Handling and Effects

1. Open the Chapter6 site if you have closed it and add a new page named **effects.cshtml**.

2. Add a reference to jQuery 1.6.2 as in the previous exercises.

3. Add the following code to the `body` element:

```
<h1>Exploring jquery Effects</h1>
<p>Some text in a paragraph element</p>
<div>Click this...</div>
<div>... and watch this</div>
<div>
    <input type="text" value="Type here" /> <span id="text"></span>
</div>
<div id="hidden" style="display:none">
    You started typing some text in the text box!
</div>
```

4. Add the following code to the `head` element, just before the closing `</head>` tag:

```
<script type="text/javascript">
    $(function(){
        $('p').hover(function(){
            $(this).fadeOut(1000).fadeIn(1000);
        });
        $('div:first').click(function(){
            $('div:contains(watch)').fadeToggle('slow');
            $(this).text('Click again!');
        });
        $(':input[type=text]').focus(function(){
            $(this).val('');
        });
        $(':input[type=text]').keypress(function(){
            $('#hidden').slideDown('fast');
        }).keyup(function(){
            $('#text').text($(this).attr('value'));
        });
    });
</script>
```

5. Save the page and run it in the browser. It looks quite dull (see Figure 6-2).

Move your mouse over the paragraph with "Some text in a paragraph element" in it. You should notice the text fade out and back in again. If you move your mouse away, the same thing should happen. Click the page where it says to do so. The text below fades out, and the text you clicked changed. Click again, and the text below fades back in again. Finally start typing in the textbox, and you should see more text appear below, as well as what you typed appear alongside the textbox.

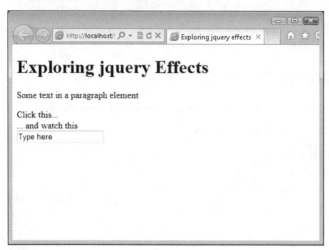

FIGURE 6-2

If your code doesn't produce the same effects, or doesn't seem to do anything at all, check your spelling and especially the arrangement of brackets, braces, and semicolons. They can be confusing when you're just starting to learn to work with jQuery.

How It Works

There isn't a huge amount of JavaScript code here, but it does quite a bit. The first segment locates all paragraph elements and applies an event handler to the hover event. Within that handler, you refer back to the element that raised the event using the `this` keyword and applied a `fadeOut` effect, followed by a `fadeIn` effect via chaining. The reason why the effects occurred twice is that the hover event includes both `mouseenter` and `mouseleave`.

Next you obtained a reference to the first `div` element on the page using the `:first` filter, and applied a click event handler to it. Within the event handler, you locate the `div` with the word `"watch"` in it, which is the one below, and cause it to fade in or out, depending on its current state. You also caused the text in the first `div` to change, again using the `this` keyword. The `text()` method provides a simple way to manipulate textual content.

Good. By now, you should not only have an idea of just how powerful jQuery is, but also how relatively easy it is to use to add a dash of effects and manipulate elements on your page. Chained methods can make things seem complicated, but you can usually unpick things by starting from the end and working backwards. It's time though to look at another side of this extraordinary library, and explore its AJAX functionality.

INTRODUCTION TO AJAX

AJAX (Asynchronous JavaScript and XML) has been around for some time. The core technologies that enable AJAX were introduced by Microsoft to power its web-enabled Outlook functionality — OWA — about ten years ago. However, it wasn't until around 2005 that the technologies gained popular attention and use, with the introduction of Google's web mail tool, Gmail. Prior to that point, the technologies were relatively unknown, and had no "stage name," as it were. The AJAX term was coined and people took notice.

AJAX eliminates the need for users to explicitly force a page request by refreshing a page, or reloading it by pressing the Enter button when focus is on the browser's address bar. In older web-based mail applications, you still have to refresh a page to see if you have new mail. Gmail, Outlook's web program, and a number of other providers use JavaScript running in the browser to make the request for you, and use it again to process the response — updating just part of the page if the response requires it, to show you that you have new mail. Facebook uses the same technology to update its news feeds.

The main technology behind AJAX is a JavaScript object called `XmlHttpRequest`, although Internet Explorer's version is called `XmlHttp`. Using jQuery, you can easily use this object to make HTTP requests asynchronously, once the page has loaded in the browser. The requests are sent in the background, and the `XmlHttpRequest` object is capable of accepting the HTTP response and loading it back into your script, from where you can use it to update just part of the page. You have just seen how easy it is to use jQuery to make changes to any part of the page you like in the last exercise. The benefit of this asynchronous approach is that the application can continue to make requests on your behalf without interrupting what you are doing with the loaded page.

Both the term AJAX and the `XmlHttpRequest` object have "XML" as part of their name, so you might wonder where in fact XML fits into all of this. It doesn't, necessarily. XML is a cross-platform text-based data format, which makes it ideal for transferring data across networks, especially the Internet. And, indeed there are plenty of AJAX-powered applications that use XML as their choice for data exchange between the browser and the server. However, XML is not required. Other data formats are available, such as plaintext, HTML, and *JavaScript Object Notation* (JSON). Plaintext is easy to work with — everyone understands it — and it can be used to pass simple values. HTTP responses can comprise snippets of HTML, which make them very easy to plug into web pages without further processing on the client, and JSON is a lightweight data format that enjoys strong support via a growing number of parsers. ASP.NET Web Pages provides helpers that make working with JSON a trivial exercise. You will see these a bit later.

Speaking of exercises, it's time for you to build your first AJAX-powered web page. This is a simple page, but it will help to illustrate just how asynchronous requests work.

TRY IT OUT Building Your First AJAX Page

1. Open the Chapter6 site if you have closed it, and add a new page named **Timer.cshtml**.

2. Add a reference to jQuery, just as you have in the previous exercises, and amend the title as follows:

```
<title>jQuery Timer</title>
<script src="@Href("~/Scripts/jquery-1.6.2.min.js")" type="text/javascript"></script>
```

3. Add the following CSS declarations just below the reference to jQuery:

```
<style type="text/css">
body {
    font: 80% Arial;
}
span {
    padding: 3px;
    background-color: #ffff80;
    border: 1px dotted black;
}
div {
    padding: 10px;
}
</style>
```

4. Just below the styles and before the closing `</head>` tag, add the following block of JavaScript code:

```
<script type="text/javascript">
    $(function(){
        $.ajaxSetup ({
            cache: false
        });
        setInterval(function() {
            $('span').load('GetTime/');
        }, 1000);
    });
</script>
```

5. Add the following code to the body element:

```
<h1>Ajax Time Demo</h1>
<div>The initial request time was @DateTime.Now</div>
<div>But the AJAX time is <span>@DateTime.Now</span></div>
```

6. Add a new page to the site and name it **GetTime.cshtml**. Remove the default markup and replace it with this one line of code:

```
@DateTime.Now
```

7. Save all your changes, ensure that Timer.cshtml is selected, and click the Run button to launch the page in the default browser. The result should look like Figure 6-3:

Notice how the time in the yellow portion of the page keeps updating each second, but the time from the server doesn't change. Now request the page again by placing your cursor in the browser's address bar and pressing Enter. The time at the top of the page should have changed when the page reloaded, but the time in the yellow box continues to change.

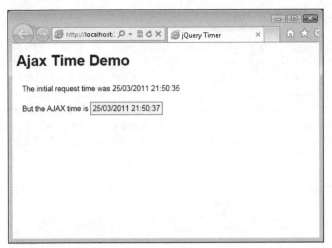

FIGURE 6-3

How It Works

At first, you declared some styles. The key part of the style declaration is the part that applies to the span element. It gives it some padding, a yellow background, and a dotted border so that it is nice and visible. This is the part of the page that is used for asynchronous updates. The next part of the code is the crucial part — the JavaScript. It begins with the shorthand way to ensure that the DOM has fully loaded, and that all elements in the page are available.

Then a jQuery ajaxSetup method is called. This method is used to set the options for all subsequent AJAX requests. The only option that has been configured ensures that the browser doesn't cache previous requests. With most browsers, caching of responses to AJAX requests isn't a problem, but it is in the most popular one — Internet Explorer. What happens is that if the AJAX request is made to the same URL as previous requests, the browser will check its cache for a local copy of the response. If one exists, it gets displayed, even though the new response would have resulted in different output. When you set cache: false, this forces jQuery to append the URL with a numeric value — a timestamp — that changes with each request, which (as far as the browser is concerned) means that the request is different each time. Consequently, the browser cannot find a match for the ever-changing URL in its cache.

The next line of code uses the setInterval method, which is not part of jQuery. It is standard JavaScript. It takes two arguments — the code or function to be executed and an interval in milliseconds. It then causes that code to be executed repeatedly with whatever delay was passed in. In this case, the function passed in will be executed every second. The function that's passed in references the span element and uses the jQuery load method, which is the simplest jQuery AJAX method. It requests the URL passed in — your GetTime.cshtml page, whose job is to return the current server time — and loads the response into the target element. Since it uses AJAX, the GetTime.cshtml page is continually requested every second, and loaded into the page without any full page refreshes or page flicker — giving the impression of a clock in the web page.

Other jQuery AJAX Methods

Before looking at other jQuery AJAX methods, it is worth examining the `load` method a little more. In the example you just saw, you called the method on a particular element on the page, and supplied a URL where the content to be loaded is retrieved from. All that came back was a string value, denoting the current server time. The `load` method can also take a *fragment* as an additional parameter. The fragment identifies a portion of the response to insert into the target element. You would use this if the resource at the URL returned an entire HTML document, for example, but you only wanted to use part of it. If you had not removed the default markup in GetTime.cshtml in the last exercise, it could have looked something like this:

```
<!DOCTYPE html>
<html lang="en">
    <head>
        <meta charset="utf-8" />
        <title></title>
    </head>
    <body>
        <span id="time">@DateTime.Now</span>
    </body>
</html>
```

Notice that the time appears in a `span` element with the ID of `time`. The existing code would still produce the same effect in most browsers, but the entire response would be loaded into the span element in the calling document, resulting in invalid HTML. To load just the fragment (the `span` identified as `time`), the revised `load` method call would look like this:

```
$('span').load('GetTime/ #time');
```

In fact, that would only work in some browsers, as the element together with its content is loaded into the target element, resulting in nested `span` elements in this example.

jQuery.get

The `get` method provides a few more options. You can send data to the URL you are calling as a query string, and specify a function that is called when the response is received. This is useful if you want to perform some processing on the response beyond just lifting out a fragment:

```
$.get('GetTime/', {param: 'somevalue'}, function(data) {
    $('#time').html(data);
    alert('Load was performed.');
});
```

This example causes a GET request to be made asynchronously to GetTime.cshtml with a query string of `?param=somevalue`. When the response is received, it is loaded into the element, and a JavaScript alert message is generated. Note that if you plan to try this in your existing page from the last exercise, you should change the milliseconds value in the `setInterval` method to longer than 1,000. Unless you have very quick hands, you won't be able to close the browser with an alert popping up at one-second intervals.

jQuery.post

The `post` method works in a similar way to `get`, except that it causes a POST request. This is useful for submitting forms using AJAX. There is a very useful jQuery method called `serialize`, which gathers up form field data and creates a request body from them. The following snippet illustrates this being done to a form with the ID of `myForm`, which is then posted to a page called Thanks.cshtml:

```
$.post('Thanks/', $("#myForm").serialize(), function(data) {
    alert('Thank you for completing the form.');
});
```

jQuery.ajax

The previous methods — `load`, `get`, and `post` — are all *shorthand methods*. The final method that you will look at briefly is a *low-level method* that enables you to exercise much finer-grained control over all aspects of the asynchronous request. This is the `ajax` method. The `ajax` method takes two parameters: the URL and a set of key/value pairs of `settings`. The options available to you in `settings` are pretty extensive, and the official documentation explains them all clearly. They include the ability to set the value for the `cache`, which you set in a separate method in the last exercise. They also allow you specify the data type of the response, the content-type of the request, functions on success and error, and so on. Using the `ajax` method, your code would be more verbose, but you have a lot more control. Here is the original script block rewritten using `ajax`:

```
$(function(){
    setInterval(function() {
        $.ajax({
            type: "GET",
            cache: false,
            url: 'GetTime/',
            dataType: 'text',
            contentType: 'text/html',
            success: function(data) {
                $('span').html(data);
                    alert(data);
                },
            error: function(data){
                alert('Something went wrong');
            }
        });
    }, 1000);
});
```

Not all of the settings are required, but this snippet illustrates just how some of them can be used.

JavaScript Object Notation (JSON)

Earlier, you learned that data exchange within AJAX-powered applications can take the form of a number of different formats, not just XML. You have just seen plaintext used, but one of the most popular formats is JavaScript Object Notation (JSON). JSON was inspired by JavaScript, but is independent of the language. One of the major benefits it offers is that it is very lightweight. It has a predictable structure, making it ideal for efficient AJAX communications. It is also human-readable. For example, taking the `Car` class from Chapter 4 as a starting point, this is how you would express a `car` object using JSON:

```
var car = {"Make":"Ford","NumberOfDoors":5,"YearRegistered":2003}
```

This looks very similar to the C# object initializer you saw when objects were introduced in Chapter 4.

So where does JSON come from and why would you use it? First, you can generate it yourself. When you use AJAX in your web application, you will more often than not use it to obtain data from a database. You need to present that data to client-side JavaScript in a way that is as easy to process as possible. JSON and jQuery go together very well, so converting your database results into JSON makes perfect sense. Equally, more and more services expose their data over HTTP as JSON for consumption by third parties.

The JSON Helper

WebMatrix provides a JSON helper. It has a small number of methods that make working with JSON pretty easy. The method you are likely to use most often is `Write`. The `Write` method takes an object as a parameter and attempts to serialize it into a JSON string before outputting it to a `TextWriter` object. The object to be serialized can be a collection or a simple value. In the next exercise, you will see how this works.

TRY IT OUT **Encoding a Collection to JSON**

In this exercise, you will create a collection of `Car` objects, based on the `Car` class you first saw in Chapter 4. You will convert the collection to JSON, and work with the resulting JSON using jQuery.

1. Open the Chapter6 website if you have closed it and add a new folder named **App_Code** to the root of the site.

2. Add a new C# class file to this folder and name it **Cars.cs**. Amend the default code so that it reads as follows:

```csharp
using System;
using System.Collections.Generic;
using System.Web;

/// <summary>
/// Summary description for ClassName
/// </summary>
public class Car
{
    public string Model { get; set; }
    public int NumberOfDoors { get; set; }
    public int YearRegistered { get; set; }
    public string Color { get; set; }
}
```

3. Add a new CSHTML file to the root of the website and name it **GetCars.cshtml**. Remove the default markup and replace it with the following:

```
@{
    var cars = new List<Car>{
        new Car{Model="Focus", YearRegistered=2003, NumberOfDoors=5, Color="Red"},
        new Car{Model="Viper", YearRegistered=2009, NumberOfDoors=2, Color="Blue" },
        new Car{Model="Prius", YearRegistered=2010, NumberOfDoors=4, Color="Silver" },
        new Car{Model="CR-V", YearRegistered=2006, NumberOfDoors=5, Color="White" },
        new Car{Model="Zephyr", YearRegistered=2008, NumberOfDoors=4, Color="Black" },
        new Car{Model="Vector", YearRegistered=2002, NumberOfDoors=4, Color="Green" },
        new Car{Model="A5", YearRegistered=2009, NumberOfDoors=2, Color="Silver" }
    };
    Response.ContentType = "application/json";
    Json.Write(cars, Response.Output);
}
```

4. Add a new CSHTML file to the root folder and name it **ListCars.cshtml**. Add a reference to jQuery as you have done in previous exercises, and add a <script> block just under the reference. Insert the following code:

```
<script src="@Href("~/Scripts/jquery-1.6.2.min.js")"
        type="text/javascript"></script>
<script type="text/javascript">
    $(function(){
        $(':input[type=button]').click(function(){
            $.getJSON("GetCars/", function(cars){
                $.each(cars, function(i, car) {
                    $('#list').append('<p>Model: ' + car.Model + '<br />'
                        + 'Year: ' + car.YearRegistered + '<br />'
                        + 'Doors: ' + car.NumberOfDoors + '<br />'
                        + 'Color: ' + car.Color + '</p>'
                    );
                });
            });
        });
    });
</script>
```

5. Add the following code to the <body> element:

```
<h1>List Cars</h1>
<div>Current time: @DateTime.Now</div>
<div><input type="button" value="Get Cars" /></div>
<div id="list"></div>
```

6. Launch the page and click the button. If all went well, the list of cars that you created in GetCars .cshtml should display, as shown in Figure 6-4.

FIGURE 6-4

How It Works

You created a new class definition for `Car` objects in your Car.cs file. Each object has four properties: `Model`, `NumberOfDoors`, `YearRegistered`, and `Color`. In the GetCars.cshtml file, you created a number of `Car` objects and added them to a collection — a `List<Car>`. The final two lines of code in GetCars .cshtml are the most important for this exercise. The first of those two lines sets the `ContentType` for the HTTP response by specifying the *MIME type* as `application/json`. This tells the browser to expect JSON. The second line uses the `Json.Write` method, which takes the `List<Car>` and serializes it to JSON before rendering the JSON to the HTTP response. The second parameter — `Response.OutPut` — takes care of sending the JSON to the browser, or in the case of an AJAX call, the `XmlHttpRequest` object.

The jQuery code in ListCars.cshtml uses a method that is new to you — `getJSON`. This method loads JSON-encoded data and parses it into a JavaScript object so that you can work with it without having to parse it yourself. The JSON that the jQuery receives looks like this:

```
[
    {"Model":"Focus","NumberOfDoors":5,"YearRegistered":2003,"Color":"Red"},
    {"Model":"Viper","NumberOfDoors":2,"YearRegistered":2009,"Color":"Blue"},
    {"Model":"Prius","NumberOfDoors":4,"YearRegistered":2010,"Color":"Silver"},
```

```
        {"Model":"CR-","NumberOfDoors":5,"YearRegistered":2006,"Color":"White"},
        {"Model":"Zephyr","NumberOfDoors":4,"YearRegistered":2008,"Color":"Black"},
        {"Model":"Vector","NumberOfDoors":4,"YearRegistered":2002,"Color":"Green"},
        {"Model":"A5","NumberOfDoors":2,"YearRegistered":2009,"Color":"Silver"}
    ]
```

It has been formatted for readability here, but it is easy to read. It is an array containing seven objects. Once jQuery has parsed the string, it sees a collection of seven items. You used the each function to iterate over this collection, passing each object in turn into a variable called *car*. In that way, you were able to address the properties of each *car* object and generate some HTML, which you ultimately appended to the div with the ID of list.

The JSON helper has two other methods: Encode and Decode. The Encode method converts an object to a string in JSON format. You might use this method if you want to work with JSON in your server-side code, or you could replace the Json.Write method in the previous exercise with the following:

```
    Response.Write(Json.Encode(cars));
```

The Decode method is useful if you receive JSON-encoded strings in your server-side code, and want to convert them to C# objects that you can work with.

INTRODUCING JQUERY PLUG-INS

You have looked at the basics of jQuery, and you have seen how to use it to manipulate HTML and CSS. You have also used jQuery to add AJAX functionality to a web page, combined with the very useful JSON helpers that come ready-baked in ASP.NET Web Pages. There is one topic still to cover, and that is the jQuery plug-in.

Plug-ins extend jQuery by offering a full range of additional specialist functionality. Pretty much every client-side requirement you can think of is covered by at least one plug-in. Plug-ins can be developed by just about anyone. There are currently over 4,000 plug-ins registered on the jQuery plug-in site (http://plugins.jquery.com/). Because they are contributed by anyone who cares to bother authoring one, plug-ins can vary in quality and documentation. If you want to display images in a slide show, for example, there is no shortage of options. Similarly, there are a range of plug-ins for managing forms, drag-and-drop, animations, displaying data in grids, providing menus, and so on. Many people take their contributions to the jQuery plug-in eco-system very seriously, and author a range of plug-ins. They maintain these components, updating them as new versions of jQuery are released, and maintain clear and comprehensive documentation. I suggest that you look around for a range of options when you want something extra from jQuery, and try out a number of alternative plug-ins before deciding which one you want to commit to your site.

The plug-in that you are going to take a closer look at in this section is the Validation plug-in. It was developed by Jörn Zaefferer, who is one of the jQuery Project Team members. Jörn also has a number of plug-ins available, and more details can be found at his site: http://bassistance.de/jquery-plugins/. Needless to say, Jörn's plug-ins are of the highest quality — so much so that Microsoft ships the Validation plug-in as part of the default template for ASP.NET Web Forms and MVC sites.

The Validation plug-in provides client-side form validation. You will remember from the previous chapter that client-side validation is a courtesy to your users. It saves them from having to wait for a round trip to the server to discover that they have entered the wrong data, or missed some required piece of information.

You will extend the Classifieds site's form to include client-side validation using the Validation plug-in. First, you need to get hold of the Validation plug-in file. The current version at the time of writing (1.8.1) is included in the download that comes with this chapter, but you can also make sure you get the latest version by visiting `http://bassistance.de/jquery-plugins/jquery-plugin-validation/`. You can also find a wealth of documentation and samples there too. Alternatively, you can reference one of the Microsoft CDN hosted versions. The most efficient download is the minified version, which can be found at `http://ajax.aspnetcdn.com/ajax/jquery.validate/1.8.1/jquery.validate.min.js`. Validate is one of very few plug-ins to have made it onto the Microsoft CDN.

TRY IT OUT Adding Client-Side Validation to the Classifieds Form

There are two ways to add client-side validation to forms using the Validate plug-in. One is to use jQuery code to add rules and messages. The other is to use HTML attributes to apply metadata. In this exercise, you will use jQuery code. It keeps the HTML cleaner, and it is easier to separate the JavaScript from the page by placing it in a separate file if you prefer.

1. Open the Classifieds site within WebMatrix. Bring the _Layout.cshtml file up in the Files workspace. It's in the Shared folder.

2. You need to add a reference to the Validate JavaScript file as well as the main jQuery file. How you do this will vary depending on whether you have a copy of the files available or whether you prefer to use the CDN hosted versions. If you want to use local copies, create a folder and name it **Scripts**, place the .js files there, and add the following lines just below the reference to the style sheet:

```
<head>
    <meta charset="utf-8" />
    <title>@Page.Title</title>
    <script src="@Href("~/Scripts/jquery-1.6.2.min.js")"
            type="text/javascript"></script>
    <script src="@Href("~/Scripts/jquery.validate.min.js")"
            type="text/javascript"></script>
    <link href="@Href("~/Content/StyleSheet.css")"
          rel="stylesheet" type="text/css" />
</head>
```

If you are using the CDN version, the reference will look like this:

```
<script src="http://ajax.aspnetcdn.com/ajax/jQuery/jquery-1.6.2.min.js"
 type="text/javascript"></script>

<script src=" http://ajax.aspnetcdn.com/ajax/jquery.validate/
1.8.1/jquery.validate.min.js"
 type="text/javascript"></script>
```

Whichever method you use, make sure that plug-ins are referenced after the main jQuery file.

3. Add the following code just below the existing Razor code block at the top of the page:

```
<script type="text/javascript">
$(document).ready(function(){
    $('#post-advert').validate({
        rules: {
            title: {
                required: true,
                maxlength: 200
            },
            description: 'required',
            duration: 'required',
            condition: 'required',
            price: {
                required: true,
                number: true
            },
            email: {
                required: true,
                email: true
            },
        },
        messages:{
            title: {
                required: ' *You must provide a title',
                maxlength: ' *Your title must not exceed 200 characters'
            },
            description: ' *You must provide a description',
            duration: ' *You must indicate a duration',
            condition: ' *You must specify the condition of your item',
            price: {
                required: ' *You must provide a price',
                number: ' *Your price must be a valid number'
            },
            email: {
                required: ' *You must provide your email address',
                email: ' *You must provide a valid email address'
            },
        },
        errorPlacement: function(error, element) {
            if ( element.is(":radio") ) {
                error.prependTo( $('#radio-error') );
            }
            else {
                error.insertAfter(element);
            }
        }
    });
});
</script>
```

4. Between the As New radio button and the `Html.ValidationMessage` helper, add a `span` as shown here:

```
<input type="radio" id="condition" name="condition" value="As New"
@Helpers.Checked("condition","As New") />As New
<span id="radio-error"></span>
@Html.ValidationMessage("condition")
```

5. Open StyleSheet.css in the Content folder and add the following style declarations to it:

```
.error{
    color:red;
}
input.error, textarea.error, select.error{
    border: 1px solid red;
    background-color: #ffbfbf;
    color: black;
}
```

6. Save your changes and, making sure that Sell.cshtml is selected in the Files workspace, run the page in the browser. If you attempt to submit the empty form, the resulting display should look just like Figure 6-5. You should also notice that the page did not post back.

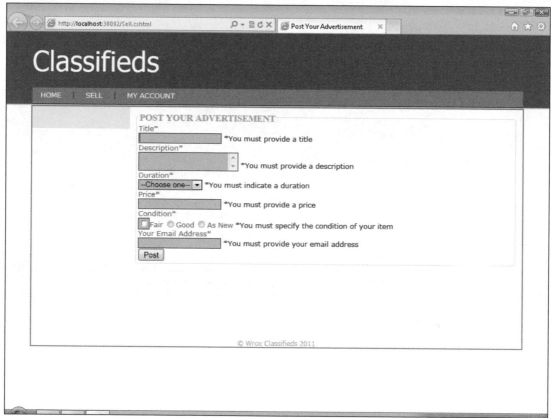

FIGURE 6-5

How It Works

When you use jQuery plug-ins, you should always reference them *after* you have referenced the jQuery core library. That is because JavaScript is executed from the top down, and since plug-ins depend on the core library, the core library has to be processed prior to the code in the plug-in. All you needed to do to get the plug-in to work was add some JavaScript code. You made a couple of other alterations, but they were not essential.

Let's examine the JavaScript code in more detail. The Validate plug-in needs to know which form it is supposed to act on, so the first method you called — the validate() method — was called on the form using its ID. The Validate plug-in works with *rules* and *messages* primarily. A rule is applied to a form element, and consists of a number of methods. The full list of methods is available in the documentation, but the main ones you have used are required, maxlength, and email. The required method states that the item must have a value supplied for it. maxlength determines the maximum number of acceptable characters permitted, and the email method ensures that the value supplied is in a valid e-mail format.

Each rule has a corresponding message, which is the customized text to be displayed if any of the rule options are not satisfied. If you do not specify your own messages, Validate will display default ones. By default, all messages are displayed after the first occurrence of the form field to which they are attached. In the case of the condition radio buttons, you have added a span after the last one. This is where you want the message to appear rather than having it insert itself after the first radio button. The errorPlacement option allows you to specify where exactly you would like a particular error message to appear.

Finally, you added some new class-based CSS rules to the style sheet. However, you have not applied these classes anywhere, so why did you add them? One of the really neat features of the Validate plug-in is that it automatically applies CSS classes to elements when rules are breached. It is always a good idea, when using plug-ins, to check to see if they apply CSS styles to elements and what they are called, otherwise you could end up with unrelated HTML elements being styled in a way that didn't expect.

PRACTICAL TIPS WHEN WORKING WITH JQUERY

jQuery is an extraordinarily powerful library, especially when combined with the huge range of plug-ins available. To get the most out of jQuery, follow this advice:

➤ Build your jQuery code in small steps — testing as you go. This will make it easier to establish when the code breaks, so you don't need to fiddle around with perfectly good code to try to fix errors. I have often used a blank HTML file to start with, just to prove a concept. If the code works there, it is usually quite simple to transfer it to a working web page.

➤ Browse the documentation at the jQuery site and familiarize yourself with the methods and options. Look at the examples and demos provided there, especially the source code.

➤ Look for ready-built jQuery code in the form of plug-ins for more advanced effects and DOM manipulation. It is a lot easier to use someone else's tried and tested code than to start from scratch yourself.

➤ Be careful about how many plug-ins and effects you add to your site. Don't stuff a lot of these into your pages just because you think they look kind of cool. Have a very good reason for using any of them and keep in mind the primary purpose of your site. Does the plug-in or effect you are considering using help deliver on that, or just add some unnecessary pizzazz?

SUMMARY

This chapter has given you an introduction to the most popular JavaScript library — jQuery. You learned that jQuery can be used to manipulate HTML elements in the browser and to create client-side effects such as animation. You learned how to obtain the library, and how to make it available to your pages, either by including the script with your files, or referencing a CDN hosted version.

The first part of the chapter introduced you to the basics behind the jQuery syntax, and showed you how to use selectors to obtain a reference to elements within the DOM. From there you were able to manipulate those elements, controlling their appearance and applying effects to them in response to events, for which you created handlers.

The second part of the chapter examined AJAX. You saw how asynchronous requests can be controlled through a number of jQuery methods, and the resulting response manipulated for updating the DOM. You also saw how the built-in JSON helper can prepare data so that it is in a format that jQuery natively understands.

In the final section, you saw how to use a plug-in in conjunction with the jQuery library to add some client-side validation to your form.

EXERCISES

1. Name two ways to incorporate jQuery in your layout pages. What is the difference between the two?

2. Which are the three most common ways to reference elements using jQuery?

3. What does the first "A" stand for in AJAX? What does it mean?

Answers to the Exercises can be found in the Appendix.

▶ **WHAT YOU LEARNED IN THIS CHAPTER**

TOPIC	KEY CONCEPTS
jQuery	A popular open source JavaScript framework library.
Selectors	A special syntax for referencing elements in the DOM.
DOM	The Document Object Model, which is an API for representing and accessing elements within a web page.
Matched set	A collection of elements returned from a jQuery selector.
Method chaining	The practice whereby method calls are appended to each other using dot notation to ensure that the result of the preceding method acts as input to the next method.
AJAX	The use of JavaScript to make asynchronous HTTP requests and manage their response.
JSON	JavaScript Object Notation, which is a data format designed along the lines of the JavaScript language structures.
Plug-in	A third-party library written to extend the functionality of the core jQuery libraries.

7

Packages

WHAT YOU WILL LEARN IN THIS CHAPTER:

➤ What packages are

➤ How to use the Package Manager

➤ The ASP.NET Web Helpers Library

➤ The FileUpload helper in detail

➤ Other notable packages

The .NET Framework is extraordinarily extensive. It contains thousands of classes that provide a huge range of functionality to cover simple and common programming needs. On top of the *Base Class Library* (the BCL), people have created thousands of *Open Source* projects to cater to more complex tasks. These libraries cover a wide range of functionality, such as generating PDF files, error logging, data access, blogging frameworks, and so on. They have been designed to save you time because you don't have to write your own code, and they are completely free. However, locating and installing such libraries can be difficult. There are a number of Open Source repositories where you might find them, or you might stumble across the source code or libraries on someone's website in a dimly lit corner of the Internet. Once you find what you are looking for, you need to download it, unzip it, figure out how to incorporate it into your application, and then configure it to get it to work. You might also find that what you downloaded relies on other libraries to work properly. These also need to be located, downloaded, and installed — sometimes in a particular order — to ensure that the entire "package" functions correctly.

INTRODUCING "PACKAGES"

Other development frameworks have offered an easy way to manage such libraries for a while, and in the middle of 2010, Microsoft joined the party with the launch of *NuGet* — a package management system for .NET developers. A package consists of a library, or a group of libraries and specially constructed instructions on how the library should be installed, and what its dependencies are. Open Source developers have been strongly encouraged to submit their projects to NuGet, and Microsoft has developed tools for Visual Studio and Visual Web Developer Express that provide integration with the NuGet repository. At the same time, Microsoft was working on the development of WebMatrix and decided to build integration with NuGet too, in the form of the ASP.NET Web Pages Package Manager. This system makes it really easy for you to find optional helpers and other components that you can make use of. Not only that, but it manages all of the installation and configuration work for you — including identifying and locating dependencies — so all you have to do is choose what you want, and let the Package Manager take care of things for you.

How to Use the Package Manager

The NuGet repository is hosted online, so you need an Internet connection to be able to access it. After you overcome that hurdle, the process is very simple. It is based on the assumption that you need specific packages for each application, which means you do not have to save code all over your machine for future use in other applications. Consequently, you access the Package Manager from within the application you are currently working on. So how do you do that?

TRY IT OUT Accessing the Package Manager

1. Create a new site within WebMatrix from the Empty Site template and name it **Packages**. Add a file named **Default.cshtml** to the site. You do not need to change the default markup in this file.

2. Switch to the Site workspace. Find the ASP.NET Web Pages Administration option in the content pane and click it. This should bring up the administration page in your browser, as shown in Figure 7-1.

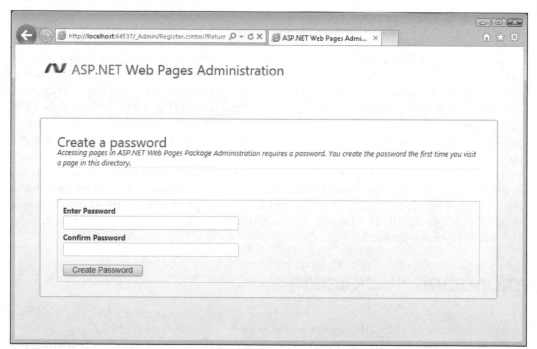

FIGURE 7-1

3. Since this is the first time you have accessed the administration area within this site, you are asked to create a password. Enter a password into the first box, and then re-enter it in the second box. Make sure you remember the password you have used. Then click the Create Password button. You should be presented with a page in your browser that looks like Figure 7-2.

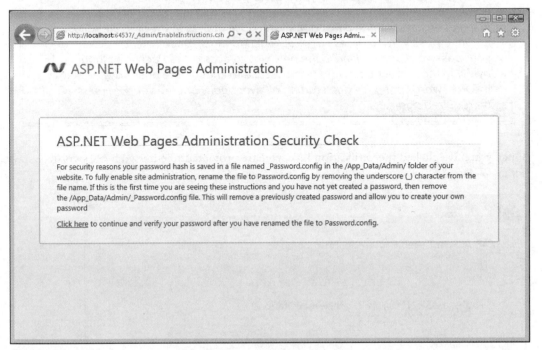

FIGURE 7-2

4. At this point, you have to move back to the Packages site in WebMatrix. If you select the Files workspace, you can see that an App_Data folder has been added to your site, and inside that is an Admin folder. The Admin folder contains a file called _Password .config (see Figure 7-3). This file contains an encrypted value.

You must rename the file to remove the leading underscore, so that it is called simply **Password.config**. Once you have done that, return to your browser and click the link to verify that you have renamed the file.

FIGURE 7-3

NOTE *Once a site has some files in it, you can access the Administration page by browsing to an address with _Admin in it, such as* www.mydomain.com/_Admin. *This could potentially open up a security hole, in that if you have not config-ured Administration access, anyone could do so once your site is in production. Forcing you to rename _Password.config is an important security feature. It helps to ensure that the only people who have access to the website's files can create a password to access the Package Manager. Once you have created your password and verified it, the only way to access the Package Manager is by using the correct password. It is possible to change the password by deleting the Password.config file and starting all over again, but the verification step will be required again.*

5. Once you have clicked the verification link, you are prompted to enter your password again (see Figure 7-4).

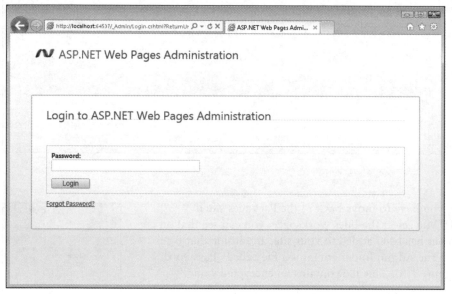

FIGURE 7-4

6. You are taken to the Package Manager, which at first defaults to showing you installed packages (see Figure 7-5). Of course, there are none at this point.

7. You can browse available packages by clicking the link as shown in Figure 7-5 or by selecting an option from the drop-down list. The Default listing will show all packages that have been identi-fied as specifically useful to ASP.NET Web Pages development. Optionally, you can choose to view Default (All) using the drop-down list. This will result in all NuGet packages being shown. At the time of writing, this numbered over 1,000, and was growing at a rapid rate. A lot of these pack-ages provide very advanced functionality that would not be appropriate in a typical Web Pages application. That's not to say you wouldn't use some packages outside of the core Web Pages listing, but the focus in this book will be the packages in the Default listing.

8. Locate ASP.NET Web Helpers Library 1.15 in the list, and click the Install button. After a moment, depending on your connection speed, you should receive a message saying that the package has been successfully installed (see Figure 7-6).

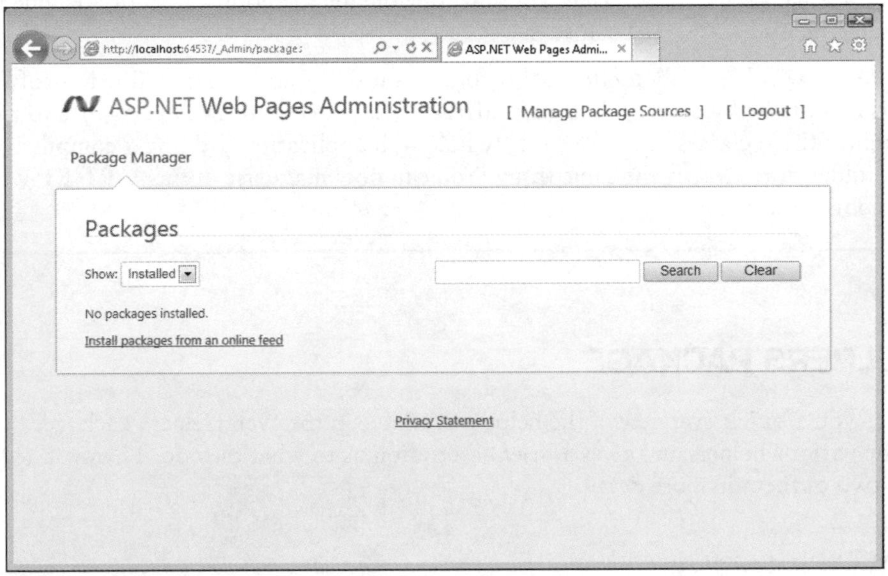

FIGURE 7-5

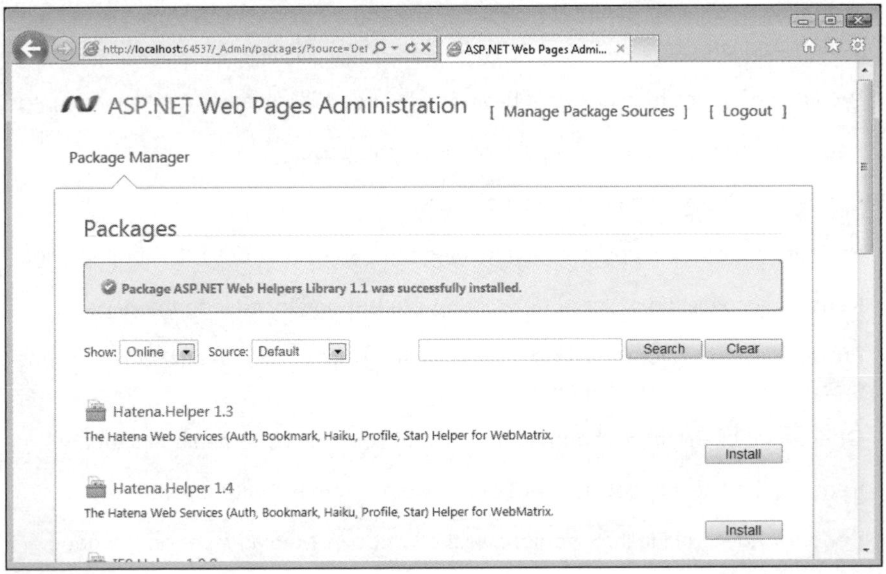

FIGURE 7-6

How It Works

Easy, isn't it? But what actually happened? If you take a look at your site folders now (you probably need to right-click and choose Refresh), you will see that a new folder has been added to App_Data called packages. In that folder is a subfolder named after the package you just downloaded, containing a file with a .nupkg extension. This file is a compressed file, which contains details of the package. If you are really interested in how a package is constructed, you can copy the file to another location, rename it so that it has a .zip extension, and extract the contents.

You also have another new folder, called *bin*. In this folder you will find a file called Microsoft.Web .Helpers.dll. This is a *compiled assembly*. You have already seen how adding C# class files to the App_Code folder makes these classes available to the whole web application. Adding a compiled assembly to the bin folder does exactly the same thing. You can now make use of the ASP.NET Web Helpers Library in your application.

THE WEB HELPERS PACKAGE

This section gives you a quick overview of the helpers available in the Web Helpers Package. Table 7-1 lists the various helpers and gives a brief description as to what they do. Then you will examine one or two of them in more detail.

TABLE 7-1: ASP.NET Web Helpers Library

HELPER	DESCRIPTION
Analytics	The Analytics helper provides a shortcut method for including Google Analytics, Yahoo Analytics, and StatCounter code in your web pages.
Bing	Provides methods that include a basic or advanced Bing search box on your page.
FileUpload	Renders one or more file upload controls on the page.
GamerCard	Renders an Xbox gaming tag on the page.
Gravatar	Renders a globally recognized avatar (see http://gravatar.com) on the page.
LinkShare	Renders a collection of social networking site buttons for sharing the page.
ReCaptcha	Provides methods for rendering and managing reCAPTCHA verification for forms (see www.google.com/recaptcha).
Themes	Offers a mechanism for changing the style of your site by switching its theme.
Twitter	Renders the latest tweets from a Twitter user or from a Twitter search result.
Video	Renders video via Flash, Silverlight, or the Windows Media Player on the page.

A number of these helpers require some sort of account creation before you can use them. For example, you need to register accounts with Google Analytics or Yahoo Analytics before you can add code to your page via the Analytics helper. ReCaptcha also requires a valid account. On the other hand, there are a number of helpers here that you can use without any kind of account set up.

Using the Twitter Helper

The Twitter helper is one of the easiest to use without registering an account. It offers two methods: `Profile` and `Search`. The `Profile` method takes a Twitter username. The Twitter username for the Wrox parent company is `WileyTech`, so if you wanted to display the most recent tweets from `WileyTech`, this is how you would use the Twitter helper to do it:

```
@Twitter.Profile("WileyTech")
```

From that single line of code, a neatly designed box appears on your page (see Figure 7-7), which displays the four most recent tweets from Wiley's Twitter stream.

FIGURE 7-7

The Search method is just as easy to use. Instead of passing in a Twitter username, you pass in a search phrase:

```
@Twitter.Search("WebMatrix")
```

This results in a slightly different display (see Figure 7-8), where the tweets are constantly updated and the content of the rendered box are looped.

FIGURE 7-8

You may decide that the default colors, or total number of tweets displayed, do not suit your purposes. No problem! The Twitter helpers have optional parameters within their methods that can be changed. Some of the more commonly used parameters are detailed in Table 7-2.

TABLE 7-2: Common Twitter Helper Parameters

PARAMETER	DEFAULT VALUE	DESCRIPTION
width	250	Width of panel in pixels
height	300	Height of panel in pixels
backgroundShellColor	#333333	Background color of top and bottom
shellColor	#ffffff	Color of text in top and bottom
tweetsBackgroundColor	#000000	Background color of tweet sections
tweetsColor	#ffffff	Font color for tweets

PARAMETER	DEFAULT VALUE	DESCRIPTION
tweetsLinksColor	#4aed05	Color of links in tweets
numberOfTweets	4	Total number of tweets to display
scrollbar	false	Show a scroll bar if needed
timestamp	true	Show the time the tweet was made
avatars	false	Show tweeters' avatars

All of these parameters are available in both the `Profile` and `Search` methods. If you wanted to change the width of the panel to 300 pixels, and show avatars, you simply need to pass your revised values to these parameters:

```
@Twitter.Search("WebMatrix", width: 300, avatars: true)
```

Adding Video to Your Pages

The Video helper manages a number of different types of video files via a selection of players. The Flash player will manage Adobe Flash (.swf files), whereas the Windows Media Player and the Silverlight player cater to a number of formats, including Windows Media Video (.wmv files), Windows Media Audio (.wma files), MP3 and 4, and Silverlight packages (.xap files).

Flash

Adobe Flash is currently the most popular video format for web pages. It is certainly the preeminent format for rich media advertising, such as banner ads. When you use the Video helper to render Flash files, the helper renders the required HTML `<object>` and `<embed>` tags for you. Both of these tags have a number of attributes, which are defined at Adobe's site.

(see `http://kb2.adobe.com/cps/127/tn_12701.html`). Each of the attributes is represented by optional parameters to the helper's method call. Only the path to the source file is required, so the simplest method call to a file named example.swf in a folder called Video would look like this:

```
@Video.Flash("Video/example.swf")
```

Since the parameters are optional, you specify values for the ones you want to set by naming them. The following code sets the width and height of the Flash player:

```
@Video.Flash("Video/example.swf", width: "200", height: "200")
```

Windows Media Player

Windows Media Player can handle a number of video and audio file formats. Just like the Flash helper, the MediaPlayer helper renders the required `<object>` tags. Again, the path to the media file is required, but all other parameters are optional:

```
@Video.MediaPlayer("Video/sample.wmv", volume: 5, width: "200", height: "200")
```

Silverlight

Silverlight is Microsoft's entry into the Rich Media space, and competes to a large extent with Adobe's Flash. When you use the Silverlight helper, three values are required — the path to the file and the width and height that the video should display at:

```
@Video.Silverlight("Video/sample.xap", "200", "200")
```

The FileUpload Helper

If you want to allow visitors to upload images to a gallery or for an avatar, or a document containing their resume for example, or any other kind of file, you can use the FileUpload helper. When rendered, FileUpload presents itself in different ways according to the browser (see Figures 7-9 through 7-13).

FIGURE 7-9

FIGURE 7-10

Users are typically presented with two buttons — one that they use to locate a file on their machine, and another to transfer that file to the web server.

FIGURE 7-11

FIGURE 7-12

Some browsers also present a text box where the filename will appear when one has been selected.

Others replace the default text, which indicates that no file has been selected, with the name of the file and an icon denoting the file type when one has been chosen (see Figures 7-14 and 7-15). By default, FileUpload also renders a hyperlink with the text Add More Files.

FIGURE 7-13

How It Works

FileUploads are one of those form elements that get passed to the server whether they contain values or not (unlike checkboxes, if you remember from Chapter 5). In the previous exercise, you assessed whether the form had been submitted using the IsPost property of the page. In this example, you determined whether the form had been submitted by examining the Request.Files collection's Count property, which is greater than zero (0) when a form has been submitted.

Having established that the form had indeed been submitted, you created a for loop that iterates the Request.Files collection. Don't forget that the value of the Count property will always result in one more than the highest index in a collection because indexes start at zero. This is why your loop executes only while the iterator is less than the value of the Count property. The ContentLength property of the current file is checked on each iteration. This returns the size of the current file in bytes. If it is zero, there is no file. If there are one or more bytes, a file exists and you used the now familiar code to save that to the Uploads folder. As each file is saved, its name is appended to a string as a list item within an unordered list, which is displayed in place of the initial message.

 WARNING *By default, the maximum file size that can be uploaded is 4MB. This is not a restriction per file. It is applied by the ASP.NET framework to the total size of the HTTP Request, and exceeding this limit will result in an exception message to the effect that the maximum request length has been exceeded. You might wonder why this limit has been put in place. It's there as a precaution against denial of service (DOS) attacks, whereby a malicious user can continuously upload huge files, swamping your web server.*

There will be times when you know that your visitors need to legitimately upload larger files. If this is the case, you can alter the default limit to any that you want by adding a web.config file to your site if you do not have one already, and adding a new configuration section within the system.web section:

```
<system.web>
  <compilation debug="true" targetFramework="4.0"/>
  <httpRuntime maxRequestLength="4096"/>
</system.web>
```

The section is httpRuntime, which has a maxRequestLength attribute. The default value of the attribute is 4096KB, or 4MB. You can alter this to a more suitable value. For example, if you wanted to increase the total to 10MB, the new value you would apply to maxRequestLength would be 10240.

As of version 7, IIS also applies a validation check against HTTP request lengths, and will not even pass requests to ASP.NET to process if they exceed 26.8MB. So, by default, if the total size of the request exceeds this limit, the result is an error message from IIS (not ASP.NET).

Other Notable Helpers

That's about it for the FileUpload helper. The next chapter covers working with files in server-side code in a lot more depth, as well as specifically working with images. Before that, the final section in this chapter summarizes some other notable packages available to you.

Visual Basic Site Templates

All of the site templates that ship with WebMatrix are also available as packages. These include the Calendar template, Bakery template, and the Starter Site template. More interestingly, Visual Basic versions can be downloaded and used. If you would like to compare the Visual Basic language with C# — especially in terms of how the language works with the Razor syntax rules — these samples provide an excellent starting point for study.

BBCode Parser and Helper

At the time of writing, this package was at version 0.3, which means that it has not reached a stage where it is thought to be stable enough for a full release. Version 1.0 is conventionally used to indicate that published software is ready for production use. Nevertheless, the BBCode package allows you to get around the problems associated with request validation discussed in Chapter 5, by allowing users to supply substitute tokens (such as [b]…[/b] for bold text) to indicate the HTML they would like applied to their text, rather than including valid HTML tags in their form post.

Facebook Helper

This is a great package if you want to apply popular Facebook widgets to your site. It comes with a clear set of reference documentation, which is downloaded into a specially created Docs folder. You can add Facebook comments boxes and simple Like buttons to your pages. At the time of writing, this helper is downloaded as a C# source code file into App_Code, which allows you the opportunity to see how it was assembled. The source code can serve as a great study aid for any student, as well as providing you with the opportunity to extend it if you want it to do things differently.

PayPal Helper

This is another great utility that allows you to very easily incorporate PayPal functionality into your site. With the minimum amount of code, you can develop a fully functioning payment system whereby users can pay for items using their PayPal accounts.

Twitter Helper

Not to be confused with the Twitter helpers in the main Microsoft.Web.Helpers package, which you learned about earlier, this package offers a wider range of Twitter widgets, such as Follow Me and Tweet buttons. Having said that, it also includes the source code in C# for the Search and Profile helpers you read about earlier.

SUMMARY

This chapter introduced you to the notion of packages within ASP.NET Web Pages. You learned that packages are libraries of code that offer solutions to common programming problems. They are accessible via the built-in Web Pages Package Manager, which you learned how to access from the Site Manager content pane within WebMatrix.

There are two kinds of packages at the moment: those that have been identified as being specifically useful to Web Pages sites and those that offer more complex or esoteric functionality. The first type of package is listed online under the Default option, and the second can be found by selecting Default — All. You saw how easy it is to download and install a package by clicking its Install button.

One of the most useful package helpers is FileUpload, and you saw how to obtain it as part of the ASP.NET Web Helpers Library and how to make use of it to allow users to upload a number of files. You also learned how to save the uploaded files to the file system. The chapter concluded with an overview of other notable packages that might help your development.

EXERCISES

1. Which two things are required to ensure that a file can be uploaded via a form?

2. What is the default size limit for uploaded files and how can you adjust it?

Answers to the Exercises can be found in the Appendix.

▶ **WHAT YOU LEARNED IN THIS CHAPTER**

TOPIC	KEY CONCEPTS
Package	A downloadable library of code designed to cater to specific requirements.
NuGet	The framework behind the Web Pages Package Management System.
ASP.NET Web Helpers Library	A package containing commonly required functionality as helpers.
FileUpload helper	Renders an `input type="file"` optionally with form tags set to the correct `enctype` for transmitting files.
maxRequestLength	A value that limits the total size of files that can be uploaded. The default limit is 4096KB, or 4MB.

Working with Files and Images

➤ How to create and modify files and folders

➤ Generating a Google sitemap

➤ How to use the WebImage helper

In the last chapter, you learned how to save text files that your users choose to upload to your site. There is a lot more to learn about files within ASP.NET Web Pages, which is why the topic deserves a chapter of its own. You can, for example, generate your own text files, or modify existing files. You can copy them and delete them. You will learn how to do this in the next few pages. You will also learn about other types of files that you can work with, and a number of ways to deliver those to your users. You will specifically learn how to create one type of XML file — a Google sitemap. Then, in the second part of the chapter, you will work in more detail with image files by using a helper specifically created to simplify these kinds of tasks.

CREATING AND MODIFYING FILES

There are three primary classes that help you work with files and folders. You met one in the previous chapter — the `Path` class. The others are the `File` class and the `Directory` class, which, like the `Path` class, are used to house a number of related utility methods. None of the classes is intended to be instantiated directly. All of the methods exposed by these classes are static methods.

There are a huge number of file types that you might want to work with when developing your Web Pages application. Any text-based file can be managed easily with the `File` class. Other file types may require additional libraries. For example, there is nothing within the .NET Framework that helps you work with Portable Document Format (PDF) files. There are third-party libraries available from the Package Manager. Select Default - All as your source option and search for PDF. The latest Microsoft Office documents are based on the OpenXML format, and although it may not be the easiest API to work with, Microsoft has produced a Software Developers Kit (SDK) for dealing with OpenXML. These APIs and libraries are not the focus of this chapter. You will look instead at working with text-based files.

There are a number of ways to create a text file using methods from the `File` class. The easiest way is to use the `File.Create` method:

```
File.Create("C:\file.txt");
```

This will create or overwrite a file at the specified location with the specified name. Generally, however, you would generate a file only if you wanted to add some content to it. There are a couple of methods that will create a file, if one doesn't already exist, and then add text to it: `File.WriteAllText` and `File.AppendAllText`. The main difference between the two is that `AppendAllText` will add text to an existing file each time it is called, whereas `WriteAllText` will overwrite the file, if it already exists. In the following exercise, you will see how these two methods differ in practice.

TRY IT OUT Creating Files

1. Start by creating a new site based on the Empty Site template, and name the site **chapter8**.

2. Add a folder to the site called **Files**, and then add a new CSHTML file to the site — in the root folder — and name it **WriteFile.cshtml**.

3. Add the following HTML to the `<body>` element:

```
<form method="post" action="">
    <div>Enter a name:</div>
    <div><input type="text" name="name" /></div>
    <div><input type="submit" value="Submit" /></div>
</form>
```

4. Add the following code block to the top of the file:

```
@{
    var location = Server.MapPath("/Files");
    var filename = "form.txt";
    var path = Path.Combine(location, filename);
    if(IsPost){
        File.WriteAllText(path, Request["name"] + Environment.NewLine);
    }
}
```

5. Run the page in the browser and enter several names into the textbox, submitting the form after each one. Then have a look at the Files folder in your site and open the form.txt file that was created. You may need to right-click on the site name and click Refresh to see the newly created file. You should see only the most recent name that you submitted via the form appear in the text file.

6. Modify the code in the code block at the top so that it looks like:

```
@{
    var location = Server.MapPath("/Files");
    var filename = "form2.txt";
    var path = Path.Combine(location, filename);
```

```
    if(IsPost){
        File.AppendAllText(path, Request["name"] + Environment.NewLine);
    }
}
```

7. Run the page in the browser and enter a number of names again. Once you have entered several names, check the Files folder again for the new form2.txt file. You should see this time that each name you entered has been written to the file on a separate line.

How It Works

The form you created should be self-explanatory by now, so the focus will be on the code block you added in Step 4. One of the first things to note is the use of a utility method from the `Path` class that you have not seen yet — `Path.Combine`. This is a very handy method that generates valid paths from strings according to the platform that the code is being run on. It will also throw an error if you attempt to include invalid path characters as part of any of the strings you want to combine into a path.

In the first example, you used the `File.WriteAllText` method, which as you learned earlier, overwrites a file if it already exists. This is why — regardless of how many names you entered into the form — you only saw the last one you entered in the file. Each time you submitted the form, the previous submission was overwritten. When you changed the code to make use of the `File.AppendAllText` method in Step 6, you saw how each name that you submitted via the form was added to the previous names.

CREATING FOLDERS

The `Directory` class contains utility methods for working with folders, including methods to create, delete, move, and copy folders. In the next exercise, you will create a new folder for each name that you enter into the form and create a text file for each folder.

TRY IT OUT Creating Folders

1. Add a new folder to the site you created in the previous exercise and name it **Folders**.

2. Add a new file to the site. Name the file **CreateFolder.cshtml**.

3. Add the following to a code block at the top of the file:

```
@{
    var location = Server.MapPath("/Folders/");
    var foldername = Guid.NewGuid().ToString();
    var path = Path.Combine(location, foldername);
    if(IsPost){
        if(!Request["name"].IsEmpty()){
            Directory.CreateDirectory(path);
            var file = Path.Combine(path, Request["name"] + ".txt");
            var text = Request["name"] + ": " + DateTime.Now;
            File.AppendAllText(file, text);
        }
    }
}
```

4. Add the same form to the `<body>` element as you added to **CreateFile.cshtml** in the previous exercise:

```
<form method="post" action="">
    <div>Enter a name:</div>
    <div><input type="text" name="name" /></div>
    <div><input type="submit" value="Submit" /></div>
</form>
```

5. Run the page in the browser and enter a number of names into the form, one at a time as in the last exercise, submitting the form with each name. Check the contents of the Folders directory in your site after you have run through a few names. It should contain a number of new folders similar to the ones visible in Figure 8-1.

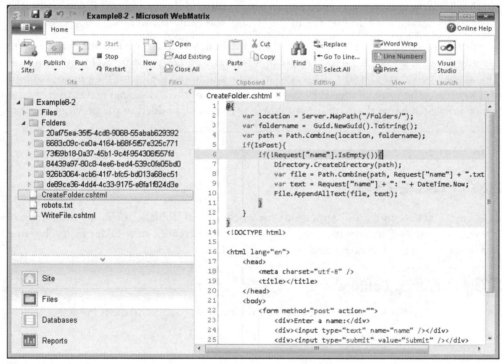

FIGURE 8-1

6. Make the following alteration to the code block at the top of the CreateFolder.cshtml file, adding the extra line at the end:

```
@{
    var location = Server.MapPath("/Folders/");
    var foldername =  Guid.NewGuid().ToString();
    var path = Path.Combine(location, foldername);
```

```
    if(IsPost){
        if(!Request["name"].IsEmpty()){
            Directory.CreateDirectory(path);
            var file = Path.Combine(path, Request["name"] + ".txt");
            var text = Request["name"] + ": " + DateTime.Now;
            File.AppendAllText(file, text);
        }
    }
    var folders = new DirectoryInfo(location);
}
```

7. Add the following code just after the form and before the closing `</body>` tag:

```
@foreach(var folder in folders.GetDirectories()){
    @:Folder: <strong>@folder.Name</strong><br />
    foreach(var file in folder.GetFiles()){
        @:File: <a href="/Folders/@folder.Name/@file.Name">
                <em>@file.Name</em></a><br />
    }
}
```

8. Run the page again in the browser, and you should see the list of folders appear together with links to the files that have been created in them like in Figure 8-2.

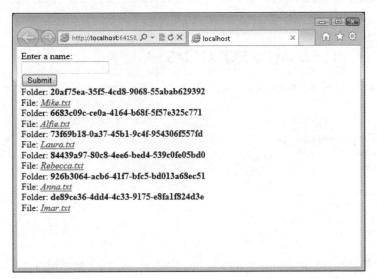

FIGURE 8-2

How It Works

Your new code block is responsible for creating a new folder every time that a value has been submitted via the form. You can see one of the static methods of the `Directory` class being used — the

CreateDirectory method. The folder's name is generated from a *Globally Unique Identifier* (GUID). GUIDs are great for generating unique names for files or folders when you don't want to run the risk of overwriting an existing one by accidentally picking a name for a file or folder that already exists at that location. Together with the folder, the code generates a file named after whatever was submitted via the form, and commits the same name together with the current date and time to the contents of the file.

You then amended the code to make use of a new class — the DirectoryInfo class. DirectoryInfo has a sibling class called FileInfo, which shares a similar relationship as that enjoyed by the Directory and File classes. DirectoryInfo and FileInfo expose many similar methods to their static counterparts — Directory and File — but the outcome of some of the methods can differ. For example, if you just want to the name of a folder using the Directory class, you have a method called GetDirectories, but it returns the entire path as well as the folder name. DirectoryInfo and FileInfo expose some properties as well as methods, which allows you to easily hone in on the folder name, or filename if you want it.

In the body of the page, you obtained a collection that holds the created folders details, and then iterated their files. As you did this, you built a hyperlink to the individual file. You built this link using the Name properties of the DirectoryInfo class and the FileInfo class. If you click on the hyperlink, you will see the content of the file displayed in the browser as plaintext.

COPYING AND MOVING FILES AND FOLDERS

You can copy and move files in a couple of ways. If you use the File class, the respective methods are Copy and Move:

```
//Copies the file example.txt in folder1 to folder2
var original = "@C:\folder1\example.txt";
var copy = "@C:\folder2\example.txt";
File.Copy(original, copy);

//Moves the file example.txt from folder1 to folder2
var source = "@C:\folder1\example.txt";
var destination = "@C:\folder2\example.txt";
File.Move(source, destination);
```

The FileInfo class has slightly different methods — CopyTo and MoveTo — which are illustrated here:

```
//Copies the file example.txt in folder1 to folder2
var original = new FileInfo("@C:\folder1\example.txt");
var copy = "@C:\folder2\example.txt";
original.CopyTo(copy);


//Moves the file example.txt from folder1 to folder2
var source = new FileInfo("@C:\folder1\example.txt");
```

```
var destination = "@C:\folder2\example.txt";
source.MoveTo(destination);
```

You can't actually copy whole folders or directories. You need to use `Directory.CreateDirectory` or the `DirectoryInfo.Create` methods to create a new directory wherever you want it, and then copy the individual files from the original to the new directory:

```
//Copies all folders and their files at folderlocation1 to folderlocation2
var source = "@C:\folderlocation1\";
var destination = "@C:\folderlocation2\";

DirectoryInfo folders = new DirectoryInfo(source);
foreach(var folder in folders.EnumerateDirectories()){
    Directory.CreateDirectory(Path.Combine(destination, folder.Name));
    foreach(var file in folder.GetFiles()){
        file.CopyTo(Path.Combine(destination, folder.Name, file.Name));
    }
}
```

You can delete folders and files quite easily with the `Directory.Delete` and `File.Delete` static methods:

```
var location = "@C:\folderlocation\";
foreach(var folder in Directory.EnumerateDirectories(location)){
    foreach(var file in Directory.EnumerateFiles(folder)){
        File.Delete(file);
        }
    Directory.Delete(folder);
}
```

OTHER TYPES OF FILES

Plaintext files are not the only type of file that you can work with. XML is a popular file format for data exchange, and is the format used for RSS feeds and sitemaps. The .NET Framework includes a relatively new set of APIs for working with XML known as LINQ to XML. LINQ — or *Language Integrated Query*, to give it its full name — was added to the .NET Framework to provide a way to query data using C# (or VB). What kind of data can you query? Well, in the LINQ world, any *sequence* can be queried — or indeed created. A sequence is another term for a collection.

XML is represented by an XDocument object, which at its most basic is a collection or sequence of XElement objects. One of the great things about LINQ is that it isn't used just for querying existing sequences; you can use it to create totally new ones as well. What this means is that using LINQ to XML, you can create an XDocument object in memory, populate it with XElement objects, and then *serialize* the result to file or a *stream*. A stream is a sequence of bytes. Serializing something means converting it to a format that can be stored and passed around.

A sitemap is a collection of URLs that search engines can use to locate content on your site for indexing. The protocol that most leading search engines support is Sitemap 0.9, which is detailed and maintained at `www.sitemaps.org/protocol`. The XML structure is not complicated, and provides the ideal example to illustrate how LINQ to XML can be used to generate a sitemap. Here's an example that shows two URLs being included in the sitemap — the home page and an about page:

```xml
<?xml version="1.0" encoding="UTF-8"?>
<urlset xmlns="http://www.sitemaps.org/schemas/sitemap/0.9">
    <url>
        <loc>http://www.domain.com/</loc>
        <lastmod>2011-04-12</lastmod>
        <changefreq>daily</changefreq>
        <priority>0.5</priority>
    </url>
    <url>
        <loc>http://www.domain.com/about</loc>
        <lastmod>2011-04-12</lastmod>
        <changefreq>monthly</changefreq>
        <priority>0.5</priority>
    </url>
</urlset>
```

The top line declares that the content of the file is XML. The second line points to a *namespace*, which references the current protocol standard. It also declares an element called `urlset`, which houses the rest of the content. Each entry appears in a `url` element, which has up to four additional elements — `loc` (the URL), `lastmod` (the date in W3C date format that the item was last modified), `changefreq` (how often the item is modified), and `priority` (how important you rank this item relative to others on the site on a scale of 0 to 1). The last three of these are optional according to the protocol. You can learn more from the documentation at the sitemaps.org site. What is of more interest here is how to construct this file structure from code.

Most of the time, a lot of the pages you would want to appear in your sitemap are generated from content stored in a database — whether they are items for sale, blog articles, news stories, or what have you. Consequently, their URLs are also generated dynamically, or at least stored in a database. Given the absence of an actual site or database at the moment, the URLs for the example code will be generated dynamically from a `List<string>`. Here's the sample code to generate the sitemap together with an explanation as to what's going on:

```
@using System.Xml.Linq;
@{
    var urls = new List<string>{
                    "home",
                    "about",
                    "contact",
                    "company",
                    "customers",
                    "corporate",
                    "products",
                    "services",
                    "locations",
```

```
                        "terms"
                };
        XNamespace ns = "http://www.sitemaps.org/schemas/sitemap/0.9";
        var baseurl = "http://www.domain.com/{0}";
        var sitemap = new XDocument(
            new XDeclaration("1.0", "utf-8", "yes"),
                new XElement(ns + "urlset",
                    from url in urls select
                    new XElement("url",
                        new XElement("loc", string.Format(baseurl, url)),
                        new XElement("lastmod",
                                    String.Format("{0:yyyy-MM-dd}",
                                    DateTime.Now)
                                    ),
                        new XElement("changefreq", "monthly"),
                        new XElement("priority", "0.5")
                        )
                    )
                );
        Response.ContentType = "text/xml";
        sitemap.Save(Response.Output);
    }
```

The first line of code imports the System.Xml.Linq namespace, which makes the XDocument, XElement, and other relevant classes available to the code. Then a List<string> is instantiated and populated with various page titles for a fictional company website.

An XNamespace object is instantiated to hold the value of the namespace that was introduced earlier, and string is also set up to hold the base URL for the site, to which all the titles will be appended to generate full URLs to specific items in the sitemap. The sitemap is created as an XDocument object (in memory at this point); and an XDeclaration object is used to specify the version and encoding of the document, as well as to indicate whether the document can "stand alone" (not rely on an external set of rules or default values for attributes to make sense).

From that point, XElement objects are added. The first is the urlset element, which encloses all other elements and includes the XNamespace object. Then the LINQ query obtains all of the items in the List<string> sequence:

```
from url in urls select…
```

As you will see when you reach Chapter 10, this looks very similar to the database query language known as SQL (Structured Query Language), but it is in fact C# code. What it does is extract each item from the *urls* collection and project it into a new form — an XElement object with the name of url, and child elements containing values for loc, lastmod, changefreq, and priority.

The last part of the code sets the correct content type for the HTTP response, and then serializes the XDocument object to a stream. In other words, the sitemap is converted to a binary format, the browser or requesting agent is notified that the MIME type for this particular format is text/xml, and then the bytes are written to the HTTP response (See Figure 8-3).

FIGURE 8-3

LINQ to XML is well worth getting to know for working with XML — both for querying and generating XML files. Just like JSON (discussed in Chapter 6), XML is a very popular format for data exchange, and you will be working with it if you want to expose data as RSS feeds, ATOM feeds, or sitemaps, as well as for a number of other purposes.

WORKING WITH IMAGES

Images give your web pages life. You may include images as part of the "furniture," which establishes a brand for your site. You might also allow your users to upload images to be used as avatars, or to illustrate an item they want to sell, or allow them to share memorable moments caught on camera. Images that you generate for your own use will be custom designed and sized, so no extra work should be needed to incorporate them into your site, but images coming from your users will invariably come in a variety of formats and sizes. They may be uploaded as .png, .bmp, .tif, or .jpg files, or something else entirely. They will need to be managed through your code regardless.

The WebImage helper has been put together specifically to help you easily manage and manipulate images. The helper enables you to grab images from uploads, copy them, crop them, resize them, rotate and flip them... and do much more funky stuff. Prior to the helper, this kind of work required a lot of code. Table 8-1 lists the main methods offered by the WebImage helper, which gives the best indication of the scope of its abilities.

TABLE 8-1: The WebImage Helper Methods

METHOD	DESCRIPTION
AddImageWatermark	Adds a watermark image to the image.
AddTextWatermark	Adds watermark text to the image.
Clone	Creates a copy of the WebImage object.
Crop	Crops an image.
FlipHorizontal	Flips an image horizontally.
FlipVertical	Flips an image vertically.
GetBytes	Returns the image as a byte array.
GetImageFromRequest	Returns an image that has been uploaded using the browser.
Resize	Resizes an image.
RotateLeft	Rotates an image counter-clockwise.
RotateRight	Rotates an image clockwise.
Save	Saves an image.
Write	Renders an image to the browser.

The best way to explore these features in depth is to try some of them in an exercise. Over the next few pages, you will build a small application that allows users to upload images into a gallery. You will create *thumbnails* (smaller versions of the original) of each image and display them using a jQuery plug-in designed specifically for managing galleries of images.

TRY IT OUT   Building an Image Gallery

1.   Create a new website based on the Empty Site Template, and name it **Gallery**.

2.   Add a new file to the site and call it **Default.cshtml**.

3.   Since you will work with the FileUpload helper, you need to download the ASP.NET Web Helpers package, which you obtained in the previous chapter. While you are installing that package, change the source to Default - All, and search for jQuery. Install the most recent version available to you. At the time of writing, it was 1.6.2.

4.   Now it's time to start adding some code to Default.cshtml. First, add the following to the `<body>` element:

```
<h1>Upload Images</h1>
<div>@message</div>
@FileUpload.GetHtml(allowMoreFilesToBeAdded:false)
```

5. Add the following to a code block at the top of the page:

```
@{
    var folderName = "";
    var path = "";
    var message = "Choose an image to upload:";

    if(Request.Cookies["folder"] != null){
        folderName = Request.Cookies["folder"].Value;
    }
    else{
        folderName = Guid.NewGuid().ToString();
    }

    path = Path.Combine(Server.MapPath("/Uploads/"), folderName);

    if(!Directory.Exists(path)){
        Directory.CreateDirectory(path);
        Response.Cookies["folder"].Value = folderName;
        Response.Cookies["folder"].Expires = DateTime.Now.AddYears(1);
    }

    if(Request.Files.Count > 0){
        WebImage image = WebImage.GetImageFromRequest();
        if(image != null){
            var imageFileName = Path.GetFileName(image.FileName);
            var imageGuid = Guid.NewGuid().ToString();
            var fileName = imageGuid + "_" + imageFileName;
            var location = Path.Combine(path, fileName);
            image.Save(location, "jpg");
        }else{
            message = "You may only upload image files: .jpg, .gif, .png, .bmp, .tif";
        }
    }
}
```

6. Add a new folder called **Uploads** to the root of the site. Now it's time to test the code as it is up to this point. To do this, run the page and select a variety of files — not just image files — and note what happens as each one is uploaded.

How It Works

When you first run the page, it initializes a number of variables. One of these is a variable called `folderName`. This variable acquires its value from one of two places. The first place that is checked is the `Request.Cookies` collection. You haven't met this collection before, but a cookie is a text file that is placed on the user's machine, and can be used to store arbitrary values. In this particular case, the value is the name of the user's personal upload folder. Each time the browser makes a request to the web server, it passes any cookies along with the request. This following line of code checks to see whether a cookie with the name `folder` exists:

```
if(Request.Cookies["folder"] != null)
```

If it does exist, the value that the cookie contains is used to identify the user's current folder. But how did a cookie with that value get there? If you follow the logic of the code from the previous line, you can see that if the cookie does not exist (that is, it hasn't been set yet), a folder name is generated from the GUID, and a folder is created using that name. Then a cookie is generated using `Response.Cookies`:

```
Response.Cookies["folder"].Value = folderName;
```

Its expiry date is set for one year from today. This makes it a *persistent cookie*. If no expiry date was set, the cookie would be removed from the browser when the browser is closed by the user. Note that cookies are browser specific. They are available only to the browser that they were set with.

 NOTE *This example isn't the greatest use of cookies, but serves to illustrate how they work. Cookies can be deleted by users, or they can set their browser to refuse them. If either of those things happened in this application, the link between the user and their folder would be lost. It would also be lost if the user accessed the application using a different browser to the one they used before, or if they used a different machine altogether. In a real world application, you would implement something a lot more robust, such as some kind of membership backed up by a database, but we haven't got to that point yet in this book.*

Now you have the folder set and its name stored in a cookie. What's needed next is some code to manage uploaded files. If there is at least one file in the `Request.Files` collection, an attempt to establish that it is a valid image file is made with the `WebImage.GetImageFromRequest` method. If you tested earlier by uploading a non-image file, such as a word processing document or a text file, for example, you would have generated the message that says only valid image files may be uploaded. If the `WebImage.GetImageFromRequest` method detects that the uploaded file is not a valid image type, the result is that the WebImage object is `null`. If the test was successful, the resulting image file is saved with a new filename, by prepending the actual filename with a GUID. There is one other thing to note here, and that is that the file type will also be converted to a .jpg. This is achieved by passing in a value for the `imageFormat` argument to the `WebImage.Save()` method call:

```
image.Save(location, "jpg");
```

This ensures that all image files are converted to JPG format before being saved. The WebImage helper will accept a range of image formats when you call the `GetImageFromRequest` method. It will happily retrieve .bmp and .tif files, for example, from the `Request.Files` collection. However, not all browsers can be relied upon to display images in these formats. Consequently, the images are saved in a format that can reliably be displayed in all known browsers.

At this stage, there is still some work to do. The images that your users upload are not constrained in any way, except to ensure that they are valid file types and they do not exceed 4MB in file size. However, any reasonable image gallery should control the size of images on display so that visitors do not have to scroll horizontally and vertically to be able to see the whole image. In the next step, you will amend the existing code to create two versions of the uploaded image. The first version will be a thumbnail version, not exceeding 200 pixels in height or width, and the second will ensure that the main image does not exceed 600 pixels in either height or width. In addition, the thumbnails will have a watermark applied to them, indicating the date that the image was added to the gallery.

Once the thumbnails are created, you need to produce a page to display them so that visitors can choose which images they would like to study more closely.

TRY IT OUT | Resizing Uploaded Images

1. Continuing with the site you were working with in the last exercise, alter the code block in Default .cshtml so that it looks like this:

```
@{
    var folderName = "";
    var path = "";
    var message = "Choose an image to upload:";

    if(Request.Cookies["folder"] != null){
        folderName = Request.Cookies["folder"].Value;
    }
    else{
        folderName = Guid.NewGuid().ToString();
    }

    path = Path.Combine(Server.MapPath("/Uploads/"), folderName);

    if(!Directory.Exists(path)){
        Directory.CreateDirectory(path);
        Response.Cookies["folder"].Value = folderName;
        Response.Cookies["folder"].Expires = DateTime.Now.AddYears(1);
    }

    if(Request.Files.Count > 0){
        WebImage image = WebImage.GetImageFromRequest();
        if(image != null){
            var imageFileName = Path.GetFileName(image.FileName);
            var imageGuid = Guid.NewGuid().ToString();
            var fileName = imageGuid + "_" + imageFileName;
            var thumbFileName = imageGuid + "_thumb_" + imageFileName;
            var location = Path.Combine(path, fileName);
            image.Resize(600, 600, preventEnlarge: true);
            image.Save(location, "jpg");
            image.Resize(200, 200, preventEnlarge: true);
            location = Path.Combine(path, thumbFileName);
            var watermark = DateTime.Now.ToShortDateString();
            image.AddTextWatermark(watermark, fontColor: "White", fontSize: 8);
            image.Save(location, "jpg");
        }else{
            message = "You may only upload image files: .jpg, .gif, .png, .bmp, .tif";
        }
    }
}
```

2. Download Tiny Carousel from the jQuery plug-in site at `http://plugins.jquery.com/project/tinycarousel`. Add the JavaScript file to a folder called Scripts, which was created when you downloaded jQuery from the Package Manager.

3. Create a new folder called **Content** and add a .css file to it. Change the filename to **tinycarousel.css**. Add the following style declarations to tinycarousel.css:

```css
#slider-code {
    height: 160px;
    overflow:hidden;
}
#slider-code .viewport {
    float: left;
    width: 220px;
    height: 220px;
    overflow: hidden;
    position: relative;
}
#slider-code .buttons {
    background:url("/Images/buttons.png") no-repeat scroll 0 0 transparent;
    display: block;
    margin: 30px 10px 0 0;
    background-position: 0 -38px;
    text-indent: -999em;
    float: left; width: 39px;
    height: 37px;
    overflow: hidden;
    position: relative;
}
#slider-code .next {
    background-position: 0 0;
    margin: 30px 0 0 10px;
}
#slider-code .disable {
    visibility: hidden;
}
#slider-code .overview {
    list-style: none;
    position: absolute;
    padding: 0;
    margin: 0;
    left: 0;
    top: 0;
}
#slider-code .overview li{
    float: left;
    margin: 0 20px 0 0;
    padding: 1px;
    height: 161px;
    border: none;
    width: 256px;
}
```

4. You might notice that the style declaration includes a reference to an image file called **buttons.png**. You can create your own image file, or simply borrow the one that comes with the download for

this book. I suggest the second option, as the positioning in the style sheet is calculated to work with the buttons.png. Create a folder called **Images** to house the buttons.png file.

5. Download jQuery FancyBox from `http://fancybox.net/home`. You should get a .zip file containing demonstration code, as well as the JavaScript and .css files. At the time of writing, the latest version was 1.3.4, and the filenames reflect that. If a newer version has been released by the time you read this, the filenames that follow may well have changed along with the newer version number. Copy the jquery.fancybox-1.3.4.css file to your Content folder, the jquery.fancybox-1.3.4 .pack.js file to your Scripts folder, and the images to your newly created Images folder.

6. At this stage, you also need to update the jquery.fancybox-1.3.4.css file to point to the correct location for the images you have just downloaded. Open the file in WebMatrix and locate the first instance of a background image reference. It should be pointed to the same folder as the jquery.fancybox-1.3.4.css file. You need to change that, and all other references to point to the Images folder. With the file open and its tab selected, press Alt, then H, then E. If all worked well, you should now have the Find and Replace dialogs visible, as shown in Figure 8-4.

You can also achieve the same result by clicking the Replace icon in the Editing menu. Once you have that, type **url('** into the Find In File box, and **url('/Images/** into Replace With, and then click Replace All. Now all the image references have been adjusted. There is another change you have to make, and that is to the location of some images for the older versions of Internet Explorer. Enter **src='fancybox/** into the Find In File box, and then **src='/Images/** into Replace With. Then click Replace All.

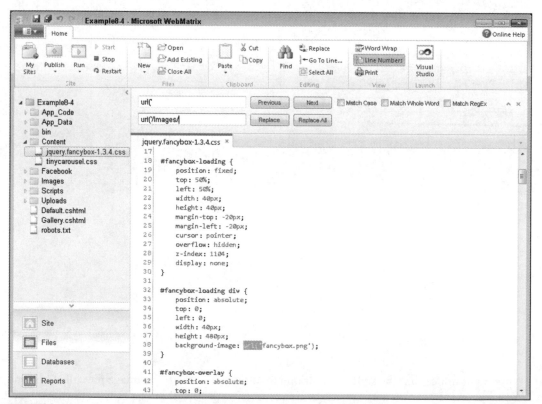

FIGURE 8-4

7. Add a new file and name it **Gallery.cshtml**. Add the following code to the `<head>` element:

```html
<head>
<meta charset="utf-8" />
<title>Gallery</title>

<link rel="stylesheet" href="@Href("~/Content/tinycarousel.css")" type="text/css" />
<link rel="stylesheet" href="@Href("~/Content/jquery.fancybox-1.3.4.css")"
        type="text/css" />
<script type="text/javascript" src="@Href("~/Scripts/jquery-1.6.2.min.js")">
</script>
<script type="text/javascript" src="@Href("~/Scripts/jquery.tinycarousel.min.js")">
</script>
<script type="text/javascript" src="@Href("~/Scripts/jquery.fancybox-1.3.4.pack.js")">
</script>
<script type="text/javascript">
    $(document).ready(function(){
        $('#slider-code').tinycarousel();
        $('.thumb').fancybox();
    });
</script>
</head>
```

8. Then add the following code to the body:

```html
<h3>Gallery</h3>
<div id="slider-code">
    <a class="buttons prev" href="#">left</a>
    <div class="viewport">
        <ul class="overview">
            @foreach(var file in files){
            <li>
            <a class="thumb" href="Uploads/@folderName/@file.Replace("_thumb", "")">
            <img src="Uploads/@folderName/@file" alt=""/>
            </a>
            </li>
            }
        </ul>
    </div>
    <a class="buttons next" href="#">right</a>
</div>
```

9. Finally, add the following code to the top of the file in a code block:

```csharp
@{
    var folderName = "";
    var path = "";
    var files = new List<string>();
    if(Request.Cookies["folder"] != null){
        folderName = Request.Cookies["folder"].Value;
        path = Path.Combine(Server.MapPath("/Uploads/"), folderName);
        foreach(var file in  Directory.GetFiles(path)){
            if(Path.GetFileName(file).Contains("_thumb_")){
                files.Add(Path.GetFileName(file));
            }
        }
    }
}
```

10. That's it. Now, assuming that you have uploaded some image files already, you should see a gallery similar to the one in Figure 8-5.

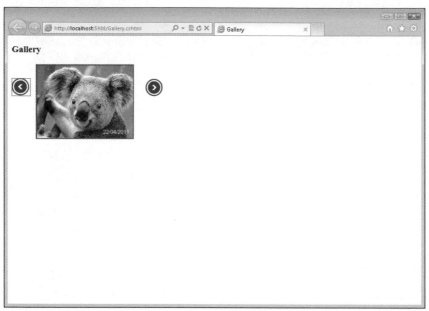

FIGURE 8-5

And if you click on one of the thumbnail images, the larger version should appear in the FancyBox, as in Figure 8-6.

FIGURE 8-6

How It Works

The first change you made was to the code that managed the uploaded file. You used the `WebImage` `.Resize` method to make two resized versions of the uploaded file. In the first version, you specified the width and height parameter values were both 600 pixels. This does not mean that your resulting image will be 600 by 600 pixels. By default, another parameter — `preserveAspectRatio` - is set to `true`. This value ensures that the proportions of the image are maintained while it is being resized. I used the sample images that come with the Windows operating system to test the code, and that is what you see in Figure 8.5. You can usually find these in C:\Users\Public\Pictures\Sample Pictures in Windows 7. All of the images there are 1024 by 768 pixels. When you set the width and height to 600 pixels, and specified that the width/height ratio should be maintained, you actually told the WebImage helper that neither the width nor the height should exceed 600 pixels. The result (assuming the starting image is 1024 by 768) will be an image that is 600 pixels wide, but (preserving the aspect ratio) 450 pixels wide. Perhaps these parameters should be named `maxwidth` and `maxheight`, as that is really what they control when setting the `preserveAspectRatio` value to `true`. If you had specified that the parameter value be `false`, the image would have been resized to 600 by 600, and would also have been distorted as a result of being stretched to fit its new aspect ratio. You also applied the value `true` to `preventEnlarge`. This ensures that if an image's width and height both fall below the resize values, the image is not increased in size to meet the (max) width or (max) height values. Increasing or enlarging images will almost always lead to a loss of quality.

The second version is saved with a maximum width and height of 200 pixels. Before it is saved, however, you generated a string with the value of today's date, and then you used the `AddTextWatermark` method to apply that string to the image as a watermark. You specified the font color (the default is black) and the font size (the default is 12 points). You left the other parameter values to their defaults, which are a normal style font, using Microsoft Sans Serif, and placed in the bottom-right corner with five pixels of padding.

Both versions of the file used the same GUID value as part of their filename. The large version had a filename constructed as before, but the change you made to this iteration ensured that the word "thumb" became part of the filename. Keeping the GUID the same for both versions makes it a lot easier to match a thumbnail to its parent.

I chose both Tiny Carousel and FancyBox for the same reason — they both offered a limited set of functionality and had easy documentation. I did not have to waste any time at all getting either of them to work. And they both work fine for this example. They may not be suitable for other projects that you work on, so you should explore other options as well. You might even want to use this little project as a basis for testing alternatives, and there are countless alternative carousel-type plug-ins available in particular.

Notice in particular the order in which the JavaScript files have been referenced in the Gallery.cshtml file: jQuery core first, followed by any plug-ins. Because all plug-ins depend on jQuery, this order is essential. The `<script>` block targets two groups of elements: It uses an ID selector to apply carousel effects to the element with an ID of `"slider-code"`. That ID was kept over from the demo code provided as part of the download. If you want to change it to something else, you will need to update the StyleSheet.css rules accordingly. This might be a useful exercise for you at some stage — make changes to the CSS one at a time, and see what breaks. It is sometimes a very useful learning exercise.

Back to the current exercise, the second group of elements are targeted using a class selector — all elements with a class of "thumb", which are actually hyperlinks. These have the FancyBox effects applied to them. But what do those hyperlinks contain? The code block at the top of the page is crucial with regards to the content of the hyperlinks. In it, you first attempt to read a cookie to see if the folder name has been set for the current user. If it has, your code uses `Directory.GetFiles`, which you saw in the previous exercise, to grab an array of all filenames in that folder. You also construct a `List<string>`, and as you iterate the array of files in the folder, you add any that have the string `"_thumb_"` in their name to the `List<string>`. Consequently, your `List<string>` will contain a nice list of all the thumbnail image filenames, and nothing else.

Once you have that collection, you iterate it in the HTML markup to generate the gallery. The hyperlink points to the large version of the image, which has the same filename as the thumbnail, except that it doesn't include "_thumb" as part of the name. Therefore, replacing "_thumb" with nothing (an empty string, in fact) gives the large version's filename. That's why the same GUID was used for both versions. The thumbnail images themselves act as the link.

SUMMARY

This chapter showed you how to work with files in your Web Pages application. You learned about the `Path`, `File`, and `Directory` utility classes and a number of their methods that help when working with both folders and files. At the beginning of the chapter, you learned the basics of file manipulation and how to create and amend text files. Then you learned how to create folders, and copy and move files.

In the next section, other file types were explored, beginning with XML. You learned that XML is really just a text-based file, and it can be generated quite easily using LINQ to XML. You saw how this relatively new .NET technology helps when it comes to constructing a valid sitemap document that search engines will understand and use as a guide to what to index on your site.

In the final section, you learned about image file types in particular, and about the WebImage helper, which is provided to make working with images easy and pain-free. You used your new knowledge on the creation and management of directories to lay the foundation of a gallery application. You also saw how the WebImage helper provides a number of very useful methods that allow you to retrieve image files from uploads, rename them, resize them, watermark them, and save them. You also learned a bonus topic in this section — all about cookies and how to read values from them and set them.

In the last exercise, you experienced first-hand how combining a couple of jQuery plugins with the WebImage helper can help you create a working thumbnail-based image gallery with the minimum amount of effort and code.

EXERCISES

1. Name at least two classes containing static methods that you are likely to use for manipulating files and folders. Explain what the classes you choose are responsible for.

2. What is LINQ to XML?

3. What is the purpose of the `preserveAspectRatio` parameter in the WebImage helper's `Resize` method? What is its default value and how are the image and height values affected by the default value?

Answers to the Exercises can be found in the Appendix.

▶ **WHAT YOU LEARNED IN THIS CHAPTER**

TOPIC	KEY CONCEPTS
File Class	A class containing static utility methods for working with files.
Path Class	A class containing static utility methods for working with file paths.
Directory Class	A class containing static utility methods for working with folders.
GUID	Globally Unique Identifier — A value that has an extremely small chance of being duplicated.
DirectoryInfo	A class containing a range of instance methods for working with folders.
FileInfo	A class containing a range of instance methods for working with files.
LINQ to XML	An API for working with XML.
Xdocument	A representation of an XML document that LINQ to XML understands.
Xelement	An element within an Xdocument.
WebImage Helper	A helper for manipulating image files.
Cookie	A text file written to the browser, which can be persisted and stored as values.

Debugging and Error Handling

By now, you have already written a fair amount of code as you worked your way through the exercises presented to you so far. If you are anything like me, and 99% of all developers, you will have made typographical mistakes and caused error pages to appear when you tried to execute your code. That is to be expected. *Bugs* and *errors* will happen, and they happen at a very high frequency when you are just learning how to program.

Before you can fix errors, you need to understand how they occurred. This chapter provides you with sufficient information to be able to understand how errors happen, prevent them from disrupting your users, and fix them quickly.

ANATOMY OF AN ERROR

Before you can defeat errors, you need to know your enemy. There are broadly two kinds of errors: those that occur when the pages compile, and those that happen at execution time, or run time. Compilation errors nearly always result from syntax errors caused by missing semicolons, missing braces, or other typing errors. Some of these errors are reported by the compiler, whereas others are reported by the Razor parser. These are generally easy to identify and fix. The second type of error falls into two categories: errors caught at run time and logical errors. Logical errors are more difficult to track and fix. These are examined a bit later in this chapter, in some detail.

Syntax Errors

When you first run a Web Pages application, each page is compiled as required. However, all content in an App_Code folder is compiled first (if you have one). Here's a snippet of code that could appear in a file called Functions.cshtml in App_Code. Can you see what's wrong with it?

```
@functions {
    public static bool IsCorrect(object o){
        return true
        }
```

If you try to run the application, you will see the page shown in Figure 9-1.

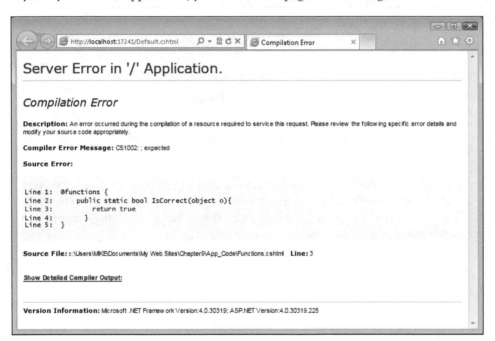

FIGURE 9-1

This is commonly referred to as the "YSOD," or the *Yellow Screen of Death*. It means your application is broken. At this stage, a lot of novice programmers panic, and search for an online forum so that they can post a question, asking if anyone knows why their website broke. You, on the other hand, are going to learn to love this page. You are going to see it as your greatest friend in helping to fix your site.

NOTE *The message provided in the error page (shown in Figure 9-1) is of enormous value to you, even if it seems obscure. You do not need to understand it to let it help you. All you need to do, if you really cannot fathom the meaning of the message, is to copy and paste it into any search engine you like. Thousands of novice programmers will have already posted a question to a forum somewhere in search of help about that particular error message, and thousands of volunteers will have translated it into plain English and provided a solution already.*

Have a look at the page closely and see what information it gives you. The first thing it tells you is that the error is a compilation error. This is followed by more detailed confirmation in the Description part of the page. Then the compiler's message appears:

```
Compiler Error Message: CS1002: ; expected
```

The message tells you that a semicolon is expected. Not only that, but the page goes on to highlight the line in the source code that caused the error message — line 3 — note that there is no semicolon after `return true`. Pop a semicolon at the end of that line, run the site again, and you'll get the page shown in Figure 9-2.

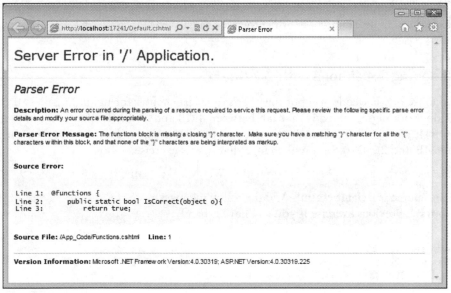

FIGURE 9-2

Oops. This is the other kind of error that can occur at compile time — the Razor parser has encountered an error on this occasion. There is a missing closing brace for the code block. If this error had occurred in a C# class file (one ending in `.cs`), the error would have been reported by the compiler. However, the point is that the YSOD is not intended to send you running to the nearest counselling service. It actually does its best to describe what the problem is, and where it occurs.

Run Time Exceptions

An *exception* is a .NET object that represents an error during application execution. There are hundreds of exception types, and you can create your own custom exception types if you like, but they all derive from `System.Exception`. If an exception is "raised" in your ASP.NET application, the result is always a YSOD unless measures are put in place to manage this. The way to manage exceptions is to try to prevent them in the first place, which is easily done once you understand what you can control and what you can't. For example, you will generate a `DivideByZeroException` if you perform a calculation in your code that attempts to divide a number by zero (0). You know you cannot do this, so you will always validate any divisor to ensure it cannot be zero. Similarly, you will generate an `IndexOutOfRangeException` if you attempt to reference an element by an array index that does not exist. As mentioned in Chapter 4, this exception is generated quite regularly until novice programmers finally grasp the fact that the value of the `Length` property of an array is always one more than the index of the last element.

Some exceptions are raised as a result of things you cannot control. Examples include attempting to reference a file or folder that doesn't exist, or a database server that is not available for some reason, or an SMTP server that's offline. You can manage these kinds of scenarios with a `try-catch` block in C#. Using this construct, you place any code that might be susceptible to failure within a `try` block. If an exception is raised while this code executes, control is passed to the `catch` block, or optionally a `finally` block.

This is easier to explain with an example. It's time to crack open WebMatrix again — you are going to write some code.

TRY IT OUT   Managing Exceptions with Try-Catch

This exercise will make use of some code you put together in the last chapter for uploading files. If you remember, ASP.NET does not permit uploads that fall between 4MB and 26.8MB. Your gallery code comfortably deals with situations where smaller non-image type files are uploaded, but does not cater for uploads between 4MB and 26.8MB. You will change that in this exercise.

1. Create a new site using the Empty Site template within WebMatrix. Name the site **Chapter 9**.

2. Add a new file and name it **Default.cshtml**. Add the following markup to the `<body>`. You can simply copy this from the previous exercise if you still have it handy:

```
<body>
    <h1>Upload Images</h1>
    <div>@message</div>
    @FileUpload.GetHtml(allowMoreFilesToBeAdded: false)
</body>
```

3. Since you are using the FileUpload helper, you need to obtain the ASP.NET Web Helpers Library 1.1 via the Package Manager. Click the Site button in the left pane, and click the ASP.NET Web Pages Administration link to create your password, locate the helpers package, and install it.

4. At the top of the file, add the following code block:

```
@{
    var message = "";
```

```
    if(Request.Files.Count > 0){
        WebImage image = WebImage.GetImageFromRequest();
        if(image != null){
            message = "Upload succeeded";
        }else{
            message = "You must upload an image file: .jpg, .gif, .png, .bmp, .tif";
        }
    }
}
}
```

5. Now test the page by uploading a regular image file of less than 4MB, a non-image file of less than 4MB, and any file you have that's over 4MB but less than 27MB. You should have received a different response depending on the file type — success in the first case, a message telling you to only upload image files in the second, and a YSOD providing details of an `HttpException` in the third case (see Figure 9-3).

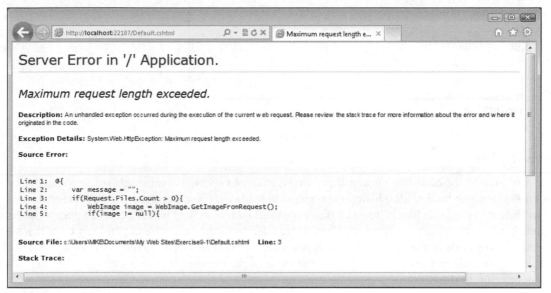

FIGURE 9-3

6. Now amend the code block so that it looks like this:

```
@{
    var message = "";
    try{
        if(Request.Files.Count > 0){
            WebImage image = WebImage.GetImageFromRequest();
            if(image != null){
                message = "Upload succeeded";
            }else{
                message = "You must upload an image file: .jpg, .gif, .png, .bmp, .tif";
            }
        }
```

```
    }
    catch(Exception ex){
        message = "Upload unsuccessful because: " + ex.Message;
    }
}
```

7. Run the page again and upload a large file between 4MB and 27MB. This time, the error message is a lot more friendly (see Figure 9-4).

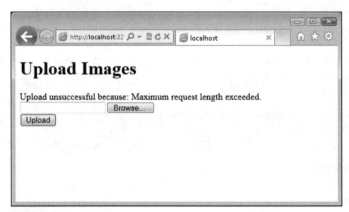

FIGURE 9-4

How It Works

Up until Step 6, the code you put together catered to some expected events such as the wrong file type or no file in the upload at all. However, oversized uploads were not managed. You amended the code to include a `try-catch` block. The `try` block contains code that may be subject to an exception. At the point that an exception occurs, control flow is transferred to the `catch` block, and any code there is executed. Any code in the `try` block that appears after the exception occurred does not get executed. In this case, the code in the `catch` block took the value of the `Exception` object's `Message` property and displayed that to the user.

You can have multiple `catch` blocks. Each one can cater to a different type of exception. You saw in the previous exercise how the `catch` block looks for a general `Exception` object, but the exception that was thrown was of type `HttpException`. If you cater to an `HttpException` as well, the code would look like this:

```
try{
    //some code that might throw an exception
}
catch(HttpException ex){
    message = "An HttpException was caught";
}
catch(Exception ex){
    message = "A general exception was caught";
}
```

The general exception will always go last in any list of catch blocks, because if an exception is thrown, the Framework looks for catch blocks and executes the code in the first one that matches the type of exception. All exceptions are based on the generic exception, so this would match all exceptions. In fact, the compiler will prevent you from placing Exception before HttpException (or any other type of exception for that matter). But why would you want multiple catch blocks looking for different types of exceptions? Well, it is so that you can narrow down the cause of any problems. For example, you might be trying to generate a file, which you then want to append to an e-mail as an attachment, and finally save the resulting document into a SQL server database. During that operation, you have the potential for an IOException, SmtpException, SqlClientException, FormatException, and probably a few others. Knowing which type of exception took place can help you shape the error message to the user, and narrow down the location of the actual problem.

> **WARNING** *In general, you should always do something in the* catch *block. You should never just catch the exception and do nothing (except in very rare circumstances). Empty* catch *blocks are the equivalent of ignoring error conditions, which can leave your application in an unstable or unknown state. The rare exceptions include a situation where you try to log an error to a database, and the database is not there. There is no point in attempting to record that exception in the database.*

When you use try blocks, you can also provide a finally block. This should contain any code that needs to be executed, regardless of whether an exception was raised. A good example of when a finally block might be used is when you create a connection to a SQL Server database, but an exception occurs. You should always make sure that connections are closed properly to conserve resources, so you would use the finally block to establish whether the connection was successfully opened, and if so, close it.

GLOBAL ERROR HANDLING

In an ideal world, you can anticipate all the areas in your code that might cause an exception to be raised, and code around those eventualities — either by validating values or by using try-catch blocks, as appropriate. However, life is not like that, and the reality is that there will always be something that you overlooked or did not think of. You are, after all, going to expose your web application to end users, and they can be fiendishly clever in doing the last thing you ever thought they would do while clicking buttons and filling out forms. The last thing you really want is for your users to be exposed to the default error page with its techie-looking messages. For one thing, it is unlikely to make any sense to them, and for another, visitors are unlikely to report the error and give detailed steps to replicate it. They'll just go away. What you need is a way to handle any error that happens on your site. In the next exercise, you will implement a mechanism that traps errors across the site and redirects users to a custom error page that you design. You will also record the details of any error, and notify yourself by e-mail when an error happens.

TRY IT OUT   Handling Exceptions Across a Site

1. Open you Chapter 9 site if you have closed it and add a new file with the name **_PageStart.cshtml**.

2. Replace the default mark-up with the following code block:

```
@{
    try{
        RunPage();
    }
    catch(Exception ex){
        var message = ex.Message + "\n";
        var stack = ex.StackTrace;

        var logentry = DateTime.Now + "\n" + message + stack;
        logentry += "\n=========================\n";
        var location = Server.MapPath("~/App_Data/");
        var filename = "errorlog.txt";
        var path = Path.Combine(location, filename);
        File.AppendAllText(path, logentry);
        WebMail.Send(
            to: "mike@mike.com",
            subject: "Error on site",
            body: "The following error occurred\n" + message + stack,
            isBodyHtml: false
        );
        Response.Redirect("~/Error/");
    }
}
```

3. Now add another new file and name it **_AppStart.cshtml**. Replace the templated content with the following:

```
@{
    WebMail.SmtpServer = "localhost";
    WebMail.From = "trouble@site.com";
}
```

4. Add a web.config (4.0) file and amend it so that it reads as follows:

```
<?xml version="1.0"?>

<configuration>

    <system.web>
        <compilation debug="false" targetFramework="4.0" />
    </system.web>
    <system.net>
        <mailSettings>
            <smtp deliveryMethod="SpecifiedPickupDirectory">
                <specifiedPickupDirectory pickupDirectoryLocation="C:\Mail\"/>
            </smtp>
        </mailSettings>
    </system.net>
</configuration>
```

5. Create a folder called **Mail** in the root of your C: drive. If you do not have access or permission to do that, create a folder where you can, and alter the code in the web.config file to point to your location.

6. Add the following line of code to the top of the code block in the Default.cshtml file:

```
throw new NullReferenceException();
```

7. Add a new file to the site called Error.cshtml and simply add `<h1>An error occurred</h1>` to the `<body>` element. Then make sure that Default.cshtml is selected in the File Explorer and run it in your default browser. If all has gone according to plan, you should be presented with the error page. You should also find that a text file has been added to App_Data, and some text has been written to it. Finally, you should find a file with an .eml extension in the Mail folder wherever you created it. If you open that file with your preferred e-mail client, you should see the e-mail message that you constructed.

How It Works

Remember from Chapter 4 that the contents of _PageStart.cshtml are executed before any file in the same folder or subfolders. You can also cause code to run after any page has been executed, by placing an explicit call to the RunPage method in _PageStart.cshtml and adding code after the method call. In this case, you placed the RunPage method call inside a `try` block. As you learned in the previous exercise, this enables you to catch any exceptions that occur and handle them within a `catch` block, so if something goes wrong during the RunPage method call (that is, while the requested page is executing), code in the `catch` block takes over. In this case, you forced something to go wrong when Default.cshtml was requested by adding a line of code that explicitly throws an exception. It could have been any exception, but you threw an exception of type NullReferenceException.

 NOTE NullReferenceExceptions *result in an error message that says "Object reference not set to an instance of an object." For some reason, this error message causes more questions in forums than most others. What it actually means is that you have attempted to reference an instance of an object in code that does not exist. A typical example of this is attempting to reference a cookie that has not been set. Do you remember the way that the cookie was referenced in the previous chapter? Each time you attempted to read the cookie value, you ensured that the cookie was not null beforehand. In nearly every case, you can cure this exception by ensuring that the object instance that causes the error is not null before you start trying to get or set its properties.*

Once the exception in Default.cshtml was encountered, no further code was processed in Default .cshtml. Control was transferred to the `catch` block, where you obtained the value of two of the Exception object's properties — the Exception.Message property and the Exception.StackTrace property. The Message property provides you with a description of what went wrong, and the StackTrace provides details of where in your code the exception occurred. You appended a line to a text file to log the error and generated an e-mail containing the details stored in these properties.

Finally, you redirected the visitor to a much friendlier page than the YSOD to explain that an error had occurred.

Another kind of error that can happen once your site is up and live is the *Page Not Found* error. Universally known as a "404" — after the HTTP status code that is generated — this error occurs when a user mistypes a URL on your site, or follows a dead link. The procedure you have just implemented will not manage this scenario for you. Instead, you need to make a small change to your web.config file:

```
<system.web>
    <compilation debug="false" targetFramework="4.0" />
    <customErrors mode="On">
        <error statusCode="404" redirect="404.cshtml" />
    </customErrors>
</system.web>
```

Add the entry for `customErrors` within the `system.web` section. This particular entry makes sure that when an HTTP error occurs with a status code of 404, the user is redirected to a page called 404.cshtml. You can actually name the file anything you like, so long as you add a file with whatever name you choose to the site, of course. This will become your custom error page. It means that you can personalize your error message for the users.

This change will only capture 404 errors generated by missing pages with file extensions that are registered to and managed by ASP.NET — those that end in .cshtml, .vbhtml, .aspx, and so on. If you want your own custom 404 error page for static content such as .htm files, you can either configure this at the web server level or talk to your web server administrators.

LOGICAL ERRORS

Logical errors are the most difficult errors to manage. Outwardly, there may be no sign that things have gone wrong. The code compiles beautifully. For most users, the site works and behaves well, but just occasionally you get reports or logs of an exception. Or things just don't appear to calculate correctly. When you try to replicate the exception, you fail. You have a logical error somewhere, which may have resulted from an incorrect calculation or an assumption about the presence of a value that has not been borne out in practice. Sometimes you can easily replicate the problem, but it is not easy to see at a glance where the cause of the problem lies. The process of identifying the cause of an error and fixing it is known as *debugging*.

Debugging tools are vital to the professional developer. Visual Studio 2010 and Visual Web Developer Express 2010 both have advanced debugging tools. Since Service Pack 1 was released for both Visual Studio 2010 and Visual Web Developer Express 2010, Web Pages development has been enabled within both environments. It is certainly worth taking a look at the enhanced development experience that full IntelliSense and debugging tools offer — especially with the free Visual Web Developer Express 2010, although neither of those tools is covered in this book. WebMatrix, certainly in Version 1, offers no formal debugging tools. That is not to say that you are left helpless. There are one or two ways that you can help yourself. You will explore those now.

Take a look at the following form:

```
<!DOCTYPE html>

<html lang="en">
    <head>
        <meta charset="utf-8" />
        <title></title>
    </head>
    <body>
        <form method="post">
            <div>First Name: </div>
            <div>@Html.TextBox("fristname", Request["firstname"])</div>
            <span style="color:red">@Html.ValidationMessage("firstname")</span>
            <div>Second Name: </div>
            <div>@Html.TextBox("secondname", Request["secondname"])</div>
            <span style="color:red">@Html.ValidationMessage("secondname")</span>
            <input type="submit" value="Submit" />
        </form>
        </body>
</html>
```

Now it may be that you can spot the deliberate mistake — or maybe not. This is a very simple form and the mistake, although perhaps not obvious at first glance, would definitely be a lot harder to spot if it was buried in a much larger form. Here is some additional code that goes at the top of the file:

```
@{
    if(IsPost){
        if(Request["firstname"].IsEmpty()){
            ModelState.AddError("firstname","Please provide a firstname");
        }
        if(Request["secondname"].IsEmpty()){
            ModelState.AddError("secondname","Please provide a secondname");
        }
    }
}
```

If you were to run this page, you would be presented with something similar to Figure 9-5.

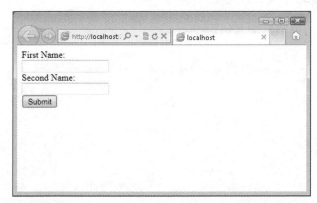

FIGURE 9-5

Furthermore, if you were to enter your first name in the first box, and your second one in the second box, and then submitted the form, you would be greeted with the result depicted in Figure 9-6.

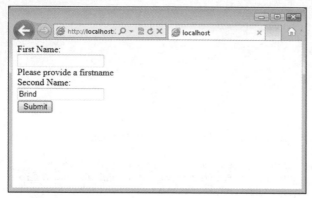

FIGURE 9-6

You know perfectly well that you submitted a value in the first name textbox, but the validation code saw it as an empty form field. You can try as many times as you like, but you cannot get past this error. Enter the ObjectInfo helper.

Using ObjectInfo to Debug Errors

ObjectInfo is a helper that is designed to output all of the details of any object that you work with in code. It has one simple method — Print. That method takes one required parameter — the object you want to analyze. It also has two optional parameters: depth, which determines the depth of nested sub-objects that can be examined (the default is 10); and enumerationLength, which limits the number of characters that will be displayed as part of an object's value. The default is 1,000 characters.

So how is it used? As an example, here are the previous code snippets combined into one file:

```
@{
    if(IsPost){
        if(Request["firstname"].IsEmpty()){
            ModelState.AddError("firstname","Please provide a firstname");
        }
        if(Request["secondname"].IsEmpty()){
            ModelState.AddError("secondname","Please provide a secondname");
        }
    }
}
<!DOCTYPE html>

<html lang="en">
    <head>
        <meta charset="utf-8" />
        <title></title>
    </head>
```

```
        <body>
            @if(IsPost){
                @ObjectInfo.Print(Request.Form)
            }
            <form method="post">
                <div>First Name: </div>
                <div>@Html.TextBox("fristname", Request["firstname"])</div>
                <span style="color:red">@Html.ValidationMessage("firstname")</span>
                <div>Second Name: </div>
                <div>@Html.TextBox("secondname", Request["secondname"])</div>
                <span style="color:red">@Html.ValidationMessage("secondname")</span>
                <input type="submit" value="Submit" />
            </form>
        </body>
    </html>
```

The only addition to the code that was previously shown is the conditional code at the top of the body element:

```
@if(IsPost){
    @ObjectInfo.Print(Request.Form)
}
```

Now, if you run the page again, you will see no difference from the previous example until you submit the form, which results in the following display illustrated in Figure 9-7.

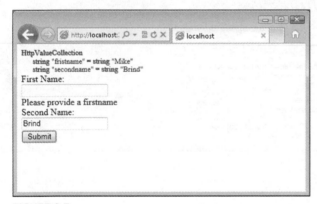

FIGURE 9-7

Notice that the object that you asked to Print in code is the Request.Form collection. The output is its type, which is an HttpValueCollection. It contains two elements (or sub-objects), which are string key/string value pairs. Each key and value is printed out too. You can see that two values were added to the collection when the form was submitted, so what happened to the firstname value? On closer inspection, you can see why it disappeared: The key for this value is fristname, not firstname. So there's the bug — a spelling mistake in the form field name.

The ObjectInfo helper's true power is evident when it is used to explore the innards of complex objects. One of the most complex objects you are likely to work with is the current page object, which can be referenced via the `this` keyword. You can have hours of fun exploring all of the properties of the `WebPage` object simply by adding the following to a page:

```
@ObjectInfo.Print(this)
```

See Figure 9-8 for an example of the output.

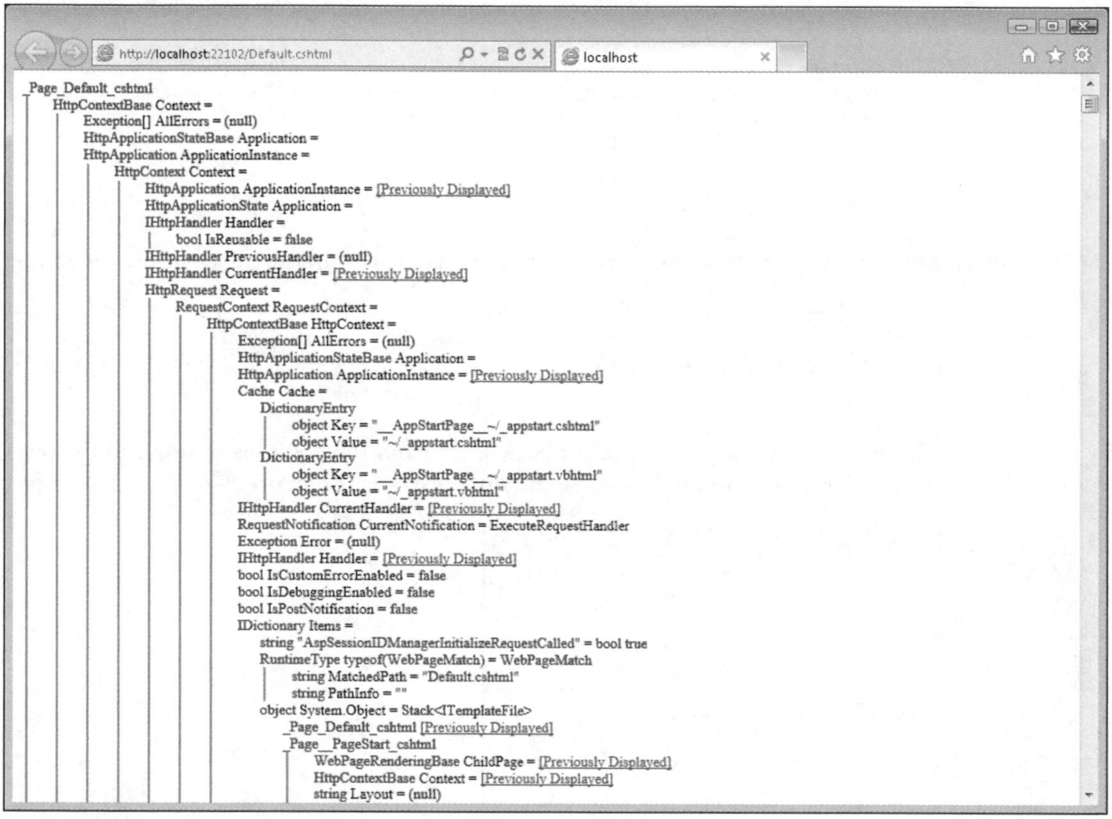

FIGURE 9-8

The ServerInfo Helper

There are times when issues arise as a result of the environment in which your site is hosted. It might be, for example, that you are trying to apply some logic that runs depending on the current Windows account that the site is running under, or you need to troubleshoot some issues concerning file paths on the server that your site is running on. The ServerInfo helper displays detailed diagnostic information covering:

➤ Server configuration

➤ ASP.NET server variables

➤ `HttpRuntime` information

➤ Environment variables

The ServerInfo helper has one method — `GetHtml`:

```
@ServerInfo.GetHtml()
```

This can be placed anywhere on a page and results in the data being printed to the browser in separate tables, as depicted in Figure 9-9.

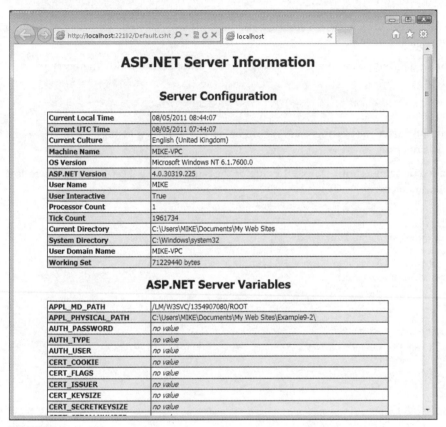

FIGURE 9-9

USING ASP.NET TRACING

In the good old days of classic ASP, the standard way to debug your application was to output tracing statements using `Response.Write` throughout the code. Each of these statements would output the values of variables so that they could be assessed throughout the execution of the page. PHP coders would do (and still do) the same thing with the `echo` statement. All of these statements had to be commented out, or removed altogether, before the page could go live as part of a site.

ASP.NET changed this with the introduction of *tracing*. Tracing is a technique that enables you to track the values of variables throughout page execution, or obtain a lot of information about the execution context of your pages. Tracing was designed to work best with ASP.NET Web Forms, but it still provides a really useful way to see what is going on as your page executes.

Tracing must be enabled for the application. You do this by adding a simple entry to the web.config file. The `TraceContext` class exposes two methods — `Write` and `Warn`. These methods are used to add entries to a trace log, which can be viewed using a special file.

In the next exercise, you will set tracing up in an application and see how it works.

TRY IT OUT **Adding Tracing to Your Site**

This exercise requires the use of the Chapter 9 site that you have already started, so if it's not open in WebMatrix at this point, please open it.

1. Open the web.config file that you added in the last exercise, and add the following entry to the `<system.web>` node:

```
<trace enabled="true" requestLimit="100" mostRecent="true" localOnly="true"/>
```

This can be placed just after the closing `</customErrors>` tag and the closing `</system.web>` tag, or just after the opening `<system.web>` tag.

2. Add a new file called **Tracing.cshtml**. Make the title of the page **Tracing Test** and add the following code to the `<body>` element:

```
<p>@message</p>
<form method="post">
<p>Choose day of week for delivery:<br />
    <select name="day">
        @foreach(var day in Enum.GetNames(typeof(DayOfWeek))){
            <option>@day</option>
        }
    </select>
</p>
<p>Morning or Afternoon?<br />
    <input type="radio" name="ampm" value="am" /> AM<br />
    <input type="radio" name="ampm" value="pm" /> PM
</p>
<p>Choose carrier:<br />
    <select name="carrier">
        <option>Speedy Boxes</option>
        <option>Comet Cartons</option>
        <option>Perilous Parcels</option>
        <option>Dicey Deliveries</option>
    </select>
</p>
<p>
    <input type="submit" name="submit" value="Submit" />
</p>
</form>
```

3. Add the following code to a code block at the top of the file:

```
@{
    var message = "";
    App.Foo = "Bar";
    Response.Cookies["MyCookie"].Value = Guid.NewGuid().ToString();
```

```
Response.Cookies["MyCookie"].Expires = DateTime.Now.AddDays(1);
if(IsPost){
    bool myBool = false;
    if(!Request["day"].Contains("s")){
        myBool = true;
    }
    if(myBool && (Request["ampm"].IsEmpty() || Request["ampm"] == "am")){
        myBool = false;
    }
    if(!myBool){
        message = "Sorry - that combination is not available";
    }else{
        message = "Success! That combination is available";
    }
}
}
}
```

4. Run the page a few times, completing the form and submitting it. Then change the address in your browser to request Trace.axd instead of Tracing.cshtml. You should see an Application Trace listing the requests you have just made to Tracing.cshtml similar to Figure 9-10.

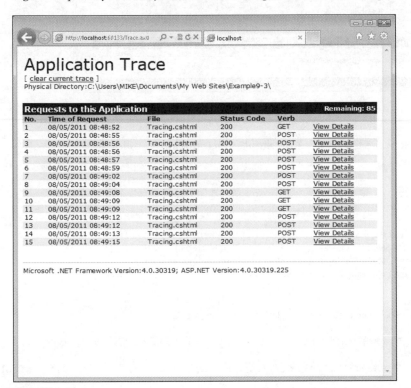

FIGURE 9-10

Choose the most recent POST request (one where you submitted the form) and examine the details, especially the section entitled Trace Information (see Figure 9-11).

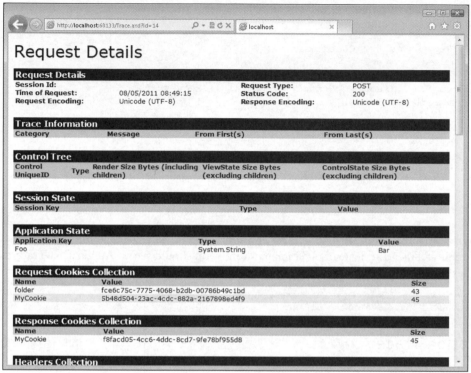

FIGURE 9-11

5. Change the code block at the top of Tracing.cshtml so that it reads as follows:

```
@{
    var message = "";
    Context.Trace.Write("Event", "Page requested");
    Context.Trace.Write("User", Environment.UserName);
    App.Foo = "Bar";
    Context.Trace.Write("Event", "Application variable set");
    Response.Cookies["MyCookie"].Value = Guid.NewGuid().ToString();
    Response.Cookies["MyCookie"].Expires = DateTime.Now.AddDays(1);
    Context.Trace.Write("Event", "Cookie set");
    if(IsPost){
        bool myBool = false;
        Context.Trace.Write("Event", "Initializing myBool...");
        if(!myBool){
            Context.Trace.Warn("Warning", String.Format("myBool is {0}", myBool));
        }else{
            Context.Trace.Write("Value Check", String.Format("myBool is {0}", myBool));
        }
        Context.Trace.Write("Event", "Checking day contains s...");
        Context.Trace.Write("Value Check", Request["day"].Contains("s").ToString());
        if(!Request["day"].Contains("s")){
            myBool = true;
        }
        if(!myBool){
            Context.Trace.Warn("Warning", String.Format("myBool is {0}", myBool));
```

```
        }else{
            Context.Trace.Write("Value Check", String.Format("myBool is {0}", myBool));
        }
        Context.Trace.Write("Event", "Checking morning...");
        if(myBool && (Request["ampm"].IsEmpty() || Request["ampm"] == "am")){
            myBool = false;
        }
        if(!myBool){
            message = "Sorry - that combination is not available";
            Context.Trace.Warn("Warning", String.Format("myBool is {0}", myBool));
        }else{
            message = "Success! That combination is available";
            Context.Trace.Write("Value Check", String.Format("myBool is {0}", myBool));
        }
    }
}
```

6. Add the following lines of code to the end of the file, just after the closing `</html>` tag:

```
@{
    Context.Trace.Write("Event","Page finished");
}
```

7. Run the page in the browser again. Complete the form and submit it one last time. Then navigate to Trace.axd and review the section titled Trace Information. You should see a number of entries in there that were not present before; they should be similar to those illustrated in Figure 9-12.

FIGURE 9-12

How It Works

The first step in this exercise was to add an entry to the web.config file. This entry enables tracing throughout the entire website. Although you were only asked to visit Tracing.cshtml as part of the exercise, if you had visited any other pages in the site, those requests would have been included in the tracing report. When you set up tracing, you specified values for a number of options. A breakdown of all of the options is provided in Table 9-1.

TABLE 9-1: Tracing Options

ATTRIBUTE	VALUES	DESCRIPTION
enabled	true or false	Switches tracing on or off for all pages in the site. If true, can be overridden at page level by adding Context .Trace.IsEnabled = false; to the page code.
requestLimit	Numeric, default is 10	This setting dictates the maximum number of page requests that will be stored in the trace log.
mostRecent	true or false	If true, only the most recent requests will appear in the trace log. The oldest ones are discarded if the requestLimit value has been reached. If false, requests are ignored once the requestLimit has been reached.
localOnly	true or false	This setting determines whether trace information will be shown on clients (browsers) running on the server (locally to the application) or to any browser. The default is true, which prevents remote clients (your users) from being able to see tracing information.
pageOutput	true or false	This setting has no effect within ASP.NET Web Pages. If set to true in a Web Forms application, the trace information is rendered at the bottom of the page.
traceMode	SortByTime or SortByCategory	Sets the sort order for tracing messages. The default is SortByTime.

You added a page with a simple form on it. The form provides the users with a small set of options relating to a fictitious delivery service. The form itself is unremarkable, except perhaps for the way that the select list for the day of the week is constructed. System.DayOfWeek is an enumeration, which is a data type. Enumerations are used to provide type safety over a set of constant values. In this case, the .NET Framework designers decided to hard-bake an enumeration of the days of the week into the framework. The Enum.GetNames method generates an array of strings from the enumerated constant values — Sunday, Monday, Tuesday, and so on — and those are iterated over to generate <option> elements. It's quite a tidy way to generate a drop-down menu containing the days of the week, and could make a good candidate for a helper, if you like.

Back to the tracing topic — the original code block you added to the page did nothing particularly amazing. You set an application variable, a cookie, and a couple of other variables, including a `bool`. Then you went through the posted form values and altered the value of the `bool` from `false` to `true` and back again, perhaps, depending on the form values. The actual logic that applies here is irrelevant. The example serves to simulate the process of having to keep track of a number of elements in a complex calculation to ensure that whatever logic has been applied actually works as intended. At the end of the processing, a message is written to the browser with the result of the calculation.

You went to the browser address bar and altered the URL to request a file called Trace.axd. You had not created this file, nor is there any sign of such a file in your website if you go back to WebMatrix and study the File Explorer; so what is it and where does it come from? Requests to Trace.axd get routed to something called `TraceHandler`, which is an ASP.NET `HttpHandler` — a component for processing the incoming HTTP request and providing a response. `TraceHandler`'s role is to obtain the logged tracing information and to output it to the browser, all nicely formatted in tables. Your attention was drawn to the second of those tables — Trace Information — when you reviewed the detail for a POST request, and you should have noticed that there was no data there.

The next change you made to the Tracing.cshtml file included numerous calls to both the `Trace.Write` and `Trace.Warn` methods. Each of these took two strings as arguments. The first is a category name, and the second is a trace message. The category is user-defined, in that you can make up your own. The message can be anything you like. When you reviewed the detail for a POST request after these statements had been added to the code, you should have had a variety of entries in the previously empty Trace Information section. You chose to use Warning as the category when you used the `Warn` method to add an entry to the trace log. However, you can probably see that isn't necessary — all items added via the `Warn` method are rendered in red. You can track how the Boolean variable changes as the code is executed.

At this stage, it's probably a good idea to review the tracing report in Figure 9-12 in more detail. It contains a wealth of information that you might find useful in the future. Starting with the Tracing Information block, you can see that the execution time for the page is displayed, but not only that — the execution time between individual log entries is also provided. If you ever have performance problems with a page and you are not sure exactly which process is causing the problem, all you need to do is log entries in the trace at various points before and after processes execute, and you should be able to narrow the issue down.

The Control Tree section is only relevant to ASP.NET Web Forms. All the time you are developing Web Pages using Razor, this will be empty. Session State will show any session level variables that you might have set, and you can see your `AppState` variable in Application State. The next two sections cover cookies — those that are sent by the browser and those that you set and send to the browser. If you check your first GET request for Tracing.cshtml, you will see Request Cookies contains no data as the cookie had not been set at that point.

The Headers section contains useful information about the HTTP Request headers, and this is followed by the Form collection. If you think back to the ObjectInfo exercise, you can see that the use of tracing would have helped diagnose the cause of the misbehaving form validation. Query string data would be shown in the next section in the same format as the Form data — name/value pairs. And the final section provides you with the server variables, which you also saw from the ServerInfo helper.

ASP.NET Tracing is a very useful utility. The key areas where it can be especially useful are in tracking values of variables throughout page execution; measuring execution time for performance reasons; and troubleshooting issues that do not cause exceptions once the site is live. Enable tracing and wait for a user to report an issue — you should have the trace information available to help identify the cause.

> **NOTE** *Tracing can be an expensive business. The trace information needs to be stored in memory until you choose to clear it, and each page that tracing is enabled within has to undergo additional processing as the trace information is generated. You must enable tracing site-wide at the web.config level, but you can also disable it on a page-by-page basis. You can disable tracing on sections of your site in a PageStart file by adding* `Context.Trace.IsEnabled = false` *to the top of the file, and then enable it on a page-by-page basis by adding* `Context.Trace.IsEnabled = true` *to each page.*

SUMMARY

Errors are an inevitable part of software development. An important part of the development process is debugging code and gracefully handling exceptions. In this chapter, you have read about a number of ways in which these tasks can be accomplished.

First of all, you learned that there are different categories of errors or bugs. You saw that there are syntax errors, which lead to compilation problems. You saw how to interpret the error message details to understand what went wrong as a prelude to being able to fix it. Runtime exceptions occur while your application is executing. You learned how to use a `try-catch` block to manage these and present controlled error messages to your users.

The final group of errors are logical errors — ones where mistakes in the logic of the code lead to unexpected results. You discovered two built-in helpers that are designed to provide diagnostic information to you — the ObjectInfo helper and the ServerInfo helper. ObjectInfo provides detailed information about values and objects in your code via its `Print` method, and ServerInfo provides detailed information about the environment in which your code is running via its `GetHtml` method.

Finally, you saw how ASP.NET Tracing allows you to track and record a wealth of information on a request-by-request basis. You saw how the `Trace.Write` method logs entries into the Tracing Information section in the trace report, and how `Trace.Warn` results in the logged information appearing in red. Execution times are logged too, which together with the other tracking information you log, helps to build up a great picture about problems — whether performance-related or resulting from logical errors.

EXERCISES

1. What is the difference between the ObjectInfo helper and the ServerInfo helper?

2. What type of code should you use `try-catch` blocks for?

Answers to the Exercises can be found in the Appendix.

► **WHAT YOU LEARNED IN THIS CHAPTER**

TERM	DEFINITION
Bug	A software error that leads to unwanted or unexpected behaviour.
Debugging	The process of locating and correcting bugs in software code.
Exception	A .NET object that represents an error that occurs at execution time.
Exception handling	The practice of anticipating exceptions and managing them gracefully in code.
ObjectInfo	A helper designed to provide details about objects in code.
ServerInfo	A helper designed to provide data about the execution environment in which your code runs.
Tracing	Enables you to log and view diagnostic information about a single HTTP request.

10

Introduction to Data and Databases

WHAT YOU WILL LEARN IN THIS CHAPTER:

➤ What a database is

➤ What tools WebMatrix provides for working with data

➤ What SQL is and how to use it

➤ How relationships work within databases

➤ How to use the Database Helper

Up to this point, most of the data you have worked with has been stored temporarily in variables within your C# code. You have persisted (saved) some data to text files, such as the exception logging that you created in the last chapter, and you have generated data that resides in e-mails in a number of exercises. You also created folders containing image data in Chapter 8. Data has so far come in many different forms, but none of it very structured or organized. As your site grows and the number of users increases, you will gather more and more data. You will need to be able to store this permanently, and you will need to be able to query it, display it, change it, and even remove it.

You will need to be able to organize your data so that it is well structured. This will make it easier to manipulate. You will also need some means of communicating how you would like to manipulate the data programmatically. In this chapter, you explore solutions to these two requirements — the structure provided by databases, and the means of communication provided by Structured Query Language (SQL).

WHAT IS A DATABASE?

A *database* is a software program designed for the storage, retrieval, and manipulation of data. Databases come in a number of forms. The most commonly used form is the *Relational*

Database Management System (RDBMS). Other types include flat-file systems (such as spreadsheets), object-oriented databases, and document-oriented databases. The type of database that ships with the WebMatrix package is SQL Server Compact 4.0, which is a relational database system. SQL Server Compact is the database system that you will use throughout the remainder of this book.

In a relational database system, data is stored in a collection of tables (relations). Each table consists of rows, with each row (also known as a *tuple*) containing a unique data item. Whenever database tables are exposed to users via a graphical interface, they resemble spreadsheets like the one shown in Figure 10-1.

Id	Title	Description	Price	CategoryId	DatePosted
1	Laptop	Refurbished	300	2	08/05/2011 0...
2	Portable Radio	Nearly New	50	1	08/05/2011 0...
3	Rowing Mach...	One previous ...	1000	3	09/05/2011 0...
4	Color Printer	As New, Can...	95	2	10/05/2011 0...
5	iPad	32GB 3G	450	2	10/05/2011 0...
6	4 Pirelli Tyres	18 Inch Unused	600	4	10/05/2011 0...
7	Hard Drive	IBM, 300GB ...	65	2	12/05/2011 0...
8	Laptop Bag	Samsonite 1...	85	2	12/05/2011 0...
9	Tom Tom Sat...	Includes cas...	125	1	14/05/2011 0...
10	Electric Mulc...	Black and De...	150	5	14/05/2011 0...
11	Pond Pump	2000 gallons ...	65	5	14/05/2011 0...
12	Xenon Bulbs	Packs of 6	10	4	14/05/2011 0...
13	Ford	Good runner	600	4	18/05/2011 0...

FIGURE 10-1

Each data item or row is organized into columns, with each column holding a specific piece of the data. In Figure 10-1, you can see that the table contains items for sale. Each item for sale has a title, description, price, and so on. You should begin to recognize these "properties" as similar to the data you captured in the form that you built in Chapter 5.

If you look at the data in Figure 10-1, you can see that each item belongs to a category. If you wanted to rename the Computers category to something like IT & Computing, you would have to make that change to every row of data that had Computers in the category column. In the sample pictured above, that's not hard — there are only a few rows of data. However, if you had thousands, or millions, of rows of data, that would be more of a problem.

The solution to this problem is to create a separate table to house the repeating information. In this case, the repeating information is the category, so you would create a table called Categories, which would contain a *unique identifier* for each category and a category name. In the Items table, instead of storing the category name for each item, you would store the category's identifier. Now the Items table has a relationship with the Categories table based on the category's identifier.

If you wanted to change the name of a category, you would only have to do it in the Categories table, and all rows of data throughout the database that reference that particular category via its identifier would be associated with the revised value. This may be a little confusing to grasp at the moment, but it should become clearer as you work through the rest of the chapter.

SQL SERVER COMPACT

There is a wide range of relational database systems you can work with in your ASP.NET Web Pages sites. You can work with Microsoft's other database systems — the full version of SQL Server, or a Microsoft Access database. You can work with other systems such as Oracle, MySQL PostGreSQL, and so on. However, you will work with SQL Server Compact throughout this book.

The full version of SQL Server, along with systems like Oracle, MySQL, and PostGreSQL, are all server-based systems. Microsoft Access and SQL Server Compact are file-based database systems. Server-based databases tend to be a lot more powerful and scalable than file-based systems. They usually feature advanced permissions and security features. On top of that, they may include a full range of development features such as the ability to create custom functions, saved queries, stored procedures, and so on. With all of those features, however, comes a lot of complexity.

Until recently, people who did not need highly scalable database systems for fairly low traffic sites, or those who simply found server-based databases too much to cope with tended to choose Microsoft Access as the database for their websites. Although Access could stand up to the rigors of smallish sites with careful programming, it was never designed to work in high availability, high-stress, high-concurrency web applications. That never prevented Access from being relatively easy to work with, and really easy to deploy to a website. You could simply copy the file across the network. As part of the WebMatrix story, Microsoft realized that they need to produce an easy-to-use, easy-to-deploy database system that would work with ASP.NET, and SQL Server Compact 4.0 is the result.

SQL Server Compact stores data in a file with a .sdf extension. These are saved to disk, which means that they become part of your website folder and file structure. In fact, they are created by default in the App_Data folder that appears when you create your password for the Package Management system. App_Data, if you recall, is a protected folder within ASP.NET, which means that users cannot browse its contents.

Perhaps one of the most significant things about SQL Server Compact is that it runs within the ASP.NET application's memory process. All other database systems, including Access, run in their own processes. What this means is that the .NET Framework has no control over them, and this fact can be the cause of memory leaks, as resources, such as connections, are not managed properly. The SQL Server Compact engine, on the other hand, starts when your website starts, and stops when the site stops again. In the meantime, it is always available as part of the application itself.

USING THE DATABASES WORKSPACE

You were briefly introduced to the Databases Workspace in Chapter 1. This area of WebMatrix is the primary tool for working with SQL Server Compact databases. Figure 10-2 shows the main screen and menu options when no database has been added to the site. You can create a new SQL Server Compact database by either clicking the New Database button on the ribbon at the top, or by clicking the link in the middle of the screen. You also have the option to connect to an existing SQL Server (full) database using the New Connection button. You can see that the New Table button is disabled at the moment, because there is no database to add a new table to. That is about to change.

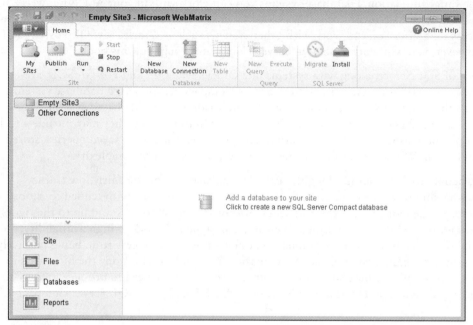

FIGURE 10-2

Creating Your First Database

In this exercise, you will use WebMatrix to create a simple database with one table. The database you create will form the basis for further exercises throughout this chapter and should eventually be suitable for use within the Classifieds site that you have been building throughout this book.

1. Create a new website based on the Empty Site template, and name it **Chapter10**.

2. Click the Databases tab in the workspace selector to bring up the Databases Workspace.

3. You should now add a database to the site. You can do this by either clicking the New Database button in the ribbon bar, or the Add a Database to Your Site link in the middle of the workspace. When you do this, the database will, by default, acquire the name of the site. Leave the database name as `Chapter10.sdf`.

4. A Tables node should become visible just below the database file entry in the File Explorer. Click that. Two things should happen: The first is that the New Table button should now be enabled, and the second is that a new tab should appear in the ribbon — Table.

5. Click either the New Table button, or click the tab at the top. The result will be the same — you will be taken to the Table menu, with the table designer ready for a table to be built (see Figure 10-3).

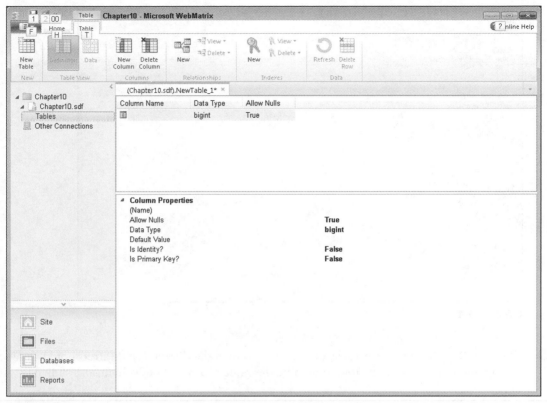

FIGURE 10-3

6. In the Column Properties section, click in the blank space next to (Name) and type **Id**.

7. Change the Data Type to `int` by using the drop-down selector, or by simply typing it where `bigint` currently appears.

8. Toggle Is Identity to `true`, and Is Primary Key to `true`.

 WARNING *At this point, you should check the name you have given the column. You are about to add a new column, and the current one will be saved automatically as soon as you do. Once the column name has been saved, you cannot change it. This is a limitation of the SQL Server Compact database. It does not apply to other database systems such as the full version of SQL Server.*

9. Click the New Column button at the top. Add the text **Name** as the column name and specify the data type as **nvarchar**. Leave the other properties as they are, and press Ctrl+S to save the table. At this stage, you will be prompted to provide a name for your table, so call it **People**. Figure 10-4 shows how your database designer should appear at this point.

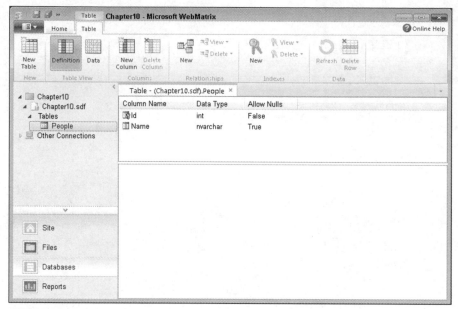

FIGURE 10-4

10. Click the Data button in the Table View menu group in the ribbon. WebMatrix should show you an empty table with one row containing the value NULL in both columns, as shown in Figure 10-5.

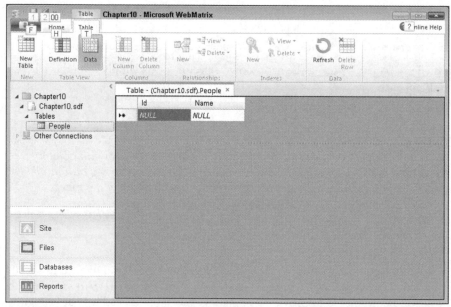

FIGURE 10-5

11. Add your name to the Name column in the first row, and press Enter. The Id column should auto-matically change to 1. See Figure 10-6.

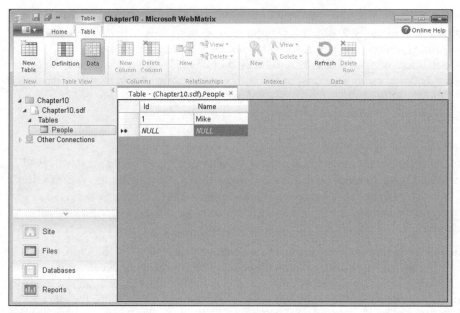

FIGURE 10-6

12. Finally, add another name to the second row and press Enter. Notice that the Id value in the new row is set to 2.

How It Works

At the outset, you learned that a relational database is composed of tables. In this exercise, you used the WebMatrix Databases Workspace to add a new blank and empty database to a website. You saw that the database filename will take the name of the site by default. You can change the name if you like by right-clicking on the filename in the File Explorer and using the Rename option. What you decide to call your database is important, as the name will form an essential part of how you connect to the database from your pages in future exercises.

Your database was created as a SQL Server Compact 4.0 database file (with an .sdf extension) and placed in a newly created App_Data folder. SQL Server Compact 4.0 is the default database for WebMatrix, and the App_Data folder is the default location for data files in ASP.NET. It is a special ASP.NET folder, in that it is protected against browsing. This means that its contents are secure from people with browsers.

You created your first table by clicking the New Table button in the menu, or by selecting the Table tab. This action took you to the Design View for a table. You saw that tables are composed of columns, which have properties. In the Table designer, you could see the definition of the columns that have been created, and in the bottom half, you set properties for two columns — Id and Name. Just like C# variables, names for database columns should describe their contents so that the *schema* becomes self-documenting. A schema is the definition of the tables, columns, relationships, and other objects that form a database.

 WARNING *It is technically possible for you to include spaces in your database column names. If you are ever tempted to sprinkle your column names with embedded spaces, take yourself to one side and have a stiff word. Do not do it. Besides this being counter to best practice, spaces in column names may break the Database Helper (which you will meet towards the end of the chapter) and this will make your WebMatrix development particularly tedious.*

On a related matter, you should also avoid using SQL Compact reserved words for table or field names. These include terms like Order, Transaction, View and many other everyday terms. You can find a full reference at `http://msdn.microsoft.com/en-us/library/ms173340(v=SQL.110).aspx`, as well as advice to wrap such terms in double quotes or square brackets in your SQL where they have been used and you have no choice but to work with them.

You also chose the data type that will be stored in those columns. Just like variables in C#, you can use data types to store different types of values. You will see more about the available data types soon. An option also exists for you to provide a default value for any column, although you did not use it in this exercise. You finally saved the table. Once you had saved the table, you switched to the Data View, and entered your name in the first row within the table. You committed (saved) that first row by pressing the Enter key. This resulted in the Id column changing from NULL to 1.

When you set the properties for the Id column, you chose to set Is Identity to `true`. When you do this, you ask SQL Server Compact to automatically generate values for the column, starting from 1, and increment-ing by 1 each time a new row is added. This ensures that each row has its own unique identity. You do not need to enter a value for an Identity column. In fact, the database will complain if you try. You also set Is Primary Key to `true`. You will learn more about primary keys later in the chapter.

SQL Server Compact Data Types

When you created your own columns, you set the data types for two columns, and met the `int` data type along with `nvarchar`. Table 10-1 looks at the most common data types that you are likely to use, and shows how they map across to the .NET types that you met in Chapter 4.

TABLE 10-1: SQL Server Compact Data Types

DATA TYPE	DESCRIPTION	.NET TYPE
bigint	Stores whole numbers between −9,223,372,036,854,775,808 and 9,223,372,036,854,775,807.	Int64
bit	Stores a value of either 1 or 0.	byte

DATA TYPE	DESCRIPTION	.NET TYPE
datetime	Stores a date and time.	DateTime
float	Stores very large fractional numbers with less precision than numeric.	double
image	Variable length binary data.	image
int	Stores whole numbers between -2,147,483,648 and 2,147,483,647.	Int32
nchar	Fixed length Unicode data.	string
nvarchar	Variable length Unicode data.	string
numeric	Stores very large fractional numbers with more accuracy than float.	decimal
uniqueidentifier	A globally unique identifier.	GUID

A full breakdown of the data types supported by SQL Server Compact can be found at MSDN: `http://msdn.microsoft.com/en-us/library/ms172424(SQL.100).aspx`.

When you set the Name column to `nvarchar` in the previous exercise, you may have noticed that the column properties offered an additional property to set: length. The value for this property defaulted to 100, which is fine for the exercise. You should be aware that the value sets a maximum number of characters that can be stored. If you attempted to enter a name that exceeded 100 characters, the value would be truncated.

The image data type allows you to save actual binary data (files) to the database. There has always been a lot of discussion about whether you should store files in a database, and while this book will not explore the arguments in any detail (a well-worded search phrase, such as "save files to database or file system" will find a lot of results on Google or Bing if you are that interested), the fact is that a SQL Server Compact database is restricted in size to 4GB. You will see how to store files in a SQL Server Compact database later in the book, but you should bear this size restriction in mind when deciding where to save your files.

STRUCTURED QUERY LANGUAGE

Structured Query Language, or SQL (pronounced "sequel"), is a language that databases understand for manipulating data. Various standards exist, with the most commonly used one being the ANSI 92 SQL standard. Database vendors choose how much of the language they support, and they can, and do, create their own extensions to the language. Microsoft's version of SQL is known as Transact-SQL, or T-SQL. SQL Server Compact 4.0 implements some parts of T-SQL, but this book will concentrate on the standard and most commonly used parts of SQL. A full reference to the T-SQL language supported by SQL Server Compact 4.0 is available on MSDN at `http://msdn .microsoft.com/en-us/library/ms173372(SQL.110).aspx`.

There are four primary data operations: Create, Read, Update, and Delete. They are together known by their acronym CRUD. Each of these operations has a SQL command: INSERT, SELECT, UPDATE, and DELETE respectively. The next sections explore each of these operations in detail. You will use the Classifieds database that comes with the download for this chapter.

Reading Data

Typically, the command you will use most frequently is SELECT for reading data. The syntax for this command in its most basic form is:

```
SELECT column_list FROM table_name
```

Column names appear in a list of columns separated by commas. You do not have to follow the order in which the columns appear in the table. If you want to select all columns, you can use a wildcard (*) as a kind of shorthand:

```
SELECT * FROM table_name
```

This will result in all columns being returned, in the order in which they appear in the table. For example, if you chose to execute this command against the Items table in the sample database, you would return the contents of the Id, Title, Description, Price, CategoryId, and DatePosted columns, as shown in Figure 10-7.

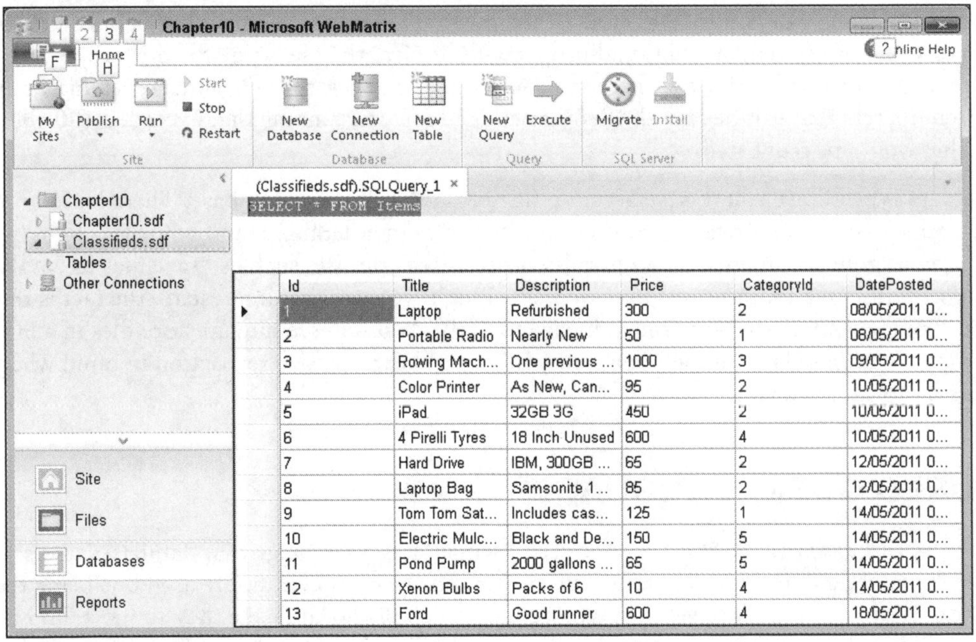

FIGURE 10-7

NOTE *You should use the * shorthand only when you actually want all columns returned as part of the query. It is considered poor programming practice to lazily use* SELECT ** just because you cannot be bothered to type the column names. When you do this, you use memory retrieving a bunch of data that you do not need, if you have no intention of using data from all the columns in the table.*

Filtering Data

Often, you will only want certain rows of data from a table — those that meet certain conditions. For example, you might only want records that were added after a certain date, or that belong to a certain category. This process of setting conditions in SQL is known as *filtering*. You filter data by adding a WHERE clause to the SQL statement. Most often, you filter on the value of a column, so if you wanted to select all rows in the Items table with a CategoryId of 2, the syntax is as follows:

```
SELECT * FROM Items WHERE CategoryId = 2
```

If you wanted to select all items with a title of iPad, the SQL is as follows:

```
SELECT * FROM Items WHERE Title = 'iPad'
```

Notice this time that the value on the right side of the operator is enclosed in single quotes. These are known as *delimiters*, and they separate string values from the rest of the SQL statement. Numeric values do not require delimiters, but since datetimes can appear in a number of valid string formats, they also need to be delimited using single quotes when they appear as part of a SQL statement.

The equals sign is not the only operator that can be used in a WHERE clause. Most of the operators you have already met as part of the C# language translate to SQL. Table 10-2 examines the most commonly used operators and describes their purposes.

TABLE 10-2: Commonly Used SQL Operators

OPERATOR	DESCRIPTION
=	Equal to
>	Greater than
<	Less than
<>	Not equal to
>=	Greater than or equal to
<=	Less than or equal to

You can combine expressions in a WHERE clause to apply multiple filters. The SQL operators you will use most often in combining expressions are AND, OR, and BETWEEN. The AND and OR operators work in exactly the same way as their C# counterparts && and ||. Look at the following two SQL statements:

```
SELECT * FROM Items WHERE CategoryId = 2 AND Price > 100
SELECT * FROM Items WHERE CategoryId = 2 OR Price > 100
```

The first statement will return rows only where the CategoryId is 2, and the price of items in that category is greater than 100. The only items matching those criteria are the Laptop and the iPad. The second statement on the other hand will return considerably more rows of data, as the criteria includes anything with a CategoryId of 2 (that's five rows) *or* a price that is in excess of 100 (that's four more rows).

The BETWEEN operator acts in the same way as a combination of <= and >= operators. For example, the following two queries will return the same results:

```
SELECT * FROM Items WHERE Price BETWEEN 85 AND 150
SELECT * FROM Items WHERE Price >= 85 AND Price <= 150
```

TRY IT OUT Selecting Data

In this exercise, you will use the sample Classifieds database that comes as part of the download for this chapter. Therefore you should ensure that you have downloaded it to a location to which you have access.

1. Open the Chapter 10 site that you created in the earlier exercise if you closed it.

2. Click the Files selector in the workspace selector (bottom-left pane). Right-click on the App_Data folder and select Add Existing File. From there, navigate to the location where you saved the Classifieds.sdf database file and select it. Now if you choose Databases in the workspace selector in the bottom-left pane, you should see the Classifieds database added to the Chapter10 database you created earlier.

3. Make sure the Classifieds database is selected by single clicking it so that the name is highlighted in blue. Notice that the New Query button in the ribbon bar has become active. Click it to open the query editor.

4. Type the following into the query editor:

```
SELECT * FROM Items
```

Then press F5, or click the Execute button in the ribbon bar. The result should look like Figure 10-6. You can move the splitter bar separating the query from the results upward if you like.

5. Change the existing SQL statement so that it looks like this:

```
--SELECT * FROM Items
SELECT Id, Title, Price FROM Items WHERE Price > 200
```

6. Press F5 or click the Execute button in the ribbon bar. Your result should resemble Figure 10-8.

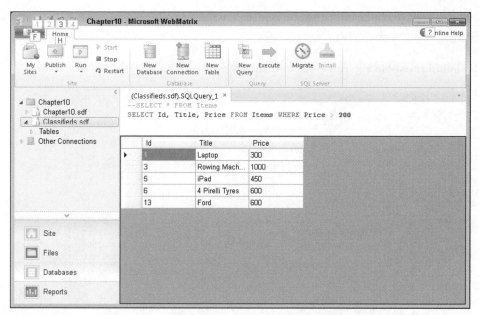

FIGURE 10-8

7. Alter the second line of SQL by adding ORDER BY Price to the end of the line:

```
--SELECT * FROM Items
SELECT Id, Title, Price FROM Items WHERE Price > 200 ORDER BY Price
```

Press F5 or click Execute so that the result looks like Figure 10-9.

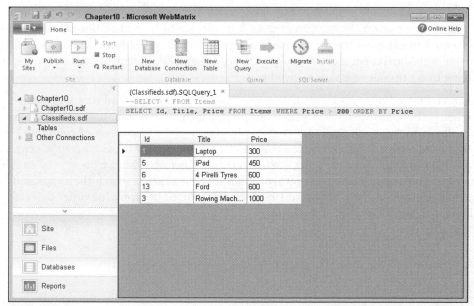

FIGURE 10-9

8. Delete all of the SQL from the top pane and replace it with the following:

```
SELECT * FROM Items WHERE Title LIKE '%or%'
```

The result should resemble Figure 10-10.

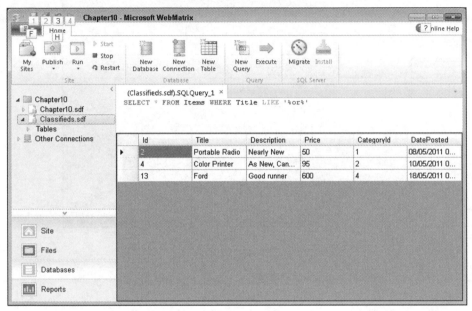

FIGURE 10-10

How It Works

In this exercise you tried out several SELECT statements with varying filters and additional statements. You also got the chance to experiment with the query designer offered by WebMatrix. This is a fairly rudimentary part of WebMatrix, but it offers you the chance to test SQL statements against your database without having to write code in a page somewhere.

The first statement you tested retrieves all records in the table. You may have had to use the splitter to bring all records fully into view. Then you commented out the initial statement using double dashes (--). This allowed you to add a new statement, which returned a limited set of columns. You applied a filter to the statement, which restricted the matching rows to only those where the price value exceeds 200. Your next amendment added an ORDER BY clause. When you ran the query, you should have noticed that the same rows of data were returned, but that the order in which they appeared had changed so that the lowest priced item appeared first. Items are sorted in ascending order by default, or if you specify the ASC argument as part of the clause:

```
...ORDER BY Price ASC
```

Adding the DESC argument to the end of the ORDER BY clause reverses the order:

```
...ORDER BY Price DESC
```

The final example introduced you to the LIKE operator. This determines whether a string matches a given pattern. The percentage sign (%) acts as a wildcard representing any string of zero or more characters. The criteria you applied sought to match any item with a title that contains the letters "or" anywhere within it. The percentage sign prior to "or" represents zero or more characters, as does the percentage sign after the string. Only titles that begin with the letters "or" would meet the condition if the leading wildcard were removed. If the leading wildcard remained but the end one were removed, only titles that end with the letters "or" would match.

Adding and Modifying Data

Learning how to retrieve data is very useful, but the data has to get into the database in the first place. The first part of the CRUD acronym is create, which is accomplished using the INSERT statement. The basic syntax for this statement is

```
INSERT INTO table_name (column_list) VALUES (value_list)
```

Each of the columns provided in the column_list part must have a matching value in the value_list part and each is separated from its predecessor with a comma. You do not need to specify the columns if you insert a value into every column in the table. Here is an example that adds a new row to the Items table:

```
INSERT INTO Items (
    Title,
    Description,
    Price,
    CategoryId,
    DatePosted
)
VALUES (
    'Ford',
    'Good runner',
    600,
    4,
    '2011-05-18'
)
```

The formatting is not necessary, but makes the statement easier to read. Values to be inserted are delimited in the same way as previously — strings and dates are surrounded with single quotes. There are a number of ways in which you can provide dates and times to be inserted. SQL Server Compact will do its best to parse a string to a datetime type. To be on the safe side however, you should always present dates in this format: yyyy-mm-dd hh:mm:ss. This will prevent any potential errors arising from differing regional settings on servers. If you want to insert the current date and time when you add a new record, you can use the built-in T-SQL function GetDate(). There are two ways this function can be applied. One is to pass GetDate() as the value in the SQL statement:

```
INSERT INTO Items (
    Title,
    Description,
    Price,
    CategoryId,
```

```
        DatePosted
    )
    VALUES (
        'Ford',
        'Good runner',
        600,
        4,
        GetDate()
    )
```

The other is to set `GetDate()` as the default value for the column when you create it using the designer. If you do this, you won't need to include the column in the INSERT statement.

The third part of the CRUD acronym stands for UPDATE, which is the command used to modifying existing data. The basic syntax for the UPDATE statement is

```
UPDATE table_name SET column_name = value, column_name = value
```

Most often, you will provide a filter via a WHERE clause to update single rows. The following example will change the price in the sample database for the iPad only:

```
UPDATE Items SET Price = 450 WHERE Title = 'iPad'
```

Just as with the SELECT and INSERT statements, string and date-time values are delimited using single quotes. The preceding example will update all rows where the title is iPad, and since you cannot guarantee that the title is a unique value, this could be dangerous. This is why most often you see the WHERE clause in an UPDATE statement pointing to a unique value, such as the primary key — unless of course you intend to update every row in the database. If, for example, you wanted to increase the price of every item in the database by 10%, you would use the following SQL. It features no WHERE clause at all, but instead includes the existing Price column as part of the calculation that provides the revised value:

```
UPDATE Items SET Price = Price * 0.1
```

Finally, the most drastic way to modify your data is to remove it altogether. Completing the CRUD acronym is the DELETE command:

```
DELETE FROM table_name [WHERE... ]
```

The DELETE command takes effect on entire rows. They are completely removed from the database, so you should think carefully about its use. Once deleted, data is non-recoverable, unless you have a back-up copy. For that reason, you may see applications implement *logical deletes* rather than *physical deletes*. A logical delete takes the form of a `bit` column in the database, which has a value set to either 0 or 1 to indicate that the row has been set to a deleted state, although all the data is still physically there.

Selecting Data from Multiple Tables

The main idea of a relational database is to avoid duplicating data by creating separate relations, or tables for repeating values. In the sample database, category information is stored in a separate table. All you have in the Items table is a category's identifier. That isn't much use if you need to work with the category's name. You need to extract data from two tables simultaneously, and the way you do this is by using a *join*.

Joins define the way that two or more tables are logically related in a query. Looking at the Items table in the sample database, and the Category table, you see that both contain a CategoryId column. This is the column that is used to relate one table to the other. The CategoryId belongs to the Category table. It is what identifies a unique category. It is the Category table's *primary key*. When it is used to associate a category to an item in the Items table, it is known as a *foreign key*. Joins typically work across primary and foreign keys (although not always). The following query will generate a list of items with their category name:

```
SELECT Title, Description, Price, DatePosted, Category
FROM Items
JOIN Categories ON
Items.CategoryId = Categories.CategoryId
```

The result of executing this query within WebMatrix can be seen in Figure 10-11.

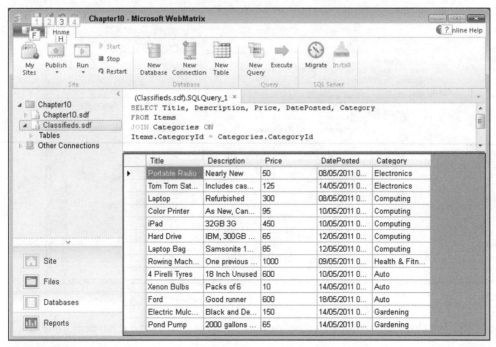

FIGURE 10-11

The default join type is an *inner join*. This returns all rows that are matched according to the *join predicate*, which in this case is where the Categories.CategoryId column has a matching entry in the Items.CategoryId column. The table named in the FROM clause is deemed to be the table on the "left side" of the join. In the previous example, that is the Items table.

Sometimes you will want to return all rows in the table on the left side of the join despite there being no matching record in the table on the right side of the join. This is best illustrated through the Bids table in the sample database. The Bids table contains details of individual bids for items. Not all items have had bids made on them, and some items have had more than one bid recorded in the Bids table. You use a `LEFT JOIN` to return all rows:

```
SELECT Id, Title, Description, Price, DatePosted, BidAmount
FROM Items
LEFT JOIN Bids ON
Items.Id = Bids.ItemId
```

All rows in the Items table have been returned in the result set (see Figure 10-12), even though some of them have no entry in the Bids table. They have no `BidAmount` value.

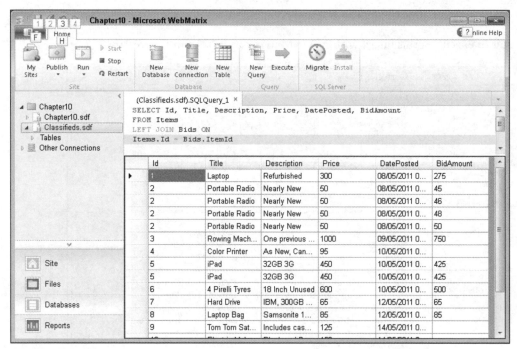

FIGURE 10-12

You can see too, that there are multiple entries for certain items — those that have multiple bids.

You can combine a `JOIN` with a `WHERE` clause too. For example, you might want to find unmatched records — those in the table of the left side of the join, which have no related record on the right side of the join. All items that have had no bids recorded against them meet this scenario. Here is the SQL to retrieve them:

```
SELECT Id, Title, Description, Price, DatePosted, BidAmount
FROM Items
LEFT JOIN Bids ON
Items.Id = Bids.ItemId
WHERE BidAmount IS NULL
```

The result is displayed in Figure 10-13.

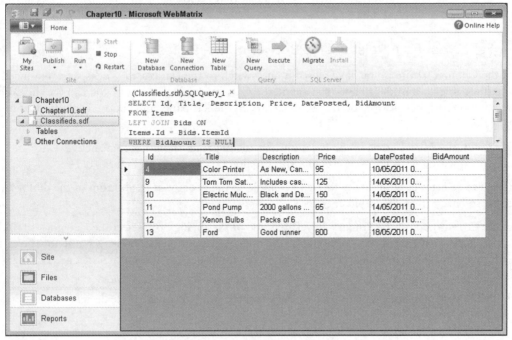

FIGURE 10-13

Relationships

If you deleted a category from the Categories table at the moment, the Items table will still hold references to a `CategoryId` value that has no matching entry in the Categories table. Your data will lose *integrity*. You create *relationships* in your database to prevent this kind of problem from occurring. Formally defined relationships are different than the temporary ones that you established in your join queries so far. They act as guardians against inconsistent data. They prevent you from deleting a `CategoryId` from the Categories table if there are existing related records in the Items table. Similarly, once you have created a relationship, you will not be able to insert a non-existent `CategoryId` value into the Items table. There would have to be a matching record in the Categories table. As the sample database stands at the moment, it is even possible to leave the `CategoryId` field in the Items table blank when you create a new Item record. A relationship will prevent this.

Relationships are created between the *primary key* column in one table and a *foreign key* in another table. The `CategoryId` in the Categories table is a primary key. It is used to uniquely identify each category. When it is used in the Items table, it is considered a foreign key there. The primary keys in the sample database are generated by setting Is Identity to `true` on the `int` or `bigint` columns. As you learned earlier, this ensures that each row obtains a different value. This isn't the only way to create primary keys, but it is the simplest to manage and use.

In the next exercise you will explore the tools available to you within WebMatrix for creating a relationship between two tables, and then you will test that relationship through SQL to see how it protects the integrity of your data.

TRY IT OUT **Creating a Relationship Between Two Tables**

1. Open the Chapter10 site if you have closed it and switch to the Databases Workspace. You need to expose the Tables tab in the ribbon, so expand the Classifieds database until you can see the tables in the left pane. Right-click on the Items table entry in the left pane, and choose Definition from the options that appear.

2. At this point, the New button in the Relationships menu group should become active. Click it. You should be presented with the New Relationships dialog box featured in Figure 10-14.

3. You need to select a column in the foreign key table as the prompt at the bottom of the dialog box suggests, so check the CategoryId checkbox.

4. From the drop-down on the Primary Key Table side of the dialog box, select the Categories table. Then check the CategoryId box. It should be the only active option available. A name for the relationship will appear in the Name box. By default, it should be FK_Items_Categories. Leave it as that.

5. Click OK, and then ensuring that you have focus on the top part of the table designer, press Ctrl+S to save your changes.

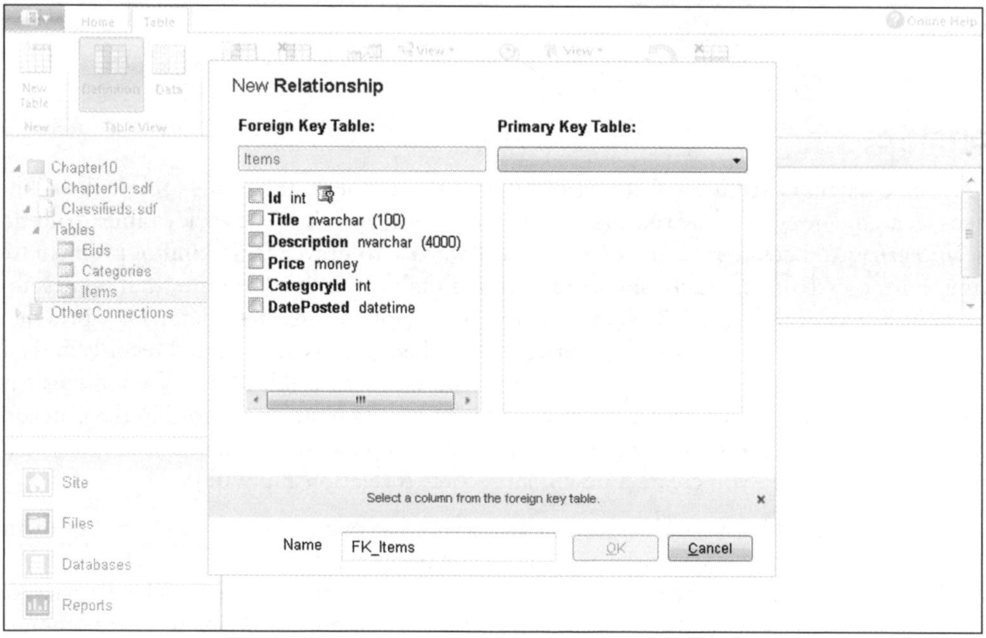

FIGURE 10-14

6. Click the Home tab and then click the New Query button. Type the following SQL and then click the Execute button to run the query:

```
INSERT INTO Items (Title, CategoryId) VALUES ('Test', 7)
```

You should receive an error dialog box with the following message:

```
A foreign key value cannot be inserted because a corresponding primary key value
    does not exist. [Foreign key constraint name = FK_Items_Categories]
```

7. Click the OK button on the error dialog box to dismiss it and replace the existing query with the following, which you should then execute by clicking the Execute button:

```
DELETE FROM Categories WHERE Category = 'Auto'
```

You should receive an error dialog box with the following message:

```
The primary key value cannot be deleted because references to this key still exist.
[Foreign key constraint name = FK_Items_Categories]
```

How It Works

When you created a relationship between the Items and the Categories tables, the relationship is enforced by the database. If you try to insert, update, or delete data and doing so would otherwise leave the data in a state where integrity is lost, the database will prevent you from doing so. In this exercise, you enforced integrity between data in the Items table and data in the Categories table. No Item can reference a non-existing category, and no category can be removed if there are matching entries in the Items table.

USING THE DATABASE HELPER

You have learned the basics involved in database design and manipulating data in it via SQL. The next step is to communicate with the database from code in your web pages. The .NET Framework includes a technology for communicating with databases from code. It is known as ADO.NET. One of the problems with ADO.NET, however, is that it takes a fair amount of code to get anything done. If you want to perform database operations on multiple pages, you need to rewrite large chunks of code on each page. The Database Helper provides a wrapper around ADO.NET, which greatly reduces the amount of code you need to produce, and makes learning how to access data from code an easier process than it otherwise would have been using ADO.NET.

The Database Helper provides a handful of methods, the most important of which is the `Open` method. This method establishes a connection to a named database and opens it so that further queries can be executed against the database. To connect to the Classifieds sample database that you have just been working with, for example, you use the following code:

```
@{
    var db = Database.Open("Classifieds");
}
```

Notice that the string you pass to the Open method is the name of the database file, without the file extension. This method will check the App_Data folder for a database file with the right name. If it cannot find such a file there, it will assume that the string passed into it is the name of a connection string stored in the web.config file. Typically, when using SQL Server Compact, you will not use the web.config file to store a connection string, but you are a lot more likely to do this if you use SQL Server. It provides a convenient way to store a connection string in one place, so that it can be altered easily. Say, for example, you need to change the connection string to reflect a different connection required for hosting compared to a development server. Here is an example of a web.config entry for a connection string:

```
<configuration>
  <connectionStrings>
   <add name="MyConnection"
     connectionString= "server=MyServer;database=MyDatabase;
     Trusted_Connection=True" providerName="System.Data.SqlClient" />
  </connectionStrings>
</configuration>
```

The Database.Open method accepts "MyConnection" as being the name of the connection string.

There are a couple of other ways to open connections to databases using the Database Helper — both of which accept the connection string. Neither of these is recommended for general use. However, it might be that you need to use one or both options. For completeness, here they are:

```
@{
    var connString = "server=MyServer;database=MyDatabase;Trusted_Connection=True";
    var provider = "System.Data.SqlClient";
    var db1 = Database.OpenConnectionString(connString);
    var db2 = Database.OpenConnectionString(connString, provider);
}
```

The first example simply takes a connection string itself, and the second option also requires the .NET Framework data provider's name.

Having established a connection to a database, you need some way to execute queries against it. The Database Helper exposes a number of methods that you can use to pass SQL commands to your database and have them executed. Table 10-3 examines these methods.

TABLE 10-3: Database Helper Query Methods

METHOD	DESCRIPTION	EXAMPLE
Execute	Used to execute an INSERT, UPDATE or DELETE statement. Returns the number of rows that were affected by the operation.	`var rowsAffected = db.Execute("DELETE  FROM Table");`
Query	Used to execute a SELECT statement that may return more than one record.	`var data = db.Query("SELECT * FROM Table");`

METHOD	DESCRIPTION	EXAMPLE
QuerySingle	Executes a SELECT statement and returns one row of data.	`var data = db.QuerySingle("SELECT * FROM Table WHERE ID = 1");`
QueryValue	Executes a SELECT statement but returns one single (scalar) value.	`var data = db.QueryValue("SELECT Count(*) FROM Table")`
GetLastInsertId	Gets the most recently created identity value.	`var id = db.GetLastInsertId();`

The Query method is the one that you are likely to use most often. The method returns a collection of DynamicRecord objects. A DynamicRecord object is one whose properties are generated dynamically at run time from the column names that are returned in the SELECT query that was executed. What this provides you with is a nice, clean way to reference data in your code. For example, consider this SQL statement:

```
SELECT Title, Description, Price FROM Items
```

When you execute this statement using the Query method, the collection of objects returned will contain the Title, Description, and Price properties. These are accessible via the familiar dot notation:

```
@foreach(var item in data){
    @item.Title<br />
    @item.Description<br />
    @item.Price.ToString("c")
}
```

If you use SELECT * to generate your data, the DynamicRecord objects are aware of what database columns were involved in the data access operation and will generate properties to match each one.

The dot notation is not the only way to access values. You can use an indexer:

```
@foreach(var item in data){
    @item["Title"]<br />
    @item["Description"]<br />
    @item["Price"].ToString("c")
}
```

Mostly, you will use the dot notation, and it is the one that you'll see in samples pretty much everywhere, but you will have to use the indexer approach if you have inherited a database with embedded spaces in the column names. For example, if a database has a column named "First Name," and the contents of that column are returned as part of a query, you will not be able to use item .First Name to reference the data, because the space in the property is illegal. You have to use item["First Name"] instead.

TRY IT OUT Using the Database Helper

In the following exercise, you will practice using the various Database Helper methods detailed earlier while working with the sample Classifieds database.

1. Open the Chapter10 site if you have closed it and add a new CSHTML file. There is no need to rename it from the default page.cshtml.

2. At the top of the file, add the following code block:

```
@{
    var db = Database.Open("Classifieds");
    var sql = "SELECT Count(*) From Categories";
    var initialCount = db.QueryValue(sql);
    sql = "INSERT INTO Categories (Category) VALUES ('Books')";
    var rowsAffected = db.Execute(sql);
    var newId = db.GetLastInsertId();
    sql = "SELECT Count(*) From Categories";
    var newCount = db.QueryValue(sql);
    sql = "SELECT * FROM Categories";
    var data = db.Query(sql);
}
```

3. In the `<body>` element, add the following code:

```
<p>The initial count of categories was @initialCount</p>
<p>The number of rows affected by the insert was @rowsAffected</p>
<p>The new Id generated by the insert was @newId</p>
<p>The new count of categories is @newCount</p>
<p>The contents of the Categories table are as follows:</p>
<table>
    @foreach(var category in data){
        <text><tr>
            <td>@category.CategoryId</td>
            <td>@category.Category</td>
        </tr></text>
    }
</table>
```

4. Run the page in a browser. The result should resemble Figure 10-15.

How It Works

In this exercise you tried out the database methods that you are likely to use most often. The first method that you used in the code block at the beginning of the page was the Open method. You passed the name of a SQL Server Compact file to the method without the file extension. That file resides in the App_Data folder. The Open method checks the App_Data folder for a file matching the string passed to it, and if successfully found, opens a connection to the database file so that further commands can be issued against it.

Once the connection was opened to the database, you were able to issue your first command against it. You obtained a count of the total number of rows in the Categories table using the SQL COUNT function. Since this returns a single scalar value, you used the QueryValue method. The next command inserted a new entry into the Categories table via the Execute method. Notice that you only had to pass a value for the Category column — the CategoryId column is an IDENTITY column and a value is generated automatically. You passed the return value from the Execute method to a variable, which stores the number of rows affected by the INSERT statement. This value can be used to confirm that the INSERT command executed successfully. If it is zero, something must have gone wrong.

Since the CategoryId column is an IDENTITY, you can use the GetLastInsertId method to obtain the new row's generated identity value, which is what you did next. This was stored in an appropriately named variable for display later. You use the QueryValue method once again to obtain a revised number for the total rows in the table. Finally, you used the Query method to obtain all rows returned from executing a SELECT command. The resulting data was passed to a variable for storage.

In the display part of the page, you wrote out the various scalar values, such as the initial count, followed by the number of rows affected by the INSERT operation along with the new row's ID value. Then you displayed the updated total number of rows and finally iterated the contents of the table using a foreach statement.

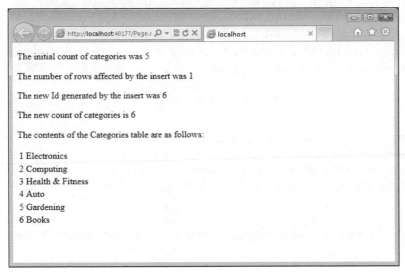

FIGURE 10-15

SUMMARY

This chapter has provided you with an overview of databases and covered how to communicate with them from a Web Pages application. You learned that a database is a structured collection of data. A relational database is composed of rows of data organized into tables, whereby repeating information is minimized or eradicated altogether. You saw that there is a range of database systems available, and that the default system that WebMatrix utilizes is SQL Server Compact Edition 4.0.

Databases respond to instructions written in Structured Query Language (SQL), which enables you to create, read, update, and delete (CRUD) data. The SQL commands for these operations are INSERT, SELECT, UPDATE, and DELETE, respectively. You can define a subset of data to perform operations on using a WHERE clause, which filters data based on the criteria passed to the WHERE clause. You can also define the order in which data is retrieved using an ORDER BY clause. When you need to read data from two or more tables, you use a JOIN to define how the tables relate to each other. You create permanent relationships between tables using the Relationships menu within the Databases Workspace. These enforce the relational integrity of your data.

The second part of the chapter looked at how to communicate with a database from your Web Pages using the Database Helper. You establish a connection to a database using the helper's Open method, and then perform CRUD operations by passing SQL statements to one of a number of methods, depending on the result of the operation. To create, update, or delete records, you use the Execute method. There are three methods available for reading data. These include Query, which returns multiple rows; QuerySingle, which returns a single row; and QueryValue, which returns one value.

This chapter has provided a very basic introduction to the SQL language. It is a very powerful language containing a range of operators and functions that can help you shape data as you retrieve it. You should spend some time familiarizing yourself with the flavour of T-SQL that SQL Server Compact supports to get the most out of it. A full reference is available at the MSDN site here: http://msdn.microsoft.com/en-us/library/ms173372(v=SQL.110).aspx.

EXERCISES

1. SQL Server Compact does not allow renaming of existing columns in a table. You have to add a new column with the new name, copy the data from the existing column, and then delete the existing column instead. Imagine that you want to change the name of a column from Forename to FirstName. What SQL would you write to transfer the data from one column to the other, assuming that the table is called Contacts?

2. What is the difference between a relationship defined in a JOIN statement and one created in the database?

3. What is so special about an IDENTITY column and which Database Helper method has been written especially for it?

Answers to the Exercises can be found in the Appendix.

▶ WHAT YOU LEARNED IN THIS CHAPTER

TOPIC	KEY CONCEPTS
Relational Database	A data storage system in which data is stored in tables, which are then related to each other.
Table	An object within the database for storing data.
Primary Key	Used to uniquely identify records. Often one column, but can be composed of multiple columns.
IDENTITY	An automatically generated number that's assigned to new records. Often used as a primary key.
Relationship	Enforces referential integrity at the database level.
Join	Defines the relationship between two or more tables in a query.
CRUD	An acronym that stands for Create, Read, Update, and Delete, which are the four basic SQL operations.
Database Helper	A Web Pages helper that enables you to connect to databases and execute SQL commands against them.
Connection String	Provides the information about a data source such as its location and the means to connect to it.
ADO.NET	The data access libraries provided as part of the .NET Framework.

11

A Deeper Dive Into Data Access

WHAT YOU WILL LEARN IN THIS CHAPTER:

➤ Secure data access

➤ How to develop forms for CRUD

➤ How to display data using the WebGrid helper

The previous chapter provided you with an introduction to databases, Structured Query Language, and the Database Helper. The last exercise provided a glimpse at how these three things come together with a web page to provide the true basis of dynamic web development: that which relies on the contents of a database to make it current and specific to the user.

You saw that you can filter data with a WHERE clause. The next step is to provide your visitors with the ability to create their own filters, or choose the order in which they can view data, or indeed how much they want to see. Since SQL commands are strings, and as you learned in Chapter 4, strings can be constructed dynamically, this opens the door to a means by which you can provide your users with a way to personalize their data access. However, as with all things powerful, there are potential dangers that you need to manage. But first, you need to understand the potential dangers.

WHAT IS SQL INJECTION?

Simply stated, SQL injection is a technique whereby a malicious user injects a SQL command with additional legitimate SQL syntax that alters the intended behaviour of the command, and potentially compromises the security of the application that makes use of the SQL command. You may well be scratching your head at the moment, and trying to read that sentence a few times to see if it makes any more sense. An illustration should provide you with some relief at this point.

Think about some of the SQL commands you met in the previous chapter. A typical example might retrieve items according to the category they are in:

```
var sql = "SELECT * FROM Items WHERE CategoryId = 2";
```

The problem with this is that it is constant. It doesn't change, which means that it will always draw items that belong to the category specified in the WHERE clause. That might indeed not be a bad thing, depending on circumstances and the requirement of your site. However, it is a common enough requirement to provide your users with a means to choose which category they would like to filter products by. The most usual means is a form, perhaps featuring a list of categories in a drop-down menu or a text box. Your server-side code would take the posted selection and combine it with the stem of the SQL to dynamically construct a working statement. It might look something like this:

```
var sql =  "SELECT * FROM Items WHERE CategoryId = " + Request["categoryId"];
```

At the moment, any value that is passed to the Request["categoryId"] value will be concatenated to the SQL string and executed against the database. There is nothing to prevent a user entering anything they like into a text box. If the user enters some rubbish into a text box, and the resulting concatenation does not produce a valid piece of SQL syntax, the site will error. Otherwise, the SQL will execute successfully. If in the previous example, the user submitted the value 2, the SQL will result in all items in the Computing category being retrieved, if the SQL was run against the sample database from the last chapter. However, the user could also enter the following into a text box:

```
2 or 1 = 1
```

When concatenated with the stem of the statement, the result would be this:

```
SELECT * FROM Items WHERE CategoryId = 2 or 1 = 1
```

That is perfectly valid SQL and it will result in all rows being returned as the condition WHERE 1 = 1 is always true.

The original intended purpose of the SQL was to provide a means to restrict results to one category, assuming that the user knew what valid categories are available, but the resulting SQL behaves in an unplanned way because the user has been allowed to modify its behaviour by injecting an additional filter. That is SQL injection, and it is one of the top two vulnerabilities that poorly written websites are exposed to.

The previous example might not seem that dangerous, so what problems can SQL injection lead to? Well, for one thing, the filter was provided for a good reason. Perhaps the filter was meant to prevent every record being retrieved from the database because there are millions and millions of them, and continually requesting all of them will hurt the site's performance. It makes a possible *denial of service* (DoS) attack easier to conduct. But there are greater dangers.

Look at the following piece of code:

```
var sql = @"SELECT Count(*) FROM Users
                    WHERE UserName = '" + Request["UserName"]  + "'
                    AND Password = '" + Request["UserPass"] + "'";
```

This is commonly seen as a way to authenticate users by matching the user name and password they provide in a log-in form. It tests to see how many rows in the database contain user names and passwords matching those supplied by the user, and if the result is greater than zero, the user is allowed to proceed further. In the previous example, you were shown a condition that is always true and results in all rows being returned. Here is another condition that's always true:

```
WHERE '' = ''
```

It is really easy for a hacker to inject code into this SQL to cause all rows in the Users table to be returned, and thus gain access to restricted areas of a website by simply inserting ' or ''=' into either the user name or password text box. The concatenation will complete the job of creating a valid piece of SQL syntax to be executed.

Fortunately, SQL Server Compact suffers some restrictions in functionality compared to its grown-up cousin, the full version of SQL Server. For example, the Compact edition doesn't support batched statements. More powerful databases do, and this exposes them to potentially serious consequences. A batched statement is one where multiple operations are passed in one SQL statement, with each separate command being executed in turn. The following provides an illustration of a batched statement:

```
SELECT * FROM Items; DROP TABLE Users
```

Running that against a SQL Server database will result in all rows in the Items table being retrieved, and then the table called Users being deleted permanently. There are even more powerful commands that can result in the entire database being deleted, or that can even result in the hacker taking full control of the server on which the database resides.

Parameters Provide Protection

Now that you understand the nature of the problem, and the potentially very serious consequences that can result, you need to learn how to protect your code properly from the threat of SQL injection. Some people suggest that using a blacklist approach is effective. This involves screening user input for SQL keywords, and if they are found, rejecting the submission. The problem with this idea is two-fold: A lot of SQL keywords are used in common everyday language (or, and, and so on) and SQL keywords are subject to change. That means that you will have to update every site you ever built if a new SQL keyword is introduced to accommodate it within your blacklist. A second suggestion involves escaping single quotes. Again, this can be effective, but is of no use if strings are not part of the SQL, such as in the first example provided earlier.

The truth is that there is only one proven and effective means to protect your site from SQL injection attacks, and that is to use *parameters*. Parameters are placeholders for dynamic values that are combined with the SQL query at execution time in a safe manner. To help explain how the concept works, here is an example that shows how the Database Helper supports the use of parameters:

```
var sql = "SELECT * FROM Items WHERE CategoryId = @0;
var data = db.Query(sql, Request["categoryId"]);
```

Notice that the dynamic value is represented within the SQL statement by a marker: @0. That is the @ sign followed by a zero. The SQL is passed in to the database Query method as usual, but this time it is followed by the source of the dynamic value. Internally, the Database Helper creates ADO.NET parameter objects and passes those to the database. That in turn checks the incoming parameter value to ensure that it is the correct data type for its target column, which prevents strings being passed in where numbers are expected, and ensures that all strings that are passed in successfully are treated literally and not as part of the SQL to be executed. Of course, the fact that this happens should not prevent you from validating the values for type as shown in Chapter 5, but you should understand now how parameters provide protection. If you relied solely on using parameters to validate data type, your application would generate a lot of exceptions.

Multiple parameters are passed in order as in this snippet:

```
var sql = "INSERT INTO items (Title, Description, Price) VALUES (@0, @1, @2)";
var title = Request["title"];
var desc = Request["desc"];
var price = Request["price"];
db.Execute(sql, title, desc, price);
```

The parameter makers start with @0 and increment by one each time. You don't have any choice about this. If you start the sequence at @1, you will generate an exception. If you omit any numbers, you will generate an exception.

Now you know how to communicate safely with your database using the Database Helper and parameters. In the next section, you will take that knowledge and apply it to the form that you built in Chapter 5 to save the submission in a database.

DEVELOPING CRUD FORMS

CRUD forms are the foundation of any dynamic website. They feature heavily in any *Content Management System* (CMS) for example, or *Line of Business* (LOB) application. More advanced web development frameworks, such as ASP.NET MVC and Dynamic Data, provide clever ways to scaffold forms from database schema information. It could well be the case that a future version of Web Pages offers something similar, but in the meantime, you have to create your own forms from scratch.

CRUD forms can vary widely in their complexity, depending on what they are intended to manage. The principle behind each type of form is the same, however. If you want to add a new item to a database, you create a form containing the required inputs — text boxes, checkboxes, select lists, and so on — for each piece of data. On submission, the form should be validated and the values passed to a parameterized query for insertion into the database. A form for updating data provides the user with a means to select the item that they want to update, make their changes, and submit those changes. The final part of the CRUD acronym — Delete — is accommodated typically by providing the users with a way to select the item or items they would like to remove from the database, and then code to delete them when the selection is posted back to the server.

It is time to have your first go at creating some forms for managing CRUD operations. You will start off with the most simple of examples that will be used to manage the Categories table in the sample Classifieds database that you met in the last chapter.

TRY IT OUT   Creating Basic CRUD Forms

This exercise will make use of the Classifieds site that you last worked on in Chapter 6, when you added client-side validation to the form you created in Chapter 5. You will extend the site to begin to work with the sample Classifieds database that you explored in the last chapter. Therefore, the first steps in this exercise walk you through adding an existing database to the site. If you prefer, you can use the download that accompanies this chapter instead.

1.   Open the Classifieds site that you last worked with in Chapter 6 and add a new folder to the root folder called **App_Data**.

2.   Right-click on the newly created App_Data folder and select the Add Existing File option. Navigate to the Classifieds.sdf file, which is in the sample site you worked on in the previous chapter. The name of the containing folder and location will depend on how you saved the previous website, but typically, it should be My Documents ⇨ My Web Sites ⇨ Chapter10. Select the file to add it to the Classifieds site.

3.   Add another folder to the root of the site, but name this one **Admin**. Within that, add a **_PageStart.cshtml** file and replace the default code with the following:

```
@{
    Layout = "~/Shared/_Layout.cshtml";
}
```

4.   Now add a file to the Shared folder and name it **_AdminLayout.cshtml**. Add the following to the `<head>` element to reference the existing style sheet:

```
<link href="@Href("~/Content/StyleSheet.css")" rel="stylesheet" type="text/css" />
```

Then add this code to the `<body>` element:

```
<div id="content">
    <h1>Admin</h1>
    <a href="@Href("~/Admin/CreateCategory")">Create Category</a>
    <hr />
    @RenderBody()
</div>
```

5.   Add a new CSHTML file to the Admin folder and name it **CreateCategory.cshtml**. Replace the default code with the following:

```
@{
    var message = "";
    if(IsPost){
        if(!Request["category"].IsEmpty()){
            var db = Database.Open("Classifieds");
            var sql = "INSERT INTO Categories (Category) VALUES (@0)";
            db.Execute(sql, Request["category"]);
            var id = db.GetLastInsertId();
            message = Request["category"] + " added with ID: " + id;
        }
    }
}
<form method="post">
```

```
    <div>@message</div>
    <fieldset>
        <legend>Create Category</legend>
        <div>
            <label for"category">Category:</label>
        </div>
        <div>
            <input type="text" name="category" />
        </div>
        <div>
            <input type="submit" value="Add"/>
        </div>
    </fieldset>
</form>
```

6. Make sure that the CreateCategory.cshtml file is selected and click the Run button to launch the page in a browser. Enter a new category and submit the form. You should receive confirmation that the new category has been created along with its ID. Figure 11-1 illustrates how this should look if you added a category for Clothes.

FIGURE 11-1

How It Works

You have now produced a Create form — the first part of CRUD. The form itself is simple, and only makes use of server-side validation. It takes just one entry; tests it for presence; and if there is a value, passes that to a parameterized SQL statement. The statement is passed to the database via the Execute method, and a new entry is added to the table. You used the GetLastInsertId method to obtain the newly created ID value to confirm that the INSERT statement has worked. You could have captured the return value of the Execute method instead. On success, the value should be 1.

In the next exercise, you will create a form that enables you to update existing categories.

TRY IT OUT   Creating an Update Form

1. Add a new file to the Admin folder in the site you are currently working on. Name the file
UpdateCategory.cshtml.

2. Replace the default code with the following:

```
@{
    var category = "";
    var message = "";
    var sql = "";
    var db = Database.Open("Classifieds");

    if(Request["categoryId"].AsInt() > 0){
        if(!IsPost){
            sql = "SELECT Category FROM Categories WHERE CategoryId = @0";
            category = db.QueryValue(sql, Request["categoryId"]);
        }
        else{
            if(!Request["category"].IsEmpty()){
                sql = "UPDATE Categories SET Category = @0 WHERE CategoryId = @1";
                db.Execute(sql, Request["category"], Request["categoryId"]);
                message = "Category changed to " + Request["category"];
            }
        }
    }
    sql = "SELECT * FROM Categories";
    var categories = db.Query(sql);
}
<form>
    <div>
        Select Category:
        <select name="categoryId">
            <option value="0">--Select Category--</option>
            @foreach(var cat in categories){
                <option value="@cat.CategoryId">@cat.Category</option>
            }
        </select>
        <input type="submit" value="Select" />
    </div>
</form>
<form method="post">
    <div>@message</div>
    <fieldset>
        <legend>Update Category</legend>
        <div>
            <label for="category">Category:</label>
        </div>
        <div>
            <input type="text" name="category" value="@category" />
        </div>
```

```
                <div>
                    <input type="submit" value="Update"/>
                </div>
            </fieldset>
        </form>
```

3.   Amend _AdminLayout.cshtml to include a link to the new file:

```
<div id="content">
    <h1>Admin</h1>
    <a href="@Href("~/Admin/CreateCategory")">Create Category</a>
    |
    <a href="@Href("~/Admin/UpdateCategory")">Update Category</a>
    <hr />
    @RenderBody()
</div>
```

4.   Make sure that UpdateCategory.cshtml is selected. Run the page in a browser and choose a category to edit and click the Select button. Notice that the URL in the browser address bar has acquired a query string at this point representing the ID of the category you want to amend. When the category name appears in the text box, make your alterations and click the Update button to submit your changes. Notice that the message confirms your change was successful, then double check that the category has in fact been changed by expanding the drop-down list and examining its new value there.

How It Works

There are two forms on this page. The top form enables the users to select the category that they would like to update from a drop-down list. The top form does not specify a method attribute value, which means that it will use the HTTP GET method (being the default method, if you recall from Chapter 5). Consequently, the selected value will be passed as a query string value when a selection is made and the form submitted. The drop-down list itself is populated from a query that returns all rows from the Categories table. The query is executed at the end of the code block. You will return to that fact a little later.

Turning now to the code block at the top of the page, you can see that a test is made of the value of Request["categoryId"]. If it is equal to zero (0) when converted to an int data type, the page has been requested for the first time (meaning that there is no query string), or the Submit button on the second form has been clicked while the default option is selected in the drop-down list. Either way, there is nothing else to do except populate (or re-populate) the drop-down list. If a query string value exists for categoryId, and it is greater than zero, a selection has been made. If that is the case, but the page has not been requested via the POST method, the user has simply chosen which category to amend. The category's name is extracted from the database using a parameterized query, and the QueryValue method (since only one scalar value is needed). The resulting value is displayed in the second form's text box, ready for amending.

If the page has been posted, you assume that the user has amended the category and is submitting that amendment. You check to see if they have in fact supplied a value, and not just emptied the text box, and then pass the new value to a parameterized query, which locates the category according to its ID (which is still available in the query string) and updates it with the new value. Just before the page is redisplayed with a confirmation message, the categories drop-down list is repopulated. It has to be done at this stage of the process, because if it is done before the update statement is executed, the category will not have been updated at that point. Figure 11-2 shows how this should have worked if you amended the previously added Clothes category to Clothing.

FIGURE 11-2

For completeness, this section will explore developing forms for the "D" of CRUD — deleting. An important part of this exercise is seeing how relationships work when you attempt to delete something that has related records in another table, so ensure that you are working with a version of the sample database where the FK_Items_Categories relationship exists. Refer to the "Creating a Relationship Between Two Tables" exercise in the previous chapter for instructions on how to create this relationship if you have not already created it.

TRY IT OUT Creating a Delete Form

In this exercise, you will begin by providing the users with a form that allows them to delete items one at a time. Following that, you will look at one way to enable users to make multiple selections and delete them in bulk.

1. Continuing with the Admin folder, add a new file called **DeleteCategory.cshtml**. Replace the default code with the following:

```
@{
    var message = "";
    var sql = "";
    var db = Database.Open("Classifieds");

    if(Request["categoryId"].AsInt() > 0){
        sql = "DELETE FROM Categories WHERE CategoryId = @0";
```

```
        try{
            db.Execute(sql, Request["categoryId"]);
            message = "Category deleted. Delete another?";
        }
        catch(Exception ex){
            message = "Category could not be deleted. Other references exist";
        }
    }
    sql = "SELECT * FROM Categories";
    var categories = db.Query(sql);
}
<form>
    <fieldset>
        <legend>Delete Category</legend>
        <div>@message</div>
        <div>
            <label for="categoryId">Select Category to delete:</label>
            <select name="categoryId">
                <option value="0">--Select Category--</option>
                @foreach(var cat in categories){
                    <option value="@cat.CategoryId">@cat.Category</option>
                }
            </select>
            <br />
            <input type="submit" value="Select" />
        </div>
    </fieldset>
</form>
```

2. Amend _AdminLayout.cshtml to include a link to your newly created page by adding the high-lighted code:

```
<div id="content">
    <h1>Admin</h1>
    <a href="@Href("~/Admin/CreateCategory")">Create Category</a>
    |
    <a href="@Href("~/Admin/UpdateCategory")">Update Category</a>
    |
    <a href="@Href("~/Admin/DeleteCategory")">Delete Category</a>
    <hr />
    @RenderBody()
</div>
```

3. Run DeleteCategory.cshtml in your browser and attempt to delete one of the original categories. You should find that the category cannot be deleted because references to it exist in the Items table. If you find that it can be deleted, you have not implemented the relationship correctly. If you attempt to delete one of the categories you created while testing CreateCategory.cshtml, you should find that it can safely be removed from the database as you have no entries in the Items table referencing it at this point.

How It Works

This page works in almost exactly the same way as the UpdateCategory.cshtml page. The form that enables the users to select a category to delete has no method attribute defined, which means that the form will use the GET verb, resulting in values appearing in a query string. The server-side code ensures that a valid category ID value has been selected before attempting to delete the corresponding entry from the database using a parameterized command. The database operation is wrapped in a try-catch block to ensure that any exception is caught, and a friendly error message is provided to the users.

The approach outlined previously is fine as far as it goes. If the user needs to delete a lot of items, picking them one by one from a drop-down will get tedious very quickly and can badly affect the usability of your application. It won't be long before your users clamour for a more elegant and efficient way to delete items in bulk. In the next exercise you will provide a way for users to select multiple categories and delete them in one go. You will also provide a little client-side addition to the form that prompts the users to confirm that they want their selection to be removed from the database permanently.

TRY IT OUT Creating a Bulk Delete Form

1. Add a new file to the Admin folder and name it DeleteCategories.cshtml. Notice the use of the plural in the filename. Replace the default code with the following:

```
@{
    var message = "";
    var sql = "";
    var db = Database.Open("Classifieds");

    if(!Request["categoryId"].IsEmpty()){
        sql = "DELETE FROM Categories WHERE CategoryId IN({0})";
        try{
            db.ExecuteIn(sql, Request["categoryId"]);
            message = "Categories deleted. Delete more?";
        }
        catch(Exception ex){
            message = "One or more Categories could not be deleted. Other
references exist";
        }
    }
    sql = "SELECT * FROM Categories";
    var categories = db.Query(sql);
}
<script type="text/javascript">
    $(function(){
        $('#delete').click(function(){
            return confirm('Are you sure you want to delete?');
        });
    });
</script>
<form method="post">
    <fieldset>
        <legend>Delete Categories</legend>
        <div>@message</div>
        <div>
            Select Categories to delete:
            <div>
```

```
                    @foreach(var cat in categories){
                        <input type="checkbox" name="categoryId"
                                value="@cat.CategoryId" /> @cat.Category<br />
                    }
                </div>
                <input type="submit" id="delete" value="Delete" />
            </div>
        </fieldset>
    </form>
```

2. Amend _AdminLayout.cshtml to include a link to this new file, and a reference to jQuery:

```
<!DOCTYPE html>

<html lang="en">
    <head>
        <meta charset="utf-8" />
        <title></title>
        <link href="@Href("~/Content/StyleSheet.css")"
                rel="stylesheet" type="text/css" />
        <script src="@Href("~/Scripts/jquery-1.5.min.js")"
                type="text/javascript"></script>
    </head>
    <body>
        <div id="content">
            <h1>Admin</h1>
            <a href="@Href("~/Admin/CreateCategory")">Create Category</a>
            |
            <a href="@Href("~/Admin/UpdateCategory")">Update Category</a>
            |
            <a href="@Href("~/Admin/DeleteCategory")">Delete Category</a>
            |
            <a href="@Href("~/Admin/DeleteCategories")">Delete Categories</a>
            <hr />
            @RenderBody()
        </div>
    </body>
</html>
```

3. Add a new file to the App_Code folder. The file type should be a C# Class File. You should name this file DatabaseExtensions.cs.

4. Adjust the existing code so that the complete file contents contain the following code:

```
using System;
using System.Collections.Generic;
using WebMatrix.Data;
using System.Linq;

/// <summary>
/// Summary description for ClassName
/// </summary>
public static class DatabaseExtensions
{
```

```
public static int ExecuteIn(this Database db, string commandText, string values)
{
    var temp = values.Split(new[]{','}, StringSplitOptions.RemoveEmptyEntries);
    var parms = temp.Select((s, i) => "@" + i.ToString()).ToArray();
    var inclause = string.Join(",", parms);
    return db.Execute(string.Format(commandText, inclause), temp);
}
}
```

5. Launch CreateCategory.cshtml in your browser and add a number of new categories. It does not matter what you name these; they are all going to go soon. Once you have added several, click the link to navigate to DeleteCategories.cshtml and select some of the new categories that you have just added together with at least one of the original categories. Click the Delete button, and notice that you are asked to confirm that you want to delete. Click OK, and see that the resulting list of categories has not changed, and that the message indicates that one or more categories are related to existing items. Now select some or all of your new categories and submit the form to delete them. Again, confirm that you would like to proceed with the delete operation. This time, you should be told that the categories you selected have been deleted. They should no longer appear in the list of items to be deleted.

How It Works

You should by now be used to how database operations are managed from form submissions, but there are two things that are worthy of note in this exercise. The first is the JavaScript that you used to prompt the users to confirm that they wish to delete something. Deleting an item from a database is a permanent thing. It is good practice to prompt your users to think about what they are doing. The script required to invoke the confirmation dialog box (which belongs to the browser, incidentally and can be seen in Figure 11-3) is simple, and probably one of the most often used on the Internet:

```
return confirm('message text')
```

In this example, that command is wired up to the click event of the Submit button using jQuery's clean, terse syntax. If you choose to click the Cancel button on the confirmation box, the form is not posted and no server-side code that relies on the form being posted is executed.

The second point of note is the C# class file that you added to the App_Code folder. This class contains an *extension method*. An extension method is a static method that extends a type to provide additional functionality. In this case, the type that's extended is the Database type, which you have been working with happily up to now. You have met the methods offered by the Database type: Query, Open, Execute, GetLastInsertId, and so on. But you have not seen a method called ExecuteIn until now. That is because it did not exist until you created it, and then extended the Database type to expose this method.

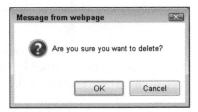

FIGURE 11-3

The key characteristic of an extension method is the this keyword in the parameter list: (this Database db...). It points to the type being extended. Additional parameters are added after the type that the method operates on. In the example you have just created, the two additional parameters are a string representing some SQL to be executed, and a string representing a series of one or more values.

So why is this additional method needed? The SQL IN operator works by allowing you to specify multiple values in a WHERE clause as a comma-separated list. It is shorthand for multiple OR statements. Look at the following:

```
SELECT * FROM Items WHERE Id = 1 OR Id = 3 OR Id = 4 OR Id = 7
```

If you use the IN operator, the revised statement is as follows:

```
SELECT * FROM Items WHERE Id IN (1,3,4,7)
```

When you group checkboxes by giving a number of them the same name value, the checked values are passed in the Request collection as a comma-separated string. You might think, therefore, that you can pass the whole lot in one parameter value:

```
var data = db.Query("SELECT * FROM Items WHERE Id IN (@0)", Request["Ids"]);
```

But that won't work. This query expects a number of separate ints to be passed separated by commas, with a matching parameter value for each int. It will receive a single string instead. Therefore, a way is needed to separate each value from the Request collection, and to dynamically generate a parameter for each one, and that is what the extension method you added does.

The first line of the extension method body takes a string and uses the string.Split method to create an array from it. If Request["Ids"] from the previous example was passed into the extension method, at this point there would be an array, with each element containing one ID. String.Split uses the character passed into it (in this case a comma) as the delimiter on which to separate items to elements within an array. The delimiter is then ignored. The second line of the method body creates another array. This time the elements are the index of the elements in the existing array preceded with the @ sign. There are four elements in this example, so the indexes of those will be 0, 1, 2, and 3. The new array will therefore contain the following values: @0, @1, @2, and @3. Finally, those values are brought together and joined, with a comma as the separator, so the resulting string looks like this:

```
@0,@1,@2,@3
```

The extension method now constructs a valid parameterized SQL statement, and passes in the comma-separated Request.Form value to be executed against the database.

The actual database call is wrapped in a try-catch block. If you include any categories with existing related records, they cannot be deleted. You get a warning to that effect. Your newly created categories with no matching records in the Items table are deleted in one go very efficiently.

You have practiced creating, updating, and deleting data in the series of exercises you have just undertaken. You have also had a brief look at displaying data on a web page. In the next section, you will explore this aspect of working with data in more detail.

DISPLAYING DATA

Data can be displayed in a number of ways. Often, you will want to display single items of data, such as a news story, or details of a particular product. You might want to display lists of data. You did this in a very simple way in the previous exercise when you rendered the names of each category next to a related checkbox. The snippets of code that you create to maintain consistency over the display of each item in a list are known as templates. You can move these templates across to helpers for code re-use and to keep your files smaller and more manageable. An example helper that renders a list of checkboxes might look like this:

```
@helper CheckList(IEnumerable<dynamic> items, string name,
                  string value, string text){
    foreach(var item in items){
        <input type="checkbox" name="@name" value="@item[value]" />
                            @item[text]<br />
    }
}
```

The calling code, assuming that you want to render categories as in the last exercise, looks like this:

```
@Helpers.CheckList(categories, "categoryId", "categoryId", "category")
```

The rendered result is identical to the example in the last exercise. This example might not save a lot of space on a page, but if your application is form-heavy, you may be rendering lists often. The helper will be a time saver and will help to minimize errors as there is only really one place for the code to go wrong.

Another common way to display data is in a tabular manner. You often see lists of data presented in rows and columns with sorting and paging features. In the really old days of classic ASP, displaying tabular data was a considerable pain. You have to take care of rendering tables, together with their rows and cells by hand. If you wanted to implement paging, that too had to be hand-crafted, as did sorting. It was a tedious and error-prone process. ASP.NET Web Forms changed that by introducing server controls that render data in tables and had paging and sorting built-in. The most popular of these controls is the GridView. There are in fact websites devoted to the topic of the GridView.

The Web Pages Framework exposes helpers instead of server controls. The helper that's designed to make working with tabular data easier is called the *WebGrid*. This helper is quite feature-rich, so it is worth exploring in detail.

The WebGrid Helper

The WebGrid Helper can accept data from a number of sources, although it has been principally designed to work with the results of a `Database.Query` call. WebGrid will attempt to identify suitable names for column headers from the data source. If the data has been obtained via the Database Helper, WebGrid will obtain information from the schema of the data and use that. If the data comes from other sources, the WebGrid Helper will use public properties as column names. For example, if you were to supply the WebGrid with a `List<Car>` from Chapter 4, it would use the public properties `Make`, `NumberOfDoors`, and `YearRegistered` as column names. But you are most likely to use the WebGrid in conjunction with data from your database so that is what you will spend more time exploring in this book.

At its most basic, all the WebGrid needs is some data. The following code is the minimum needed to display all items from the Classifieds database using the WebGrid.

```
@{
    var db = Database.Open("Classifieds");
    var data = db.Query("SELECT * FROM Items");
    var grid = new WebGrid(data);
}
<!DOCTYPE html>

<html lang="en">
    <head>
        <meta charset="utf-8" />
        <title></title>
    </head>
    <body>
        @grid.GetHtml()
    </body>
</html>
```

The first two lines in the code block are familiar to you and establish which database is to be used to obtain the contents of the Items table. The last line in the code block initializes a WebGrid. It uses the new keyword to establish an instance of the WebGrid class that's represented by the variable `grid`. The constructor takes a minimum of one parameter, and that is the data source for the WebGrid. In this case, it is the result of the `Database.Query` call. Finally, the WebGrid's `GetHtml` method is called and renders a table of data with the default settings. You can see this in Figure 11-4.

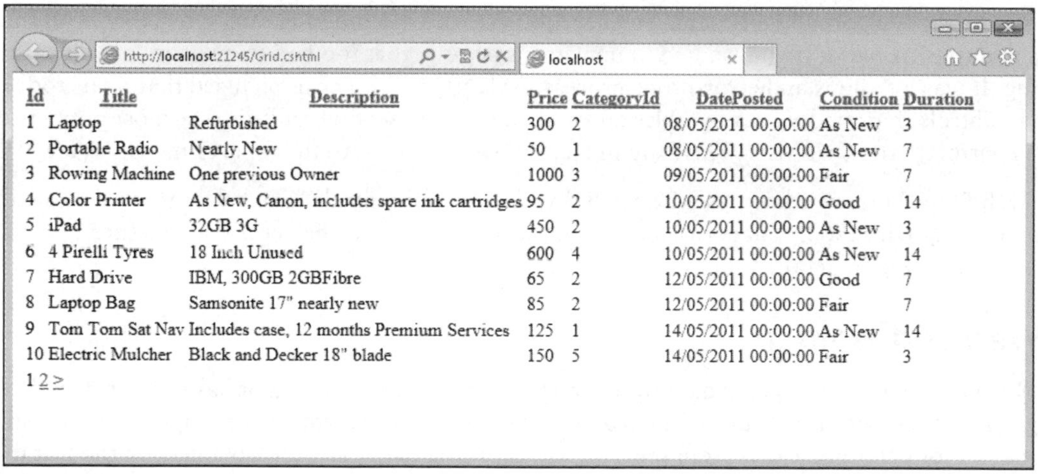

Id	Title	Description	Price	CategoryId	DatePosted	Condition	Duration
1	Laptop	Refurbished	300	2	08/05/2011 00:00:00	As New	3
2	Portable Radio	Nearly New	50	1	08/05/2011 00:00:00	As New	7
3	Rowing Machine	One previous Owner	1000	3	09/05/2011 00:00:00	Fair	7
4	Color Printer	As New, Canon, includes spare ink cartridges	95	2	10/05/2011 00:00:00	Good	14
5	iPad	32GB 3G	450	2	10/05/2011 00:00:00	As New	3
6	4 Pirelli Tyres	18 Inch Unused	600	4	10/05/2011 00:00:00	As New	14
7	Hard Drive	IBM, 300GB 2GBFibre	65	2	12/05/2011 00:00:00	Good	7
8	Laptop Bag	Samsonite 17" nearly new	85	2	12/05/2011 00:00:00	Fair	7
9	Tom Tom Sat Nav	Includes case, 12 months Premium Services	125	1	14/05/2011 00:00:00	As New	14
10	Electric Mulcher	Black and Decker 18" blade	150	5	14/05/2011 00:00:00	Fair	3

1 2 ≥

FIGURE 11-4

Notice in the illustration that the column headings are underlined. This is because by default, they act as links that manage sorting in the grid. If you click on one of the headings, the page is posted back to the server, and the data is re-ordered based on the contents of the column you clicked. The number of items displayed is 10 by default, and since there are more than 10 items in your Items table, a paging mechanism at the bottom of the grid enables the users to view more data. You can affect all of this behaviour, and more, by passing in values for optional parameters when you initialize the WebGrid. Table 11-1 details the full range of parameters that are available to you.

TABLE 11-1: The WebGrid's Parameters

PARAMETER (DEFAULT VALUE)	TYPE	DESCRIPTION
source	IEnumerable<object>	The data source for the grid.
columnNames (null)	IEnumerable<string>	The columns to display.
defaultSort (null)	string	The column that you want to have the grid sorted on by default.
rowsPerPage (10)	int	The number of rows you want per page.
canPage (true)	bool	If this is true, paging is enabled.
canSort (true)	bool	If this is true, sorting is enabled.
ajaxUpdateContainerId (null)	string	The ID of the element for Ajax paging and sorting support.
fieldNamePrefix (null)	string	A value that prefixes the default query string fields, such as "sort" and "sortdir."
pageFieldName (null)	string	A custom value to replace the default query string "page" field.
selectionFieldName (null)	string	A custom value to replace the default query string "row" field.
sortFieldName (null)	string	A custom value to replace the default query string "sort" field.
sortDirectionFieldName (null)	string	A custom value to replace the default query string "sortdir" field.

The first parameter is the only one that is required. All others are optional. As such, they can be placed in any order that you like so long as you use named parameters. The columnNames argument can be used to specify the order of columns and also to limit the data to be displayed. The following code alters the previous example by providing a List<string> to the columnNames parameter:

```
var data = db.Query("SELECT * FROM Items");
var columns = new List<string>{"Price","CategoryId","Title","Id"};
var grid = new WebGrid(data, columnNames: columns);
```

Figure 11-5 clearly illustrates how, despite the fact that the query returns all columns in the Items table, only those specified in the `columnNames` argument are displayed, and the order in which they appear follows the order in which they are added to the `List<string>`.

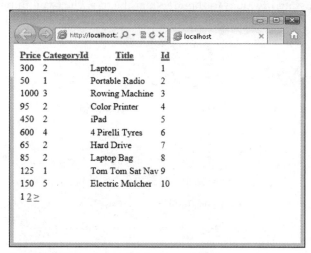

FIGURE 11-5

At the moment, the data is sorted according to how it sits in the table, although you might not be able to always rely on that fact. If you wanted to sort the data by price, you would add that as the value for `defaultSort`:

```
var grid = new WebGrid(data, defaultSort: "Price", columnNames: columns);
```

This ensures that items will be placed according to price in ascending order. If you wanted items to be ordered by price in descending order (most expensive first) you have two options. One is to add an `ORDER BY` clause to the SQL statement. The other is to chain the `Database.Query` method call with an `OrderByDescending` extension method call:

```
var orderBy = "Price";
var data = db.Query("SELECT * FROM Items").OrderByDescending(c => c[orderBy]);
```

The benefit of taking this second approach is that it leaves you room for dynamically altering the default sort column and the order in which the data is sorted based on user selection safely. However, if you want to select data from the database based on its ordered position, you must include the `ORDER BY` as part of the SQL.

When you click on one of the headers in this example, the grid redisplays with data sorted in ascending order of whichever column you chose to sort by. Those pieces of information are represented in the URL as query string values. If you sort by price, the query string that gets generated is as follows:

```
?sort=Price&sortdir=ASC
```

You can see the default `sortFieldName` and `sortDirectionFieldName` values here: `sort` and `sortdir`. You can change those completely by setting your own values for these parameters in the WebGrid's constructor. For example, take a look at the following code:

```
var grid = new WebGrid(data,
                defaultSort: "Price",
                columnNames: columns
                sortFieldName: "fieldToSortBy",
                sortDirectionFieldName: "UpOrDown"
                );
```

This produces the following query string:

```
?fieldToSortBy=Price&UpOrDown=ASC
```

You could instead use the `fieldNamePrefix` to alter the values in the query string:

```
var grid = new WebGrid(data,
                defaultSort: "Price",
                columnNames: columns
                fieldNamePrefix: "grid1"
                );
```

This will result in the default field names being prefixed with `grid1`, as in the following example:

```
?grid1sort=Price&grid1sortdir=ASC
```

Why would you want to do this? Well, for one thing, you might have multiple grids on a page with similar column names. You will need to customize the field names to prevent all grids being sorted on the same field. More importantly, if you have multiple grids on the same page without customizing their respective fieldnames, they will all be affected by each other's paging links. Paging links are rendered by default if the total number of items in the data source exceeds the `rowsPerPage` value.

Some AJAX Spice

So far, sorting and paging has required a full-page refresh. The links that are generated by default are straightforward HTML links. If you click one of them, the entire page is replaced with the target of the link. The WebGrid offers support for AJAX sorting and paging, which results in a partial page refresh. This functionality relies on jQuery, so that needs to be available to and referenced within the page that houses a grid. The grid itself needs to be placed within an HTML element that has an ID attribute. The value of the ID attribute is the `ajaxUpdateContainerId`. In the next exercise, you will build a page that makes use of this functionality.

TRY IT OUT An AJAX Powered WebGrid

1. Continuing with the Classifieds site that you worked with earlier in this chapter, open the Default.cshtml file.

2. Add the following to the existing code block at the top of the file:

```
var db = Database.Open("Classifieds");
 var sql = @"SELECT Id, Title, Description, Price, Items.CategoryId,
```

```
            Category, DatePosted FROM Items JOIN Categories ON
            Items. CategoryId = Categories.CategoryId";
    var data = db.Query(sql).OrderByDescending(c => c.DatePosted);
    var grid = new WebGrid(data, ajaxUpdateContainerId: "grid");
```

3. Add the following code to the content part of the page, replacing the paragraph that exists there:

```
<h2>Latest Items at @DateTime.Now</h2>
<div id="grid">
    @grid.GetHtml()
</div>
```

4. Run the page in your browser, and click some sorting and paging links. You should notice that the grid contents change according to the paging or sorting options that you choose but that the time in the Latest Items heading remains the same.

How It Works

The standard WebGrid paging and sorting functionality is driven by simple HTML hyperlinks. This behaviour changes when you specify a value for the `ajaxUpdateContainerId` parameter. HTML hyperlinks are still produced, but now their destination anchors (the `href` value) are set to a hash sign (#). The hyperlinks also acquire a JavaScript `onclick` event handler which fires a jQuery load function call. You should remember from Chapter 6 that this function makes an asynchronous request and loads either the whole response, or a fragment from the response into the specified part of the DOM. In this case, jQuery requests the current page, passing sorting and paging instructions in the query string. The response consists of the HTML for the entire page. However, only a fragment of the response is required — the `ajaxUpdateContainerId` element and its contents — and this fragment is loaded into the existing element, denoted by the `ajaxUpdateContainerId`.

Here is a decoded example of the click event handler that's added to the link at the top of the Id column, and which controls sorting for that column:

```
    $('#grid').load('/Default.cshtml?sort=Id&sortdir=ASC&__=634436543370524609 #grid');
```

This example clearly shows the element that will receive the content to be loaded, the URL for the request, which includes a timestamp value to prevent caching of results. You can also see the fragment identifier after the timestamp.

Working with Styles and Columns

The grid that you have just worked with is cool in an AJAX way, but it looks kind of default and bland. It needs some styles applied to it. The `GetHtml` method accepts a large number of optional parameters that control a range of grid features, including style. Table 11-2 details the parameters available to you.

TABLE 11-2: WebGrid GetHtml Style Parameters

PARAMETER	DESCRIPTION
tableStyle	CSS class that contains style rules for the whole table
headerStyle	CSS class for styling the header
footerStyle	CSS class that styles the footer
rowStyle	CSS class for styling rows
alternatingRowStyle	CSS class providing the style for alternating rows
selectedRowStyle	CSS class for setting the style of selected row

The following style sheet provides a typical set of CSS classes relating to styling various aspects of a grid. It has already been added to the style sheet that comes with this chapter's download:

```css
/*
--------------------------------------------------
GRID
--------------------------------------------------
*/
.grid
{
    background: #fff;
    width: 650px;
    border-collapse: collapse;
}
.grid th
{
    font-size: 1.1em;
    font-weight: normal;
    color: #039;
    padding: 10px 8px;
    border-bottom: 2px solid #728059;
    text-align: left;
}

.grid td
{
    border-bottom: 1px solid #ccc;
    padding: 4px 6px;
}

.alternate{
    background: #d3ff80;
}

.gridheader, .gridfooter{
    background: #9ebf60;
}
.gridheader a, .gridfooter a{
```

```
        color: #fff;
        text-decoration:none;
    }
    .dateWidth{
        width: 100px;
    }
```

The various styles are applied via the `GetHtml` method in the following way:

```
@grid.GetHtml(
    tableStyle : "grid",
    alternatingRowStyle : "alternate",
    headerStyle : "gridheader",
    footerStyle : "gridfooter"
)
```

Figure 11-6 illustrates how these styles affect the grid you have just created in the previous exercise. As an additional exercise, add the style declarations to your existing style sheet and alter the `GetHtml` method in the code you have just created so that it resembles the previous snippet.

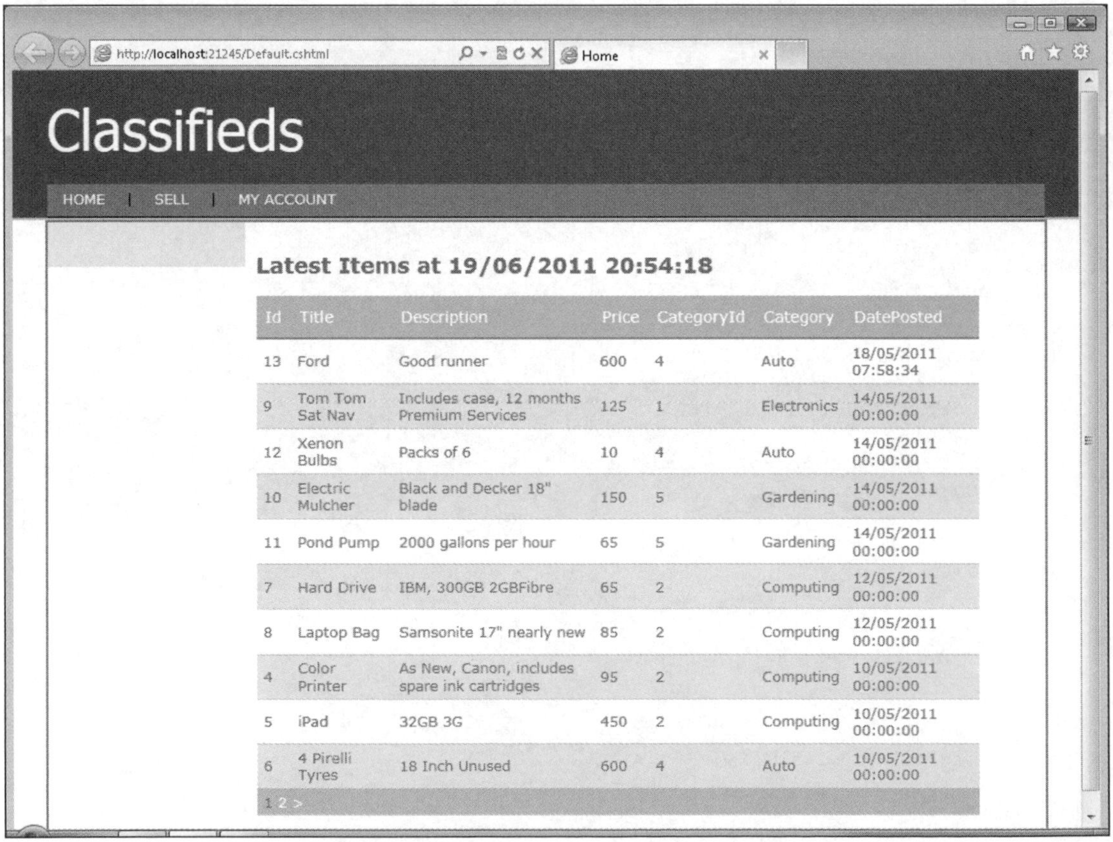

FIGURE 11-6

Table 11-3 details more parameters that provide access to other display-related properties.

TABLE 11-3: Additional WebGrid Display-Related Parameters

PARAMETER	DESCRIPTION
caption	The text you want to display as a table caption. The result will appear within a `<caption>` element.
displayHeader	True by default. If false, the table header is not displayed.
fillEmptyRows	False by default. If true, this ensures that empty rows are added to ensure that the `rowsPerPage` value is met when there are insufficient rows of data to do so.
emptyRowCellValue	If `fillEmptyRows` is set to true, the `emptyRowCellValue` determines what is displayed in the cells of any empty rows that are added. By default, it is an HTML non-breaking space (` `).

The grid is coming along nicely now and looks a lot better, but there are still some aspects of it that can be improved. If you look at the column headers, they replicate the database column names. That might not always be desirable. For example, the final column has a header containing two words concatenated into one: *DatePosted*. That's not particularly user-friendly. The contents of the column itself are displayed using the default `DateTime` as a string setting. The column also needs a CSS style applied to it to ensure that the date doesn't break over two lines, and the price is not displayed as a currency. Finally, there is a column in the grid for every field returned by the SQL query, although you might not want all of them displayed in the grid.

Column-specific properties are accessible via the `columns` parameter. This represents a collection of individual `WebGridColumn` objects that represent each column in the grid. Each column exposes a number of properties, as detailed in Table 11-4.

TABLE 11-4: WebGridColumn Properties

PROPERTY	DESCRIPTION
ColumnName	The name of the data item associated with a particular column. Most often this is the database field name.
CanSort	True by default, if sorting is enabled on the grid as a whole, but you can disable sorting on specific columns by setting this to false.
Header	The value you want to appear in the column header, if not the database field name.
Style	The CSS class you want to apply to the column.
Format	A function that formats the item displayed in the column.

The first four properties are easy to follow. The final one (Format) is not quite so straightforward. You will explore that in more detail shortly, but first, you need to understand how these properties are set as part of the GetHtml method.

Here's the relevant code that you should have so far:

```
@grid.GetHtml(
    tableStyle : "table",
    alternatingRowStyle : "alternate",
    headerStyle : "header",
    footerStyle : "footer"
)
```

The WebGrid.Columns() method gives you access to the collection of columns, which can be manipulated individually via another method, WebGrid.Column():

```
@grid.GetHtml(
    tableStyle : "table",
    alternatingRowStyle : "alternate",
    headerStyle : "header",
    footerStyle : "footer",
    columns: grid.Columns(grid.Column(),grid.Column(),grid.Column()etc…)
)
```

You must reference all the columns that you want to appear, even if you do not want to set any of the properties that are available to you in Table 11-4. You must also provide the columnName parameter value unless you specify an argument to the format parameter. If, for example, you simply didn't want the Id column to show a header, but you wanted all fields from the database displayed except for the CategoryId field, this is the minimum that you need:

```
@grid.GetHtml(
    tableStyle : "table",
    alternatingRowStyle : "alternate",
    headerStyle : "header",
    footerStyle : "footer",
    columns: grid.Columns(
        grid.Column(
            columnName: "Id",
            header: string.Empty
            ),
        grid.Column(
            columnName: "Title"
            ),
        grid.Column(
            columnName: "Description"
            ),
        grid.Column(
            columnName: "Price"
            ),
        grid.Column(
            columnName: "Category"
            ),
        grid.Column(
            columnName: "DatePosted"
```

```
            )
        grid.Column(
            columnName: "Condition"
            )
        grid.Column(
            columnName: "Duration"
            )
        )
    )
```

You can see that the properties of the column object are accessible via parameters that have the same name, but with a lowercase first letter. If you wanted to remove sorting from the Id column and set a CSS style, the following code will arrange that:

```
grid.Column(
    columnName: "Id",
    canSort: false,
    style: "specialClass"
    ),
```

That just leaves formatting cell values. Earlier, you learned that the Format property's data type is a function. It is actually an inline Razor Template. It is a snippet of Razor syntax, just like you have seen before, which determines the way that the data item is presented for display. Inline Razor templates can take one of a number of forms. Technically, it is a delegate that takes a single parameter called item, which represents the data for the current row. Since it is a delegate, it will take a lambda expression. For example, if you wanted to display a Long Date version of the DatePosted value, you could pass this to the format parameter:

```
(item) => string.Format("{0:D}", item.DatePosted)
```

More often than not, you will see the terser Razor syntax used in examples, and that is what this book recommends. The following two lines are functionally equivalent and equally as valid:

```
@:@item.DatePosted.ToString("D")
@<text>@item.DatePosted.ToString("D")</text>
```

If you want to include HTML, you can do so easily. The following line will result in the content of the column being rendered bold:

```
@<strong>@item.DatePosted.ToString("D")</strong>
```

Putting all of this together, the following revised version of the GetHtml method call will resolve the outstanding issues that were identified earlier:

```
@grid.GetHtml(
    tableStyle : "grid",
    alternatingRowStyle : "alternate",
    headerStyle : "gridheader",
    footerStyle : "gridfooter",
    columns: grid.Columns(
        grid.Column(
            columnName: "Id",
            header: string.Empty
```

```
    ),
grid.Column(
    columnName: "Title"
    ),
grid.Column(
    columnName: "Description"
    ),
grid.Column(
    columnName: "Price",
    format: @<text>@item.Price.ToString("c")</text>
    ),
grid.Column(
    columnName: "Category"
    ),
grid.Column(
    columnName: "DatePosted",
    header: "Date Posted",
    style: "dateWidth",
    format: @<text>@item.DatePosted.ToString("D")</text>
    )
    )
)
```

Figure 11-7 illustrates the finished grid.

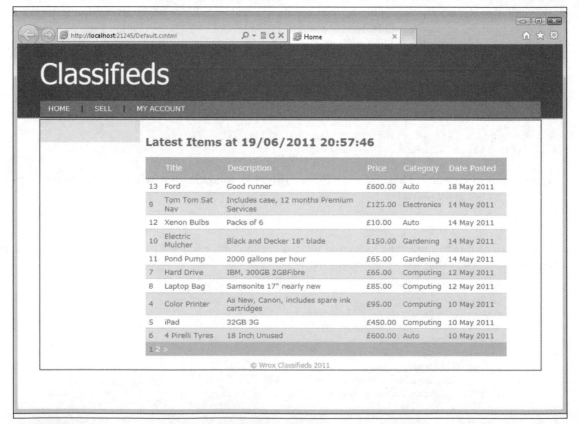

FIGURE 11-7

Selecting Items

Most often, grids are used to display summary data as in the previous example. Visitors usually need a way to drill down to more detail. In the Classifieds site, the visitor will want to examine the description of any item that interests them, and perhaps make a bid on it. You can present this detailed information in a number of ways, but first you must provide the visitors with a way to select particular items.

There are a number of ways to enable selection. Which one you choose largely depends on whether you have AJAX paging and sorting enabled. If you do, your options are restricted somewhat. The simplest way to enable selection is to use the WebGridRow's `GetSelectLink` method, which acts on the `item` parameter you met before. This method works by generating a hyperlink with a query string indicating the current row. You can detect whether a row has been selected using the WebGrid's `HasSelection` property, which is true if a selection link was clicked. Since this approach relies on hyperlinks, it cannot be used with AJAX paging and sorting. In the following exercise, you will alter the existing grid to try out the built-in selection feature.

TRY IT OUT   Enabling Selection

1. Open the Classifieds site if you have closed it, and remove the `ajaxUpdateContainerId` value from the grid's constructor. The relevant line of code should now simply read as follows:

```
var grid = new WebGrid(data);
```

2. At the same time, alter the `<h2>` element to remove the reference to the time. That should now read as follows

```
<h2>Latest Items</h2>
```

3. Amend the column initializer for the Id column to remove the `columnName` and `header` parameter values and replace them with a value for the `format` parameter as follows:

```
columns: grid.Columns(
    grid.Column(
        format: @<text>@item.GetSelectLink()</text>
),
```

Ensure that the `format` parameter is separated from the header value by a comma.

4. Add the following code just after the closing `</div>` tag:

```
@if(grid.HasSelection){
    dynamic Item = grid.SelectedRow;
    <p>The selected item is @Item.Title with an ID of @Item.Id</p>
}
```

5. Launch the page in a browser by clicking the Run button or pressing F12, and click any one of the Select links. Notice just below the grid that the title of the item in the selected row is displayed along with its ID.

How It Works

You removed the `columnName` parameter value from the Id column along with the header value. This didn't really have much effect, except that it demonstrates that you can add arbitrary columns to the WebGrid, which are not linked to fields in the database or other data-related items. Then you applied the `GetSelectLink` method. This generates a hyperlink in the cell, which features "Select" as the text. You can pass any string value you like to the `GetSelectLink` method to alter the default text value of the generated link. The anchor for the hyperlink is the current page with a query string value. Each row of the grid generates a different query string value based on its ordinal position, starting from 1 and incrementing by 1 each time. The query string field is called `row` by default. This can be altered through the `selectionFieldName` parameter within the WebGrid's constructor, as detailed in Table 11-1. It is also subject to the `fieldNamePrefix` parameter value.

If a link has been clicked, the `HasSelection` property will be `true`. The `SelectedRow` property of the WebGrid represents the currently selected `WebGridRow` object. You can access the values of the grid cells by passing the `SelectedRow` to a dynamic object.

From there, you could render a content page using the `RenderPage` method, passing the dynamic object as `PageData`. Within the content page, you would access the ID of the object, and query the database for more details. For example, you can replace the code that displays the title and ID of the selected row with something like the following:

```
@if(grid.HasSelection){
    dynamic row = grid.SelectedRow;
    @RenderPage("~/Shared/_Details.cshtml", new { Item = row } )
}
```

The page _Details.cshtml will contain a call to the database to obtain details of the item, which has been passed via the page dictionary:

```
@{
    var db = Database.Open("Classifieds");
    var sql = "SELECT * FROM Items WHERE Id = @0");
    var data = db.QuerySingle(sql, Page.Item.Id;);
    // and so on
}
```

An alternative way to drill down to an item's details is to generate links that navigate the user to a separate page altogether. Since this works with AJAX paging and sorting, it is the method that you will implement in the Classifieds site. It means modifying the page you have just worked with again, but the changes are limited.

TRY IT OUT Creating a Details Page

1. The first thing to do is to restore the AJAX paging and sorting functionality. This is easily accomplished by adding the `ajaxUpdatecontainerId` parameter value to the WebGrid constructor:

```
var grid = new WebGrid(data, ajaxUpdateContainerId: "grid");
```

2. Alter the first column's `format` value to the following:

```
grid.Column(
    format: @<a href="@Href("~/Details.cshtml?id=" + item.Id)">Details</a>
),
```

3. Add a new file to the root folder and name it **Details.cshtml**. Replace the default code with the following:

```
@{
    dynamic item = null;
    if(!Request["id"].IsEmpty() && Request["id"].IsInt()){
        var db = Database.Open("Classifieds");
        var sql = "SELECT * FROM Items, Categories WHERE Id = @0";
        item = db.QuerySingle(sql, Request["id"]);
    }
}
@if(item != null){
    <h2>Details</h2>
    <h3>@item.Title</h3>
    <p>@item.Description</p>
    <p>Price: @item.Price.ToString("c")</p>
    <p>Condition: @item.Condition</p>
    <p>Posted on @item.DatePosted.ToString("D") in the @item.Category category</p>
}
```

4. Make sure that Default.cshtml is selected in the File Explorer and press the F12 key to launch the site as a browser. The first column of the grid should contain a link with the text "Select." Choose any product to view, and click the link. You should be taken to a page that displays more detail for that item.

How It Works

The principle behind the links that you generated in the first column is that they use the query string to pass values from one page to another. You were able to easily generate query strings dynamically based on the individual item's identity value. Once the user is taken to the target page, the identity can be retrieved from the query string and, once validated, passed to a parameterized SQL query. The `QuerySingle` method is used to obtain one row of data that's displayed on the page.

You have spent a lot of time learning how to manipulate the items in the Classifieds database, but the one thing that you have not completed yet is to create a means by which the data gets there in the first place. So in this final exercise, you will extend the form you created in Chapter 5 and enhanced in Chapter 6 to save the submitted item in your database. There isn't a lot of work to do. You need to add a select list for categories, and to fill that for the database. Validation will be needed on that select list too. Then, once all items have passed validation, you need to insert them into the database.

TRY IT OUT Finishing the Classifieds Form

1. Open the Sell.cshtml file in the Classifieds site you have been working on. At the top of the code block, add the following three lines of code:

```
var db = Database.Open("Classifieds");
var sql = "SELECT * FROM Categories";
var categories = db.Query(sql);
```

2. Amend the server-side validation logic so that it includes validation for categories. You can place the following lines of code anywhere in the validation block, but I have placed it at the end, just before the check to determine if the ModelState IsValid:

```
if(Request["categoryId"].IsEmpty()){
    ModelState.AddError("categoryId", "Please choose a category your item");
}
```

3. At the end of the code block, just after the WebMail helper has sent a confirmation e-mail, replace the line of code that sets a value for the message variable with the following code:

```
sql = @"INSERT INTO Items (Title, Description, Price,
    CategoryId, DatePosted, Condition, Duration) VALUES
    (@0, @1, @2, @3,GetDate(), @4, @5)";
var parameters = new[]{Request["title"], Request["description"],
                    Request["price"], Request["categoryId"],
                    Request["condition"], Request["duration"]};
db.Execute(sql, parameters);
Response.Redirect("~/Default.cshtml");
```

4. Alter the client-side validation code by adding the following line to the rules:

```
categoryId: 'required',
```

Add the following line to the messages section:

```
categoryId: ' *You must choose a category for your item',
```

5. Add the following code to the form between the "condition" radio buttons and the "e-mail" text box:

```
<div>
    <label for="categoryId">Category*</label>
</div>
<div>
    <select name="categoryId">
        <option value="">--Choose Category--</option>
            @foreach(var category in categories){
            <option value="@category.CategoryId"
                @(category.CategoryId == Request["categoryId"].AsInt() ?
                    " selected=\"selected\"" : "")>
                @category.Category</option>
            }
    </select>
    @Html.ValidationMessage("categoryId")
</div>
```

6. Run the page in a browser and ensure that you enter valid values into all the required fields. Submit the page to check that it works. If the submission has been successful, you should be presented with the home page, featuring your newly added item at the top of the grid.

How It Works

By now, you should understand what is going on as you applied these changes to the existing code. You added the select list for categories, which is driven by the database. This is exactly the same principle as the one you used to select a category for editing when you built your admin screens. There is nothing new here. You applied validation to the new field very easily by simple modifications to the existing validation code, and then you inserted the valid details in the database using a straightforward piece of SQL. The one thing to note is the final line you added to the code block at the top of the page:

```
Response.Redirect("~/Default.cshtml");
```

`Response.Redirect` tells your browser to request another page — the one denoted by the string in the method call. Why would you want to make the user's browser request a different page? For one thing, the users can immediately see the result of their successful form post — the item they just added is at the top of the grid! But more importantly, it reduces the possibility of a double-post. If you redisplay the form, the values will persist and the user can easily click the Submit button again, thus causing a duplicate entry. Or they might refresh the page, which will have the same effect. Redirecting them to another page reduces the chances of this happening dramatically (although they could still use the browser's Back button to go back to the form and press Refresh). This technique is known as Post/Redirect/Get or PRG. The user makes a POST request, which results in a Redirect command forcing a GET request.

SUMMARY

This material has built on the database and SQL basics that you learned in the previous chapter, and covered the Database Helper's usage in a lot more detail. You now understand the serious dangers posed by SQL injection, one of the top two threats to websites. You were shown how it works and how the Database Helper protects your application from this danger if you use parameters.

The chapter then covered developing simple forms for CRUD operations. You generated a series of forms that allows users to create, update, and delete categories in the Classified site. You learned how to apply secure data access using parameters in these exercises.

The next section of the chapter introduced the WebGrid Helper, which is designed for displaying tabular data on a web page. You saw how the default configuration includes sorting and paging capabilities out-of-the-box. It is also AJAX-capable so that sorting and paging operations do not necessarily result in a full-page postback. You learned how to set the properties of the WebGrid as a whole, and also how to set properties on a column-by-column basis.

In the final part of the chapter, you learned about the Post/Redirect/Get pattern, which is used to help prevent accidental form submission, and the subsequent duplication of data.

Together with Chapter 10, this chapter has provided you with a good grounding in data access within ASP.NET Web Pages development. The skills and principals you have learned here are core to being able to develop great dynamic websites. The best news is that these skills and techniques are not limited to WebMatrix development. They are just as applicable at a basic level to website development using any other framework, such as Web Forms or MVC, or indeed PHP, or any other kind of development that involves interaction with databases.

EXERCISES

1. What is the main cause of successful SQL injection attempts?

2. Why might you need to set a value for `fieldNamePrefix`?

3. Imagine that you are using the WebGrid, and that one of the columns in the database is used to store an image filename. The column is called FileName, conveniently. The actual image files are stored in a folder called "images" in the root folder of the site. Which parameter would you need to use to get the associated image to display in each row of the grid, and what code or markup would you need?

Answers to the Exercises can be found in the Appendix.

▶ **WHAT YOU LEARNED IN THIS CHAPTER**

TOPIC	KEY CONCEPTS
SQL injection	The alteration of the behaviour of a SQL command by injecting additional SQL syntax into it.
Parameter	A placeholder for a value to be sent with a SQL command to the database.
Extension method	A method that extends the behaviour of an existing type.
WebGrid	A helper for displaying tabular data.
Post/Redirect/Get	A technique used to prevent duplicate submissions of forms.

12

Security

WHAT YOU WILL LEARN IN THIS CHAPTER:

- ➤ An overview of website security

- ➤ Services offered by the WebSecurity Helper

- ➤ How to retrofit security features to an existing site

- ➤ How to manage access to parts or all of a website

- ➤ How to let users create accounts

- ➤ How to manage the display of content based on the user's role

At this point, you have a site that is capable of storing items for sale, and notifying the person who posted the item by e-mail that their item is listed. You also have a way of managing categories with a series of CRUD forms in an administration area. However, the site is completely open, which means that anyone can access your CRUD forms and add or alter existing categories. This is likely to be unacceptable, because people will add duplicate items, or worse. You need some way to restrict access to the administration area to only people whom you trust. You need to be able to identify those people when they visit the site, and more importantly, you need to be able to prevent untrusted visitors from being able to access trusted areas.

MEMBERSHIP AND ROLES MANAGEMENT

The ASP.NET security model is built on two pillars — *Membership* and *Roles Management*. The next sections examine these concepts in more detail and explain what they incorporate.

Membership

A lot of sites these days invite visitors to register with them — to submit personal details in a form in order to take advantage of some of the features the site offers. For example, I have an account at the official ASP.NET forums. I created an *identity* with the site by completing a registration form and providing some information about who I am along with an e-mail address. The site used that e-mail address to verify my identity. It sent an e-mail to that address which contained a link I had to click in order to confirm I own that e-mail address. When I visit the forums, I have to provide my details in a login form to identify myself. Once I have done that, I have access to my existing threads, and can post new questions or answers. I am a *member* of the forums. The features responsible for managing the creation of my account, storing my personal details, and *authenticating* me (confirming who I am) when I return to the site are delivered via a *membership provider.*

Roles

Most of the members at the ASP.NET forums have the same set of privileges. They can start threads by posting a question, edit their posts, mark other posts as the answer if they appear in a thread started by them, or reply to another member's thread. If you are a Microsoft Most Valuable Professional (MVP) you enjoy some additional privileges. You can mark any post as an answer, and you have access to an MVP-only forum. Moderators have a considerably wider set of permissions. We can move posts from one forum to another, delete them, merge duplicate threads, and ban users. An ordinary member, an MVP, and a moderator all have different *roles* within the forums. Once the member has authenticated his or herself, the system determines what they are *authorized* to do based on the permissions allocated to their role within the site. This functionality is managed by a *role provider.*

The Provider Pattern defines a base set of behaviors, which are then implemented by specific components. There is SqlMembershipProvider, which is the default implementation for managing membership services via SQL Server databases. Other membership providers include one for Access and another for Active Directory.

The Web Pages Framework introduces a new membership provider called SimpleMembershipProvider. It features a range of methods for managing common tasks such as creating accounts, validating users, resetting passwords, and so on. The Web Pages Framework also introduces a new role provider called SimpleRoleProvider. Again, this features a range of methods for creating roles, adding users to roles, checking whether a given user is in a particular role, and so on. You will explore how to manage roles later in the chapter.

THE WEBSECURITY HELPER

The WebSecurity Helper wraps the most commonly used membership properties and methods to make them easier to work with. The Starter Site template site has been designed to illustrate how the WebSecurity Helper can be used, and offers a view of the typical workflow required to create and implement a membership. It is worth creating a site from the Starter Site template to explore these features in more detail.

The WebSecurity Helper needs initializing, which is best done in an _AppStart file. You can see this in the _AppStart.cshtml file within the Starter Site template:

```
@{
    WebSecurity.InitializeDatabaseConnection("StarterSite", "UserProfile", "UserId",
                                             "E-mail", true);
    // WebMail.SmtpServer = "mailserver.example.com";
    // WebMail.EnableSsl = true;
    // WebMail.UserName = "username@example.com";
    // WebMail.Password = "your-password";
    // WebMail.From = "your-name-here@example.com";
}
```

The `InitializeDatabaseConnection` method takes five arguments. The first is the name of the database that holds user information. This must be an existing database. Just as with the `Database.Open` method, the string can point to a connection string within the web.config file, or to a SQL Server Express or SQL Server Compact 4.0 database filename within the App_Data folder. The second argument is the name of the table that houses the user profile information. The absolute minimum information that this table must store is a unique integer identity and a user name value. The columns within the table that holds this data are specified in the third and fourth arguments. The final argument indicates whether the table and its columns should be created automatically if they do not already exist.

When the `InitializeDatabaseConnection` method is called, it checks to see if the specified table and columns exist. If they do not, it will create them in the specified database. It will also add three other tables: webpages_Membership, webpages_Roles, and webpages_UsersInRoles. These tables are used by the SimpleMembershipProvider to store information that enables the management of users and their roles. The tables are useless without some way to capture user data in the first place. For that, you need a registration form.

All of the Starter Site membership logic including a registration form is housed in files with the Account folder. Within that, you can see the following files depicted in Figure 12-1:

➤ **Register.cshtml:** Contains the registration form so that users can create an account

➤ **Confirm.cshtml:** Used to confirm creation of an account based on a confirmation e-mail

➤ **Login.cshtml:** Allows existing account holders to log in to the site

➤ **Logout.cshtml:** Enables the users to log out of the site

➤ **ChangePassword.cshtml:** Enables the users to change their passwords

➤ **ForgotPassword.cshtml:** Enables users to apply to reset their password if they have forgotten it

➤ **PasswordReset.cshtml:** Enables the users to reset their passwords

➤ **Thanks.cshtml:** A POST/Redirect/GET destination to prevent duplicate form submission when the user applies for an account

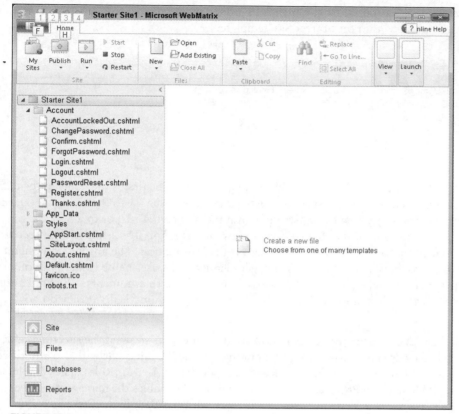

FIGURE 12-1

Individual pages can be protected to allow only currently authenticated users access by adding a call to the WebSecurity.RequireAuthenticatedUser() method at the top of the page. You can see this in ChangePassword.cshtml. If you attempt to browse this page directly, having just created the site without registering, you will be redirected to Login.cshtml. You can also protect an entire folder and its subfolders by adding WebSecurity.RequireAuthenticatedUser() to a _PageStart file.

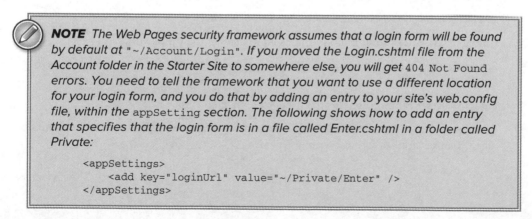

> **NOTE** The Web Pages security framework assumes that a login form will be found by default at "~/Account/Login". If you moved the Login.cshtml file from the Account folder in the Starter Site to somewhere else, you will get 404 Not Found errors. You need to tell the framework that you want to use a different location for your login form, and you do that by adding an entry to your site's web.config file, within the appSetting section. The following shows how to add an entry that specifies that the login form is in a file called Enter.cshtml in a folder called Private:
>
> ```
> <appSettings>
>     <add key="loginUrl" value="~/Private/Enter" />
> </appSettings>
> ```

The code in the Starter Site's registration form may at first glance look a little daunting. It includes some commented-out lines that take care of validating a ReCaptcha control. Part of the Starter Site's purpose is to demonstrate the use of the ReCaptcha Helper. You won't be exploring that in any detail in this book, but it is a device that prevents automated bot submission of forms. If you want to explore the ReCaptcha Helper in more detail, it is available in the ASP.NET Web Pages Helpers library that you worked with in Chapter 7.

The registration form contains an input for an e-mail address, which will serve as a user name. It also asks the registrant to provide their chosen password twice. When the form is posted back, the code block initially ensures that there is a user name and a password, and that the second password matches the first. This is basic validation, which you should be used to seeing by now. The form uses the first method of creating and displaying error messages that you worked with in Chapter 5 — the one based on building up a string as opposed to using the Html.Validation Helpers. The code then connects to the database and determines if anyone has already registered an account with the same user name, assuming that all validation passes. If no results are found, the code uses SQL to add the user to the users table, which is called UserProfile in this site.

This is the point at which the *user* has been created. However, an *account* is created only after a corresponding entry for that user is added to the webpages_Membership table. The definition of the webpages_Membership table is illustrated in Figure 12-2.

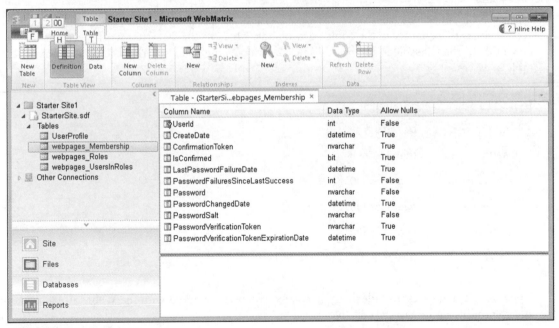

FIGURE 12-2

It is the place where passwords are stored as a hashed value along with account confirmation tokens and fields for managing password resetting. The account is created in the Starter Site via the

WebSecurity.CreateAccount method. There is an alternative method that negates the need for creating the user via SQL. This is the WebSecurity.CreateUserAndAccount method. You will use this method soon.

Both the CreateAccount and the CreateUserAndAccount methods return a string. This string is a token that's generated by the SimpleMembershipProvider and is used for confirming an account — if you decide to implement that feature. The Starter Site implements it, and sends out an e-mail containing a link that new users must follow to validate their accounts. Part of the link URL consists of a query string that features the token. This confirmation feature is based on the theory that only people who have access to the e-mail account that the user registered with can verify the account — thus increasing the likelihood that the account is genuine.

Creating a Registration Form

In the following exercise, you will create a registration form for the Classifieds site. The workflow that you introduce will be based on the Starter Site example that you have just looked at. As well as a registration form, the workflow requires a page to redirect to after successful submission, and a page for confirming registration.

TRY IT OUT   Creating a Registration Form

1. Open the Classifieds site that you last worked with in the previous chapter, or use the version that accompanies this chapter in the book's downloads. Move to the Database workspace and add a new table to the Classifieds database. Table 12-1 details the columns you need to add. Save the table as Users.

TABLE 12-1 User Table Columns

NAME	DETAILS
UserId	Identity, int
UserName	nvarchar 100
FirstName	nvarchar 100
LastName	nvarchar 100
E-mail	nvarchar 100

2. Open the _AppStart.cshtml file that you created when you worked with the WebMail Helper and add the following line to the code block:

```
WebSecurity.InitializeDatabaseConnection("Classifieds",
                                         "Users",
                                         "UserId",
                                         "UserName",
                                         true);
```

This doesn't need to be broken over multiple lines. It is presented like that in this book because the pages aren't wide enough sometimes.

3. Add a new folder named Account to the root folder. Create a new page in this folder called **Register.cshtml**. Replace the existing code with the following:

```
@{
    Page.Title = "Create an account";
    var sql = string.Empty;
    var firstname = Request["firstname"];
    var lastname = Request["lastname"];
    var username = Request["username"];
    var password = Request["password"];
    var email = Request["email"];
    var email2 = Request["email2"];
    if(IsPost){
        if(firstname.IsEmpty()){
            ModelState.AddError("firstname", "Please provide a first name");
        }
        if(lastname.IsEmpty()){
            ModelState.AddError("lastname", "Please provide a last name");
        }
        if(username.IsEmpty()){
            ModelState.AddError("username", "You must provide a user name");
        }
        if(password.IsEmpty()){
            ModelState.AddError("password", "You must provide a password");
        }
        if(email.IsEmpty()){
            ModelState.AddError("email", "Please provide your email address");
        }
        if(!email.IsEmpty() && !Functions.IsValidEmail(email)){
            ModelState.AddError("email", "Please provide a valid email address");
        }
        if(email2 != email){
            ModelState.AddError("email2", "Your email addresses must match");
        }
        if(!ModelState.IsValid){
            ModelState.AddFormError(@"Please fix the errors
                                below before resubmitting the form");
        }
        else{
            var db = Database.Open("Classifieds");
            var user = new {FirstName = firstname, LastName = lastname, Email = email};
            try{
                var token = WebSecurity.CreateUserAndAccount(username, password,
                                                    user, true);
                var hostUrl = Request.Url.GetComponents(UriComponents.SchemeAndServer,
                                                    UriFormat.Unescaped);
                var queryString = HttpUtility.UrlEncode(token);
                var confirm = "~/Account/Confirm?confirmationCode=";
                var confirmationUrl = hostUrl +
                            VirtualPathUtility.ToAbsolute(confirm + queryString);
                var message = "<p>Your confirmation code is: " + token + "</p>" +
```

```
                          "<p>Visit <a href=\"" + confirmationUrl + "\">" +
confirmationUrl + "</a>" +
                      " to activate your account.</p>";
                  WebMail.Send(
                          to: email,
                          subject: "Please confirm your account",
                          body: message,
                          isBodyHtml: true
                      );
                  Response.Redirect("~/Account/Thanks");
              }
              catch(MembershipCreateUserException ex){
                  if(ex.StatusCode == MembershipCreateStatus.DuplicateUserName){
                      ModelState.AddError("username",
                          "That user name is already in use. Please choose another.");
                      ModelState.AddFormError(@"Please fix the errors below
                              before resubmitting the form");
                  }else{
                      ModelState.AddFormError("Something went wrong. Please try again");
                  }
              }
          }
      }
}
<h2>Create an account</h2>
<p>Use the form below to create an account with the site.
    Then you can post items for sale and bid on other items.
    Please ensure that you complete all fields
    marked with an asterisk *</p>
<form method="post">
    <fieldset>
        <legend>Register</legend>

        @Html.ValidationSummary(true)
        <div>
            <label for="firstname">First Name*</label>
        </div>
        <div>
            <input type="text" id="firstname" name="firstname"
                    value="@firstname" />
            @Html.ValidationMessage("firstname")
        </div>
        <div>
            <label for="lastname">Last Name*</label>
        </div>
        <div>
            <input type="text" id="lastname" name="lastname" value="@lastname" />
            @Html.ValidationMessage("lastname")
        </div>
        <div>
            <label for="username">User Name*</label>
```

```
            </div>
            <div>
                <input type="text" id="username" name="username" value="@username" />
                @Html.ValidationMessage("username")
            </div>
            <div>
                <label for="password">Password*</label>
            </div>
            <div>
                <input type="password" id="password" name="password" />
                @Html.ValidationMessage("password")
            </div>
            <div>
                <label for="email">Email*</label>
            </div>
            <div>
                <input type="text" id="email" name="email" value="@email" />
                @Html.ValidationMessage("email")
            </div>
            <div>
                <label for="email2">Re-enter your email*</label>
            </div>
            <div>
                <input type="text" id="email2" name="email2" value="@email2" />
                @Html.ValidationMessage("email2")
            </div>
            <div>
                <input type="submit" name="Submit" value="Register" />
            </div>
        </fieldset>
</form>
```

4. Add another file to the newly created Account folder and name it **Thanks.cshtml**. Replace the existing code with the following:

```
@{
    Page.Title = "Thanks for registering";
}
<h2>Thanks</h2>
@if (!WebSecurity.IsAuthenticated) {
    <p>
        An email with instructions on how to activate
        your account has been sent to you.
    </p>
} else {
    <p>
        Please use the navigation to find your way around.
    </p>
}
```

5. Add another file to the Account folder. Name this one **Confirm.cshtml** and replace the default code with the following:

```
@{
    Page.Title = "Registration Confirmation Page";

    var message = string.Empty;
    var confirmationToken = Request["confirmationCode"];

    WebSecurity.Logout();
    if (!confirmationToken.IsEmpty()) {
        if (WebSecurity.ConfirmAccount(confirmationToken.Trim())) {
            message = @"Registration Confirmed!";
            message += "Click <a href=\"/Account/Login\">here</a>"
            message += "to log in to the site.";
        } else {
            message = "Could not confirm your registration info";
        }
    }
}

@if (!message.IsEmpty()) {
    <p>@Html.Raw(message)</p>
} else {
    <form method="post" action="">
        <fieldset>
            <legend>Confirmation Code</legend>
            <label for="confirmationCode">
                Please enter the confirmation code sent to you via email and
                then click the <em>Confirm</em> button.
            </label>
            <input type="text" id="confirmationCode" name="confirmationCode" />
            <input type="submit" value="Confirm" />
        </fieldset>
    </form>
}
```

6. Open the _Navigation.cshtml file in the Shared folder and alter the link to My Account so that it points to the newly created Register.cshtml file:

```
<div id="nav">
    <a href="@Href("~/")">Home</a> |
    <a href="@Href("~/Sell")">Sell</a> |
    <a href="@Href("~/Account/Register")">Register</a>
</div>
```

7. Make sure that your WebMail Helper is set up correctly. If you are using the `SpecifiedPickupDirectory` method for managing e-mail while testing, ensure that the specified directory still exists. Once you have verified all is working, launch the Register.cshtml page in your browser. Enter valid values into the form and submit the form. You should be transferred to the Thanks.cshtml page you created. Check your e-mail (or pickup folder) for the confirmation e-mail, and click the link within it to confirm the account. Now click the Register link in the navigation menu and attempt to create another account, entering the same user name that you just used. Submit the form and notice the error message that appears in Figure 12-3.

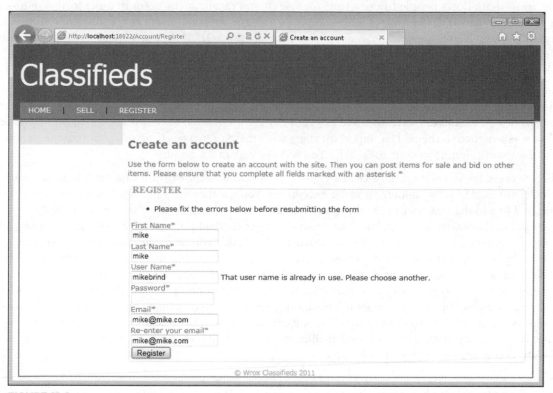

FIGURE 12-3

How It Works

The first step you took was to create your own user table within the existing Classifieds database. The schema for the table exceeds the minimum requirements, which is an integer column for the User's ID and a unique user name value. It also provides for a first name, last name, and an e-mail address. There is no limit to the amount of information you can collect from users, but these additional fields serve to illustrate the point sufficiently.

The next step was to initialize the WebSecurity Helper. You did this in the _AppStart file, which as you might remember is executed once when the application starts. The parameter values that the `InitializeDatabaseConnection` method takes are the database to use, the user table, the unique integer identity column in that table, the unique user name, and whether to create all tables if they do not exist. In this case, the user table exists, but the other membership and roles tables do not. When you first requested a page in the application, this method took care of creating the extra tables in the nominated database for you.

The bulk of the work went into creating the registration page. It contains a form, with server-side validation using the Validation Helpers and `ModelState`, just like you worked with in Chapter 5 when creating the form that allows people to post items for sale. If you recall, at the point that the form submission is deemed to be valid, the Starter Site example queries the database to see if the submitted user name is already in use. It uses `QuerySingle` to obtain the result of a SQL `SELECT` statement. (`QueryValue` would be more correct...). Your code didn't do this. First, you created an anonymous object:

```
var user = new {FirstName = firstname, LastName = lastname, Email = email};
```

An anonymous object is like a temporary container for values. In this case, you gave your object three properties: `FirstName`, `LastName`, and `Email`. They are all deemed to be strings, based on the value that was assigned to them. The important thing with these properties is that they mimic the names of the database columns in your user table. You will see why in a second.

The next section of code takes place in a `try-catch` block. Remember from Chapter 9 that `try-catch` blocks are used to safely manage possible exceptions. You use the `WebSecurity.CreateUserAndAccount` method to add the new user to the database. This does more than the `CreateAccount` method that you see used in the Starter Site template. The `CreateAccount` method populates the webpage_Membership (the accounts) table only. You have to populate the user table yourself. The `CreateUserAndAccount` method populates the user and the account tables. The parameters this method accepts are the user name, password, an object containing further user details (your anonymous object), and true or false indicating whether you want to generate an account confirmation token or not. Internally, the method will examine your anonymous object and attempt to match values to be inserted against database column names taken from the names of the object's properties. It will construct a SQL statement based on the property names, so it is vital that you double check your spelling and ensure that your property names are identical to the database column names in your user table.

The `CreateUserAndAccount` method (and the `CreateAccount` method for that matter) checks to see if the user name value it has been asked to insert is in use. If it is, the method returns an exception of type `MembershipCreateUserException`. This particular exception has a status code of `MembershipCreateStatus.DuplicateUserName`. There are other possible status codes, such as `InvalidUserName` (if you don't pass a value to the user name parameter, for example). Consequently, your code checks to see if the exception has the `DuplicateUserName` flag, and if it does, you present the users with a friendly error message asking them to choose another user name. Since the WebSecurity Helper performs these checks for you, there seems little point in executing your own SQL to determine if a user name is already in use. There is also a WebSecurity method called `UserExists`, which takes a string representing the user name you want to check:

```
if(WebSecurity.UserExists(username){
    //it's already in the database
}
```

Since you indicated that you want to use confirmation tokens, the successful execution of the `CreateUserAndAccount` method generates and returns an appropriately hashed and encoded value for that purpose. The value is also stored in the account table against the user. Your code used the confirmation token value as part of an e-mail message that it constructs and sends to the owner of the e-mail address that the user registered with. An example of the resulting e-mail can be seen in Figure 12-4.

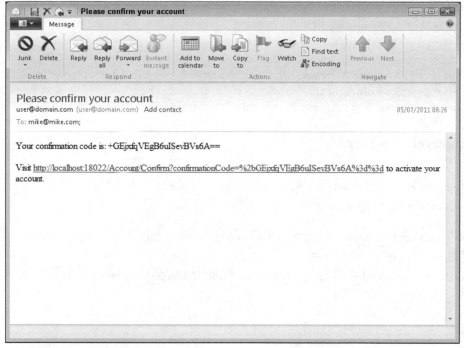

FIGURE 12-4

The code in this section is largely identical to the Starter Site template, except that your version creates an HTML-based e-mail by specifying the WebMail's `isBodyHtml` parameter value as `true`. Once the e-mail has been generated and sent, the code takes the visitor to the Thanks.cshtml page.

The account confirmation page examines `Request["confirmationcode"]` and uses the `WebSecurity.ConfirmAccount` method, which simply updates the account table (webpages_Membership) to set `IsConfirmed` to 1 where it finds a matching confirmation token. If it cannot match the query string value to a value in the database, the form displays instead. This might happen if the link in the e-mail breaks across more than one line and some of the last characters are not included in the link. In that event, the user can copy and paste the token from the e-mail. The only difference between your implementation of the confirmation page and the Starter Site is your use of the `Trim()` method on the confirmation code. This removes leading and trailing whitespace from the strings, which might get picked up when copying.

Creating a Login Form

At this point, you have created a registration page and a database for storing user account information. Your site is still wide open, in that none of the pages are protected from unauthenticated users, and if they were, your users have no way to authenticate themselves. There is no form for them to use to log in. The key part of the site that needs protecting at this point is the Admin folder and its contents. As you learned earlier, a folder can be protected from prying eyes by adding a _PageStart file to the folder and including a single line of code:

```
@{ WebSecurity.RequireAuthenticatedUser(); }
```

There is little point in doing this just yet, because the WebSecurity Helper will attempt to redirect unauthenticated users to a login form, and that still needs to be created. Therefore, in the next exercise, you will continue with protecting your site by adding a login form.

TRY IT OUT Adding a Login Form

1. It is time to protect that Admin folder. Open the existing _PageStart.cshtml file that currently resides in the Admin folder and add the following line to the code block:

```
WebSecurity.RequireAuthenticatedUser();
```

Test that it works by trying to browse to any of the other files in the folder. You should be met with an HTTP Error 404 Not Found page.

2. Add a new file to the Account folder and name it **Login.cshtml**. Replace the existing code with the following:

```
@{
    Page.Title = "Log In";

    var username = Request.Form["username"];
    var password = Request.Form["password"];
    var rememberMe = false;
    if (IsPost) {
        rememberMe = Request.Form["rememberMe"].AsBool();

        if (username.IsEmpty()) {
            ModelState.AddError("username", "You must specify a username.");
        }
        if (password.IsEmpty()) {
            ModelState.AddError("password", "You must provide your password");
        }

        if(!ModelState.IsValid){
            ModelState.AddFormError(@"Please fix the errors below
                                    before resubmitting the form");
        }
        else {
            if (WebSecurity.Login(username, password, rememberMe)) {
                var returnUrl = Request.QueryString["ReturnUrl"];
                if (returnUrl.IsEmpty()){
                    Response.Redirect("~/");
                } else {
                    Context.RedirectLocal(returnUrl);
                }
            }
            else{
                ModelState.AddFormError(@"Your credentials did not match
                                        a valid account. Please try again");
```

```
            }
        }
    }
}
<p>
    Please enter your username and password below. If you don't have an account,
    visit the <a href="@Href("~/Account/Register")">registration page</a> and
    create one.
</p>
<form method="post">
    <fieldset>
        <legend>Log In to Your Account</legend>
        @Html.ValidationSummary(true)
        <div>
            <label for="username">User Name*</label>
        </div>
        <div>
            <input type="text" id="username" name="username" value="@username" />
            @Html.ValidationMessage("username")
        </div>
        <div>
            <label for="password">Password*</label>
        </div>
        <div>
            <input type="password" id="password" name="password" />
            @Html.ValidationMessage("password")
        </div>
        <div>
            <input type="checkbox" name="rememberMe" value="true"
                        @(rememberMe ? "checked=\"checked\"" : string.Empty) />
            <label for="rememberMe">Remember Me</label>
        </div>
        <div>
            <input type="submit" value="login" title="Login"/>
        </div>
    </fieldset>
</form>
```

3. Add another new file to the Account folder and name it **Logout.cshtml**. Replace the default code with the following:

```
@{
    WebSecurity.Logout();
    var returnUrl = Request.QueryString["ReturnUrl"];
    if (returnUrl.IsEmpty()) {
        Response.Redirect("~/");
    } else {
        Context.RedirectLocal(returnUrl);
    }
}
```

4. Alter the _Navigation.cshtml file in the Shared folder to read as follows:

```
<div id="nav">
    <a href="@Href("~/")">Home</a> |
```

```
    <a href="@Href("~/Sell")">Sell</a> |
    <a href="@Href("~/Account/Register")">Register</a> |
        @if(WebSecurity.IsAuthenticated){
        <a href="@Href("~/Account/Logout?returnUrl=" +
        Server.UrlEncode(Request.ServerVariables["SCRIPT_NAME"]))">Log Out</a> @:|
            <span style="color: white">You are currently logged in as
        @WebSecurity.CurrentUserName</span>
    } else {
        <a href="@Href("~/Account/Login")">Login</a>
    }
</div>
```

5. Alter the _AdminLayout.cshtml file to include a link to the home page of the site:

```
<h1>Admin</h1>
<a href="@Href("~/Admin/CreateCategory")">Create Category</a>
|
<a href="@Href("~/Admin/UpdateCategory")">Update Category</a>
|
<a href="@Href("~/Admin/DeleteCategory")">Delete Category</a>
|
<a href="@Href("~/Admin/DeleteCategories")">Delete Categories</a>
|
<a href="@Href("~/")">Main site</a>
<hr />
@RenderBody()
```

6. Make sure that you have a valid account registered and confirmed. Select a file other than _PageStart in the Admin folder, and launch it in your default browser. Notice now that you land on the Login form (see Figure 12-5).

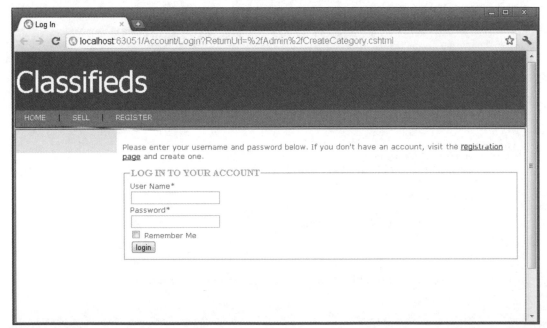

FIGURE 12-5

Use the valid account details to log in to the site, and you should be redirected to the page you first attempted to browse to. Now click the link to the Main site, and notice that your user name appears in the navigation bar, next to the Log Out link. Click the Log Out link so that the text changes to Login. Now click that link and log in all over again. Once you have done so, close the browser entirely. Re-launch the site in the same browser that you just used and notice that you are not logged in according to the navigation bar. Log in once more, this time ensuring that you check the Remember Me box. Notice that you are logged in according to the navigation bar (shown in Figure 12-6).

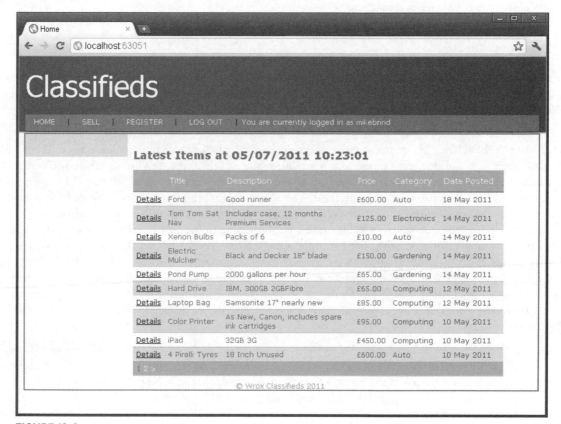

FIGURE 12-6

Now close the browser. This time, when you launch the site, you should see that you are logged in to it.

How It Works

A lot of functionality is provided here in relatively few lines of code. The login form requires that the user enter just their user name and password. Just these two items are subject to validation. The WebSecurity.Login method does all the hard work. It takes the user name, password, and a Boolean value to indicate whether Remember Me was checked, and checks that there is a matching name/password combination in the database. If there is, it sets the user to authenticated. If the Remember Me box was checked, the WebSecurity Helper sets a *persistent cookie* on the client's browser. By default, this cookie expires after 30 minutes, but it will keep the user authenticated in the meantime. You may decide that 30 minutes is not enough, and that your visitor might come back to the site only once every few days. If you want to extend the lifetime of the cookie that the membership provider sets, you can do so in your web.config file as follows:

```
<system.web>
  <compilation debug="false" targetFramework="4.0"/>
  <authentication mode="Forms">
    <forms timeout="10080"/> <!--one week-->
  </authentication>
</system.web>
```

You should add an authentication element within the system.web section, and set the mode to Forms. The type of authentication you are using by default is known as *forms authentication* (as opposed to Windows authentication, for example), and you set the timeout value in minutes within the forms element.

Once the WebSecurity Helper has authenticated the user, the code checks to see if there is a value for the returnUrl parameter in the query string, which might indicate you attempted to access a protected resource without being logged in. If there is, the code will try to get you there using the HttpContextBase.RedirectLocal method. This extension method is a security feature. It protects your visitors against *open redirection attacks*. This type of attack takes advantage of the fact that people rarely look at query string values when they attempt to log in to a site. Query string values are open to being tampered with. For example, imagine that you operate a site www.wroxbank.com. I'm an evildoer and I know that you use a returnUrl or similar in your query string to redirect users once they have logged in. I send a lot of e-mails out to potential customers of Wrox bank, asking them to log in to confirm they approve of the revised terms and conditions, or something similar. The link in the e-mail is www.wroxbank.com/Account/Login?returnUrl=http://www.worxbank/ Account/Login.

Notice that the returnUrl points to Worx Bank — the letters "o" and "r" are the wrong way round. If the e-mail gets to an existing customer who is taken in by my ruse, they will click the link and land on the legitimate login page for Wrox Bank. On successful login, they will be redirected to the returnUrl, or phony Worx Bank site. I control that site, and I will present them with a page that looks identical to the legitimate Wrox Bank login form, with a message saying they got the user name or password wrong, and that they should attempt to login again. This time, I hit pay dirt as I obtain their user name and password. The RedirectLocal method prevents this attack. It checks to see if the URL that is being redirected to is local to the site. If it is not, the user is redirected to the home page of the site instead. Under no circumstances will the user be redirected to an external domain.

The Logout page that you created doesn't present any interface to the user. When the page is requested, the WebSecurity.LogOut method is called, which simply signs the user out of the site, setting them to an unauthenticated state. The code uses the safe RedirectLocal method to safely transfer the user back to the returnUrl or the default page. When you created the link to Logout.cshtml in the navigation page, you constructed the returnUrl value by using Request.ServerVariables["SCRIPT_NAME"]. This value returns the virtual path to the page that is currently executing, or anything after the domain part of the current URL. It means that wherever you are in the site, when you click the logout link, you will stay on the same page — unless you are in an area that requires you to be logged in, of course.

These two exercises have given you a hands-on introduction to the WebSecurity properties and methods you will use most often. There are two features within the Starter Site template that have not been covered so far, and those are the ability to allow users to reset their passwords if they have forgotten them, and the ability to lock accounts for a period of time if too many unsuccessful attempts are made to log in.

Resetting Passwords

If you want to incorporate a mechanism that allows users to reset their passwords in the event they have forgotten them, the WebSecurity Helper makes this quite easy. The first thing you need to do is provide a form for the user to submit the user name and/or e-mail address associated with the relevant account. You need both of these values. You need the e-mail address in order to send an e-mail, and you need the user name to identify the account. If the user name and e-mail address are one and the same, that makes life a lot easier.

The `WebSecurity.GetUserId()` method will return the identity of the account that the user name belongs to. If it cannot find a matching user name, it returns -1. You can use `WebSecurity.IsConfirmed()` to ensure that the account was activated before you permit resetting of passwords. This method requires the user name as well. Once you have the account identity, you can use that to query the user table for the e-mail address if you have not obtained it already. If you have obtained it from the user, you might still want to check that it belongs to the account whose identity you have. You can do this by executing your own SQL against the user table.

The `WebSecurity.GeneratePasswordResetToken()` returns a secure hashed value, much like the confirmation token. This method also requires the user name to be passed as a parameter. You can also optionally provide another integer value to set the number of minutes that the reset password token will be valid for. The default value is 1,440 minutes, or 24 hours. From that point, you follow the workflow that you used previously when sending a link by e-mail to the owner of the account. Your receiving page will be slightly different than the one that confirmed the account. You need to provide the user with a means to provide a new password. Then a simple method does all the hard work: `WebSecurity.ResetPassword`. This method needs the token, which is obtained from the query string or the user can paste it into a text box. It also needs a proposed new password. The method will return false if it cannot find a match for the reset token, or if the reset token has expired. It will return true if the operation was a success.

Locking Accounts

When your users get their passwords wrong, the `PasswordFailuresSinceLastSuccess` field in the membership table automatically increments in value by one. The time of the failure is also updated in the `LastPasswordFailureDate` field. When the users get their passwords right, the `PasswordFailuresSinceLastSuccess` field reverts back to its default value of 0. These two fields form the core of a locking account strategy. You decide how many failures you will accept. You may decide that you will allow users to get their passwords wrong an unlimited number of times and never lock their accounts, but this opens a potential security hole — it allows hackers to use brute force to guess the password of an account. You might think that it would take ages for someone to guess a password, and you are probably right. That's why hackers use computers to do the work for them.

When the user attempts to log in, you can check to see the value of `WebSecurity` `.GetPasswordFailuresSinceLastSuccess()`, passing in the current user's name. It will return the value of the `PasswordFailuresSinceLastSuccess` field. You can also obtain the value of the `LastPasswordFailureDate` by using the `WebSecurity.GetLastPasswordFailureDate()` method. If the number of failures exceeds the limit that you set, you can choose to lock the account for a predetermined period. Locking the account means that you will not allow the user to log in, so any attempt to do so will be met with a redirect to a page that explains that the user has been locked out. The lockout period expires when the `LastPasswordFailureDate` together with the lockout period is no longer greater than the current time. If, for example, you decide to apply a lockout period of five minutes, you would use the following code to establish whether the time had expired:

```
if(WebSecurity.GetLastPasswordFailureDate(username).AddMinutes(5) >
                    DateTime.Now){
        //the lockout period has not expired yet} else {
        //the last time a wrong password was entered was more than 5 minutes ago
    }
```

Managing Roles

At the moment, when a user posts an item for sale, you are reliant on them providing a valid e-mail address so that you can identify them. If you forced users to register prior to being able to post an item, you enforce proper authentication mechanisms on them. You know who they are when they post an item, because they will have had to log in to the site to do so. But there will be no way to differentiate between people who can post items and people who can administer categories. One of the reasons that you implemented security over the category administration area was to prevent untrusted users from messing around with them. You need a way to differentiate between these two differing sets of authorized users. The mechanism you will use is called *roles*.

Roles are common throughout software. Windows employs roles-based permissions. You can belong to a number of groups, such as Administrator, Guest, Power User, and so on. You can define permissions at the role level, which means that all members of the role have the same permissions. You can apply the same concepts to your site. People who have access to the Admin folder and the category management pages can be placed in a role called *Administrator*. People who can post items will be placed in a different role — *Seller* perhaps. You have a table in your database for logging bids against items. If and when you develop the site to allow people to place bids, you might only allow people in the *Bidder* role to do so.

When WebSecurity is initialized in a site, it generates at least three tables. Two of these have the word "role" in their name, and they are where role information is stored. The first table — webpages_Roles — consists of two columns. The first, RoleId, is an Identity column; and the other, RoleName, is a column for storing the names of your roles. This is where you create your roles. The second table — webpages_UsersInRoles — is what is known variously as a *bridge table* or a *junction table*. Its job is to resolve *many-to-many relationships*, such as the case where many users can be in many roles. The typical pattern for these tables is that they contain two foreign keys, each pointing to a primary key on one side of the relationship. These two foreign keys are then combined to form a *composite primary key* on the table itself. As you create roles in the webpages_Roles table, you enter the RoleId value that is generated together with the selected UserId into the webpages_UsersInRoles table.

The SimpleRoleProvider

The SimpleRoleProvider has been introduced specifically for the Web Pages Framework to work with the two database tables you have just been introduced to. The provider offers 10 useful methods for adding users to roles, determining if a given role exists, creating roles, and so on. These are listed in Table 12-2.

TABLE 12-2: SimpleRoleProvider Methods

METHOD	DESCRIPTION
AddUsersToRoles	Enables you to add one or more users to a role
CreateRole	Creates a new entry for a role in the Roles table
DeleteRole	Removes an entry from the Roles table
FindUsersInRole	Returns the specified users in the specified role
GetAllRoles	Returns a list of all roles
GetRolesForUser	Returns a list of all roles that the specified user is in
GetUsersInRole	Returns all users in a role
IsUserInRole	Indicates whether the specified user is in the specified role
RemoveUsersFromRoles	Disassociates users from the specified roles
RoleExists	Indicates whether the specified role exists

In the next exercise, you will use a number of these methods to create new roles and add users to them as part of your administration area.

TRY IT OUT Creating Roles and Adding Users to Them

1. Open the _AdminLayout.cshtml file in the Shared folder of your Classifieds site. Add the following two hyperlinks to it before the link to the main site that you just added in the last exercise:

```
<br />
<a href="@Href("~/Admin/CreateRole")">Create Role</a>
|
<a href="@Href("~/Admin/AddUsersToRoles")">Add User To Role</a>
```

2. Add a new file to the Admin folder and name it **CreateRole.cshtml**. Replace the existing code with the following:

```
@{
    var message = "";
    var role = Request["role"];
    if(IsPost){
        if(!role.IsEmpty()){
            if(!Roles.RoleExists(role)){
                Roles.CreateRole(role);
                message = role + " added as Role";
            }else{
                message = "That role already exists";
            }
        }
    }
}
<form method="post">
    <div>@message</div>
    <fieldset>
        <legend>Create Role</legend>
        <div>
            <label for="role">Role:</label>
        </div>
        <div>
            <input type="text" name="role" value="@Request["role"]" />
        </div>
        <div>
            <input type="submit" value="Add"/>
        </div>
    </fieldset>
</form>
```

3. Run the page in a browser. You will be redirected to the Login form but once you have logged in, you can enter a new role. Add a role called **Admin** to check that the form works. Try submitting the same role again if it works, and note the message. Don't close your browser at this stage to prevent having to log in again.

4. Add another new page to the Admin folder. This time, name the page **AddUsersToRoles.cshtml**. Replace the default code with the following:

```
@{
    var message = "";
    var db = Database.Open("Classifieds");
    var sql = "SELECT UserName FROM Users";
    var users = db.Query(sql);
    var roles = Roles.GetAllRoles();
    if(IsPost){
        var user = Request["user"];
        var role = Request["role"];
        if(!user.IsEmpty() && !role.IsEmpty()){
            if(!Roles.IsUserInRole(user, role)){
                if(Roles.RoleExists(role)){
                    Roles.AddUsersToRoles(new []{user}, new[]{role});
                    message = user + " added to the " + role + " Role";
                } else {
```

```
                message = role + " no longer exists!";
            }
        } else {
            message = user + " is already in the " + role + " Role";
        }
    }
}
}
<form method="post">
<div>@message</div>
    <fieldset>
        <legend>Add User To Role</legend>
        <div>
            <label for="user">Select User:</label>
            <select name="user">
                <option value="">--Choose user--</option>
                @foreach(var user in users){
                    <option>@user.UserName</option>
                }
            </select>
        </div>
        <div>
            <label for="role">Select Role:</label>
            <select name="role">
                <option value="">--Choose role--</option>
                @foreach(var role in roles){
                    <option>@role</option>
                }
            </select>
        </div>
        <div>
            <input type="submit" value="Add"/>
        </div>
    </fieldset>
</form>
```

5. Navigate to this page using the link in your still-open browser, or launch it via the Run button and log in again. You should have a "user" select list containing one or more user accounts, depending on how many you have created so far. You should also have at least one role — the Admin role you just created. Select your first user account and the Admin role, and click the Add button. You should receive a confirmation message indicating that the user has been added to the role. If you try adding the same user to the same role, a different message appears. Finally, try adding a new role to the system using the first form you created, and then run the second form to add a user to this new role. However, just before you click the Add button, remove the role from the database by switching to the Database workspace, opening the webpages_Roles table in Data view, selecting the line that the new role is on, and pressing Delete. Once you have done that, go back to the form in the browser and click the Add button. Notice the message you get.

How It Works

These two forms are quite uncomplicated. One features a text box and a Submit button, and the other just two select lists and a button. The code blocks are equally simple, in that the SimpleRoleProvider via the static System.Web.Security.Roles class does all the heavy lifting. The CreateRole form is interesting in that it obviously adds a record to the database, and yet there is no Database.Open call, or any suggestion of

SQL at all. The database operations are managed on your behalf by the SimpleRoleProvider. It knows what tables and columns it expects to find in the database that has been initialized in the AppStart file, and internally, it attempts to perform an INSERT operation, taking the value that you provided. First, you checked the database to ensure that the role you are attempting to add doesn't already exist. This is the job of the RoleExists method, which returns true or false depending on the result. The CreateRole method actually inserts the new role into the database.

In the second form, you create two select lists. The first is populated with all the current users. The second list is populated with all the current roles. The GetAllRoles method retrieves all roles from the database. It returns an array, which is iterated through to generate the select list options. When the form is posted back, the code uses the IsUserInRole method to ascertain whether the selected user is already in the chosen role. The code also uses the RoleExists method to establish that the selected role hasn't been removed since it was first presented in the form (by another user, perhaps). Once those tests have been passed, the AddUsersToRoles method takes care of assigning the selected user to the selected role. AddUsersToRoles is designed to take care of adding multiple users to multiple roles at the same time, which is why you had to put both the user and the role into arrays before feeding them to the method. You could have added multiple="multiple" attributes to the select lists:

```
<select name="user" multiple="multiple">
```

Doing so would enable the user to select multiple users and multiple roles by holding down the Ctrl key. When they post the form back, the selected user and the selected roles will appear in the Request collection as comma-separated values, just like the grouped check boxes in the last chapter. You can use the string.Split method on the incoming form values and pass the result directly to AddUsersToRoles:

```
Roles.AddUsersToRoles(user.Split(','), role.Split(','));
```

Programmatically Applying Roles

Having created some roles, you will want to apply them to protect areas of the site, or to optionally show or hide pieces of content based on the role that the user is in. You will use the IsUserInRole method to determine whether the current user is in a specific role. You may decide, for example, to show a link in the navigation to the Administration area that you have built. You only want users who are in the Admin role to be able to see this link. The following code, added to the _Navigation.cshtml file, will accomplish that:

```
@if(Roles.IsUserInRole("Admin")){
    @:| <a href="@Href("~/Admin/")">Admin</a>
}
```

In the final exercise of this chapter, you will create a role for sellers so that only logged in members of this new role will be able to access the form to post items for sale. You will also apply a different protection over the Administration folder, so that only users in the Admin role can access the pages there.

TRY IT OUT Restricting Access Based on Roles

1. In the last exercise, you should have added a user account to the Admin role that you created. Use that account to log in to the Classifieds site, and add another role named Seller, using the CreateRole page that you created earlier.

2. Add the following highlighted line to the code in Account/Register.cshtml just before the line that redirects the user to Thanks.cshtml:

```
Roles.AddUsersToRoles(new[]{username}, new[]{"Seller"});
```

3. Switch to the database workspace and open the Items table. Switch to definition view and add a new column to the Items table. The column should be called **UserId**, and should be an **int** data type. You will have to allow nulls initially since none of the existing values have a UserId associated with them. Save the changes and then switch to Data view. Enter a valid UserId value for each of the existing items, and then change back to definition view. Amend the UserId column so that it no longer accepts nulls, and save your changes once more.

4. Amend the _PageStart file in the Admin folder so that it reads as follows:

```
@{
    Layout = "~/Shared/_AdminLayout.cshtml";
    //WebSecurity.RequireAuthenticatedUser();
    if(!Roles.IsUserInRole("Admin")){
        Response.Redirect("~/");
    }
}
```

5. The Sell.cshtml page needs a number of alterations. They begin with the removal of the text box for inputting an e-mail address from the form itself, and all the validation (client-side and server-side) related to the e-mail address. In the code download that accompanies this chapter, these elements have been commented out rather than deleted so that you can more easily see which parts need removing. Following that, change the code in the else block that sends the e-mail and stores the item in the database so that it reads as detailed here:

```
var message = "<p>Details of your item for sale:</p>";
message += "Title: " + Request["title"] + "<br />";
message += "Description: " + Request["description"] + "<br />";
message += "Duration: " + Request["duration"] + " days<br />";
message += "Price: " + String.Format("{0:c}", Request["price"].AsFloat());
message += "<br />";
message += "Condition: " + Request["condition"];
var id = WebSecurity.GetUserId(WebSecurity.CurrentUserName);
sql = "SELECT Email From Users Where UserId = @0";
var email = db.QueryValue(sql, id);
WebMail.Send(
            to: email,
            subject: "Advertisement confirmation",
            body: message,
            isBodyHtml: true
            );
sql = @"INSERT INTO Items (Title, Description, Price,
    CategoryId, DatePosted, Condition, Duration, UserId) VALUES
    (@0, @1, @2, @3,GetDate(), @4, @5, @6)";
var parameters = new[]{Request["title"], Request["description"],
                    Request["price"], Request["categoryId"],
                    Request["condition"], Request["duration"], id.ToString()};
db.Execute(sql, parameters);
Response.Redirect("~/Default.cshtml");
```

6. At the beginning of the HTML, just after the closing `</script>` tag, add the second line of code below:

```
</script>
@if(Roles.IsUserInRole("Seller")){
<div> @result</div>
```

7. Finally, add the following lines after the closing `</form>` tag at the end of the file:

```
}else{
    <p>You need to be <a href="@Href("/Account/Login")">logged in</a>
        to post items for sale.
        If you do not have an account, please
        <a href="@Href("/Account/Register")">register</a> first.</p>
}
```

8. If you still have the site open in the browser, click the Log Out link to log yourself out. Now click the Sell link. You should be told that you need to log in or register, as shown in Figure 12-7.

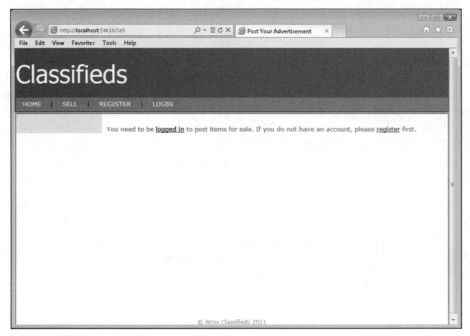

FIGURE 12-7

9. Log in to the site with the account you just created. Now navigate to the Sell page, and you should be presented with the form. Add an entry and submit the form. Once you have submitted the item successfully, check whichever e-mail method you are using to see the confirmation e-mail. Notice that it was sent to the e-mail address associated with the user account you created. Then check the Items table in the database in Data view. See your newly added item, and verify that it was given the correct UserId value. Finally, attempt to navigate to the Admin folder. You should be redirected to the home page.

How It Works

In this exercise, you have used roles to manage different levels of access to different groups of people. It is no longer good enough just to be an authenticated user to be able to access the Admin area. You have to be a member of the Admin role. Additionally, you have to be a member of the Seller role to be able to see and use the form for posting items for sale. Since this is the case, you must be logged in, which means that you no longer have to identify yourself to the site every time you want to post an item. The WebSecurity Helper already knows your user name. It is therefore able to obtain your UserId from the database via the `GetUserId` method. From that, your registered e-mail address is available via SQL. You wouldn't actually use the `GetUserId` method in this way in the real world, as it resulted in two calls to the database when you could have passed the user name as a parameter to the SQL instead. This contrived example serves purely to illustrate another WebSecurity Helper method that you haven't seen.

On the topic of the WebSecurity Helper, notice that since you are now using roles to manage access to resources, you no longer need to use the `RequireAuthenticatedUser` method. In fact, you commented it out in the Admin folder's _PageStart file.

SUMMARY

Security in an ASP.NET Web Pages application is implemented by default through a mechanism called *forms authentication*. The three concepts behind the security model are identity, authentication, and authorization. Identity represents you on a website. It determines who you are. Authentication is a process whereby you confirm your identity by providing some proof, such as a user name and password combination. Authorization manages your access to features within the site based on the permissions you have been granted, or more often, permissions that people in a similar role to you have been granted.

The WebSecurity Helper is a component that includes numerous features for simplifying identity and authentication. It is a wrapper around the SimpleMembershipProvider class, which encompasses standard and extended ASP.NET membership properties and methods. The helper greatly simplifies the tasks of writing code to create accounts, managing logging in, logging out, and other related tasks such as resetting passwords and generating appropriate database tables for managing membership.

Authorization is managed via the SimpleRoleProvider class, which includes methods to create roles, establish whether the current user is in a role, add users to roles, remove users from roles, and so on. Through determining which role the current user is in, you can programmatically control what they see on a page, and which resources they can access within the site.

EXERCISES

1. What is the difference between authentication and authorization?

2. Imagine that you want to enhance the Details page to display a link to a page called Bid.cshtml, but you only want that link to be visible to users in the Bidder role. What is the code you would add to achieve this?

3. What is the difference between the membership table and the user table in your database?

Answers to the Exercises can be found in the Appendix.

▶ **WHAT YOU LEARNED IN THIS CHAPTER**

TOPIC	KEY CONCEPTS
Authentication	The process whereby you identify yourself to a website.
Authorization	The system that determines what permissions you have.
Identity	Who you are.
Membership	The system that manages creating identities and authenticating them.
WebSecurity	A helper that simplifies common membership programming tasks.
Roles	The system that manages groups of permissions and controls how they are applied to individuals.
Open Redirection Attack	A security flaw that allows hackers to spoof the redirection URL to fool the user into providing sensitive information.

13
Optimizing Your Site

WHAT YOU WILL LEARN IN THIS CHAPTER:

➤ Optimizing for search

➤ How the WebMatrix Reports area works

➤ How to create SEO-friendly URLs

➤ Optimizing for performance

➤ Gathering visitor data

If the site you have built is a public site, you want people to come and visit it often. You want the site to perform well on search engines, which is the primary way that people find out about new sites, and when you have attracted traffic to the site, you want your site to perform well on the server. It's also important to know about your *traffic*, such as who your visitors are, where they came from, how long they spent on your site, and how they found out about it.

Search engine optimization (SEO) is the process by which you configure your site so that it is as search engine friendly as possible. This chapter looks at some of the tools that WebMatrix offers to help you optimize your site for search engines, as well as providing some basic SEO advice. You will also explore some ways in which you can improve the performance of your site on the server, thus ensuring maximum availability when people do come visiting. Finally, this chapter looks at the Analytics helper, which is designed to make working with free traffic analysis services as easy as possible.

SEARCH ENGINE OPTIMIZATION

A lot of people believe that SEO is a black art, which only people "in the know" can successfully practice. Everyone who manages a commercial site wants to get to the top of the search engine results pages (SERPS) for relevant search terms. Of course, only one site can ever be at the top of any search result at any one time, so competition to be that site is fierce.

A large part of SEO is easy. There is no mystery behind it at all. In fact, the leading search engines (Google, Bing, and Yahoo) publish guidelines on how to improve your site's performance in search results. The first rule is to publish original, interesting, and relevant content. That way, you provide a reason for people to visit your site. If visitors find your content of value, they will link to it. They might link to it from forums, or their own site, but you soon find that links coming into your site grow in number. Generating and maintaining quality content is hard work, but you should have the tools to update your site easily and regularly now that you know how to develop CRUD forms and store content in a database.

The second part of SEO is technical. All search engines follow similar rules with regards to *spidering* web pages and assessing their content. Spidering is the process where automated programs (known as spiders, bots or crawlers) make HTTP requests to web pages, and parse the response (HTML code) to establish the content of the page. The content may be indexed for later retrieval in search results. As part of the process, the spider or bot will extract the URLs contained in any links within the page, and add them to a list of URLs to visit. Search engine bots are only interested in HTML. They ignore JavaScript, CSS, images, and video content to a large extent — although the people at Google in particular are working hard to develop algorithms that can make some sense of images. That said, the same advice is offered by all search engines — ensure that your HTML is valid and used appropriately. You can get free help ensuring that your HTML is valid and follows the rules laid down for its `doctype` from the W3C, which provides a markup validation service at `http://validator.w3.org/`. Figure 13-1 shows that you can provide a URL for validation, although that won't work for `http://localhost`, of course. You can upload a file instead, or paste your HTML source code straight into the third tab.

Figure 13-2 shows the result of validating the Classifieds site home page. The site was launched in a browser and then the View Source option was chosen from the context menu that appears when you right-click anywhere on the rendered page. The resulting markup was copied and pasted into the validation tool. You can see that the tool automatically detected the `doctype` correctly as HTML5. There are two warnings — one general warning covering the fact that HTML5 is not a Recommendation yet, so the tool may be subject to change, and the other is a minor matter related to Unicode encoding being assumed when you paste text directly into the tool. But the key thing is that the HTML is valid — according to the current specification for HTML5.

If there are errors in the HTML, the tool will provide details of them, including where they appear within the source code and what you should do to correct the errors.

Why do you need to ensure that your HTML is valid? Often, browsers will be quite forgiving with invalid or incorrect HTML. They ignore errors and attempt to do their best to display a page. Browser developers build extensive parsing engines which are designed to guess how the page was intended to display. Search engine crawlers do not have these features. They attempt to identify content as the stuff between opening and closing tags according to the rules of HTML. If you forget to close a tag, for instance, the search engine may assume that everything after the opening tag is part of a tag, and not content. Basically, invalid HTML can hide your content from search engines. If search engines can't see your content, they won't index it or rank your site for it.

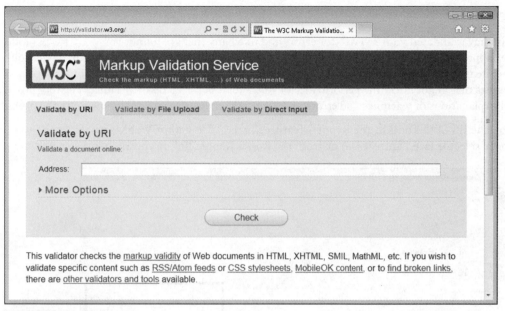

FIGURE 13-1

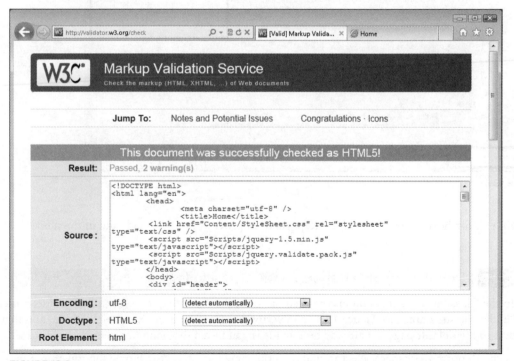

FIGURE 13-2

SEO Reports

Once you have validated your HTML for errors and fixed any that are found, you need a way of identifying inappropriate use of HTML. WebMatrix provides a fantastic reporting tool that crawls your pages or site in exactly the same way as a search engine, and reports back to you on SEO errors as well as any issues that might affect the performance of your site. It doesn't stop there either. The tool provides detailed explanations of warnings and errors and offers comprehensive advice on how to fix the problems.

Based on the IIS SEO Toolkit, the Reports feature is accessible within WebMatrix from the Reports workspace selector (see Figure 13-3) or from the Run a Report link in the Site workspace.

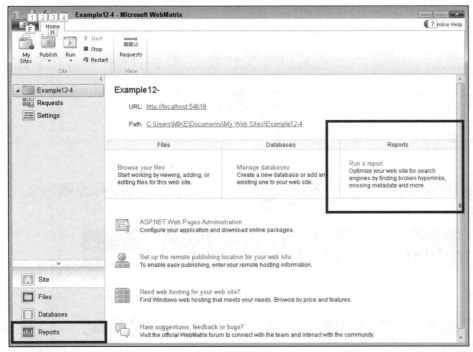

FIGURE 13-3

You will explore how to use WebMatrix Reports to improve your Classifieds site in the next exercise.

TRY IT OUT Running an SEO Report on the Classifieds Site

1. Open the Classifieds site that you last worked on in the previous chapter. Click the Requests button just under the site name (see Figure 13-4) and verify that Capture Requests is highlighted, and that a request to the default page has already been made if you tested the online validation tool yourself.

2. Click the Reports workspace selector, and then the New button on the Home tab illustrated in Figure 13-5.

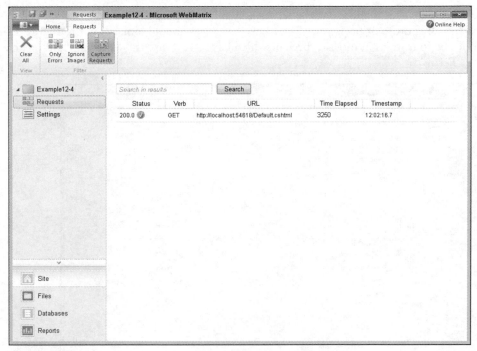

FIGURE 13-4

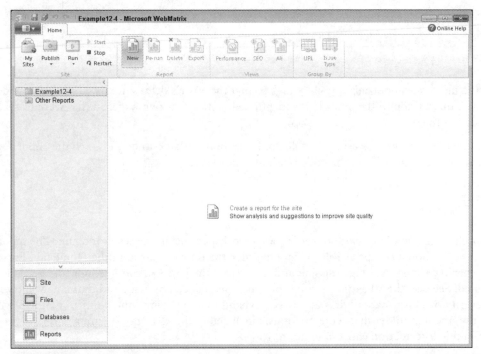

FIGURE 13-5

3. Leave the Start URL as it is and name the report **Classifieds Report #1** in the New Report dialog box. Click the OK button or press your Enter key. The result should look similar to Figure 13-6. There should be four items in the list, three of which have a severity of "Warning" and one has a severity of "Error".

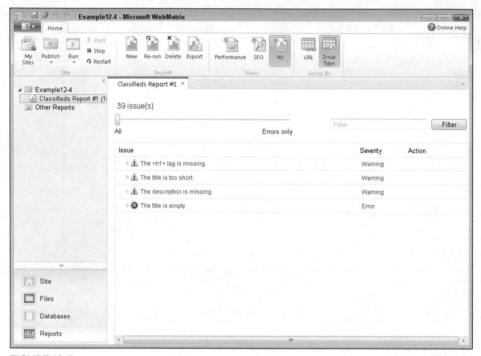

FIGURE 13-6

4. Expand the first issue about missing `<h1>` tags so that the error's details are listed, as illustrated in Figure 13-7. In addition to the other items mentioned, notice that two pages in the Account folder are included in the list.

5. Switch to the Files Workspace using the selector in the bottom-left corner and open the `robots.txt` file. Amend the contents so that the code reads as follows:

```
# WebMatrix 1.0
User-agent: *
Disallow: /Account
```

6. Save your changes and then switch to the Reports workspace using the selector again. The report you just created should still be visible. This time, click the Re-run button in the Home tab. Expand the first warning about `<h1>` tags missing and notice that the pages in the Account folder are no longer listed. See also that the total number of issues has reduced by two, and that a new entry with a severity of "Information" has appeared. Expand that new entry and confirm that the two pages in the Account folder that were previously included in the `<h1>` tag warning entry are now included in this Information entry (see Figure 13-8).

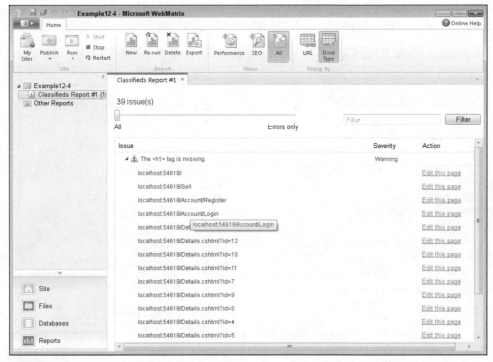

FIGURE 13-7

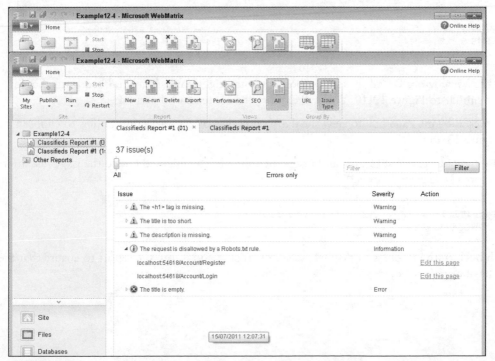

FIGURE 13-8

7. Expand the error related to the `title` being empty, and click once on the first entry. Notice how more details appear on the right side, as illustrated in Figure 13-9.

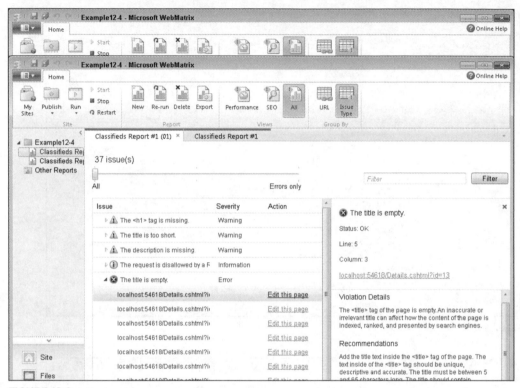

FIGURE 13-9

8. Click the View More Details link at the bottom of the right pane. A new tabbed form should appear similar to Figure 13-10. You will explore the contents of this soon.

9. Click the Edit This Page link to view the dialog box that offers a selection of files to choose from (see Figure 13-11).

10. Choose the `Details.cshtml` file and insert the following highlighted line to the page just after the line that reads `@if(item != null){`:

```
@if(item != null){
    Page.Title = "For Sale: " + item.Title;
    <h2>Details</h2>
```

11. Switch back to the Reports workspace, select the report and re-run the report to ensure that the error has been resolved.

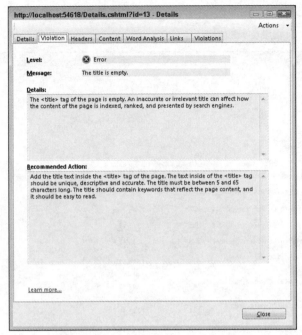

FIGURE 13-10

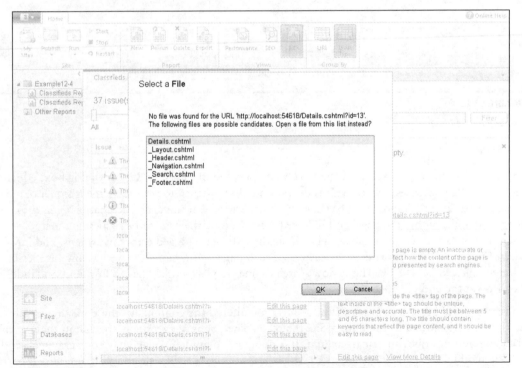

FIGURE 13-11

12. Switch back to the Site workspace and verify that the Requests log is substantially longer than it was at the beginning (see Figure 13-12)

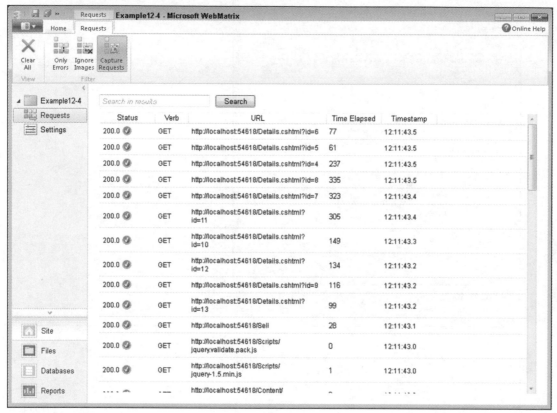

FIGURE 13-12

How It Works

The Reports engine crawler began with the URL that appeared in the New Report dialog box, which was http://localhost:xxxx, where xxxx is the port number assigned to your Classifieds site. It requested that page and examined the rendered HTML, logging any errors, warnings, or information items it found. It also logged all links within the page, and followed them, causing the page to be requested. As it followed each link, it examined the rendered HTML again, and again logged errors, warnings, and information item. The Requests report demonstrated that each page on the site — as well as any JavaScript files — were requested via HTTP. This is how search engine crawlers work. They follow links and index what they find at the end of those links.

Between the first and second running of the report, you altered the contents of the robots.txt file, which is the only file added to the Empty Site template. The robots.txt file is special, in that compliant search engines will obey instructions in it. It is designed to guide user agents (bots, crawlers, and other automated HTTP request agents) as to which parts of the site they should visit and which parts they should avoid. The instruction you gave when you amended the file was to tell all user agents to stay away from the Account area. The Reports crawler honored that instruction, but `robots.txt` is not a mandatory protocol and is not followed by all bots or crawlers. It should not be used to protect sensitive pages or areas. That's the job of the WebSecurity helper. You can learn more about `robots.txt` at `www.robotstxt.org/`.

Entries in the report are entered under one of three headings: Error, Warning, or Information. You had just one error if you have followed along correctly — there was nothing in the `<title>` tag on the `Details.cshtml` page. You were able to view more details on why that was considered an error, and what impact it might have on the SEO of your site. You were also provided with instructions on how to fix the error, which was easily accomplished by clicking the Edit This Page link next to the entry in the report.

NOINDEX AND NOFOLLOW

There are other ways to instruct search engine crawlers how to behave when indexing and following links besides using a `robots.txt` file. You can, for instance, add a `noindex` meta tag to the `head` section of a page:

```
<meta name="robots" content="noindex" />
```

This will not prevent crawlers from visiting the page, but it should stop them from indexing the page and listing it among the search results. In addition, you can apply the `"nofollow"` value to the `rel` attribute of a hyperlink:

```
<a href="/Account/Register" rel="nofollow">Register</a>
```

This does not prevent the crawler or bot from actually following the link. Different crawlers behave in different ways, but most of the leading search engine crawlers will not include the link in their calculations for assessing the value of the target. `nofollow` is more often used for external links than internal links.

During Step 8 in the previous exercise you clicked on a View More Details link, which opened a tabbed dialog box similar to the one shown in Figure 13-10. It's time to look at that series of tabs in greater depth, as there is a wealth of useful information hidden in this dialog box.

The first tab — Details — provides basic information about the HTTP response that resulted from the request to the URL. It shows the content-length value, or the number of bytes that were returned, along with the time taken for the response to reach the tool. These times should be pretty quick because all the requests are local. However, since you can also run the tool against your live site, this information can be useful for checking performance on the production server. To run a report against a live site, just enter the address of the home page in the Start URL box when you create a new report.

The Details tab also shows the title, description, heading, and keywords for the page. In this example, you are missing all but the title. These pages are not very SEO friendly at the moment. The description is taken from the `meta` tag for description. Search engines use the description as part of their SERPS (search engine results pages) to describe your site. If they cannot find a description, they try to infer one from the text on the page. You can create descriptions in much the same way as you created titles: You can use the `PageData` dictionary to set the value on a page-by-page basis, including dynamic content if you like. Where your layout page includes the `head` element, you add the following `meta` tag:

```
<meta name="description" content="@Page.Description" />
```

 Headings are `<h1>` elements. You have not used any of these in the site so far. They should represent the top-level heading for each page, and there should only be one per page. Keywords are taken from another `meta` tag called `keywords`:

```
<meta name="keywords" content="comma separated list of keywords" />
```

The next tab — Violation — provides the same details as the right pane when you select an entry in the report. It explains the reason that the item was flagged in the first place, and provides information about how the problem can be resolved. The Headers tab shows the Response headers, and the Content tab displays the source HTML that came back as the response body. The last two tabs — Links and Violations — are self-explanatory. The remaining tab — Word Analysis — is very useful. It performs analysis on the textual content of the page, providing you with a report covering word density. The title, description, keywords, and heading are redisplayed on this tab so that you can assess whether your chosen keywords appear often enough on the page, and in the most important parts of the page, such as the title, description, and main heading.

Search

As well as appealing to search engines, you might also want to provide your users with a means to search your site contents. You can build your own search engine, and it really isn't that difficult to build a simple one that can search database contents using the `LIKE` keyword in SQL and wildcard characters, as you saw in Chapter 8. There is another approach, which involves the use of Microsoft's search engine, Bing. A Bing helper is available in the ASP.NET Web Helpers Library, which makes it easy to add search capability to your site.

The following code sample shows the Bing helper being added to `_Search.cshtml`, which is in the Shared folder. The example assumes that you have downloaded and installed the ASP.NET Web Helpers Library:

```
<div id="search">
    <h3>Search</h3>
    <p>Use the search box below to search this site, or the entire web!</p>
    @Bing.SearchBox("170", "www.mysite.com", "Classifieds")
</div>
```

The result is illustrated in Figure 13-13.

The first value that the `SearchBox` method expects is the width in pixels of the box. The second is the URL of your site, and the third is a friendly name for that site. Note that Bing must have first indexed the site before you can get any results from a site search.

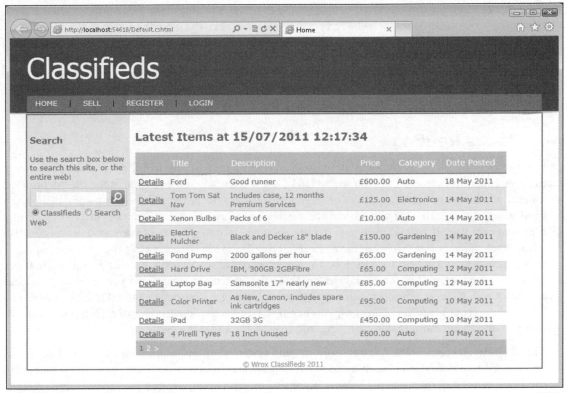

FIGURE 13-13

URLS AND ROUTING

You have used two different URL formats throughout this book. Sometimes, you have added the file extension to the filename and other times you haven't. For example, the link to the Sell page in the main navigation omits the file extension:

```
<a href="@Href("~/Sell")">Sell</a>
```

The following would work just as well:

```
<a href="@Href("~/Sell.cshtml")">Sell</a>
```

The links from the grid on the home page to `Details.cshtml` all include the file extension. So how does this work? And how can you take advantage of this system to improve SEO?

Apart from the software engineers who develop the algorithms that the search engines work to, no one really knows how much weight is placed on each individual aspect of a web page in terms of how it influences that page's performance on search engines. The title and description, for example, are known to be important, but which one is more important? Similarly, there are questions about the value of keywords in the URL of a page. Do the search engines take any notice of them? Well, according to Google (`www.youtube.com/watch?v=gRzMhlFZz9I`), having key words in the URL can help your SEO a little bit. They don't say what a "little bit" actually means, but the fact that keywords in the URL help at all is enough reason to try to work them in. Beyond that, if you can create more descriptive URLS, such as `www.mysite.com/Details/2432/LapTop-For-Sale` instead of `www.mysite.com/Details.cshtml?Id=2432`, you immediately improve the usability of your URLs. They become self-describing.

Web Pages Routing

In a typical ASP.NET application, all incoming requests map to physical files on disk. That is why the filename and extension appear in the URL, apart from when the request is for the "default" document, which might be `index.aspx` or `default.aspx`, or both. One of the results of this is that you need to use query strings if you want to pass arbitrary pieces of data as part of the URL. Taking the previous example. If you want to pass details about the product being offered, you might construct a link such as `www.mysite.com/Details.cshtml?Id=2432&Product=LapTop-for-Sale`. Now that is fine, and it kind of does the job. However, there are warnings from search engines that you should keep query strings short, and name/value pairs few in number. When you combine this kind of approach to URL construction with a grid that has paging and sorting enabled (which generates its own query string values, as you saw), you begin to tread into dangerous waters. No one knows how many query string name/value pairs are "too many" for a search engine.

The Web Pages Framework has a built-in routing system that, although it still requires URLs to be mapped to physical files on disk, allows for additional information to be passed as segments in the URL instead of query string values. What this means is that you can use `www.mysite.com/Details/2432/LapTop-For-Sale` as the URL in a link, and it will find the `Details.cshtml` file and work as before. So how does this work and how can you use it?

Web Pages routing assumes that the URL represents path information to a file or a folder containing a default document. At some stage within the URL, one of the segments must match either a filename or a folder name in which there is an `index.cshtml` or `default.cshtml` file. This matching process is initially a little confusing, but becomes quite clear. In the following exercise, you explore how it works.

TRY IT OUT Matching Web Page Routes

1. Create a new site from the Empty Site template and name the site **Testing Routes**.

2. Add a file named **_Layout.cshtml** with the following content:

```
<!DOCTYPE html>

<html lang="en">
    <head>
        <meta charset="utf-8" />
        <title>Testing Routes</title>
    </head>
    <body>
        @RenderBody()
        <div>
```

```
@if(UrlData.Count() > 0){
    <text>UrlData:</text>
        for(var i = 0; i < UrlData.Count(); i++){
            <div>UrlData[@i]: @UrlData[i]</div>
        }
    }
    </div>
</body>
</html>
```

3. Add a **_Pagestart.cshtml** file to the site with the following code:

```
@{
    Layout = "_Layout.cshtml"
}
```

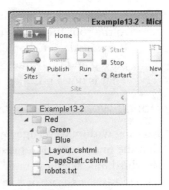

FIGURE 13-14

4. Create a folder called **Red**, and in that create a folder called **Green**, and in that create a folder called **Blue**. The structure should follow the one shown in Figure 13-14

5. In the Red folder, add these four files: **Green.cshtml**, **Blue.cshtml**, **Index.cshtml** and **Default.cshtml**. Replace the default code with the following in each of them:

```
<div>
    @VirtualPath.Replace("/", " > ").Replace("~", "Root ")
</div>
```

6. In the Green folder, add these two files: **Blue.cshtml** and **Default.cshtml**. Again, replace the default markup with the same code as the previous three files:

```
<div>
    @VirtualPath.Replace("/", " > ").Replace("~", "Root ")
</div>
```

7. Add a file named **Default.cshtml** to the Blue folder. You can probably guess what code this file should contain:

```
<div>
    @VirtualPath.Replace("/", " > ").Replace("~", "Root ")
</div>
```

8. Add a folder to the root of the site called **Blue**. In that folder, add a folder called **Green**, and in that folder, add a folder called **Red**. Add a new **Index.cshtml** file to the Red folder, and replace the default code with the same as all the other files.

9. Finally create a new file called **Default.cshtml** to the root folder, and replace the existing code with the following:

```
<div>
    @VirtualPath.Replace("/", " > ").Replace("~", "Root ")
</div>
<div>
    <a href="@Href("~/Red")">~/Red</a><br />
```

```
    <a href="@Href("~/Red/Green")">~/Red/Green</a><br />
    <a href="@Href("~/Red/Green/Blue")">~/Red/Green/Blue</a><br />
    <a href="@Href("~/Red/Green/Blue/123/456")">~/Red/Green/Blue/123/456</a><br />
    <a href="@Href("~/Red/Blue/Green")">~/Red/Blue/Green</a><br />
    <a href="@Href("~/Blue/Green/Red")">~/Blue/Green/Red</a><br />
    <a href="@Href("~/Blue/Green/Red/123")">~/Blue/Green/Red/123</a><br />
</div>
```

The final site structure should resemble Figure 13-15.

10. Launch the site, making sure that the `Default.cshtml` file you just added to the root folder is selected. Click each link in turn, noting the path and filename depicted on each page. Pay attention to any `UrlData` that is displayed and the values shown. The final link should result in a 404 error. That is not a mistake.

How It Works

Routing within Web Pages works by trying to match file paths. It will assume that the final segment represents a filename without the extension. If you take the third link as an example, the routing system will attempt to locate a file named `Blue.cshtml` in a folder called Green in a folder called Red. When you click that link, the resulting path is `Root` ⇨ `Red` ⇨ `Green` ⇨ `Blue.cshtml`. You can see this principle working in the second link too, where a file called `Green.cshtml` within the Red folder is located. Now look at the fourth link, called `~/Red/Green/Blue/123/456`. Working on the same principle, the routing system will attempt to match the following path: `Root` ⇨ `Red` ⇨ `Green` ⇨ `Blue` ⇨ `123` ⇨ `456.cshtml`. There is no file named `456.cshtml`, so routing considers 456 to be `UrlData` — an arbitrary value passed as part of the URL — and will attempt to match the remainder of the URL to a file path: `Root` ⇨ `Red` ⇨

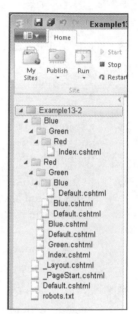

FIGURE 13-15

`Green` ⇨ `Blue` ⇨ `123.cshtml`. Again, there is no match so the final segment is added to `UrlData`, and an attempt to match `Root` ⇨ `Red` ⇨ `Green` ⇨ `Blue.cshtml` is made. This time, there is a match. Two items have been added to the `UrlData` collection, and they can be referenced by their indexes (which as usual in C#, is zero-based). 123 is the first item in `UrlData` and 456 is the second. You can pass as many values you like as `UrlData`. There is no limit — except for that imposed on the size of URLs (which is generally around 2,000 characters).

Take another look at the first and sixth links. These links illustrate what happens when no match is made to a file path. In that event, one final attempt is made to find a default document (first `Default.cshtml` and then `Index.cshtml`) in the folder structure suggested by the URL segments. The first link, according to the rules, might represent a file called `Red.cshtml` in the root folder. No such file exists, so an attempt is made to match a default document in a folder called Red. There are two candidates — `Default.cshtml` and `Index.cshtml`. When you click the link, the file path is shown as `Root` ⇨ `Red` ⇨ `default.cshtml`, thus demonstrating that a match with `Default.cshtml` is attempted before a match with `Index.cshtml`. You can confirm that `Index.cshtml` is also matched by clicking the sixth link. If you use the default document approach to URL construction, you cannot add `UrlData` to the URL. Of course, you can use `UrlData` if the default document is included as part of the URL.

The final link results in a `Page Not Found` error. The URL doesn't meet either of the previous patterns. It is not a file path (with or without `UrlData`) and it doesn't point to a folder containing either a `Default.cshtml` file or an `Index.cshtml` file. To get this URL to resolve to an existing file, you can change it to `~/Blue/Green/Red/Index/123`, which results in the `Index.cshtml` file in the inner-most Red folder being found, and `UrlData` of 123.

The ability to add any number of arbitrary values as `UrlData` is what makes Web Pages routing such a flexible and easy-to-use system. Just before the exercise, you were shown an example of a friendly URL that is possible to achieve with Web Pages: `Details/2432/LapTop-For-Sale`. How would you generate such a URL? This URL is similar to the one that you already created in your WebGrid, which takes people to the details pages for products. It is generated as part of the format argument to the first column like this:

```
<a href="@Href("~/Details.cshtml?id=" + item.Id)">Details</a>
```

You can instead create the following function and use it to generate the friendly URL:

```
@functions {
    public static string SeoFriendly(string page, int id, string title){
        return "~/" + page + "/" + id + "/" + title.Replace(" ", "-")
            + "-For-Sale";
    }
}
```

It can be used in a WebGrid as follows:

```
format: @<a href="@Href(Functions.SeoFriendly("Details",
                    item.Id, item.Title))">Details</a>
```

On the receiving page (`Details.cshtml`), you can replace `Request["id"]` with `UrlData[0]`. The rest of the code will work as-is. You may, however, want to check that the value of `UrlData[1]` (which is the human readable part of the URL comprising the item title minus the `"-For-Sale"`, also is known as a *slug*) matches the actual item title. If you only rely on matching the ID value to an item in the database, you run the risk of becoming a victim of *link bombing*. This is the practice whereby people with malicious intent plant links to your site with the last segment altered to convey a poor impression of the site. I could, for example, go to a forum somewhere and plant links like `http://domain.com/Details/3422/This-site-will-rip-you-off`. The link will be indexed by search engines, and will appear nice and bold. It will also appear to describe the content found at the page, and will not cause any errors to happen when the link is clicked, because the current code relies purely on the ID portion being correct.

To prevent this from happening, you should ensure that the slug is a valid one, and if it is not, redirect the visitors to a valid URL using the `Response.RedirectPermanent` method. This is how code in the Details page might handle that if you applied the `SeoFriendly` function to generate your URL:

```
@{
    dynamic item = null;
    if(!UrlData[0].IsEmpty() && UrlData[0].IsInt()){
        var db = Database.Open("Classifieds");
```

```
var sql = "SELECT * FROM Items, Categories WHERE Id = @0";
item = db.QuerySingle(sql, UrlData[0]);
if(!UrlData[1].Contains(item.Title.Replace(" ","-"))){
    var validUrl = Functions.SeoFriendly("Details", item.Id, item.Title);
    Response.RedirectPermanent(validUrl);
}
    }
}
```

This is not production-ready code, but it illustrates the logic: Ensure a match between what the URL contains and what you expect it to contain. If that match doesn't exist, reconstruct the URL and permanently redirect users to the valid version.

NOTE esponse.RedirectPermanent *is a new method to ASP.NET, introduced in Version 4.0. It was introduced to cure an inherent problem with the traditional way of sending a visitor to another page through the* Response.Redirect *method, and illustrates Microsoft's fairly recent focus on providing a much better range of SEO tools to developers. When you use either of these methods, they send response headers that tell the "user agent" (browser or search engine, for example) the status of the requested resource. Most often, the status codes are* 200, *meaning* OK, *or* 304, *meaning* Not Modified, *(typically for images, style sheets, and other resources cached by the browser).* Response.Redirect *issues a* 302 *status code, which has this definition:* "The requested resource resides temporarily under a different URI". *Note the use of the word* temporarily. Response.RedirectPermanent *issues a different status code:* 301, *which has this definition:* "The requested resource has been assigned a new permanent URI and any future references to this resource SHOULD use one of the returned URIs". *This clearly instructs user agents, particularly search engines crawlers, to disregard the URL they have just followed in the future and to replace it with the one your code has just presented them with. In other words, by using* Response.RedirectPermanent, *you defeat any attempts to get the malicious link indexed and published by search engines.*

You have a site that is full of rich original content. It has been validated for error-free HTML and CSS, and optimized to ensure that it is search engine and user friendly. All pages have titles, headings, descriptions, and descriptive URLs. People start visiting. You still have two tasks remaining: You need to do your best to ensure that the site is available when they visit, and you need to measure and track the site visitors. In the next section, you will look at one of the tools provided by the Web Pages Framework specifically to help you optimize for performance.

PERFORMANCE OPTIMIZATION

Each time a page is requested on your site, the web server has to do some work in order to generate a response. Often, this work includes calls to databases, the generation of variables, possibly computations on those values, and so on. Servers can be extremely powerful beasts, but if your data-driven content rarely changes, there is little point in retrieving it fresh from a database on every page request. The less work you ask your server to do, the quicker it can complete what it has to, and the more responsive your site appears to visitors.

The ASP.NET Framework includes a mechanism known as *caching*. This allows you to effectively save all or part of a page so that it can be reused, without being processed again. Items are stored in the cache, which is a collection and can contain all kinds of data, including strings, integers, and even complex objects. In this way, the cache is similar to the `PageData` or `AppData` collections that you have already learned about.

Web Pages provides a simple helper — the WebCache helper — which enables you to use caching easily within your application. It has just three methods — `Get`, `Set`, and `Remove`. The `Get` method takes a string, which is the key to the item to be retrieved from the cache. The `Remove` method similarly takes a string, which is the key to the item that is to be removed from the collection. The final method, `Set`, adds an item to the cache and takes a number of parameters. The first is a string representing the key for the item. The second is the item itself, which can be any kind of object. The third is the number of minutes that the item should be stored for, and the final argument is a Boolean, representing whether *sliding expiration* should be applied. If you decide to store an item for 60 minutes, that period will elapse one hour after the item was committed to the cache if you pass `false` to this parameter. If you pass `true` (or pass no value as `true` is the default), the expiration time is reset every time an item is accessed, so the 60 minutes period begins again when the item is retrieved. This expiration feature is the primary difference between using the WebCache helper and `AppData` (global) variables.

The home page of your Classifieds site makes a good candidate for the WebCache helper. At the moment, every time someone lands on your home page, the server-side code connects to the database and retrieves all items for display in the WebGrid. However, that data may not change for a while. Sellers might only post one item every 10 minutes on average, but buyers might be visiting the home page 10 times a minute. So for every 10-minute period, there are 100 database calls, and just one change in the data. In the following exercise, you will amend the Classifieds site to incorporate the use of caching through the WebCache helper. The goal in doing so is to reduce the load on your server.

TRY IT OUT   Adding Caching with the WebCache Helper

1.   Open the Classifieds site if you closed it and turn to the `Default.cshtml` file. Amend the existing code block at the top of the file so that it looks like this:

```
@{
    Page.Title = "Home";
    var data = WebCache.Get("cachedData");
    var fromCache = " From Cache!";
```

```
    if(data == null){
        fromCache = " Not From Cache!";

      var db = Database.Open("Classifieds");
        var sql = @"SELECT Id, Title, Description, Price, Items.CategoryId,
                Category, DatePosted FROM Items JOIN Categories ON
                Items. CategoryId = Categories.CategoryId";
        data = db.Query(sql).OrderByDescending(c => c.DatePosted);
    }
    WebCache.Set("cachedData", data, 1, true);
    var grid = new WebGrid(data, ajaxUpdateContainerId: "grid");
}
```

Notice that the `data` variable has been declared at the top of the code block now, so the `var` keyword has been removed where `data` is assigned the return value of the `Database.Query` method call.

2. Modify the `<h2>` heading so that it looks like this:

```
<h2>Latest Items @fromCache</h2>
```

3. Run the Default page in the browser. Confirm that the heading says "Latest Items Not From Cache!." Then click the Home link and confirm that the heading now reads "Latest Items From Cache!."

4. Wait for at least one minute, and then click the Home link again. The heading should say that the items in the grid did not come from the cache.

5. Amend the line that begins `WebCache.Set` so that the expiry interval is set to 10 minutes and sliding expiration is enabled:

```
WebCache.Set("cachedData", data, 10, true);
```

6. Turn to the `Sell.cshtml` file and add the following line of code just before the `Response .Redirect` call at the end of the code block:

```
WebCache.Remove("cachedData");
```

This line should be preceded by the `db.Execute()` method call.

7. Click the Restart button on the Site menu. Then re-launch the site in your browser. Check that the cache was populated by refreshing or reloading the home page, and then log in to the site using one of your existing user accounts in the Seller role. Navigate to the Sell page and add a new item. When you have successfully submitted the new item, notice that you are redirected to the home page. At this point you should check the heading to see whether the data came from the cache or not.

How It Works

Your initial code changed how the `data` variable is declared and first assigned. You used the `WebCache .Get` method to obtain an item from the cache that has a key of `cachedData`. The value of the retrieved item is assigned to the `data` variable. A string is assigned a value suggesting that the data came from the cache. However, there is no guarantee that an entry with that key exists, so the value is tested for `null`. If the value is `null`, the string is amended to say that the value did not come from the cache, and data is obtained from the database. Once it has been retrieved, it is added to the cache using the `WebCache.Set` method. In the first instance, it was given a key of `cachedData` and set to expire after one minute. Once this period has elapsed, the item will be removed from the cache regardless of whether it has been accessed within the previous 60 seconds, as sliding expiration was not enabled.

You then amended the code so that the item stays in the cache for 10 minutes after it was last accessed, by changing the interval and the Boolean to enable sliding expiration. Because your theoretical site is being accessed 10 times a minute, this 10-minute expiration time is continually being reset, which means that the data stays in the cache. That is not helpful if someone wants to post a new item. Their item will not be displayed, because the database is not being called all the time that the data is in the cache. That's why you added a line that forces removal of the data from the cache just after the new item was added to the database.

During this exercise, you saw two ways to remove items from the cache. The first is to allow the expiration period to pass, and the second is to call the `WebCache.Remove` method. There is also a third method, and that is to restart the site. When your site is running on a live server, your cache is cleared when the server is stopped and restarted. The server might decide to clear the cache for reasons of its own, such as a dangerous lack of resources. In that case, it will reclaim as much memory as it needs at the expense of your cache. What this means is that you can never rely on an item being retained in the cache. Whenever you attempt to retrieve an item from the cache, you should always check to ensure that it is not `null` before trying to do anything with it. Otherwise, your website will throw `NullReferenceExceptions`: `"Object reference not set to an instance of an object"`.

VISITOR TRACKING

When I first started in web development, getting good analysis on visitors to a website was expensive. Web hosting companies used to resell traffic analysis software at a healthy profit. It was the only way that you could get a meaningful picture of the volume of traffic you got, as well as its behavior when it got to your site, and where it came from. Nowadays, highly advanced analytics software is given away free. Google is the primary source of free analytics software, but Yahoo also offers a free service for some eligible groups. It should therefore come as no surprise that there is a helper for that.

The Analytics helper can be found in the ASP.NET Web Helpers Library along with the Bing helper discussed earlier. Before you can use the Analytics helper, you need a relevant account with whichever provider you choose. Google provides you with a site identity, as does Yahoo. You need that information when you use the Analytics helper. In both cases, all you need to do is to pass the account name to the relevant method call:

```
@Analytics.GetGoogleHtml("account_id")
@Analytics.GetYahooHtml("account_id")
```

Both of these render JavaScript, so the code must be placed before the closing `</body>` tag on the page.

SUMMARY

This chapter discussed a number of ways in which the Web Pages Framework offers help for optimizing your site. You began this chapter by examining ways in which you can optimize your site for search engines. You learned about the importance of valid HTML and quality content. Then you looked at how the Reports area of WebMatrix provides invaluable help with its SEO, or Search Engine Optimization, analysis reports. You learned how to interpret the reports and categorize the importance of any details provided in a report. You also saw how you can make changes and instantly get feedback by re-running the report.

Keywords in URLs have some effect on the way a site is indexed, by Google, at least. Therefore, you need to understand how the Web Pages routing system works, and how you can take advantage of it to produce both user friendly and search engine friendly URLs. You saw how the routing system tries to match file paths. You also learned how trailing segments of URLs are stored in `UrlData`, and can be used to provide very descriptive URLs and parameter information.

In the next section of the chapter, you explored how to optimize your site for performance using the WebCache helper. You learned how to add items to a cache and retrieve them, as well as the benefits of doing so in terms of minimizing the load on the server.

Finally, you learn about the Analytics helper, which is available from the ASP.NET Web Helper Library, and which takes care of rendering the right code for Google and Yahoo analytics services on your site.

Your site is finished. It is optimized and ready. The only thing you need to do now is make it publicly available. In the final chapter, you will explore the options available for deploying your site, as well as look at some of the key things you should prepare to ensure your site works in its new environment.

EXERCISES

1. What is the purpose of a `robots.txt` file?

2. A site has a Pages folder within an Admin folder, which is in the root folder. Within the Pages folder, there is a page called `Edit.cshtml`, which needs to know which page (identified by a numeric ID) it should display for editing. Which of the following URLs can be used to reach this page, and pass the appropriate information for editing page 29?

```
~/Admin/Pages/Edit/29

~/Pages/Admin/Edit/29

~/Admin/Pages/Default/29

~/Admin/Pages/Edit/?id=29
```

3. What can cause items to be removed from the cache?

Answers to the Exercises can be found in the Appendix.

▶ **WHAT YOU LEARNED IN THIS CHAPTER**

TOPIC	KEY CONCEPTS
SEO	Search Engine Optimization — the process of optimizing websites to improve their visibility to search engines.
Spider	An automated program designed to parse HTML and index the content.
Crawler	An alternative term for spider.
Routing	A mechanism within the ASP.NET framework that maps URLs to physical files on disk.
UrlData	Segments of a URL consisting of arbitrary data that do not form part of a file path.
Caching	Storage of data in memory on the web server which is intended to reduce the need for processing to create it.
WebCache Helper	A component that is designed to make working with caching easy.

14

Deploying Your Site

WHAT YOU WILL LEARN IN THIS CHAPTER:

➤ Exploring your hosting options

➤ Deployment using Web Deploy

➤ Deployment via FTP

➤ Common deployment problems

This is a short chapter. In most ASP.NET books, a chapter on deploying your site to a web server so that it can go live usually covers a fair amount of ground. There are a number of things you need to do and options you can choose in terms of how you deploy your site. WebMatrix simplifies the whole process so dramatically that there isn't much to write about. This is good news for you.

This chapter examines your hosting options and explains the differences among each one. It will cover the small amount of work you need to do to ensure that your site works on the server just as it did on your local machine. You will learn about the built-in tools offered by WebMatrix for locating a suitable hosting company and ensuring that it offers a compatible service. Finally, you will walk through the two deployment options offered by WebMatrix.

WEB HOSTING SERVICES

If you want to expose your site to a public audience, you need to deploy it to a public facing web server. Most often, you will use the services of a company that provides web hosting on a commercial basis. This chapter assumes that you will take this approach as opposed to installing and configuring your own web server. If you are interested in deploying to your own server and you need assistance in obtaining, installing, and configuring Internet Information Server (IIS), the official IIS site at www.iis.net contains a wealth of articles and other resources designed to help you.

Most web hosting providers offer a range of products and services. The options available to you can be a little bewildering at first. To begin, you need to understand the different ways in which server space is made available to you.

Shared Hosting

Under shared hosting, your website shares space on a server with hundreds or thousands of other websites. None of the sites has access to the files of the others, but they all share the resources of the server, such as CPU and RAM. Typically, each site will have a maximum amount of resources allocated to it. Invariably, hosting companies offer a range of options with shared hosting packages, which includes a range of additional services, memory, space, and so on. You cannot install any software on these shared servers, such as Microsoft Office, for example.

Dedicated Server

Dedicated servers are servers that are provisioned solely for your use. They may be virtual or physical servers, and the cost will likely vary depending on which option you take. Dedicated servers provide a lot of freedom, in that you can install anything you like on them. You are then fully responsible for patching and supporting the server software, although the hosting company is responsible for the physical machine, which they own. The server is effectively leased to you as the customer, so it is a lot more expensive than shared hosting.

Colocation

With Colocation, you buy the server, set it up any way you like, and then ship it to the hosting company. The company then plugs it into their infrastructure and makes it available on the Internet. This is the most powerful, but most expensive, way to host a website. All the hosting company does is to provide you with physical space for your box, and they will ensure that power and connectivity are maintained.

FINDING A HOSTING COMPANY

Now that you understand some of the jargon behind the different packages, it is time to find a company that can offer a cost-effective and reliable service for your site. Where to start? One place is a search engine, but with over half a billion search results to the keywords "web hosting" on Google alone, that approach is akin to locating one needle somewhere in Kansas. The task is further complicated by the fact that you need to ensure that your chosen provider actually provides the right kind of hosting, since Web Pages sites require the Microsoft .NET 4.0 Framework to run, and even now, not all web hosting companies have moved to Version 4.0.

WebMatrix simplifies this process for you, removing the risk and confusion. The Sites workspace provides an option to help you find web hosting for your site. This option is also available from the Publish button on the Home tab. You can see both of these options illustrated in Figure 14-1.

Whichever option you choose, a browser will launch and you will be taken to the Microsoft Hosting Gallery, illustrated in Figure 14-2.

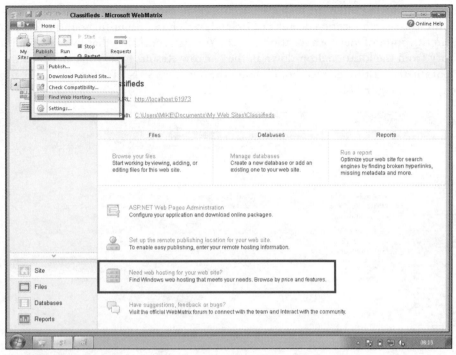

FIGURE 14-1

FIGURE 14-2

You can see that various hosting offers are displayed according to their type, cost, features, and so on. From where I am, the search location defaults to Ireland, which is a beautiful country to be sure, but inaccurate from the point of view of a location search. You can soon alter that by selecting the appropriate territory from the location drop-down in the Narrow Results tool. You can also alter a number of other parameters, although you should retain the default ASP.NET 4.0 option. The tool is shown in more detail in Figure 14-3.

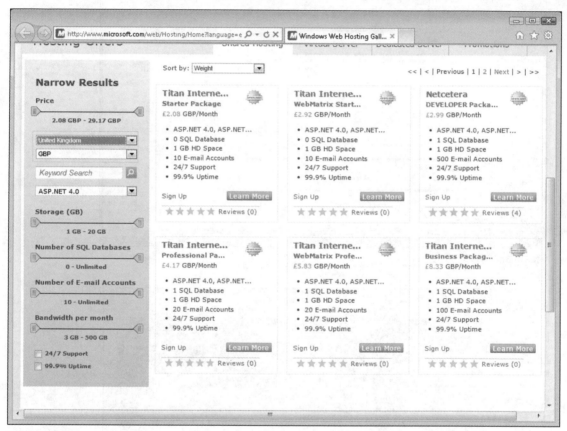

FIGURE 14-3

Each hosting company provides more details about their offer from the Learn More button, and Figure 14-4 illustrates the details offered by Netcetera. Once you have chosen your provider, you are almost ready to deploy your site.

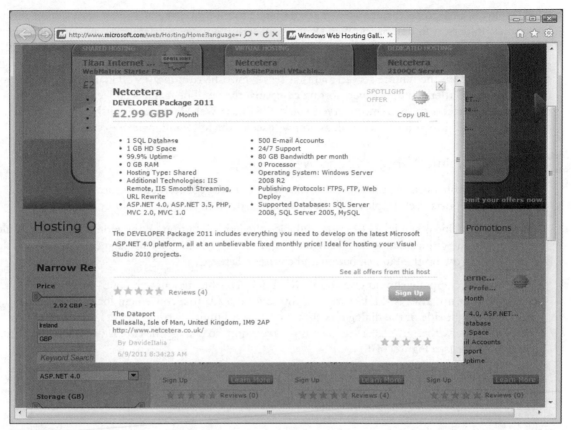

FIGURE 14-4

DEPLOYMENT OPTIONS

WebMatrix offers two ways to deploy your site: via Web Deploy and via FTP. FTP, or File Transfer Protocol, is the traditional way to upload files to a piece of web space. FTP is a standard, and there are countless FTP client applications available — many of them free. WebMatrix adds to this pool of FTP clients. Clients contain varying levels of functionality, but essentially, FTP is a process that copies files across networks. FTP can also ensure that directories are created on the server, but it cannot affect the Access Control List (ACL) permissions on those directories. FTP does not include anything that helps you configure a server-based database file, either. Typically, you have to FTP the database files and ask the hosting company to attach them to the database server, and then set appropriate permissions. Some hosting companies provide remote access to the SQL Server itself, so that you can perform maintenance and management tasks yourself, using SQL Server Management Studio or similar.

Web Deploy is a Microsoft framework that's designed to minimize the work you need to do to configure files, folders, and databases. Web Deploy will script SQL Server databases and populate them with data. It will ensure that the correct permissions are set on folders that are created, and it will keep track of what has changed between the server and your local files. For Web Deploy to work, it must be enabled on the remote server, and that server must be running IIS 7. Chances are that if you use the Hoster Gallery to find a web hosting company, they will be using Web Deploy, but if you only have FTP access to the remote server, you can still use WebMatrix to publish your site. In fact, the two processes are almost identical, as you will see in the following pair of exercises

TRY IT OUT   Using WebMatrix and Web Deploy

1. Obtain a suitable hosting account as described earlier in the chapter, and ensure that the package you select supports Web Deploy. All packages labelled "WebMatrix" should do this.

2. Open the Classifieds site in WebMatrix and click the Publish button on the Home tab. You should see the Publish Settings dialog box (shown in Figure 14-5), which you can also get to by clicking the expansion arrow on the Publish button and choosing Settings.

3. Your hosting company should give you an XML file. This file may have a `.publishsettings` extension, but not always. Make sure that you save your file to a convenient location and click the link on the right side of the dialog box that says Import Publish Settings. By default, WebMatrix looks for a file with `.publishsettings` as an extension, so change the extension if necessary and select your file (see Figure 14-6).

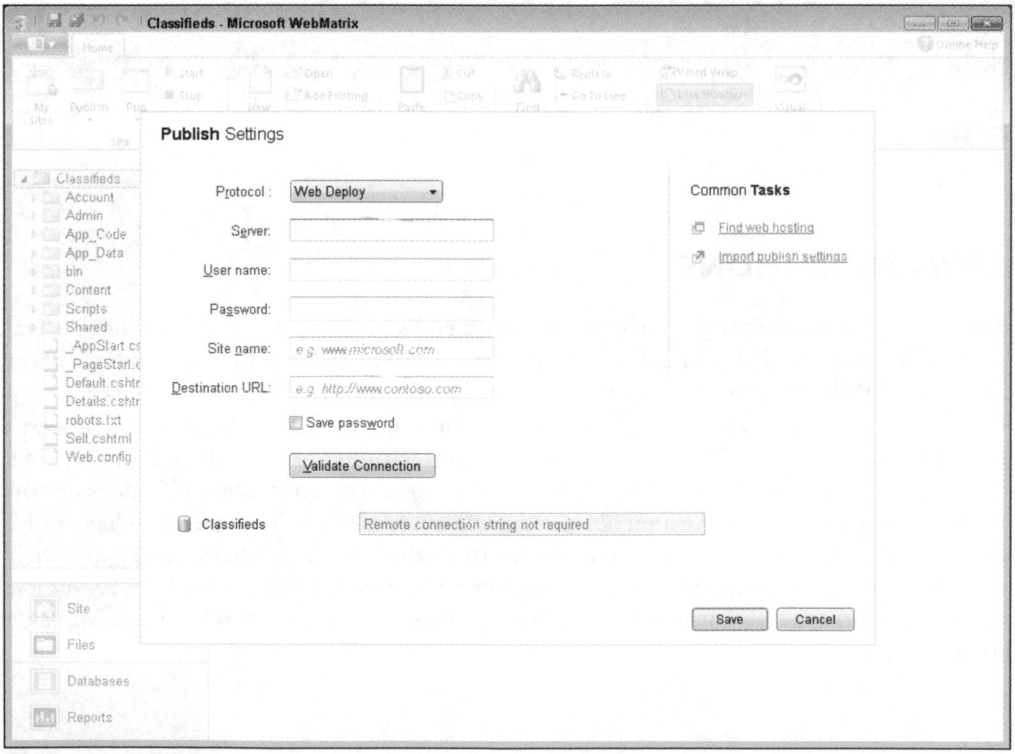

FIGURE 14-5

FIGURE 14-6

4. The form fields should auto-populate from the information provided in the imported file. At this point, it is a good idea to test that they work. You can do this by clicking the Validate Connection button (see Figure 14-7).

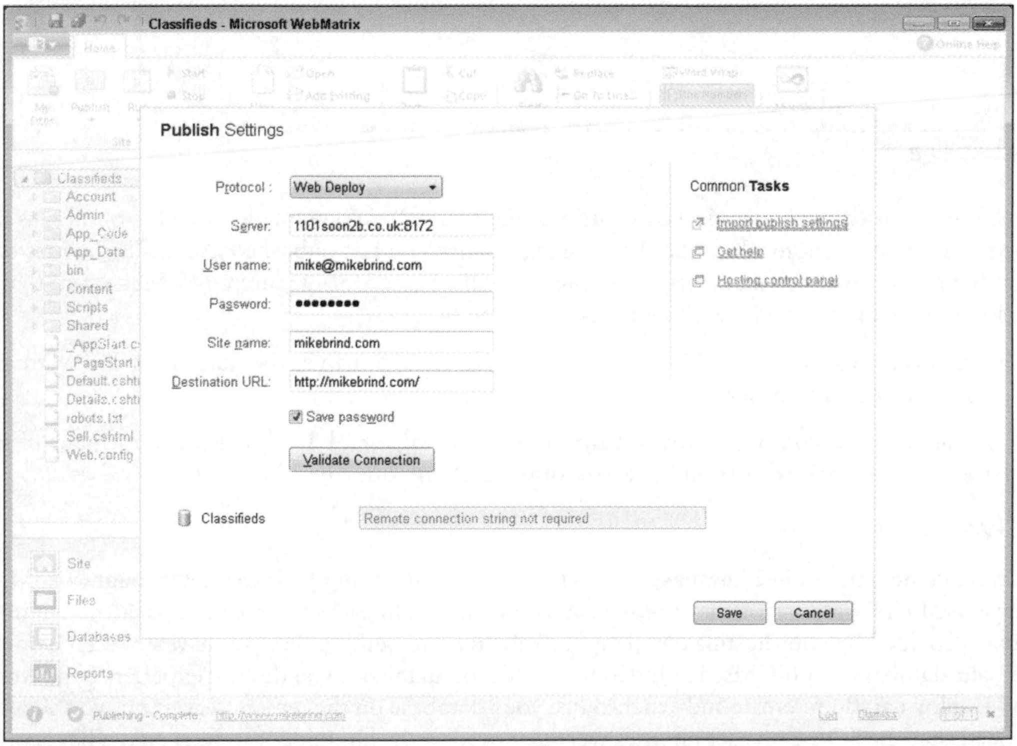

FIGURE 14-7

5. Click Save after the connection is validated. You will be asked if you would like WebMatrix to perform a compatibility test (see Figure 14-8). This only happens the first time you add new connection details, and it is advisable that you perform the test to ensure that the hosting package is set up correctly.

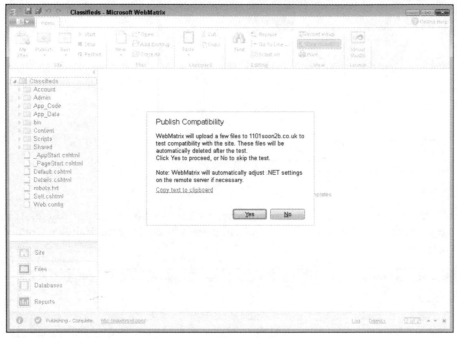

FIGURE 14-8

6. Assuming that the test passed, click Continue and you will be presented with a list of all files in the site on your local machine that have changed since you last published. As this is the first time you have published the site, every file in the site will be listed. See Figure 14-9. Make sure that you include the database file by clicking the appropriate box.

7. Click Continue to start the publishing process. The message strip at the bottom of WebMatrix will keep you informed of progress.

8. Once publishing is complete, browse to your new site. Figure 14-10 shows the home page of my version of the Classifieds site under a temporary URL provided by Netcetera.

How It Works

This exercise demonstrated just how easy it is to publish your site using Web Deploy through WebMatrix. If you have used FTP before, you may not have noticed a lot of difference in the process, although importing settings provided by your hosting company is likely to be something that you have not seen before. Because your database is a file-based SQL Compact Edition database, you did not experience the work that Web Deploy can do to create and synchronize your database on the remote server, but you should have noticed that the SQL Compact binaries were deployed to the bin folder on the server. That is one of the key features of SQL Compact Edition — you do not need a database engine to be installed on the server. They are shipped as part of your application.

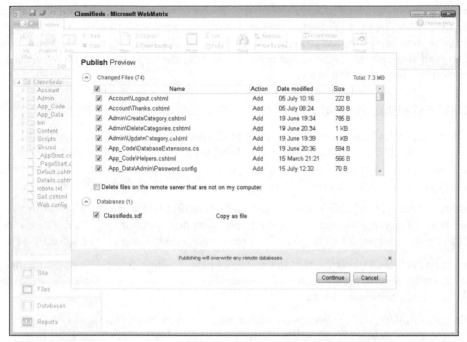

FIGURE 14-9

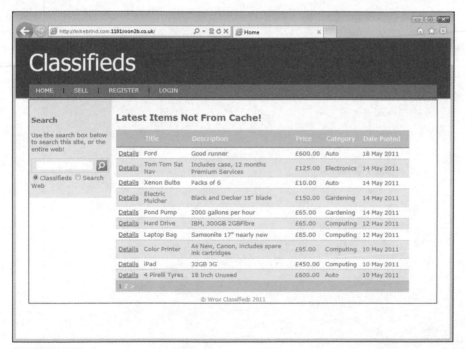

FIGURE 14-10

In the next exercise, you will use FTP to deploy your site. If you only have one web hosting package and have already used Web Deploy to publish your site to that, you may want to consider deleting all of the files from the remote server so that you can follow along step by step. On the other hand, you might just want to read through this exercise and note how similar the steps are to those required by the Web Deploy method, for future reference.

TRY IT OUT Using WebMatrix and FTP

1. Ensure that you have a valid FTP site that you can publish your site to. If you obtain a suitable hosting account from the Hosting Gallery, you might be able to set up an FTP site via a control panel, or your hosting company might set one up for you. I chose Titan Internet for this exercise. They provided an XML file that contains FTP account settings as well as WebDeploy settings.

2. Click the Settings option on the Publish button, and make sure that you select the FTP protocol. Manually enter the FTP account details, or use the Import Settings option if your FTP settings have been provided in an appropriate XML file. Test that the connection validates (see Figure 14-11)

3. Click Save and then click the Publish button again. The Publish Preview dialog box appears, displaying all files since none have been transferred yet. Again, ensure that the database file is selected, and then click Continue. See Figure 14-12.

4. Once publishing is complete, you are presented with a message in the status bar and a View Log link. When you click that link, a log of transfer activity it displayed (shown in Figure 14-13).

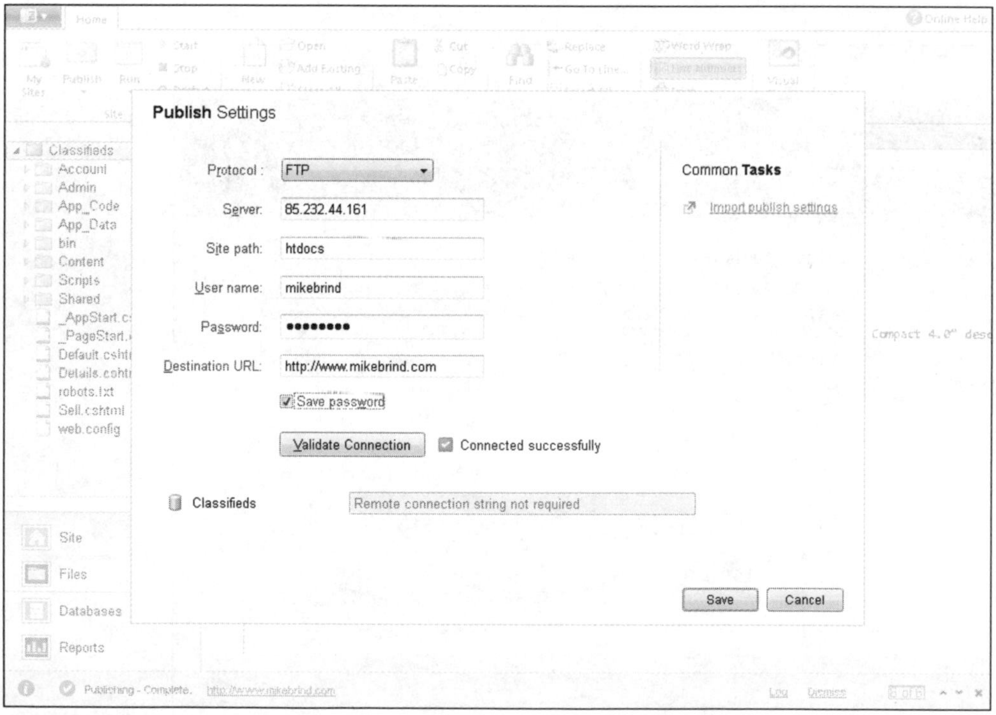

FIGURE 14-11

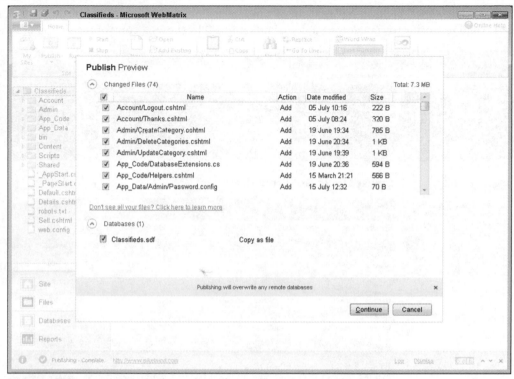

FIGURE 14-12

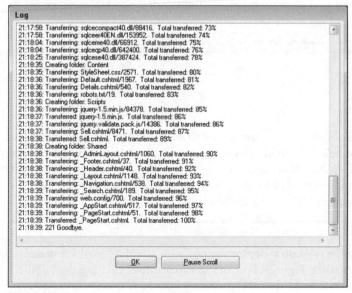

FIGURE 14-13

5. Navigate to the URL of your deployed site. Titan Internet provided me with a temporary URL so that I could test prior to transferring a domain. Figure 14-14 shows a copy of the site on first run.

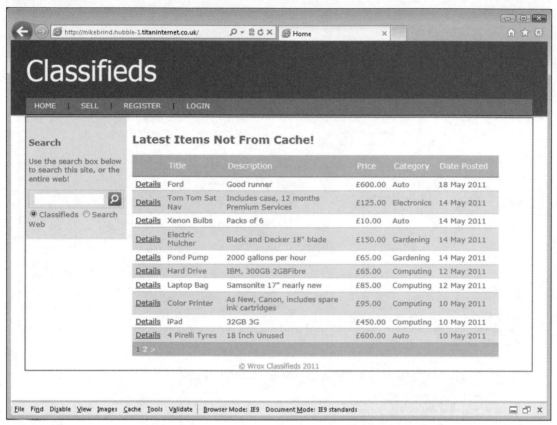

FIGURE 14-14

How It Works

This walkthrough illustrates how to publish your site using FTP through WebMatrix. As mentioned previously, if you have used an FTP client before, you may not have noticed a lot of difference in the process, although importing settings provided by your hosting company is likely to be something that you have not seen before. Just like the Web Deploy version, FTP knows that it should include the binaries required to run the SQL Compact Edition database, and so they are uploaded as part of the deployment.

The publishing tool isn't used just for the initial deployment of your site. It is used for maintaining the site content as you develop it further. Figure 14-15 shows the result of clicking the Publish button when a new file is added to the site and three of the existing files have been amended.

You can see clearly which files are new and which files have been changed by looking at their entries in the Action column. New files are set to Add and existing files are set to Update.

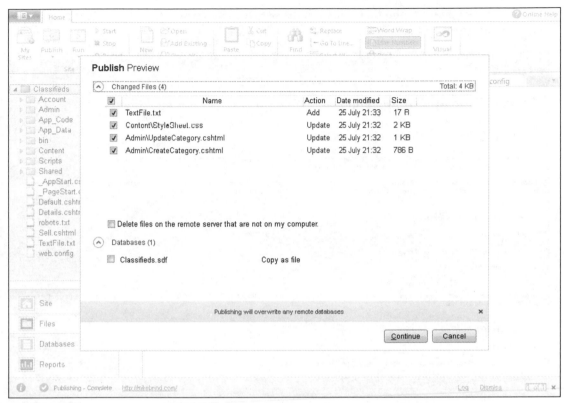

FIGURE 14-15

COMMON DEPLOYMENT ISSUES

Despite your best efforts, there is always the possibility that something goes wrong when deploying the site. Often, the first inkling that you get that something is not right with the deployment is when you receive an error page. If you have not implemented application-wide error handling or logging as described in Chapter 9, you will most likely get an error message that gives no details at all, as shown in Figure 14-16.

Every time you got an exception while developing your site, you got a lot of detail, so why doesn't the error page provide detail now? The reason is security. Error messages can reveal sensitive information such as user names, passwords, connection string details, and other pieces of data that might be useful to people of ill intent. By default, you can get detailed error messages only when you are browsing to the site on the machine on which it is deployed. It might not be possible for you to remote onto the web server and use a browser to get error details. So you need to temporarily enable details of the specific error to be viewable from a remote machine. You do this by adding a web.config file to the site (if you have not done so already) and adding an attribute to the <system.web> section:

```
<customErrors mode="Off" />
```

Once you have done this and then republish the site, you can browse to the offending page again and view the error details.

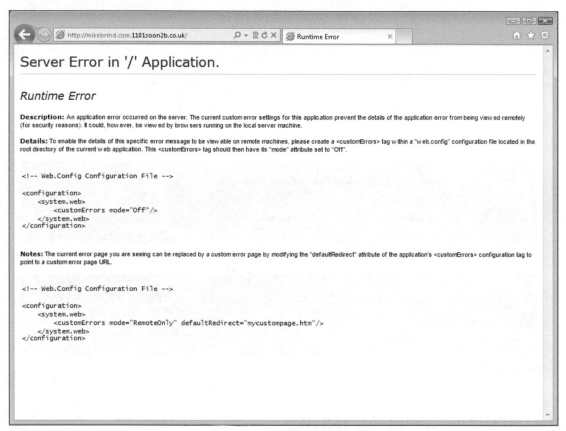

FIGURE 14-16

File Paths and URLs

The web server is a completely different environment to your development machine. It has a different file system for starters, and this difference is often enough to cause problems in deployment. If you have hardcoded any file paths in your application, they are unlikely to exist on the development server (unless you are very fortunate). If you need to reference a file path, you should always use `Server.MapPath` to obtain the actual path. You saw this method being used throughout Chapter 8. `Server.MapPath("/")` will always return the full file system path to your application's root folder.

If you need to work with the URL, you will have to cope with the differences between the localhost URL that you developed against, and the site's full URL when live. You saw how to handle URLs in an agnostic way when you explored the Starter Site's registration page, and implemented your own registration page in the Classifieds site. The secret is to use the `Uri.GetComponents` method on the current URL, and then deconstruct or reconstruct as necessary.

Other Issues

Deploying Web Pages sites to hosting servers has caused relatively few problems, if the forums are much to go by. However, two issues have come up a few times. The first revolves around the correct version of the .NET Framework being set on the website. The Web Pages Framework needs Version 4.0, and this can be set on a site-by-site basis. The following symptoms indicate that the hoster has targeted the site at the wrong version of ASP.NET:

➤ HTML pages work, but CSHTML pages result in 404 not found errors.

➤ Could not load file or *assembly* error messages. The file or assembly will be one of the DLLs required by Web Pages, such as System.Web.WebPages or Microsoft.Web.Helpers. The error message will also say "This assembly is built by a runtime newer than the currently loaded runtime and cannot be loaded".

The solution is to ask the hoster to target the site at Version 4.0 of the .NET Framework.

The second issue results in the following error message: "The connection name 'LocalSqlServer' was not found in the applications configuration or the connection string is empty". The LocalSqlServer connection string belongs to the SqlMembershipProvider, and some hosting companies remove it from the central configuration file, because it references a SQL Server Express database (which they do not support). If you suffer from this error, the solution is to add the following to the configuration section of your web.config file:

```
<connectionStrings>
  <remove name="LocalSqlServer" />
  <add name="LocalSqlServer" connectionString="none" />
</connectionStrings>
```

What Next?

You have completed and published your site. Your work here is done. However, this is just your first site, and there is a lot more that you can add over time. For example, you can add a mechanism by which account holders can bid for items. The database table structure is there already. You can include Facebook Like buttons, or the Linkshare helper to each item. Most obvious of all perhaps, you can add a FileUpload to the Sell page and allow users to upload an image of the item they want to sell. Then you can start looking toward enhancing your skills for the next project.

There are several key topics that you should master if you want to pursue a career as an ASP.NET developer. It is difficult to place priority on these topics, but they are as follows:

➤ HTML

➤ CSS

➤ SQL

➤ JavaScript/jQuery

➤ C#

This book can only provide a very basic introduction to these topics. Each one merits a book on its own, not just a chapter. In fact, Wrox has published books that do cover each of these subjects. I have purchased many of them myself, if that's any kind of a recommendation, and the following titles should be useful to you:

➤ *Discovering SQL: A Hands-On Guide for Beginners* (ISBN: 978-1-118-00267-4)

➤ *Beginning CSS: Cascading Style Sheets for Web Design, 3rd Edition* (ISBN: 978-0-470-89152-0)

➤ *HTML5 24-Hour Trainer* (ISBN: 978-0-470-64782-0)

➤ *Beginning JavaScript and CSS Development with jQuery* (ISBN: 978-0-470-22779-4)

➤ *Beginning Visual C# 2010* (ISBN: 978-0-470-50226-6)

You can also find help on the Internet. The following URLs provide access to communities and resources targeted at the ASP.NET developer:

➤ `http://p2p.wrox.com`: This is the public discussion forum from Wrox where you can go for all your programming-related questions. This book has its own category on that site, enabling you to ask targeted questions.

➤ `www.mikesdotnetting.com`: This is my own website where I post articles on ASP.NET, and in particular, Web Pages development.

➤ `www.asp.net`: This is the official Microsoft community site for ASP.NET technology. The site includes tutorials, news, articles, and ASP.NET downloads. It also includes a community forum where I am a moderator.

➤ `www.asp.net/web-pages`: This is the home of Web Pages content, including downloads and tutorials.

➤ `http://msdn.microsoft.com/asp.net`: This is the official home for ASP.NET at the Microsoft developer's website and gives you a wealth of information on ASP.NET.

➤ `www.microsoft.com/web/`: This is another Microsoft resource for Web Pages development. This site also includes a range of walkthroughs and tutorials.

SUMMARY

As I said in the introduction, this chapter is short. Deploying your ASP.NET website has never been easier with the introduction of WebMatrix, so it does not take much to cover this topic. The Web Pages deployment model relies on compilation on first run, which means that there are no complicated steps to undertake prior to getting your site on a web server. WebMatrix includes tools to deploy your site via Web Deploy or FTP. Web Deploy includes some great features for tracking changes between your local site and the live site on a remote server. It also manages the configuration of security on files and folders for you. FTP is a well-known and popular file transfer mechanism that will work with nearly every host.

Although WebMatrix makes deploying your site a relatively simple process, there are some potential pitfalls to avoid, and this chapter finished with a discussion of some areas you need to watch, such as managing file path and URL differences between local and live sites.

This book has provided you with a good grounding in WebMatrix and the Web Pages framework. The chapter finished with a round-up of the technologies you should focus on if you want to improve your web development skills and maximize your productivity with WebMatrix.

▶ **WHAT YOU LEARNED IN THIS CHAPTER**

TOPIC	KEY CONCEPTS
Shared hosting	Multiple customer sites deployed on the same server.
Dedicated server	A web server made available for the use of one customer.
Colocation	The hosting company makes your physical server available to the Internet.
Web Deploy	A framework that simplifies the deployment of websites to IIS servers.
FTP	File Transfer Protocol, a standard for transmitting files across networks.
PublishSettings	A file format for distributing and managing settings for Web Deploy or FTP accounts on web servers.

APPENDIX

Exercise Answers

CHAPTER 1

Exercise 1 Solution

The easiest way to download and install WebMatrix is using the Web Platform Installer, which you can download from www.microsoft.com/web.

Exercise 2 Solution

A file with a CSHTML extension is called a C# Razor file. It typically contains a mix of plain markup (such as HTML, CSS, and JavaScript) and server-side code that uses the Razor syntax. A file with a CS extension contains pure C# code and cannot contain HTML or other markup directly. The same differences apply to VBHTML and VB files.

Exercise 3 Solution

There are at least three special folders you typically use in an ASP.NET Web Pages application. The App_Data folder is used to store data consumed by the application, such as database and XML files. The App_Code folder is used to store your code files (files with a CS or VB extension). Finally, the Bin folder is used to store your own or third-party assemblies (files with a DLL extension). Because these folders contain files that you don't want your users to download, the web server blocks access to these folders for end users. Obviously, your application files and code can access them just fine.

Exercise 4 Solution

Static files are files that require no special processing and are served to the client by the web server directly. Dynamic files are processed by some other component first. For example, CSHTML files are processed by the ASP.NET run time first, executing the server-side code they contain to build up the final markup (HTML, CSS, and JavaScript).

CHAPTER 2

Exercise 1 Solution

Block-level elements occupy the entire width of the containing element, and force a new line. Inline elements do not force a new line, and only occupy the space designated by their start and end tags.

Exercise 2 Solution

The first method of applying CSS to HTML elements is by their tag name or the type selector. You provide the name of the tag, and then within curly braces, set values for the properties you want to style. The following snippet illustrates setting styles for all paragraph elements:

```
p{
    padding: 5px;
    color: blue;
}
```

The second method is by referencing the element's id attribute or the ID selector. You prefix the name of the ID with a pound or hash sign (#) and set the values of properties within curly braces as before. The next snippet illustrates this being done to an element with the ID of myId:

```
#myId{
    padding: 5px;
    color: blue;
}
```

Finally, you can reference elements by their class name or the class selector. In the style sheet, the name of the class is prefixed with a dot (.), and the rules are specified within curly braces. The following snippet illustrates this being affected on any element with a class of myClass applied to it:

```
.myClass{
padding: 5px;
    color: blue;
}
```

Exercise 3 Solution

The HTML for the page is as follows:

```
<!DOCTYPE html>

<html lang="en">
<head>
<meta charset="utf-8" />
<link href="/3-col.css" rel="stylesheet" type="text/css" />
<title></title>
</head>
<body>
<div id="wrapper">
<div id="header">Header</div>
```

```
    <div id="col1">Some text in red</div>
    <div id="col2">Some text in blue</div>
    <div id="col3">Some text in green</div>
    <div id="footer">Footer</div>
    </div>
    </body>
    </html>
```

The CSS for this page is as follows:

```
body {
    padding: 0;
    margin:0;
}

#wrapper{
    width: 900px;
}

#col1, #col2, #col3{
    width: 290px;
    margin: 5px;
    float: left;
}

#col1{
    color: Red;
}

#col2{
    color: Blue;
}

#col3{
    color:Green;
}
```

CHAPTER 3

Exercise 1 Solution

You should always prefix the layout filename with a leading underscore. This prevents the layout page from being requested directly via the browser.

Exercise 2 Solution

The RenderBody method, when placed in a file, defines the position at which default content will appear. It also ensures that the file in which it is placed will act as a layout page. RenderPage requires a name to be passed to it, which dictates which file contents should be rendered. A layout page will not work without a call to RenderBody, but will do so without any calls to RenderPage.

Exercise 3 Solution

You can pass an extra argument to the `RenderSection` method called `required: false` or you can use `IsSectionDefined`. The first option provides a means for you only to choose to display the content of a section or not. The second option works in the same way, but also allows you to specify default content to be displayed if no section has been defined.

Exercise 4 Solution

You need to use the `RenderPage` method and provide the data as a second argument to the method call. The data is passed as an anonymous type, which is created through the following syntax:

```
new {key1 = value1, key2 = value2}
```

CHAPTER 4

Exercise 1 Solution

The most common way to mix Razor syntax and HTML is to ensure that the HTML is enclosed in opening and closing tags, or includes a self-closing tag such as `<br />`. For example, the following uses matching HTML tags:

```
@foreach(var item in collection){
    <p>@item</p>
}
```

Alternatively, you can use the `@` symbol followed immediately by a colon to identify literal strings, if you do not include HTML tags:

```
@foreach(var item in collection){
    @:You chose @item
}
```

Finally, you can wrap the item to be rendered in matching `<text>` tags:

```
@foreach(var item in collection){
    <text>You chose @item</text>
}
```

Exercise 2 Solution

The interval between 65 and 90 is 26, which is the number of letters in the alphabet. It would therefore be logical to assume that you need to iterate from 65 to 90, incrementing the digit part of the HTML entity by one within each iteration to render the complete alphabet. Since you know the number of iterations required in advance, the `for` loop is the preferred choice:

```
@for(var i = 65; i <= 90; i++){
    <text>&#@i; </text>
}
```

Exercise 3 Solution

You should start by creating an App_Code folder if you haven't already created one, and then add a CSHTML file suitably named so that its intent is clear; *Helpers.cshtml* is always a good choice. Within that file, you should use the @helper syntax to create a method that accepts an array and generates an ul element, adding each item in the array within li elements:

```
@helper DisplayAsList(string[] values)
{
    <ul>
    @foreach(var value in values){
        <li>@value</li>
    }
    </ul>
}
```

When you want to use the method, you use the filename plus your method name, separated with a dot:

```
@Helpers.DisplayAsList(new[]{"Pulp Fiction", "The Long Good Friday", "Snatch"})
```

CHAPTER 5

Exercise 1 Solution

Server-side validation is essential. Client-side validation is only a courtesy to the users and can be by-passed, which means that invalid data could get through. The three things you should test for are presence, data type, and range.

Exercise 2 Solution

POST is preferred for form data as GET appends values to the query string. Most browsers limit the size of query strings, which makes GET unsuitable for submitting large amounts of data. POST adds the form data to the body of the HTTP request where there is no size limit for the request.

Exercise 3 Solution

By default, all output is HTML-encoded by Razor, which means that you cannot display formatted HTML. This is a security measure that helps to prevent cross site scripting (XSS) attacks. It also helps to prevent your page from being broken by the addition of uncontrolled invalid HTML. The Html.Raw helper prevents the output from being HTML-encoded so that, if necessary, you can choose to include HTML within your output.

Exercise 4 Solution

You use the AddError or AddFormError methods to register errors with ModelState. Doing this sets the ModelState.IsValid property to false, which is what you test to see if validation failed.

Exercise 5 Solution

You can set it when you initialize the helper, for example within _AppStart.cshtml. When you do this, you set the value for all e-mails that your application sends. Alternatively, you can set it when you create an e-mail, by passing a value to the `from` parameter in the WebMail's `Send` method. This allows you to change the value for each e-mail, offering more flexibility.

CHAPTER 6

Exercise 1 Solution

You can download the file locally and store it in a location within your website. In that case your link would point to a relative location within the site, for example:

```
<script href="@Href("~/Scripts/jquery-1.6.2.min.js")"></script>
```

Or you can reference a copy of jQuery hosted by a Content Distribution Network (CDN):

```
<script src="http://ajax.aspnetcdn.com/ajax/jQuery/jquery-1.6.2.min.js"
        type="text/javascript"></script>
```

The benefit of using a CDN hosted version of jQuery is that if your visitor has visited previous sites that make use of the CDN you have chosen, they already have a copy of the JavaScript file cached locally on their machine, which means that it does not need to be downloaded from your site. This increases the load time of your pages, and decreases the bandwidth that your web server is required to use in serving content.

Exercise 2 Solution

You can select elements according to their tag name (element selectors). For example, you would reference all paragraph elements using

```
$('p')
```

You can also reference specific elements via their ID selectors. You would reference an element with an ID of myId in the following manner:

```
$('#myId')
```

You can also reference elements according to their CSS class name. All elements that have a CSS class name of special would be referenced using the following syntax:

```
$('.special')
```

Exercise 3 Solution

The first "A" in AJAX stands for asynchronous. It represents the model whereby requests or processes are managed in the background without having to interrupt the users while they are involved in their primary task — typically viewing a web page.

CHAPTER 7

Exercise 1 Solution

The enctype of the form tag must be set to multipart/form-data, and the form must contain at least one input type="file".

Exercise 2 Solution

The default maximum request length is 4MB, which you can alter in the web.config file. To do this, you add a configuration section called httpRuntime if one doesn't already exist, and set its maxRequestLength attribute to a more suitable value in kilobytes.

CHAPTER 8

Exercise 1 Solution

The three classes are the File class, the Path class, and the Directory class. The File class exposes methods related to working directly with files. The Path class exposes methods that enable you to work with file paths. The Directory class exposes methods that enable you to work with folders.

Exercise 2 Solution

LINQ to XML is an Application Programming Interface for working with XML in memory. It provides a means to query and create XML using C# (or VB).

Exercise 3 Solution

It is used to determine whether an image should retain its proportions when it is resized. The default value is true, which ensures that the image will be resized either to the height value or the width value, but neither will be exceeded during resizing.

CHAPTER 9

Exercise 1 Solution

ObjectInfo displays details of objects to the browser including their data type, values, and any nested objects that they might contain. ServerInfo displays a range of details about the environment in which the code is executing. This includes the server configuration, environment variables, and HTTP runtime information.

Exercise 2 Solution

The `try` block should house code that could cause an exception to be raised, and the `catch` block should contain a handler for that exception. However, `try - catch` blocks should not be used to manage just any possible exception. They should only be used to manage exceptions that result from things that you cannot control in code, such as the availability of a mail server, database, or file. They should not be used to replace validation of acceptable values coming from the user.

CHAPTER 10

Exercise 1 Solution

This is kind of a trick question in that the way it is phrased rather obscures the operation you need to perform. Often, novice developers will attempt to insert the data into the new column. `INSERT` operations always result in new rows, whereas the end result of this exercise should be a change in the data for each existing row or an `UPDATE`. The SQL needed is therefore:

```
UPDATE Contacts SET FirstName = Forename
```

Exercise 2 Solution

A relationship defined in a `JOIN` statement is created purely for that query and does not persist. It has no bearing on how data is managed or maintained. A relationship defined in the database itself is permanent and protects the integrity of data on either side of the relationship by enforcing it at database level.

Exercise 3 Solution

`IDENTITY` columns—those that have Is Identity set to `true` in the column properties—create their own values by incrementing a number and using that value for each row. You cannot insert a value of your own into such a column.

The `GetLastInsertId` method retrieves the value of the most recently created row containing an `IDENTITY` column.

CHAPTER 11

Exercise 1 Solution

SQL injection attempts are successful when the programmer concatenates user input directly into a command that will be executed against a database. The database is unable to differentiate between what the programmer intended to be the command, and one that has been manipulated to behave in a different way. All the database sees is a valid SQL statement presented as a string.

Exercise 2 Solution

The `fieldNamePrefix` parameter allows you to provide a prefix to the default query string field names that identify the column that sorting depends on—the sort direction, the page number, and the selected row. If you have multiple grids on the same page, any paging operation is likely to affect all of the grids by default, as they will all generate the same sorting and paging links. Consequently, when the grids "see" query string values that tell them how to sort, or page, or which row has been selected, they will all try to react to the instructions provided by the query string values. The `fieldNamePrefix` allows you to personalize query string values on a grid-by-grid basis, so there will be no confusion as to which grid the query string should be read by.

Exercise 3 Solution

You need to use the `format` parameter of the column constructor. This is because you need to take the database value and format it into another string to render an HTML `img` tag. Here's what you would pass to the format parameter:

```
@<img src="@Href("~/images/" + item.FileName)" alt="" />
```

The format parameter accepts any HTML so long as the tags are balanced (closed or self-closing) and the argument is prefixed with the `@` sign.

CHAPTER 12

Exercise 1 Solution

Authentication is the process whereby you establish your identity by providing some proof of who you are, such as a user name and password. Authorization is the process by which your permissions are determined based on who you are.

Exercise 2 Solution

The following code will result in the link to the Bid page being displayed only if the currently logged in user is a member of the Bidder role:

```
@if(Roles.IsUserInRole("Bidder")){
    <p><a href="@Href("~/Bid/" + item.Id)">Bid on this item</a></p>
}
```

You would place this code in the code block that establishes whether the item is null.

Exercise 3 Solution

The membership table is automatically generated by the WebSecurity Helper as part of its initialization. The user table will be generated automatically if one does not exist. However, you can reference an existing table instead, so long as the table has a numeric identity column and a column for unique user name values. You specify these two columns as parameters to the `InitializeDatabaseConnection` method of the WebSecurity Helper.

CHAPTER 13

Exercise 1 Solution

The `robots.txt` file provides instructions to compliant user agents (search engine crawlers) on which part of a site it should visit and index, and which parts it should not enter. It is not a replacement for the WebSecurity helper and should not be used to protect sensitive areas of a site.

Exercise 2 Solution

The first and fourth URLs will work.

The first URL passes 29 as `UrlData` to a page called `Edit.cshtml` in the Pages folder, within the Admin folder. The second URL has the folders the wrong way around, so the URL does not reflect the file path. The third URL requires a page called `Default.cshtml`, which doesn't exist. The fourth option is more interesting in that this wasn't covered in the chapter. The question mark denotes a query string, which works as usual with routing. The page number is not identified from `UrlData` as in the first example, but it can be obtained from the Request collection: `Request["id"]`.

Exercise 3 Solution

Items can be removed programmatically via the `WebCache.Remove` method. They can also exceed the time they are set to persist in the cache. Also, a number of events on the server can cause the cache to be emptied, including restarts, application pool recycles, and the server reclaiming memory.

INDEX

X

Y

Z

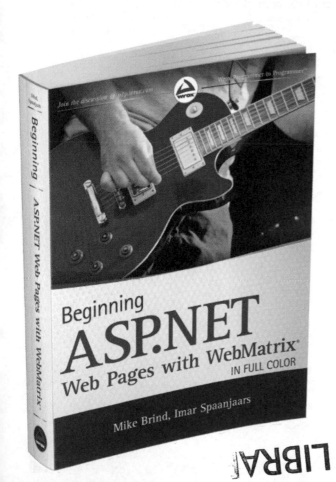